CONCEPTUAL AND PROCEDURAL KNOWLEDGE: THE CASE OF MATHEMATICS

edited by JAMES HIEBERT

CONCEPTUAL AND PROCEDURAL KNOWLEDGE: THE CASE OF MATHEMATICS

LAWRENCE ERLBAUM ASSOCIATES, PUBLISHERS

1986   Hillsdale, NJ   London

Lawrence Erlbaum Associates, Inc., Publishers
365 Broadway
Hillsdale, New Jersey 07642

Library of Congress Cataloging-in-Publication Data

Conceptual and procedural knowledge.

   Bibliography: p.
   Includes index.
   1. Mathematics—Study and teaching.   2. Concept
learning.   I. Hiebert, James.
QA12.C65   1987   370.15′6   86-4599
ISBN 0-89859-556-8

Printed in the United States of America
10 9 8 7 6 5 4 3

Contents

Preface

This book is intended for those people who are interested in how mathematics is learned. It is intended especially for those who are interested in the mental processes involved in becoming mathematically competent and the mental processes that inhibit such competency from developing. Insights into the nature of these processes is provided by focusing on a central issue in mathematics learning—the relationship between conceptual understanding and procedural skill. The issue has had an informative past, but work presented in this volume reveals a relatively recent appreciation for the complexities of the issue and a new sense of the appropriate questions to address.

The volume opens with an overview of the issue and then traces the relationships between conceptual and procedural knowledge in mathematics from preschool days through the years of formal schooling. Mathematics educators and cognitive psychologists from a variety of perspectives contribute theoretical arguments and empirical data to illuminate the nature of the relationships and, in turn, the nature of mathematics learning.

The book owes its success in furthering our understanding of these issues to the contributing authors. A personal note of thanks is extended to the authors for their graciousness in dealing with editorial suggestions and for the uniformly high quality of their work.

Many of the chapters are updated versions of the 1985 colloquium series of the College of Education, University of Delaware. Thanks are due to the series sponsors: the Unidel Foundation through the Interdisciplinary Committee on Education, The Cognitive Science Group, the Visiting Women Scholars Fund, and the College of Education. Associated with the colloquium series was a graduate seminar in which the colloquium content and initial drafts of some chapters were examined further. The comments of Kathleen Cauley, Neil Haldeman, Pat Lefevre, Sally Orr, Barbara Piech, Debbie Smith, Tim Smith, and Susan Taber are gratefully acknowledged. Pat Lefevre receives particular thanks for her untiring efforts in ensuring that the series ran smoothly. Special acknowledgment is given to Frank Murray, Dean of the College of Education and Chair of the Interdisciplinary Committee on Education, for his support of the colloquium series and this book.

James Hiebert

Foreword

The relationship between our ability to perform a task and to understand both the task and why our action is appropriate appears—even with only a little reflection—to be complicated. On the one hand, there may be no functional relationship at all between action and understanding, especially in the basic behavioral areas that are critical for the continuation of the species. The development of our species, let alone the individual's development, surely requires that certain actions and procedures be carried out nonreflectively and without any appreciation of the meaning or explanation of the action. For example, our ability to speak a language, a critical survival competence, is acquired fairly easily, without deliberate instruction, and, in the end, is quite independent of any formal knowledge on our part of the syntactic rules that in fact describe our speaking. Native English speakers of school age can, like mature speakers, pluralize regular nonsense nouns they have never seen before (e.g., wug, gutch, zot) with high agreement and speed and yet have no coherent knowledge of how they were able to do it.

Still their speaking behavior is lawful and rule driven, even if as speakers and knowers they are unaware of the rules; and were they shown the rules, they might not even acknowledge or recognize the very rules they act as though they knew. Moreover, we ordinarily would not find a speaker deficient owing to his failure to know a set of rules that is, by and large, known only by professional linguists, because the speaker at least acts as if he knows the set of rules, even though it is perfectly clear that he does not. It does not seem to be the case either that linguists, who do know the rules, speak the language better than those who remain ignorant of the appropriate rules. And so it is in any number of behavioral areas—from baseball players, who adhere to several laws of Newtonian mechanics without knowing any of them, to all state-of-their-art professionals, who operate on the frontier edges of their disciplines and professions without any firm theoretical base to guide them.

On the other hand, there are the well-worn examples from the experimental psychology literature on the transfer of training and recall. It is quite clear that both performance of a sequence of discrete skills and recall of independent items are enhanced when a person acquires a concept or principle that allows the person to organize, structure, and make sense of the heretofore unrelated items. There is a demonstrably close interaction in many domains between one's successful actions and one's theoretical knowledge of them—each, on occasion, facilitates the development or exhibition of the other.

From an historical perspective, similar relationships are found; the formulation of Euclidean geometry extended, for example, the practical power of the Pythagorean theorem, which was known to pre-Euclidean surveyors and others as merely a set of empirical attributes of the right triangle. As well, the atheoretical discovery of the Pythagorean relationship certainly shaped and conditioned the eventual invention of geometry as a codified deductive system. Similarly and closer to our own time, the creation of the early intelligence tests, which were built with no supporting theory of intelligence, have facilitated the development of current theories of the intellect. The symbiotic relationship between practice and theory or understanding is undeniable from either the historical perspective of the development of the academic disciplines or from the perspective of one who is able to solve a novel problem, never encountered before, based upon one's notions of how other things work.

The fact that the relationship between practice and understanding is complicated and seems to encompass instances that run from the closest symbiosis to functional independence means only that the work of the school is more difficult than is ordinarily thought. It is simply not obvious what the schools should strive for in this area. On the one hand, many children have uniform and persistent difficulty with several straightforward algorithms and their simple extensions (e.g., those that are applied to decimals, fractions, or percentages). On the other hand, there are some children who can flawlessly compute arithmetical functions with virtually no idea of the logic of the algorithms they employ. What accounts for those persistent computational errors children make? How is it that some children who do not make computational errors seem to understand so little about what they are doing? These are the questions of this book and the subject, one way or another, of a year-long colloquium series at the University of Delaware. The book's thesis is that the relationship between conceptual and procedural knowledge is the key to further advances in our understanding of how children and adults do mathematics and how they think about what they do.

John Dewey noted that intellectual progress on a difficult matter that presents itself as an "either/or" dichotomy of polar opposites can be made if a way can be found to link the two putative opposites (computational skill and understanding, for example) on a common dimension. It is a good beginning to realize that the object of the search is the "relationship," or the dimension upon which the opposites are merely the poles. It is a good sign of progress when the dimension can be named and conceptualized so that the nature of the relationship can be examined and tested. Several candidates are put forward in this book. The dimension can be seen as an Ausubelian scale of meaning, ranging from rotely acquired and unconnected items to items that have ever increasing connections to other mental events. Or the scale may be more profitably seen as a developmental one in which the initial mathematical actions are themselves the objects of other actions or "operations" in the Genevan sense. Or the scale may be viewed as a scale of conscious awareness of the rules for doing mathematics in which at one pole is represented the easily taught and perfectly explicit algorithms of the discipline and at the other pole are the rules for doing mathematics superbly— those rules that elude formal explication and are thereby relatively unteachable. Along the scale, presumably, are the rules for doing mathematics well, rules (heuristics) that are reasonably well formed and teachable, but less exact and certain in the outcome of their application. Whether the relationship or dimension is best thought of as a scale of meaning, of more abstract and internalized actions, of more explicit rules, or of some other cognitive factor is taken up in the following chapters.

Frank B. Murray, Dean
H. Rodney Sharp, Professor
The University of Delaware
The College of Education

CONCEPTUAL AND PROCEDURAL KNOWLEDGE: THE CASE OF MATHEMATICS

1 Conceptual and Procedural Knowledge in Mathematics: An Introductory Analysis

James Hiebert
Patricia Lefevre
University of Delaware

Conceptual and procedural knowledge of mathematics represents a distinction that has received a great deal of discussion and debate through the years. Questions of how students learn mathematics, and especially how they should be taught, turn on speculations about which type of knowledge is more important or what might be an appropriate balance between them. Additionally, discussions of conceptual and procedural knowledge extend beyond the boundaries of mathematics education. The distinction between concepts and procedures plays an important role in more general questions of knowledge acquisition. In some theories of learning and development, the distinction occupies center stage. Although the types of knowledge that are identified from theory to theory are not identical, there is much overlap. The differences are primarily in emphasis rather than kind. For example, Piaget (1978) distinguishes between conceptual understanding and successful action; Tulving (1983) distinguishes between semantic memory and episodic memory; Anderson (1983) distinguishes between declarative and procedural knowledge. Parallel distinctions are made in philosophical theories of knowledge. For example, Scheffler (1965) distinguishes between the propositional use of "knowing that" and the procedural use of "knowing how to." The distinction between conceptual and procedural knowledge that we elaborate in this chapter is not synonymous with any of these distinctions, but it draws upon all of them.

Mathematics, with its tightly structured and clearly defined content, has provided an arena for much discussion of conceptual and procedural knowledge. Over the past century, considerations of these two kinds of mathematical knowledge have taken different forms using different labels. Probably the most widely recognized distinction has been that between skill and understanding. Often the discussions of skill and understanding have taken the form of a debate about which should receive greater emphasis during instruction. McLellan and Dewey

1

(1895) argued for understanding and presented a mathematics curriculum they felt would raise the level of understanding beyond that existing in classrooms at the time. Thorndike (1922) presented the case for skill learning and described in detail how skills should be taught to maximize retention. Brownell (1935) opposed the emphasis on learning isolated skills and argued forcefully for an increased emphasis on understanding. Essentially the same debate was carried on periodically through Gagné's (1977) emphasis on skill learning versus Bruner's (1960) case for understanding. Along the way there have been many additional voices addressing the issue from a variety of perspectives (see Jones, 1970; Shulman, 1970).

Currently, cognitive psychologists and mathematics educators are looking again at conceptual and procedural knowledge in mathematics learning. Sometimes, the discussions are couched in terms different from those used in the past. For example, Resnick (1982) talks about semantics and syntax, and Gelman and Gallistel (1978) distinguish between principles and skills. Even within this volume, a variety of terms are used to differentiate between types of knowledge. Baroody and Ginsburg describe differences between meaningful and mechanical knowledge, and VanLehn distinguishes between schematic and teleologic knowledge. But, regardless of the labels, the division between types of knowledge lies in approximately the same place today as it has in the past.

There are, however, three important differences between current discussions of conceptual and procedural knowledge and the historic discussions of understanding and skill. First, the essays of the past have treated understandings and skills as instructional outcomes and have dealt with them in the context of advocating instructional programs. The issue has been whether skills, or understandings, or both should be emphasized during classroom instruction. The context for addressing the question of the relative importance of skills and understandings often has been the *prescription* of instructional programs. Today, many of the writings *describe* the acquisition of knowledge and the relationships between different kinds of knowledge. The implicit assumption is that more complete descriptions are a first step on the road to better prescriptions. Detailed descriptions are believed to provide a sound basis from which to develop effective instructional programs.

The second difference between past and current discussions of conceptual and procedural knowledge is found in the current attention to *relationships* between concepts and procedures. Historically, the two kinds of knowledge have been viewed as separate entities, sometimes competing for the teacher's attention, at best coexisting as disjoint neighbors. Little interest has been shown in studying the relationships between the two kinds of knowledge. In contrast, there is a growing interest today in how concepts and procedures are related. Current discussions treat the two forms of knowledge as distinct, but linked in critical, mutually beneficial ways. The new language of cognitive science has facilitated this approach because a single language can now be used to deal with both forms of knowledge (Anderson, 1983; Davis, 1984; Norman & Rumelhart, 1975). It is no longer the case that different theories are needed to express the principles guiding the acquisition and application of each kind of knowledge; a single theoretical orientation can handle both conceptual and procedural knowledge.

The third difference between past and present discussions is that past distinctions between conceptual and procedural knowledge focused on mathematics learning in school, whereas recent discussions of the issue have broadened the scope to include preschool mathematics learning in informal settings. Although it has long been recognized that children enter school with significant mathematical competencies (Brownell, 1941; McLaughlin, 1935), it is only recently that these competencies have been analyzed in great detail. Some of the analyses have revealed that the distinction between conceptual and procedural knowledge is as appropriate and useful for understanding the acquisition of informal mathematics as for formal mathematics. Preschool children acquire certain procedures or skills along with concepts, understandings, or intuitions about mathematics. The relationships between these kinds of knowledge, even at this level, appears to be complex.

Although the recent orientation to the issue of conceptual and procedural knowledge promises to provide significant insights into mathematics learning and performance, the relationship between these forms of knowledge are not yet well understood. A primary reason for the intractable nature of the problem is that the types of knowledge themselves are difficult to define. The core of each is easy to describe, but the outside edges are hard to pin down.

Our position is that the distinction between conceptual and procedural knowledge is useful for thinking about mathematics learning, and the clearer we can be about the distinction, the better. We do not believe, however that the distinction provides a classification scheme into which all knowledge can or should be sorted. Not all knowledge can be usefully described as either conceptual or procedural. Some knowledge seems to be a little of both, and some knowledge seems to be neither. Nevertheless, we believe that it is possible to distinguish between the two types of knowledge and that such a distinction provides a way of interpreting the learning process that helps us better understand students' failures and successes.

DEFINITIONS OF CONCEPTUAL
AND PROCEDURAL KNOWLEDGE

Conceptual Knowledge

Conceptual knowledge is characterized most clearly as knowledge that is rich in relationships. It can be thought of as a connected web of knowledge, a network in which the linking relationships are as prominent as the discrete pieces of information. Relationships pervade the individual facts and propositions so that all pieces of information are linked to some network. In fact, a unit of conceptual knowledge cannot be an isolated piece of information; by definition it is a part of conceptual knowledge only if the holder recognizes its relationship to other pieces of information.

The development of conceptual knowledge is achieved by the construction of relationships between pieces of information. This linking process can occur between two pieces of information that already have been stored in memory or between an existing piece of knowledge and one that is newly learned. It may be helpful to consider each of these phenomena in turn. The literature of psychology and education is filled with accounts of insights gained when previously unrelated items are suddenly seen as related in some way. Such insights are the bases of discovery learning (Bruner, 1961). We characterize this as an increase in conceptual knowledge. Two illuminating accounts of this kind of conceptual knowledge growth in elementary mathematics are found in Ginsburg (1977) and Lawler (1981). Ginsburg describes many points in the learning of number and arithmetic where understanding involves building relationships between existing bits of knowledge. For example, Jane (age nine) understood multidigit subtraction for the first time when she recognized the connection between the algorithm she had memorized and her knowledge of the positional value of each digit (p. 155). Relationships can tie together small pieces of information or larger pieces that are themselves networks of sorts. When previously independent networks are related, there is a dramatic and significant cognitive reorganization (Lawler, 1981).

A second way in which conceptual knowledge grows is through the creation of relationships between existing knowledge and new information that is just entering the system. The example of Jane cited above would fit here if Jane had recognized the connection between algorithm and place value immediately upon being taught the algorithm. Again, this phenomenon has been described with a variety of labels. Perhaps "understanding" is the term used most often to describe the state of knowledge when new mathematical information is connected appropriately to existing knowledge (Davis, 1984; Skemp, 1971; Van Engen, 1953). Other terms, like "meaningful learning," convey similar sentiments (Ausubel, 1967; Brownell, 1935; Greeno, 1983b). Regardless of the term used, the heart of the process involves assimilating (Piaget, 1960) the new material into appropriate knowledge networks or structures. The result is that the new material becomes part of an existing network.

It is useful to distinguish between two levels at which relationships between pieces of mathematical knowledge can be established. One level we will call primary. At this level the relationship connecting the information is constructed at the same level of abstractness (or at a less abstract level) than that at which the information itself is represented. That is, the relationship is no more abstract than the information it is connecting. The term abstract is used here to refer to the degree to which a unit of knowledge (or a relationship) is tied to specific contexts. Abstractness increases as knowledge becomes freed from specific contexts.

An example may help to clarify the idea of primary level relationships. When students learn about decimal numbers, they learn a variety of things about decimals, including the following two facts. First, the position values to the right of the decimal point are tenths, hundredths, and so on; second, when you add or subtract decimal numbers you line up the decimal points. Usually, it is expected that students will relate these two pieces of information and recognize that when you line up decimal points in addition you end up adding tenths with tenths, hundredths with hundredths, and so forth. If students do make the connection, they certainly have advanced their understanding of addition. But a noteworthy characteristic of this primary relationship is that it connects two pieces of information about decimal numbers and nothing more. It is tied to the decimal context.

Some relationships are constructed at a higher, more abstract level than the pieces of information they connect. We call this the reflective level. Relationships at this level are less tied to specific contexts. They often are created by recognizing similar core features in pieces of information that are superficially different. The relationships transcend the level at which the knowledge currently is represented, pull out the common features of different-looking pieces of knowledge, and tie them together. In the example cited earlier, the learner might step back mentally and recall that you line up numerals on the right to add whole numbers and end up adding units with units, tens with tens, hundreds with hundreds. When adding common fractions, you look for common denominators and end up adding the same size pieces together. Now the connection between the position value and lining up decimal points to add decimal numbers is recognized as a special case of the general idea that you always add things that are alike in some crucial way, things that have been measured with a common unit. Lining up decimal points results in adding together the parts of the decimal fractions that are the "same size." This kind of a connection is at a reflective level because building it requires a process of stepping back and reflecting on the information being connected. It is at a higher level than the primary level, because from its vantage point the learner can see much more of the mathematical terrain.

There are other ways to describe the different kinds of relationships that are part of one's conceptual knowledge in mathematics, but the primary and reflective levels provide a useful distinction. The analysis is similar in some important ways to the different types of understanding described by Greeno (1980, 1983b) and the different types of intelligence proposed by Skemp (1971). Although this distinction is not always made explicit in the remaining discussion, it is important to remember that not all relationships are of a single kind.

Procedural Knowledge

Procedural knowledge, as we define it here, is made up of two distinct parts. One part is composed of the formal language, or symbol representation system, of mathematics. The other part consists of the algorithms, or rules, for completing mathematical tasks. The first part is sometimes called the "form" of mathematics (Byers & Erlwanger, 1984). It includes a familiarity with the symbols used to represent mathematical ideas and an awareness of the syntactic rules for writing symbols in an acceptable form. For example, those who possess this aspect of procedural knowledge would recognize that the expression $3.5 \div \square = 2.71$ is syntactically acceptable (although they may not know the "answer") and that $6 + = \square 2$ is not acceptable. At more advanced levels of mathematics, knowledge of form includes knowledge of the syntactic configurations of formal proofs. This does not include the content or logic of proofs, only the style in which proof statements are written. Notice that, in general, knowledge of the symbols and syntax of mathematics implies only an awareness of surface features, not a knowledge of meaning.

The second part of procedural knowledge consists of rules, algorithms, or procedures used to solve mathematical tasks. They are step-by-step instructions that prescribe how to complete tasks. A key feature of procedures is that they are executed in a predetermined linear sequence. It is the clearly sequential nature of procedures that probably sets them most apart from other forms of knowledge. The only relational requirement for a procedure to run is that prescription n must know that it comes after prescription $n - 1$. Actually, at the barest minimum it needs to recognize as input only the outcome of prescription $n - 1$.

The procedures we are describing can be characterized as production systems (Anderson, 1983; Newell & Simon, 1972) in that they require some sort of recognizable input for firing. For the completion of a task, the initial procedure operates on the input and produces an outcome that is recognized by the next procedure in sequence. In this way, the sequence of procedures moves the given state (the statement of problem) to a goal state (the answer).

It is useful to distinguish between two kinds of procedures by noticing the objects upon which they operate. A basic distinction can be drawn between objects that are standard written symbols (e.g., 3, $+$, $\sqrt{}$) and objects that are nonsymbolic (e.g., concrete objects or mental images). After students have been in school for a few years, the objects often are symbols. Students are presented with problems in the form of symbol expressions, such as adding whole numbers, translating from common to decimal fraction notation, or solving algebraic equations. The task is to transform the symbol expression from the given form to an answer form by executing a sequence of symbol manipulation rules. In production system terms, the given state is a pattern of symbols (e.g., $\frac{1}{3} + \frac{3}{4} = \square$). Each step in the procedure recognizes the pattern it receives and changes it to another pattern, which in turn is recognized by the next step, and so on until a number is produced that is recognized as the answer. Procedures whose input and output are visual symbol patterns have been labeled "visually-moderated sequences" (Davis, 1984, p. 35). Such procedures make up the lion's share of school mathematics.

That school tasks most often involve symbol manipulation procedures is a fact whose importance should not be underestimated. It means that examinations of students' procedural knowledge often deal with a rather narrow but critical kind of procedure. Because of their importance in school learning, we believe it is useful to distinguish procedures that essentially are syntactic maneuvers on symbols. Chapters in this volume that focus on school-age children reflect this emphasis, especially those by VanLehn, Hiebert and Wearne, and Silver.

A second kind of procedure is a problem-solving strategy or action that operates on concrete objects, visual diagrams, mental images, or other objects that are not standard symbols of our mathematical systems. Such procedures are used extensively by preschool children, by older children on "nonschool" tasks, and occasionally by students in school. Young children, for example, use a variety of counting strategies to solve verbally presented addition and subtraction problems (Carpenter, this volume). More elemental counting and number procedures are described by Gelman and Meck, Sinclair and Sinclair, and Baroody and Ginsburg (this volume). Examples of school tasks that require nonsymbol procedures are straightedge and compass constructions in geometry (Schoenfeld, this volume). The important point here is that procedures, like concepts, are not all of one kind. Some procedures manipulate written mathematical symbols, whereas others operate on concrete objects, visual diagrams, or other entities.

An important feature of the procedural system is that it is structured. Procedures are hierarchically arranged so that some procedures are embedded in others as subprocedures. An entire sequence of step-by-step prescriptions or subprocedures can be characterized as a superprocedure. The advantage of creating superprocedures is that all subprocedures in a sequence can be accessed by retrieving a single superprocedure. For example, to apply the superprocedure "multiply two decimal numbers" (e.g., 3.82 × .43) one usually applies three subprocedures: one to write the problem in appropriate vertical form, a second to calculate the numerical part of the answer, and a third to place the decimal point in the answer. The second of these is itself made up of lower level subprocedures for (whole number) multiplication. Often it is possible to identify several levels of subprocedures that comprise a single superprocedure. The subprocedures are accessed as a sequential string once the superprocedure is identified.

In summary, procedural knowledge of mathematics encompasses two kinds of information. One kind of procedural knowledge is a familiarity with the individual symbols of the system and with the syntactic conventions for acceptable configurations of symbols. The second kind of procedural knowledge consists of rules or procedures for solving mathematical problems. Many of the procedures that students possess probably are chains of prescriptions for manipulating symbols. However, procedural knowledge also includes strategies for solving problems that do not operate directly on symbols. Perhaps the biggest difference between procedural knowledge and conceptual knowledge is that the primary relationship in procedural knowledge is "after," which is used to sequence subprocedures and superprocedures linearly. In contrast, conceptual knowledge is saturated with relationships of many kinds.

Meaningful and Rote Learning

Lurking just below the surface is the question of how the notions of conceptual and procedural knowledge are related to the issue of meaningful versus rote learning. There are some clear similarities, to be sure, but there are also some important differences. In addition to settling (momentarily) the question of how these ideas are related, a discussion of their similarities and differences may help to clarify our view of conceptual and procedural knowledge.

Meaningful learning, as we indicated earlier, often has been used to convey many of the same ideas that we presented as part of conceptual knowledge (see Brownell, 1935; Davis, 1984; Greeno, 1983b). Meaning is generated as relationships between units of knowledge are recognized or created. Conceptual knowledge, by our definition, must be learned meaningfully. Procedures, on the other hand, may or may not be learned with meaning. We propose that procedures that are learned with meaning are procedures that are linked to conceptual knowledge. This is such an important idea in mathematics learning that its discussion takes up most of the remaining part of this chapter.

Rote learning, on the other hand, produces knowledge that is notably absent in relationships and is tied closely to the context in which it is learned. The knowledge that results from rote learning is not linked with other knowledge and therefore does not generalize to other situations; it can be accessed and applied only in those contexts that look very much like the original. Conceptual knowledge, as we have described it, cannot be generated directly by rote learning. Facts and propositions learned by rote are stored in memory as isolated bits of information, not linked with any conceptual network. Of course at some later time the learner may recognize or construct relationships between isolated pieces of information. In this case, conceptual knowledge is created from information that was learned initially by rote.

In contrast, procedures can be learned by rote. Procedures can be acquired and executed even if they are linked tightly to surface characteristics of the original context. In fact, many procedures, especially those that operate on symbol patterns, are triggered by surface features similar to those of the original context. The sequential nature of procedures also is not violated by rote learning. In fact, learning a predetermined linear sequence of actions seems to lend itself to rote memorization as an instructional method. Thus procedures can be learned by rote and probably often are learned by rote since they seem especially susceptible to this form of instruction.

No sooner than we propose definitions for conceptual and procedural knowledge and attempt to clarify them, we must back up and acknowledge that the definitions we have given and the impressions they convey will be flawed in some way. As we said earlier, not all knowledge fits nicely into one class or the other. Some knowledge lies at the intersection. Heuristic strategies for solving problems, which are themselves objects of thought, are examples. Rather than operating on symbols, heuristic strategies seem to have concepts as their arguments. Consider young children who invent strategies to solve addition problems (e.g., $8 + 9 = \square$) by combining their knowledge of doubles (e.g., $8 + 8 = 16$) with their knowledge of number relationships (e.g., 9 is one more than 8) (Carpenter, this volume). Here it is not always clear where conceptual knowledge ends and procedural knowledge begins.

Furthermore, it is difficult to imagine someone possessing conceptual and procedural knowledge as *entirely* independent systems. Some connections are inevitable (Nantais, Herscovics, & Bergeron, 1984). In fact, although it is possible to consider procedures without concepts, it is not so easy to imagine conceptual knowledge that is not linked with some procedures. This is due, in part, to the fact that procedures translate conceptual knowledge into something observable. Without procedures to access and act on the knowledge, we would not know it was there.

A final caveat about our definitions is that not everyone working in this area—even the contributors to this volume—will agree with them. There are explicit differences between our definitions and those contained in other chapters, and some contributors suggest other distinctions that are not part of our definition. For example, Gelman and Meck distinguish between conceptual, procedural, *and* utilization competence, and Schoenfeld discusses differences between empiricism and deduction, a distinction that has some similarities but certainly is not identical with our discussion of concepts and procedures. Rather than viewing these differences as a statement of discord, we believe they are a sign of a healthy, vital discussion about very complex issues.

POTENTIAL RELATIONSHIPS BETWEEN CONCEPTUAL AND PROCEDURAL KNOWLEDGE

Mathematical knowledge, in its fullest sense, includes significant, fundamental relationships between conceptual and procedural knowledge. Students are not fully competent in mathematics if either kind of knowledge is deficient or if they both have been acquired but remain separate entities. When concepts and procedures are not connected, students may have a good intuitive feel for mathematics but not solve the problems, or they may generate answers but not understand what they are doing. Critical links between conceptual and procedural knowledge not only would prevent these deficit cases from developing but also would contribute in many other ways to the development of a sound knowledge base.

Benefits for Procedural Knowledge

Linking conceptual and procedural knowledge has many advantages for acquiring and using procedural knowledge. The advantages apply to both kinds of procedural knowledge identified earlier. Building relationships between conceptual knowledge and the formal symbol system of mathematics is the process that gives meaning to symbols. Building relationships between conceptual knowledge and the procedures of mathematics contributes to memory (storage and retrieval) of procedures and to their effective use.

Developing Meaning for Symbols. Few would deny that meaningful symbols provide an essential foundation for genuine mathematical competence. But students do not always establish meanings for the symbols they use. Given our description of procedural knowledge, it is possible to acquire knowledge of symbols purely as visual patterns that conform to certain syntactic constraints. Symbols acquired in this way make no demands on conceptual knowledge. For symbols to develop meaning they must be connected to the conceptual knowledge they represent.

The process of relating symbols to conceptual knowledge is described by Van Engen (1949). Symbols like 5.2, $+$, $=$, $\frac{3}{4}$ all represent ideas that can be encountered in concrete or real-world experiences. Once experienced, the ideas can be represented as conceptual knowledge. It is these conceptual, concretely based ideas that provide the referents for symbols. For example, the symbol "$+$" represents the joining idea in the story, "Sue has three marbles. Her mother gave her five more marbles. How many marbles does Sue have altogether?" If the joining idea is connected with "$+$," the symbol takes on meaning. Similar links must be made between each symbol and appropriate referents in order for the formal language of mathematics to become meaningful.

The notion of connecting symbols with their referents is presented in a more formal way by Schoenfeld (this volume). Schoenfeld identifies a reference world, a symbol world, and mappings between them. The mappings connect the referents and operations on them with symbol representations and analogous operations on the symbols. A critical part of mathematical competence stipulates that entities in the symbol world must represent (for the learner) entities in the reference world.

Recalling Procedures. Doing mathematics requires the execution of hundreds of different procedures, probably too many to memorize as individual pieces of information. In order to make the task manageable, the learner must call on some additional intellectual equipment. A good choice would be the available store of conceptual knowledge. If procedures are related to the underlying rationale on which they are based, the procedures begin to look reasonable. It is possible to understand how and why the procedures work. Because it is easier to remember things that make sense (Chase & Simon, 1973; Chi, 1978), procedures that are meaningful, that are understood by their users, are more likely to be recalled.

There are several reasons to believe that connecting procedures with their conceptual underpinnings is the key in producing procedures that are stored and retrieved more successfully. First, if procedures are linked with conceptual knowledge, they become stored as part of a network of information, glued together with semantic relationships. Such a network is less likely to deteriorate than an isolated piece of information, because memory is especially good for relationships that are meaningful (Anderson, 1983; Rohwer, 1973; Skemp, 1976) and highly organized (Baddeley, 1976; Bruner, 1960; Hilgard, 1957). Second, retrieval is enhanced because the knowledge structure, or network, of which the procedure is a part comes equipped with numerous links that enable access to the procedure. The ''conceptual'' links increase the chances that the procedure will be retrieved when needed, because they serve as alternate access routes for recall (Anderson, 1983). For example, suppose students are learning to add decimal numbers and the teacher says, ''When you add decimals you must first line up the decimal points.'' If this is all the information students acquire about setting up decimal addition problems, the line-up-the-decimal-points rule likely will be stored as an isolated piece of information with retrieval dependent on retracing a single link between the procedure and the perception of an addition problem as one involving decimal numbers. However, if students also learn that the concept underlying the procedure is the adding together of things that are alike, and they are able to recognize the similarity between this rationale and that used in adding whole numbers or common fractions, they are in a much better position to remember the rule. The likelihood of recalling the appropriate procedure is increased, partly because now the retrieval process can be triggered by several external *and* internal cues, and the procedure can be accessed by crossing a number of different conceptual bridges (e.g., ideas about place value or about common denominators, or intuitive notions about relative sizes of quantities). In fact, with this sort of conceptual base, the rule could be reconstructed extemporaneously.

Using Procedures.   There also is reason to believe that in addition to enhancing memory for procedures, linking conceptual and procedural knowledge facilitates the effective use of procedures. This may occur in at least three different ways. If conceptual knowledge is linked to procedures it can: (a) enhance problem representations and simplify procedural demands; (b) monitor procedure selection and execution; and (c) promote transfer and reduce the number of procedures required.

The logic behind the first claim, that related conceptual knowledge enhances problem representations and thus makes the problems easier to solve, is as follows. Problems are solved by building mental representations of the problems and then dealing with the representations to select appropriate procedures. Relevant conceptual knowledge can be brought to bear on the task by elaborating the problem context (Silver, 1982). Related conceptual knowledge is accessed, and the problem representation is enriched (Larkin, 1983). The advantage of representing the problem conceptually is that it allows one to reason directly about the quantities involved rather than reasoning about the symbols of a mediating language (Greeno, 1983a). In this way, conceptual knowledge can turn a difficult problem into a simpler one, which can be solved by available procedures (Davis, 1984).

Data supporting the importance of problem representations that are heavily conceptual come from two different sources. First, comparisons between experts and novices suggest that expert problem solvers in a particular domain represent problems by using underlying structure and conceptual features of the problem context, whereas novices focus more on superficial features and specific symbol manipulation rules that might apply (Chi, Feltovich, & Glaser, 1981; Larkin, McDermott, Simon, & Simon, 1980; Silver, this volume). The implication is that conceptually enriched problem representations facilitate successful performance.

A different data source that delivers the same message comes from observing adults solve what they perceive to be "real-life" problems (Lave, Murtaugh, & de La Rocha, 1984; Lesh, Landau, & Hamilton, 1983). It appears that problem representations drawing on conceptual knowledge to place the problem in a meaningful context influence the selection of procedures and raise the accuracy and efficiency of the applied procedures. More specifically, problems that lack a conceptual representation, that are solved only by selecting and applying memorized procedures, are more susceptible to error than problems for which a rich conceptual knowledge representation can be built (Carraher & Schliemann, 1985; Lave et al., 1984).

A second way in which links with conceptual knowledge can enhance the use of procedures is by executive control. Conceptual knowledge, if linked with a procedure, can monitor its selection and use and can evaluate the reasonableness of the procedural outcome. With regard to selection, conceptual knowledge serves (a) as an aid in the choice of appropriate procedures (Gelman & Meck, this volume; Piaget, 1978) and (b) as a constraint that discourages the selection of unacceptable procedures (Gelman, 1982; Gelman & Meck, this volume; Greeno, 1980). Piaget (1978) argues that when conceptual knowledge is on par with procedural actions, the conceptualization of a task enables one to anticipate the consequences of possible actions. This information can be used to select and coordinate appropriate procedures.

Conceptual knowledge can also inform a user that a procedure is inappropriate. This happens when the procedure itself violates conceptual principles. Gelman and Meck (this volume) argue that children learn to count relatively early in life *because* conceptual principles provide constraints against which they can evaluate their counting behaviors and reject them or alter them to conform to the conceptual principles. For an example later in life, consider again the student who is adding decimals (Hiebert & Wearne, this volume). Suppose the student is presented with 3.5 + 1.76. One procedure that specifically would be rejected by conceptual considerations is adding the 5 to the 6 and the 3 to the 7. It would be rejected because these operations would combine quantities of different denomination or size. So, in addition to assisting with the selection of an appropriate procedure, conceptual knowledge acts as a screening agent to reject inappropriate procedures.

A second and related executive control function for conceptual knowledge is monitoring procedural *outcomes*. Conceptual knowledge fulfills this function by playing the role of a validating critic (Brownell, 1947; Davis & McKnight, 1980). The critic judges the reasonableness of the answer; it checks whether the answer "makes sense." Consider, for example, a word problem described by Silver (this volume) that involves long division. The problem asked students to find how many buses would be needed to transport a given number of people. Most eighth-grade students computed correctly but consistently provided answers (involving remainders) that were unreasonable solutions to the problem. Conceptual knowledge of the problem situation would warn students that their answers were inappropriate. Another example comes from an earlier National Assessment of Educational Progress (Post, 1981). Students were asked to estimate the answer to $\frac{12}{13} + \frac{7}{8}$ and were given choices of 1, 2, 19, 21, and "I don't know." A conceptual knowledge critic would warn the student that 19 and 21, the two most frequent responses, were unreasonable. Ideally, the warnings in both of these examples would encourage the student to reevaluate the solutions and perhaps the choice of procedures.

On complex mathematical problems, executive decisions must be made at a macroscopic strategic level as well as at the tactical level (Schoenfeld, 1983). Both functions described above, selecting a procedure and checking its outcome, are tactical decisions. Strategic decisions involve planning the direction in which a solution will be pursued and managing intellectual resources to keep the pursuit running. Conceptual knowledge undoubtedly plays a strong role in strategic decision making as well. Schoenfeld (1983) has illustrated that effective use of procedures requires conceptually informed decisions at both the tactical and the strategic levels.

Up to this point, the ways in which conceptual knowledge can improve the use of procedures have dealt with using procedures on a single problem. Another benefit has to do with using procedures across two or more problems. It has long been recognized that if procedures are understood, or learned in a meaningful way, they transfer more easily to structurally similar problems (Brownell, 1947; Dewey, 1910). It now is possible to describe the phenomenon in more detail. Problems that are structurally similar have problem representations with some conceptual elements in common. The links between the procedure and related concepts connect the procedure, by way of the common elements, to many problem representations. Therefore, the appropriateness of the procedure for many superficially different problems is recognized, and the procedure "transfers" from one problem to another (Greeno, 1983a). In other words, conceptual knowledge releases the procedure from the surface context in which it was learned and encourages its use on other structurally similar problems.

An example of how conceptual knowledge facilitates transfer of procedures is provided by Carpenter (this volume). As young children's concept of subtraction is enriched to include different interpretations (such as take away, difference, and adding on), they are able to use a particular strategy learned for solving one type of problem to solve problems of a different type. The key is building a rich store of conceptual knowledge that covers a variety of task situations and, through its interconnections, becomes linked to a single, efficient procedure.

The real significance of increasing transfer of procedures is that it reduces the number of procedures that must be learned. Procedures that can be used flexibly, that are not tied to specific tasks, are procedures that have at least some generality. Generalized procedures eliminate the need to learn different procedures for each task, thereby reducing the number of procedures that must be learned and remembered. For instance, consider the process of multidigit subtraction with regrouping. If the process is learned at a purely syntactic level, different procedures must be learned for different kinds of problems (e.g., borrowing across zeros is syntactically different from borrowing across nonzeros). However, at the semantic level a single process of regrouping governs all cases. The slight syntactic variations that are executed for different tasks need not be treated as different procedures to be memorized independently; instead they simply appear as syntactically different manifestations of the same process applied to structurally similar tasks. Mathematics is filled with examples of a single, conceptually linked procedure that replaces numerous syntactically distinct ones.

To reiterate, a linking relationship between conceptual and procedural knowledge appears to increase the usefulness of procedural knowledge. The benefits accrue for both kinds of procedural knowledge, symbols and procedures. Linking conceptual knowledge with symbols creates a meaningful representation system, an essential prerequisite for intelligent mathematical learning and performance. Linking conceptual knowledge with rules, algorithms, or procedures reduces the number of procedures that must be learned and increases the likelihood that an appropriate procedure will be recalled and used effectively.

Benefits for Conceptual Knowledge

Linking conceptual and procedural knowledge benefits conceptual knowledge as well as procedural knowledge. The benefits for conceptual knowledge are cited less often but are equally significant. Under an organizational scheme similar to the previous section, some benefits for conceptual knowledge arise from the formal language system and syntax conventions, whereas others emerge from the use of rules and procedures.

Symbols Enhance Concepts. The formal language system of mathematics provides a powerful tool for dealing with complex ideas. Symbols that have been connected with meaningful referents can be used to think about the concepts they represent. "It is largely by the use of symbols that we achieve voluntary control over our thoughts" (Skemp, 1971, p. 83). Thought is aided by the fact that symbols can represent complex or densely packed concepts; in these cases, cognitive effort in dealing with the concepts is reduced by focusing on the symbols. In fact, one of the powerful features of mathematics is the effortlessness with which complex ideas can be manipulated by moving symbols.

Viewed as cognitive aids, symbols help to organize and operate on conceptual knowledge. But that is not all. The symbol system can also *produce* conceptual knowledge. Byers and Erlwanger (1984) draw attention to the fact that the notation system, or syntax of mathematical symbols, is responsible for the development of some key mathematical concepts. Place-value notation and Leibniz's integral notation are two especially apt examples. Advances in form often bring with them advances in related concepts (Struik, 1967).

Procedures Apply Concepts to Solve Problems. Conceptual knowledge is useful for solving mathematical tasks only when it is accessed and converted into appropriate form. Anderson (1983) describes one way in which this might happen. Problems for which no routine procedures are available are solved initially by applying facts and concepts in an effortful, laborious way. As similar problems are solved repeatedly, conceptual (declarative) knowledge is gradually transformed into set routines (condition-action pairs) for solving the problems. The condition-action pairs constitute the basic elements of the procedural system. Thus knowledge that is initially conceptual can be converted to knowledge that is procedural.

Gelman and Gallistel (1978) describe another way in which procedures can bring conceptual knowledge into the problem-solving arena. They believe that young children possess a significant store of conceptual knowledge about counting and number. However, they can only use their conceptual knowledge to reason about specific numerosities, about quantities to which a numerical value has been assigned. Counting *procedures* bring number within the purview of conceptual knowledge by generating specific numerosities with which conceptual knowledge can reason.

Third, procedures can facilitate the application of conceptual knowledge because highly routinized procedures can reduce the mental effort required in solving a problem and thereby make possible the solution of complex tasks. Case

(1985) explains this phenomenon by pointing out that efficient procedures require less of one's limited cognitive processing capacity. This frees additional space for more effortful processes, such as planning (Kotovsky, Hayes, & Simon, 1985), or looking for relationships between novel aspects of a problem and relevant conceptual knowledge. In other words, automated and efficient strategies make room for applying conceptual knowledge.

Procedures Promote Concepts.   Just as new symbol notation occasionally generates or advances concepts in the discipline of mathematics, new procedures can trigger for individuals the development of concepts. It is clear that during the early years, relationships between conceptual and procedural knowledge are intricate and dynamic (Baroody & Ginsburg, this volume; Gelman & Meck, this volume; Sinclair & Sinclair, this volume). It appears that on occasion procedural knowledge takes the lead and spurs the development of new concepts. For example, Gelman and Meck (this volume) present a scenario in which children use already acquired counting skills to promote the development of an ordinal concept of number. Baroody and Ginsburg (this volume) describe other instances in which young children's conceptual development is motivated by the application of procedures.

Summary

Linking conceptual knowledge and procedural knowledge has many advantages. Usually the advantages are claimed for procedural knowledge. Procedural knowledge that is informed by conceptual knowledge results in symbols that have meaning and procedures that can be remembered better and used more effectively. A closer look reveals theoretical advantages for conceptual knowledge. Procedural knowledge provides a formal language and action sequences that raise the level and applicability of conceptual knowledge. These are the theoretical claims. In reality, the advantages are not always realized.

ACTUAL RELATIONSHIPS BETWEEN CONCEPTUAL AND PROCEDURAL KNOWLEDGE

If students of mathematics naturally and routinely connected their conceptual and procedural knowledge, the issue (and this book) would be of little interest. The skill versus understanding debate of the past would certainly not have persisted and probably would not have arisen at all. Examining the relationships between conceptual and procedural knowledge is a worthwhile pursuit only because students often fail to recognize or construct the relationships. Being competent in mathematics involves knowing concepts, knowing symbols and procedures, and knowing how they are related. Why is it that the relationships frequently are not constructed? What are the factors that inhibit the creation and recognition of relationships between conceptual and procedural knowledge?

Factors That Inhibit the Construction of Relationships

Building relationships between pieces of information does not always occur spontaneously. Even if the relationships are made explicit, they are not always recognized or internalized. Many factors may contribute to the failure to establish relationships between units of knowledge; we address three of them that may have special importance for mathematics learning.

Deficits in the Knowledge Base. Relationships between items of knowledge cannot be constructed if the knowledge does not exist. This observation is obvious, but it is worth elaborating because of its importance in mathematics learning. Three examples illustrate the point. Silver (this volume) argues that the common error in adding fractions of adding numerators and adding denominators (e.g., $\frac{1}{2} + \frac{1}{3} = \frac{2}{5}$) may not be due so much to a separation of concepts and procedures as to an erroneous and incomplete conceptual base. Many visual diagrams and other conceptual models unwittingly contribute to a conceptual structure that *reinforces* (rather than discourages) this error. Hiebert and Wearne (this volume) suggest that a critical relationship in decimal fractions is the equivalence relation between a decimal fraction and its associated common fraction. For many students, such relationships are impossible to establish because the students enter instruction on decimals with deficient knowledge of common fractions. A final example, from a slightly different perspective, comes from Carpenter (this volume). Carpenter points out that children's increasing proficiency in solving simple addition and subtraction problems can be traced to increases in conceptual knowledge. Furthermore, meaning for procedures cannot be developed unless a rich conceptual knowledge base is in place.

All three examples suggest that a sound knowledge base is necessary for useful relationships to be established. Deficiencies in concepts or procedures, although sometimes hidden, can be the source of weak or missing connections.

Difficulties of Encoding Relationships. A second factor that inhibits the construction of relationships is young children's tendency to overlook or fail to encode relationships that may be obvious to adults. Research on young children's encoding of information, specifically studies on elaboration in paired-associate learning, suggests that sometimes children have trouble constructing relationships between items of information (Ackerman, 1985; Pressley, 1982; Rohwer, 1973). Even when conceptual relationships between items are obvious to adults, children do not readily encode them. It may be that the failure to encode and construct relationships between units of information is not limited to these rather special paired-associate tasks but extends to more complex school learning tasks as well. Relationships between units of mathematical knowledge, although taught by adults using seemingly appropriate methods, may not be picked up and internalized by children.

Tendency to Compartmentalize Knowledge.   A third general factor that seems to impede the construction of relationships between units of knowledge is that knowledge just acquired often is context bound (Bruner, 1973; Tulving, 1983). Things learned in a particular context are initially tied to surface characteristics of that context. This prevents one from noticing similarities between the newly acquired knowledge and previously acquired knowledge held in memory. Context-bound knowledge is not looking for relationships outside the immediate context. The phenomenon is illustrated well by Lawler's (1981) description of a young child learning to compute in several different contexts. "Different" methods were learned in each context, and the methods remained faithful to the context in which they were acquired. Money methods were used only with money, LOGO methods with LOGO, paper and pencil methods with paper and pencil. For some time the methods remained encapsulated by the context. Later, similarities between the methods were recognized, but then only by detecting regularities in the outcome of the different methods rather than by detecting similarities in the methods themselves.

The experience of acquiring information as isolated, context-specific bits of knowledge is known to both older and younger learners and pervades all content domains. In whole numbers (Carpenter, this volume), fractions (Silver, this volume), decimals (Hiebert & Wearne, this volume), algebra (Kaput, 1982), and geometry (Schoenfeld, this volume), students acquire knowledge in one context and hold it separate from knowledge acquired in other contexts. Knowledge compartments can remain isolated even when they are well developed individually. Furthermore, the content of these knowledge compartments can be mutually incompatible, a condition that does not necessarily fluster the learner. Evidence for the isolated nature of students' knowledge often is collected by observing students solve the same problem in two different contexts, produce conflicting solutions, and not reconcile the differences. Indeed, most investigators report that many students do not recognize that the differences must be reconciled.

A further explanation for students' tendency to compartmentalize knowledge is offered by Posner, Strike, Hewson, & Gertzog (1982). They suggest that because learners often resist conceptual change, the new knowledge is compartmentalized so that it does not interfere with existing concepts. This is especially true when new knowledge is perceived to be unrelated to or conflicts with existing knowledge. Specific compartments are accessed only when surface characteristics of the problem context are recognized as similar to those in which the knowledge was acquired.

The effects on mathematics learning of acquiring units of knowledge but not establishing relationshps between them are serious. Important insights into the acquisition and application of mathematical competencies can be gained by examining the nature of these breakdowns and the points at which they occur. On the basis of recent work in this area, it now is possible to trace the changing nature of the relationships between conceptual and procedural knowledge as children proceed through the preschool and school years. What follows is a simplified sketch. The remaining chapters in this volume describe in more detail the nature of the relationships at succeeding points in a person's mathematical career.

Ontogeny of Relationships
During the Mathematical Learning Years

Preschool Years. During the earliest years, conceptual knowledge and procedural knowledge are closely related. In fact, Sinclair and Sinclair (this volume) suggest that at this point concepts and procedures are so closely related that they become nearly indissociable. Before children enter school, their mathematical knowledge is limited mostly to knowledge about counting (Ginsburg, 1977). How conceptual and procedural knowledge interact as children learn to count is a matter of current debate. Some investigators believe that the development of concepts or principles of counting precedes the acquisition of skills needed to count accurately (Gelman, 1982; Gelman & Gallistel, 1978; Gelman & Meck, 1983, this volume). Children know more conceptually than they are able to demonstrate procedurally. Other researchers believe that some counting skills are acquired initially as rote procedures and later become informed by conceptual knowledge (Baroody, 1984; Baroody & Ginsburg, this volume; Fuson & Hall, 1983; Fuson, Richards, & Briars, 1982). Either way, concepts and procedures are closely intertwined as children learn to count.

During the preschool years, children also are learning about numerical print (Sinclair & Sinclair, 1984, this volume). They acquire meanings for numerical symbols from environmental print and gradually refine and enrich their meanings to correspond to adult conventions. The important point is that the process seems to involve concepts *and* procedures that are closely connected.

The connections between conceptual and procedural knowledge still are in place as children enter school. By this time children have learned to use their counting abilities to solve simple addition and subtraction problems, if they are presented in words rather than symbols. The kinds of strategies they use to solve the problems is the clue to the link between their procedures and their conceptualization of the problem (Carpenter, this volume; Carpenter, Hiebert, & Moser, 1981; Carpenter & Moser, 1984; De Corte & Verschaffel, 1984). For example, if concrete counters are available, almost all beginning school children will solve a missing-addend story by adding on, and a take-away story by taking away. That is, the child's counting strategy matches the semantic structure of the story. It is as if the child's conceptual knowledge of the situation guides the selection of a solution procedure.

Additional weight for the argument that conceptual and procedural knowledge are closely related at this point is provided by two models proposed to account for children's performance on addition and subtraction word problems (Briars & Larkin, 1984; Riley, Greeno, & Heller, 1983). Although there are some important differences between them, both models assume that increases in procedural skill are tied to advances in conceptual knowledge. Improvements in performance are related to improvements in understanding, not merely to increases in memorized procedures. Students have not yet learned algorithms that take them beyond their level of conceptual knowledge. At this point in their mathematical careers, students do not get right answers for problems they do not understand.

School Years.   Classroom instruction in arithmetic introduces students to the formal symbolic language of mathematics. If students connect the symbols with conceptually based referents, the symbols acquire meaning and become powerful tools for recording and communicating mathematical events. Unfortunately, many students seem to learn symbols as meaningless marks on paper (Hiebert, 1984a). The symbols are separated from the conceptual knowledge they are supposed to represent. For instance, after instruction on writing number sentences (equations), many first graders still do not see the connection between the story problems and the number sentences that represent them (Carpenter, Hiebert & Moser, 1983; Lindvall & Ibarra, 1980; Matthews, 1983). They view the process of solving a story problem and solving the related number sentence as two separate, independent events. Their conceptual knowledge of addition and subtraction accessed through story problems is not connected with the symbolism of arithmetic.

For many children, the effect of initial instruction on arithmetic symbols is to pry apart conceptual and procedural knowledge and send them in different directions. Up to this point both types of knowledge seem to develop in close synchrony, continually informing each other. But with the introduction of written symbols whose meanings are not well established, the dynamic interaction is broken. Probably due to the emphases of conventional instruction (see chapters in this volume by Baroody and Ginsburg, by Carpenter, by VanLehn, and by Schoenfeld), the focus of attention shifts to the procedural level. New symbols are introduced, and rules for manipulating the symbols are heavily emphasized. Students learn to execute the rules and algorithms according to syntactic constraints, and the rules produce current answers if they are fed the problems in familiar form. But the rules are tied only to the symbols, not to the conceptual knowledge that provides their rationale.

By the time students are in third and fourth grade, they have acquired a large array of symbol manipulation rules. In general, the rules are more sensitive to syntactic constraints than to conceptual underpinnings. Even if conceptual under-standings exist, they have little effect on the selection or execution of procedural skills (Davis & McKnight, 1980; Resnick, 1982). The nearly exclusive reliance on procedural knowledge is evidenced in two ways. First, most of students' behavior on arithmetic computation tasks can be described in purely syntactic terms (Brown & VanLehn, 1982; VanLehn, 1983, this volume). Second, students' computation errors reflect attempts to repair broken procedures according to syntactic constraints rather than semantic or conceptual considerations (Van-Lehn, this volume).

As students move through elementary and junior high school, conceptual knowledge and procedural knowledge continue to develop along separate tracks. The focus of instruction remains on procedural knowledge, and students acquire new rules for new symbol systems such as common and decimal fractions (Hiebert & Wearne, this volume). As with whole numbers, there are few connec-tions apparent between procedures and concepts. For example, students' behav-ior on decimal computation problems can be modeled well by appealing only to procedural, symbol manipulation rules (Hiebert & Wearne, 1985). Also, the errors students make often are produced by rules that mildly distort the syntactic guidelines but greatly violate the relevant concepts. As an illustration, an earlier National Assessment of Educational Progress confirms that many students add common fractions by adding numerators and adding denominators (Post, 1981). From a procedural point of view, it is easy to explain why students do this, but conceptually it makes no sense.

Reliance on syntactic symbol manipulation rules continues into high school. Students' behavior on algebra tasks can be characterized by identifying a list of syntactic rules together with distortions of the rules triggered by surface features of the tasks (Matz, 1980). Notably absent from the use of algebraic symbols is a link with conceptual content (Kaput, 1982; Rosnick & Clement, 1980). In geom-etry, the separation between types of knowledge can be characterized somewhat differently (Schoenfeld, this volume), but the theme remains the same. Students learn rules for solving specific kinds of problems, and the rules remain isolated from students conceptual knowledge of the subject.

In spite of the fact that students' procedural rules often become flawed, the rules can take them well beyond their level of conceptual understanding. Stu-dents are able to get correct answers for many problems they do not understand. Studies have shown that students from elementary school through college can perform successfully on routine paper and pencil problems but lack essential, underlying conceptual knowledge. This happens in mathematics (e.g., Erl-wanger, 1975; Rosnick & Clement, 1980), in science (see Gentner & Stevens, 1983), and undoubtedly in other disciplines as well.

The problem with learning procedures without concepts is that the procedures become likely victims of all the maladies identified earlier. Procedures that lack connections with conceptual knowledge may deteriorate quickly and are not reconstructable; they may be only partially remembered and combined with other subprocedures in inappropriate ways; they often are bound to the specific context in which they were learned and do not transfer easily to new situations; and they can be applied inappropriately without the benefit of a validating critic to check the reasonableness of the outcome. Hence, although routinized procedural skills are essential for efficient problem solving, related conceptual knowledge is needed to give procedures stability and effectiveness. "Without these meanings to hold skills and ideas together in an intelligible, unified system, pupils in our schools for too long a time have 'mastered' skills which they do not understand, which they can use only in situations closely paralleling those of learning, and which they must soon forget" (Brownell, 1947, p. 260).

Formal mathematics instruction seems to do a better job of teaching procedures than concepts or relationships between them. There are undoubtedly many reasons for this. Chapters in this volume by Baroody and Ginsburg, by Carpenter, by Schoenfeld, and by VanLehn discuss some of these, and the literature on classroom processes and teacher decision making identifies others (Brophy, 1982; Doyle, 1983; Good, 1984). An examination of instructional processes lies beyond the scope of this chapter. Nevertheless, it should be recognized that the preeminence of procedures over concepts and the lack of relationships between the two can be explained in part by the nature of formal school instruction.

THE MISSION OF THE BOOK

"The relationship between computational skill and mathematical understanding is one of the oldest concerns in the psychology of mathematics" (Resnick & Ford, 1981, p. 246). Relationships between procedural and conceptual knowledge have had a long history for two reasons. First, the issue has been recognized as an important one by many psychologists and educators through the years. It is important because it seems to hold the key to many learning processes and problems. If we understood more about the acquisition of these kinds of knowledge and the interplay between them in mathematical performance, we surely could unlock some doors that have until now hidden significant learning problems in mathematics. Second, the issue has been extremely difficult to resolve. Relationships between conceptual and procedural knowledge change over time and are influenced by many forces, both internal and external to the learner. Describing such complex relationships is a monumental task.

Why should we think that this book will succeed in describing the relationships between conceptual and procedural knowledge? Certainly, it will not succeed in explicating all of the issues surrounding the conceptual and procedural knowledge debate. We simply don't know everything needed to finish the discussion. But we do believe that the remaining chapters take us significantly further in our understanding of conceptual and procedural knowledge than we have come so far.

We are optimistic for two reasons. One is that there is a clearer understanding of the questions that need to be asked, a clearer focus on the issues that will yield useful insights. Building on past work, it now is evident that it is the *relationships* between conceptual and procedural knowledge that hold the key. The skills and understanding issue is important, to be sure, but not because instruction should choose between them. Rather, skills and understandings are important because they signal two kinds of knowledge that play crucial, interactive roles in the development of mathematical competence. It is understanding the relationships between these two forms of knowledge that will provide the real payoff (Glaser, 1979).

Our second reason for optimism is the convergence in focus of several lines of research. Two dimensions of this joining of forces are especially significant. One is the coming together of two previously separate paradigms of psychology research: Gestalt psychology, with an emphasis on concept learning and development; and behavioral psychology, with its emphasis on skilled performance. Studying the *relationship* between concepts and procedures focuses these two perspectives on the same issues. A second form of convergence is that of two disciplines: mathematics education and cognitive psychology. The nature of the relationships between conceptual and procedural knowledge is receiving concentrated attention by researchers from both fields, using a nearly common language. The broad field of cognitive science provides much common ground that facilitates and encourages serious communication and collaborative efforts among those from various research traditions. Past experience suggests that joint efforts by mathematics educators and psychologists are especially productive in providing insights in children's learning of mathematics (Hiebert, 1984b). This book represents such an effort.

REFERENCES

Ackerman, B. P. (1985). Children's retrieval deficit. In C. J. Brainerd & M. Pressley, *Basic processes in memory development: Progress in cognitive development research* (pp. 1–46). New York: Springer-Verlag.

Anderson, J. R. (1983). *The architecture of cognition.* Cambridge, MA: Harvard University Press.

Ausubel, D. (1967). *Learning theory and classroom practice.* Toronto: Ontario Institute for Studies in Education.

Baddeley, A. D. (1976). *The psychology of memory.* New York: Basic books.

Baroody, A. J. (1984). More precisely defining and measuring the order-irrelevance principle. *Journal of Experimental Child Psychology, 38,* 33–41.

Briars, D. J., & Larkin, J. H. (1984). An integrated model of skills in solving elementary word problems. *Cognition and Instruction, 1,* 245–296.

Brophy, J. E. (1982). How teachers influence what is taught and learned in classrooms. *Elementary School Journal, 83,* 1–13.

Brown, J. S., & VanLehn, K. (1982). Towards a generative theory of "bugs." In T. P. Carpenter, J. M. Moser, & T. A. Romberg (Eds.), *Addition and subtraction: A cognitive perspective* (pp. 117–135). Hillsdale, NJ: Lawrence Erlbaum Associates.

Brownell, W. A. (1935). Psychological considerations in the learning and teaching of arithmetic. In *The teaching of arithmetic. Tenth yearbook of the National Council of Teachers of Mathematics.* New York: Teachers College, Columbia University.

Brownell, W. A. (1941). Arithmetic in grades I and II. *Duke University Research Studies in Education* (No. 6). Durham, NC: Duke University Press.

Brownell, W. A. (1947). The place of meaning in the teaching of arithmetic. *Elementary School Journal, 47,* 256–265.

Bruner, J. S. (1961). The act of discovery. *Harvard Educational Review, 31,* 21–32.

Bruner, J. S. (1960). *The process of education.* New York: Vintage Books.

Bruner, J. S. (1973). *Beyond the information given.* New York: Norton.

Byers, V., & Erlwanger, S. (1984). Content and form in mathematics. *Educational Studies in Mathematics, 15,* 259–275.

Carpenter, T. P., Hiebert, J., & Moser, J. M. (1981). Problem structure and first-grade children's initial solution processes for simple addition and subtraction problems. *Journal for Research in Mathematics Education, 12,* 27–39.

Carpenter, T. P., Hiebert, J., & Moser, J. M. (1983). The effect of instruction on children's solutions of addition and subtraction word problems. *Educational Studies in Mathematics, 14,* 55–72.

Carpenter, T. P., & Moser, J. M. (1984). The acquisition of addition and subtraction concepts in grades one through three. *Journal for Research in Mathematics Education, 15,* 179–202.

Carraher, T. N., & Schliemann, A. D. (1985). Computation routines prescribed by schools: Help or hindrance? *Journal for Research in Mathematics Education, 16,* 37–44.

Case, R. (1985). *Intellectual development: Birth to adulthood.* New York: Academic Press.

Chase, W. G. & Simon, H. A. (1973). The mind's eye in chess. In W. G. Chase (Ed.), *Visual information processing.* New York: Academic Press.

Chi, M. (1978). Knowledge structures and memory development. In R. Siegler (Ed.), *Children's thinking: What develops?* (pp. 73–96). Hillsdale, NJ: Lawrence Erlbaum Associates.

Chi, M., Feltovich, P., & Glaser, R. (1981). Categorization and representation of physics problems by experts and novices. *Cognitive Science, 5,* 121–152.

Davis, R. B. (1984). *Learning mathematics: The cognitive science approach to mathematics education.* Norwood, NJ: Ablex.

Davis, R. B., & McKnight, C. (1980). The influence of semantic content on algorithmic behavior. *Journal of Mathematical Behavior, 3,* (1), 39–87.

De Corte, E., & Verschaffel, L. (1984). First graders' solution strategies of addition and subtraction word problems. In J. M. Moser (Ed.), *Proceedings of the sixth annual meeting of the North American Chapter of the International Group for the Psychology of Mathematics Education* (pp. 15–20). Madison: Wisconsin Center for Education Research.

Dewey, J. (1910). *How we think.* Boston: Heath.

Doyle, W. (1983). Academic work. *Review of Educational Research, 53,* 159–199.

Erlwanger, S. H. (1975). Case studies of children's conceptions of mathematics—Part I. *Journal of Children's Mathematical Behavior, 1* (3), 157–183.

Fuson, K. C., & Hall, J. W. (1983). The acquisition of early number word meanings: A conceptual analysis and review. In H. P. Ginsburg (Ed.), *The development of mathematical thinking* (pp. 49–107). New York: Academic Press, 1983.

Fuson, K. C., Richards, J., & Briars, D. J. (1982). The acquisition and elaboration of the number word sequence. In C. J. Brainerd (Ed.), *Children's logical and mathematical cognition* (pp. 33–92). New York: Springer-Verlag.

Gagné, R. M. (1977). *The conditions of learning* (3rd ed.). New York: Holt, Rinehart, & Winston.

Gelman, R., & Gallistel, C. R. (1978). *The child's understanding of number.* Cambridge, MA: Harvard University Press.

Gelman, R. (1982). Basic numerical abilities. In R. J. Sternberg (Ed.), *Advances in psychology of human intelligence* (Vol. 1) (pp. 181–205). Hillsdale, NJ: Lawrence Erlbaum Associates.

Gelman, R., & Meck, E. (1983). Preschoolers' counting: Principles before skill. *Cognition, 13,* 343–359.

Gentner, D., & Stevens, A. L. (Eds.). (1983). *Mental models.* Hillsdale, NJ: Lawrence Erlbaum Associates.

Ginsburg, H. (1977). *Children's arithmetic: The learning process.* New York: Van Nostrand.

Glaser, R. (1979). Trends and research questions in psychological research on learning and schooling. *Educational Researcher, 8* (10), 6–13.

Good, T. L. (1984, April). *Recent studies of teaching: Implications for research and policy in mathematics education.* Invited address to the Special Interest Group for Research in Mathematics Education at the annual meeting of the American Educational Research Association, New Orleans.

Greeno, J. G. (1980). Analysis of understanding in problem solving. In R. H. Kluwe & H. Spada (Eds.), *Developmental models of thinking* (pp. 199–212). New York: Academic Press.

Greeno, J. G. (1983a). Conceptual entities. In D. Gentner & A. L. Stevens (Eds.), *Mental models* (pp. 227–252). Hillsdale, NJ: Lawrence Erlbaum Associates.

Greeno, J. G. (1983b). Forms of understanding in mathematical problem solving. In S. G. Paris, G. M. Olson, & H. W. Stevenson (Eds.), *Learning and motivation in the classroom* (pp. 83–111). Hillsdale, NJ: Lawrence Erlbaum Associates.

Hiebert, J. (1984a). Children's mathematics learning: The struggle to link form and understanding. *Elementary School Journal, 84,* 497–513.

Hiebert, J. (1984b). Complementary perspectives. [Review of *Acquisition of mathematics conepts and processes, Children's logical and mathematical cognition: Progress in cognitive development research,* and *The development of mathematical thinking*]. *Journal for Research in Mathematics Education, 15,* 229–234.

Hiebert, J., & Wearne, D. (1985). A model of students' decimal computation procedures. *Cognition and Instruction, 2,* 175–205.

Hilgard, E. R. (1957). *Introduction to psychology* (2nd ed.). New York: Harcourt Brace.

Jones, P. S. (Ed.). (1970). *A history of mathematics education in the United States and Canada: Thirty-second yearbook.* Washington, DC: National Council of Teachers of Mathematics.

Kaput, J. (1982, March). *Intuitive attempts at algebraic representation of quantitative relationships.* Paper presented at the annual meeting of the American Educational Research Association, New York.

Kotovsky, K., Hayes, J. R., & Simon, H. A. (1985). Why are some problems hard? Evidence from Tower of Hanoi. *Cognitive Psychology, 17,* 248–294.

Larkin, J. H. (1983). The role of problem representation in physics. In D. Gentner & A. L. Stevens (Eds.), *Mental models* (pp. 75–98). Hillsdale, NJ: Lawrence Erlbaum Associates.

Larkin, J., McDermott, J., Simon, D.P., & Simon, H. A. (1980). Expert and novice performers in solving physics problems. *Science, 208,* 1335–1342.

Lave, J., Murtaugh, M., & de La Rocha, O. (1984). The dialectical construction of arithmetic in grocery shopping. In B. Rogoff & J. Lave (Eds.), *Everyday cognition: Its development in social context* (pp. 67–94). Cambridge, MA: Harvard University.

Lawler, R. W. (1981). The progressive construction of mind. *Cognitive Science, 5,* 1–30.

Lesh, R., Landau, M., & Hamilton, E. (1983). Conceptual models and applied mathematical problem-solving research. In R. Lesh & M. Landau (Eds.), *Acquisition of mathematics concepts and processes* (pp. 263–343). New York: Academic Press.

Lindvall, C. M., & Ibarra, C. G. (1980). Incorrect procedures used by primary grade pupils in solving open addition and subtraction sentences. *Journal for Research in Mathematics Education, 11,* 50–62.

Matthews, J. (1983). A subtraction experiment with six and seven year old children. *Educational Studies in Mathematics, 14,* 139–154.

Matz, M. (1980). Towards a computational theory of algebraic competence. *Journal of Mathematical Behavior, 3* (1), 93–166.

McLaughlin, K. L. (1935). Number ability in preschool children. *Childhood Education, 11,* 348–353.

McLellan, J. A., & Dewey, J. (1895). *The psychology of number and its applications to methods of teaching arithmetic.* New York: D. Appleton.

Nantais, N., Herscovics, N., & Bergeron, J. C. (1984). The skills-understanding dilemma in mathematics education. In J. M. Moser (Ed.), *Proceedings of the sixth annual meeting of the North American Chapter of the International Group for the Psychology of Mathematics Education* (pp. 229–235). Madison, WI: Wisconsin Center for Education Research.

Newell, A., & Simon, H. A. (1972). *Human problem solving.* Englewood Cliffs, NJ: Prentice-Hall.

Norman, D. A., & Rumelhart, D. E. (1975). *Explorations in cognition.* San Francisco: Freeman.

Piaget, J. (1960). *The psychology of intelligence.* Totowa, NJ: Littlefield, Adams.

Piaget, J. (1978). *Success and understanding.* Cambridge, MA: Harvard University Press.

Posner, G. J., Strike, K. A., Hewson, P. W., & Gertzog, W. A. (1982). Accommodation of a scientific conception: Toward a theory of conceptual change. *Science Education, 66,* 211–227.

Post, T. R. (1981). Fractions: Results and implications from National Assessment. *Arithmetic Teacher, 28* (9), 26–31.

Pressley, M. (1982). Elaboration and memory development. *Child Development, 53,* 296–309.

Resnick, L. B. (1982). Syntax and semantics in learning to subtract. In T. P. Carpenter, J. M. Moser, & T. A. Romberg (Eds.), *Addition and subtraction: A cognitive perspective* (pp. 136–155). Hillsdale, NJ: Lawrence Erlbaum Associates.

Resnick, L. B., & Ford, W. W. (1981). *The psychology of mathematics for instruction.* Hillsdale, NJ: Lawrence Erlbaum Associates.

Riley, M. S., Greeno, J. G., & Heller, J. I. (1983). Development of children's problem-solving ability in arithmetic. In H. P. Ginsburg (Ed.), *The development of mathematical thinking* (pp. 153–196). New York: Academic Press.

Rohwer, W. D., Jr. (1973). Elaboration and learning in childhood and adolescence. In H. W. Reese (Ed.), *Advances in child development and behavior* (Vol. 8) (pp. 1–57). New York: Academic Press.

Rosnick, P., & Clement, J. (1980). Learning without understanding: The effect of tutoring strategies on algebra misconceptions. *Journal of Mathematical Behavior, 3* (1), 3–24.

Scheffler, I. (1965). *Conditions of knowledge: An introduction to epistemology and education.* Chicago: University of Chicago Press.

Schoenfeld, A. H. (1983). Episodes and executive decisions in mathematical problem-solving. In R. Lesh & M. Landau (Eds.), *Acquisition of mathematics concepts and processes* (pp. 345–395). New York: Academic Press.

Shulman, L. S. (1970). Psychology and mathematics education. In E. G. Begle (Ed.), *Mathematics education: The sixty-ninth yearbook of the National Society for the Study of Education* (pp. 23–71). Chicago: University of Chicago Press.

Silver, E. A. (1982). Knowledge organization and mathematical problem solving. In F. K. Lester & J. Garofalo (Eds.), *Mathematical problem solving: Issues in research* (pp. 15–25). Philadelphia: Franklin Institute Press.

Sinclair, A., & Sinclair, H. (1984). Preschool children's interpretation of written numbers. *Human Learning, 3,* 173–184.

Skemp, R. R. (1971). *The psychology of learning mathematics.* Middlesex, England: Penguin.

Skemp, R. R. (1976). Relational understanding and instrumental understanding. *Mathematics Teaching, 77,* 1–7.

Struik, D. J. (1967). *A concise history of mathematics.* New York: Dover.

Thorndike, E. L. (1922). *The psychology of arithmetic.* New York: Macmillan.

Tulving, E. (1983). *Elements of episodic memory.* New York: Oxford University Press.

Van Engen, H. (1949). An analysis of meaning in arithmetic. *Elementary School Journal, 49,* 321–329; 395–400.

Van Engen, H. (1953). The formation of concepts. In H. F. Fehr (Ed.), *The learning of mathematics: Its theory and practice. Twenty-first Yearbook of the National Council of Teachers of Mathematics* (pp. 69–98). Washington, DC: NCTM.

VanLehn, K. (1983). On the representation of procedures in repair theory. In H. P. Ginsburg (Ed.), *The development of mathematical thinking* (pp. 201–252). New York: Academic Press.

2 The Notion of Principle: The Case of Counting

Rochel Gelman
Elizabeth Meck
University of Pennsylvania

We have proposed that learning to count skillfully is initially directed by the implicit knowledge of some counting principles (e.g. Gelman & Gallistel, 1978; Gelman & Meck, 1983). Here we develop the thesis that this is so because principles both set constraints on the nature of counting procedures and provide clues about relevant learning environments. More generally, the idea is that much of early cognitive development proceeds as a function of some domain-specific principles that define domains, focus attention on domain-relevant inputs, and play a central role in the selection and generation of the class of domain-appropriate behaviors. In this chapter, we expand on the notion of principle, taking up both what it does and what it does not entail. In doing so, we hope to clarify the nature of principled or conceptual competence and its relation to the generation of behavior which is governed by procedural competence.

INITIAL CONSIDERATIONS

One can attribute to individuals knowledge of principles without requiring that they be able to articulate those principles. The distinction here is between *implicit* and *explicit* knowledge and is central to discussions in linguistics and psycholinguistics. We honor principles of syntax when listening to and producing utterances that are in the language, as well as when deciding that strings like "Who did John see Mary and ?" are not in the language. Yet we are not able to articulate the linguistic principle governing the selection or rejection of acceptable utterances (the present unacceptable string violates the Coordinate Structure Constraint [Ross, 1967]).

Knowledge of the correct principles does not guarantee correct performance. As we will see, principles specify characteristics that a correct performance must possess, but they do not provide recipes for generating a plan for correct performances. Nor do they guarantee correct execution of a plan. As a consequence, a competence-performance distinction is central to our treatment of development. This is one reason Greeno, Riley and Gelman (1984) distinguish between *conceptual, procedural* and *utilization competence.*

Although principles do not provide recipes for generating successful procedures under particular circumstances, they do play a fundamental, indispensable role in the synthesis of these procedures. This is because they provide the constraints procedures must reflect if they are to yield acceptable counting behavior. Conceptual competence or principled knowledge is coordinated with the planning- and procedure-generation system that makes up procedural competence and thus helps determine the actual procedures used.

We postulate that some principled understanding precedes skilled counting both because we think the data support the view and because we believe that were there no early competence, children might never learn to count or do arithmetic. The initial competence guides the development of initial procedures. Once the system is on its way, it is inevitable that there will be an interaction between procedural and conceptual competence. We begin our discussion of the relation between conceptual and procedural competence by presenting the case that some principles antedate correct performance and make possible the acquisition of the knowledge required for correct performances. We end with a consideration of a case where the use of a procedure supports the development of further principled understanding. This makes clear that only some counting principles are available to young children before they produce counting behaviors. It also illustrates how conceptual, procedural, and utilization competence can interact to produce new learning (see Baroody & Ginsburg, Carpenter, Sinclair & Sinclair, and Schoenfeld, this volume).

A Concrete Case: The Counting Principles

Counting to assess the cardinal value of a set is governed by five principles. These are: (a) one-one correspondence—every item in a set must be assigned a unique tag; (b) the stable order principle—the tags used must be drawn from a stably ordered list; (c) the cardinal principle—the last tag used in a count has a special status; it represents the cardinal value of the set; (d) the item-indifference (or irrelevance) principle—there are no restrictions on the collection of items that can be counted; and, (e) the order-indifference principle—the order in which items are tagged is irrelevant; a change in the order of the items in the display does not change the consequence of applying the first three principles. Note that the last two principles are principles of permissibility, statements about the wide range of conditions to which the first three "how-to-count" principles can apply.

This or some subset of this list of principles is the one we suggest as a possible candidate for the initial competence children bring to the task of acquiring skill at counting. Note that it does not cover all principles about counting. To do this, it at least needs to be expanded to account, for example, for our knowledge of the relationship between counting and the ordinal number of some object in a display (Botman, 1981; Fuson, Richards & Briars, 1982) or our knowledge that *every* count number has a successor (Evans & Gelman, 1985). We do not include knowledge of such principles in the initial competence, because we can propose ways in which these principles could be learned—given the assumption of what is already in conceptual competence.

We believe that the function of the early principles is to guide the assemblage of procedures and the development of skill at using these procedures. Other researchers maintain that initially children memorize, by rote and without understanding, various counting behaviors and only eventually induce principles or components of the counting principles (e.g. Briars & Siegler, 1984; Fuson & Hall, 1983). These authors point out that young children lack general skill and that what skills they do have appear only in limited situations. Additionally, they note children do best on tasks that use conventional counting behaviors, for example, counting things in a row as opposed to a circle. In learning theory or S-R terms, the argument is that children's habits are built up as children are reinforced for copying conventional demonstrations; initial habits are weak, and performance and generalization levels are low. This account of early number skill is developed in detail in Briars and Siegler (1984) and Siegler and Shrager (1984).

We show here that although it is true that young children have limited and variable skill, this is not definitive evidence for the rote-learning position. The fact that initial skills are variable fits well, indeed is predicted, by the position that principles guide but do not guarantee successful performance (see also Wilkinson, 1984). Further, we show that it is difficult to explain why young children learn count sequences at all unless we grant them a structure that guides this learning. We attempt to show that it would be exceedingly difficult for learning about counting to get off the ground in the first place were children not able to take advantage of some counting principles.

Why Postulate Principles?

To Help Solve the Problem of Stimulus Attention and Stimulus Definition. Recent research converges on a rather surprising generalization: babies and very young children attend to numerically relevant information in the environment. For example, 6- to 8-month-old infants match the number of drumbeats they hear (two or three) with the number of items they see in a colored photograph of a haphazard collection of small household objects (Starkey, Spelke, & Gelman, in press). Twelve-month-olds can learn to compare a paired sequence of displays of one, two, three, or four items on the basis of whether the displays have an equal number of items, one has more items, or one has fewer items (Cooper, Campbell, & Safady, 1985). This is a surprising generalization, because not long ago even preschoolers were said to be unable to achieve true numerical (as opposed to perceptual) representations of sets. Matters pertaining to number were assumed to be too abstract for the young mind (see Gelman, 1982, for further discussion). There has been considerable debate over the way to interpret the fact that babies, toddlers, and preschoolers respond to numerically relevant information. But given the explosion of research on this topic (see Ginsburg, 1983, Sophian, 1984, for many examples), it can be concluded that such information is especially salient to young children. The same cannot be said for chimpanzees (Premack, 1976).

Why the salience? Although it is true that children in our culture encounter a number-rich environment, this will not suffice as an account. Infants are unlikely to have encountered much of this environment, yet they respond on the basis of the number of items in a display or sequence. Further, there is an infinitude of stimuli in the environment to which infants might attend and yet do not. That something is in the environment is no guarantee that it will be attended to. The child's focus on number words at an early age (Fuson, Richards, & Briars, 1982; Gelman & Gallistel, 1978; Saxe, Guberman, & Gearhart, 1984) is a real puzzle, especially in view of the difficulty that the same age children have learning color terms (e.g. Bartlett, 1977; Bornstein, 1985; Landau & Gleitman, 1985; Rice, 1980). Afterall, color terms are also omnipresent in the environment. Young children watch Sesame Street; play with colored stacking blocks and colored rings; draw with crayons that produce colors. Surely adults use some of these occasions to tell children the names of the colors they are seeing or working with. It will not do, therefore, to argue that number words are attended to and memorized because they are heard frequently and used in relevant contexts—so are color terms. Yet color terms are not learned early—even though color differences are perceived (Bornstein, 1985).

At the sensory level, it is easy to account for the fact that we attend to some ranges of the light frequency spectrum but not others or that we hear some sounds and not others; the structure of our sense organs plays the controlling role. Similarly, the structure of our knowledge base can determine whether or not we attend to an aspect of our environment. Piaget made this point repeatedly. For example, Inhelder and Piaget (1964) argued that young children fail to notice the orderliness in an ascending series of lengths because they lack the seriation structures needed to assimilate such information. Without taking sides in the debate about whether young children can or cannot seriate lengths, we can endorse the general point. Information of a particular kind is assimilated only if a suitable structure is available to support the assimilation. Indeed, it is often the availability of a structure that makes a stimulus salient; the structure carries with it a characterization of the kind of input it will attend to and process.

We propose that it is the availability of the counting principles that makes children sensitive at an early age to number relevant information, including the counting words. The principles also help the child to sort verbal inputs that resemble each other, thereby allowing the child to match correctly the use of terms to the functions they are meant to serve. Sinclair and Sinclair develop a similar argument in their chapter in this volume.

To illustrate how principles help children match terms and functions, consider the problem of children learning two kinds of words, labels for objects and numerals (numerlogs in Gelman & Gallistel's (1978) terminology) for counting. The theorist who prefers a rote learning account of the ability to learn to count with words will point out that children hear the count words in a variety of contexts and see people pointing to objects, one at a time, as they use the items in the list. The rote learning advocates suggest that these experiences are sufficient for learning to use the count words. The problem with this observation, however, is that the same environment can occur for the names of the objects. Consider a parent "reading" from a picture book: "horse, dog, chair, baby." Why doesn't the child who sees an adult pointing to objects in a set while reciting the count list assume that this is a lesson in object naming? The possibility that there may be more frequent demonstrations of counting than recitations of particular words to match particular objects is an inadequate explanation. Color words are recited frequently in response to the ever present set of toys that vary in color; yet children who have mastered from three to six words in an ordered count list and can use at least three of these in a meaningful way (Fuson et al., 1982; Gelman & Gallistel, 1978) have enormous difficulty learning to use even a few color names when given explicit instruction (Bornstein, 1985; Rice, 1980).

So the problem remains. Why is it that children do not seem to think that number words are labels for objects?[1] We suggest that it is the presence or absence of principles that provides the child with clues to what conditions or constraints the use of the terms must meet.

The initial learning of labels for objects benefits from three assumptions children make. First, they assume that it is the object as whole, rather than any of its parts or its surround, which is its referent (Spelke, 1984). Second, they assume that once an object in a class has been assigned a label, that label applies to other members of the class (Markman & Hutchinson, 1984; Waxman & Gelman, 1985). Finally, they assume that unique objects (e.g., dogs, cats, birds,

---

[1]The child's problem goes beyond determining which class of words support which function. Quine (1960) drew attention to the fact that truly naive learners of a language have no way of knowing whether a label, used in conjunction with a point, refers to the object or parts of that object, what that object can do, the environment surrounding the object, and so forth. Spelke's assumption that children are constrained first to assume that labels refer to objects goes a long way toward solving their problem regarding labels. See Landau and Gleitman (1985) for a discussion of the possible constraints on verb meaning.

etc.) have unique names; different objects cannot be assigned the same name (Markman, 1984). Contrast these implicit assumptions with the potential use of number words given the counting principles.

One way to satisfy the stable order principle is to use a list to tag items. On the assumption that this principle is available to structure the environment, ordered lists of words should be salient to the child. But this principle by itself cannot tell the child how to *use* the lists. This depends on the availability of further principles. During counting, the same words *must* be used with different objects (the abstraction or item-indifference principle) and assigned to but one item at a time (the one-one principle).

In the absence of the stable order principle and item indifference principles, children's assumptions about labels should lead them to think the count words are labels for objects (as indeed they are when used in reference to the symbols 1, 2, 3, etc.). Thus, it is a combined consideration of the stable order and item-irrelevance principle that leads to the conclusion that number words are not names for objects. So the answer to our question about how it is that children might manage to keep the tasks of vocabulary and number-word learning separate, is that they are guided by principles from each of these domains. The principles in each domain define the domain-relevant items in the environment. The counting principles dictate that the child has to learn a list and provide clues for recognizing what is to be assimilated from the verbal environment. Thus, to account for the failure of the young child to confuse number-relevant with language-relevant inputs, one needs to grant the presence of implicit principles that carry with them constraints on what is to be assimilated from the environment.

Returning to the problem of color terms: inasmuch as these, like nouns, refer to a particular set of stimuli and do not have to be ordered, they should not be confused with the class of count words. If anything, color terms may be confused with labels for things if children do not yet know a label for an object (Landau & Gleitman, 1985; Markman, 1984). Additionally, the learning of color terms may be at risk because the young may assume that attribute terms come in polar opposites (Landau & Gleitman, 1985) and because they have a bias to treat objects integrally (Smith & Kemler, 1978).

In the absence of principled clues about the use of color terms, young children can still learn them by rote. If learning to use count words benefits from principles, and learning to use color terms does not, two predictions follow. First, the onset of the correct use of color terms should be more variable than the onset of the correct use of count words. Second, most children should use some count words correctly before they use color terms correctly. (Interestingly, once the learning starts, the standard demands of serial learning could force a crossover in the two acquisition curves.)

In an initial effort to test these predictions, Rochel Gelman, Eve Clark, and Steve Pinker analyzed the language acquisition transcripts from Adam, Eve, and

Sarah (Brown, 1973).[2] All three children were reinforced by the adult they were talking to for correct usage of their first three count words *before* they were reinforced for their first correct use of one color term. Age of onset of correct counting ranged from 1:7 to 2:6. The age of onset for correct use of a color term ranged from 1:9 to 3:2.

We know of no evidence on how early children treat labels for things differently from count words. Some data on 3- and 4-year-olds comes from Gelman, Meck and Merkin (1986), who asked those children who completed the first order-irrelevance experiment whether (a) the "baby" (in a row they had been counting) could be 1, 2, and so on; (b) the "chair" could be 1, 2, and so on; and (c) "the baby" could be "the chair," or vice versa. Of 19 3-year-olds and 36 4-year-olds (N = 40/age group) asked this series, 79% and 80%, respectively, answered *yes* to the first two questions and *no* to the third. They readily tolerated the reassignment of counting tags while resisting the reassignment of labels for things. Children were not very good at explaining their judgments. A few talked about counting in response to questions on why it was okay to say "2" for both objects but not okay to use the same label for both objects. Explanations about labels included "The baby does not have enough legs," "People sit in chairs," "A baby is a human being and not a chair," "She is not made like a chair" and once even "A chair is furniture." These explanations read like definitions of basic concepts or object classification statements; the very activities presumed to constrain the child to label things exclusively.

Admittedly, these lines of evidence are preliminary. Still, they are consistent with the idea that a fundamental reason for postulating principles is to capture the proposition that the acquisition of early knowledge can be aided by the availability of domain-specific mental structures. This is because children's reactions to their learning environments are mediated by domain-specific principles that specify, to some degree, the relevant inputs for that domain. The general argument is that just as syntax-based principles lead the child to attend to syntax-relevant inputs as opposed to number-relevant inputs when learning syntax, number- and object-relevant constraints on names for things lead children to learn the correct interpretation of word classes and items within them. For the reader who remains skeptical that children work with principles that generate assumptions about whether they interpret language data as relevant to the way they learn to count words, we offer the following summary of a portion of Eve Clark's diary of her son's language acquisition.

---

[2] I thank Steve Pinker for agreeing to search the computerized language data bank being assembled by Brian McWhinney and Katherine Snow. He searched for the word "color," the phrase "how many," and all instances of counting-words and color-terms—providing both child and adult utterances. Counting and coloring activities occurred at relatively high and quite comparable rates. What distinguished the color sequences was the ubiquitous tendency for the adult to do most of the talking about color. Eve Clark graciously consented to go through the transcripts with me, serving thus as both an expert, and, in a sense, a source of reliability.

D. C.'s first way of marking plurals was to use the word "two," as for example in "I have two shoe" (for "I have shoe*s*"). Having assigned this syntactic function to the term "two," he refused to include it in his counting list despite repeated efforts on the part of a determined adult friend (an engineer, no less) visiting the household. Thus, he counted items with the list "one, three, four, five, six" and did so repeatedly over trials. When, several months later, he discovered the conventional plural morpheme "s," he inserted the missing "two" between "one" and "three"! A term that once had to be applied in a consistent way as a particular syntactic type was now free to enter a count list where it now met the requirement that it *not* apply to anything in particular.

To say learning is guided by implicit principles is not to say that there are no input requirements. To the contrary, in addition to drawing attention to the relevant environment, the principles characterize the form of the input requirements. They help detect and sort inputs in accord with the functions they can serve. In their absence, the child must rely on rote memorization, and the learning becomes more difficult, variable, and protracted.

To Define a Domain.   One need not use the standard count list in a given natural language in order to count. Computers count with 0s and 1s; some cultural groups in Africa count with different hand positions; various groups in New Guinea count while touching body parts in sequence; letters of the Greek and Hebrew alphabets are also number words; hatch marks and the abacus have existed since time immemorial. Nor does one have to touch or point to each item, start counting a given set in the same place each time a count of it is to be rendered, or arrange the items in any particular way. In addition, there are many ways to keep track of the number of items used in a count-on strategy of arithmetic (Fuson, 1982); indeed there are many count strategies that can be used to solve a variety of arithmetic problems (see Carpenter, Moser & Romberg, 1982; Ginsburg, 1983). What renders order to these different acts we call counting? What permits us to say they are all, in fact, examples of behavior in the common domain of counting? The answer must be that it is principles of counting which define the domain. In all these cases, at the very least, the principles of one-one correspondence, stable ordering, cardinality, item-irrelevance, and order irrelevance must hold. To be sure, in the case of complex counting algorithms, we may have to recognize further principles. But these depend on the availability of the ones already listed.

Thus, just as principles of syntax help define the language domain, principles of number help define the domain of counting as well as other numerical skills.

To Account for Variable Performance.   Many have drawn attention to the way limited processing abilities in young children can interfere with the display of an ability (e.g. Case, 1984; Shatz, 1978). This is one way to account for the failure of children to reveal their conceptual competence. Our notion of principle leads to another account of how conceptual competence can be masked. In turn, this account makes clear why the some-principle-first theory of counting predicts variable performance—especially for the youngest children. It is developed here much as it was in Greeno et al. (1984), where distinctions are made between conceptual, procedural, and utilization competence.

In the Greeno model of counting, conceptual competence characterizes knowledge of the counting principles; utilization competence deals with the ability to assess the performance requirements of a particular task in light of the constraints imposed by conceptual competence; and procedural competence deals with planning knowledge about the relations between actions and goals and the ability to make use of constraints. More generally, procedural competence plans the course of action, which satisfies the constraints imposed on it by conceptual and utilization competence. Successful generation of a performance plan, then, depends on the coordinated applications of conceptual, procedural, and utilization competence.

In distinguishing between procedural and conceptual competence, we introduce the idea that the counting principles represent a set of abstract constraints the mind places on procedures. They place constraints on procedures in the sense that the counting procedures must satisfy them if they are to be recognized as instances of counting. Principles, however, do not dictate how to put the principles into practice in any setting. Instead the counting principles provide the specifications that define the classes of acceptable procedures and number-specific goal structures, much as do rewrite rules in linguistics. For example, in the Greeno et al. (1984) computer model, the schemata MATCH and KEEP-EQUAL-INCREASE specify the properties a procedure must exhibit if it is to be consistent with the one-one principle. Since the MATCH schemata takes two sets as arguments, the sets can be (1) some particular items to count and (2) the words in the conventional count list. The sets could also be words, abstract thoughts, or the like on the one hand, and the alphabet or hatch marks on the other. KEEP-EQUAL-INCREASE requires that the two sets remain equal throughout a count and indicates a general way of keeping the sets equal; the idea is that two initially empty sets, remain equal if each is increased by a single member. These schemata together capture the fact that the child will have to generate procedures to partition to-be-counted and already counted items and coordinate the use of count words and the partitioning of items. But they do not dictate how this will happen. Their characterization in terms of abstract action schemata makes it possible to detail the constraints involved in their use and formally describe the class of acceptable procedures. It is the work of procedural competence to generate the particular instances of this class.

Although principles do not themselves generate counting procedures, they do play an indispensable role in their generation, this because they are referred to by the planning or executive part of the procedural competence system, the part that must produce and monitor the production of competent or effective behaviors. For a child to succeed, procedural competence must produce a competent plan of action. Because the quality of the planner sets the limits on procedural competence, children can fail a task because of a deficit in their procedural competence.

The generation of procedures also requires a utilization competence, the ability to assess a particular setting in terms of the task demands relevant to putting a plan of action into effect. The items in front of a child could be in a circle, in which case the task introduces a counting-relevant feature, that is, the beginning or end of the set must be clearly marked in order to avoid double-counting items and violating the one-one principle. Since children may know that they are not supposed to double-count, yet lack the resources to deal with the problem, a distinction should be drawn between these abilities. To recognize the problem, children have to appreciate the difference between displays that have a clear beginning and end; but this is a problem in perception and is not unique to counting. Deficiencies in the detection or construction of perceptual groupings will influence counting whether or not children possess the requisite conceptual competence: Hence, the Greeno et al. (1984) argument is that these are best represented as deficiencies in utilization competence. Similarly, tendencies to misinterpret instructions, memory problems, and the like will influence the quality of a plan of action because of the limits they place on the child's utilization skill at the moment.

But even if the child has the wherewithal to assess all that matters in a task setting and correctly interpret instructions, there is no guarantee that success will follow. In the case at hand, the child also has to generate an acceptable counting procedure. This might involve moving items; it might also involve putting a piece of paper on an item. Neither of these skills is counting-specific: they could be used to improve the perception and memory of other material as well. Still, a plan which fails to include them or other components which reflect the needs of a setting would be inadequate. For accurate performance to occur, children have to refer their assessment of the task requirements to the planner, which has to coordinate these with the constraints given to it by its conceptual competence.

The foregoing analysis leads to a renewed defense of the ''competence-performance'' distinction in developmental accounts. Since principles do not spell out how conceptual competence will be put into practice, it follows that there must be a distinction between ''competence'' and ''performance.'' Our use above of the terms ''principled'' or ''conceptual competence'' substitute for what is standardly taken as ''competence'' in the phrase competence-performance, this being the underlying rules of knowledge of a domain. However, we characterize the competence more broadly, in terms of the requirements a plan must meet. It is not a passive structure. It offers guidelines for connecting knowledge constraints to plans of action.

Our discussion of what influences performance is different from ones that consider limits on memory, attentional capacities, or processing space (e.g.

Case, 1984; Chomsky, 1957). We also consider the child's ability to plan actions consistent with the constraints set down by the principles. The principles do not guarantee that the child will use the relevant goals; this must be part of the planning activity. Faulty planning could cause a child to fail.[3] Further, a consideration of planning competence requires considering the separate ability to assess task settings and relate them to these constraints. Making a distinction between procedural and utilization competence allows us to begin to classify in a systematic way the different kinds of variables that will influence the selection and production of actions and the consequent performance. We begin this classification in the Evidence section of this chapter.

To Begin to Explain Learning.   Since principles set constraints on the acceptability of a chosen procedure, they are a potential source of feedback to children when they are learning to count or are trying to solve a problem that requires a novel behavior. Procedures used can be monitored and checked for violations of the constraints. If there is a discrepancy between the constraints' requirements and an output, the child can obtain information about negative efforts and then reject or alter them to conform more closely to the requirements of the constraints. If there is no discrepancy, the child can use the procedure again and, thus, develop skill as a function of practice. In this sense, then, principles both guide and help determine the acquisition of skill. Procedures that honor the requisite constraints can be used again and gain strength.

The foregoing might lead one to conclude that we give the very young child the conscious ability to monitor cognitive processes and capacities. We do not and see no need to do so. We understand, however, why others might reach this conclusion. The reason is that discussion of the development of metacognitive skills often deals with the ability to monitor one's cognitive processes as if they were on the same plane as the ability to think about the nature of the contents of one's memory. To talk about the ability to monitor is to talk about the regular state of affairs for any case of active learning. Following Piaget (1976, 1978), the argument is that any learning governed by a structure will self-regulate. To capture the tendency of children to self-correct their language errors (Clark & Clark, 1977), their motor errors (Bruner, 1973), their counting errors (Gelman & Gallistel, 1978), or their search errors (Deloache, 1984), one can use Piaget's phrase "autonomous regulation" without ever referring to matters of consciousness (Piaget, 1976, 1978). Over and over again we find that the development of conscious knowledge of one's implicit knowledge and abilities develops relatively late (Brown, Bransford, Ferrara, & Campione, 1983). But, likewise, there is evidence that very young children monitor, rehearse, and self-correct their performances (Brown et al., Deloache, 1984; Siegler & Schrager, 1984).

---

[3]The Greeno et al. analysis of competence bears a close resemblance to ones about speech planning.

One can recognize the generality of monitoring tendencies without reaching the false conclusion that the very young must, therefore, be metacognitive (see Brown et al., 1983 for more on this issue). Whether or not they possess metacognitive skills, young children do monitor and correct their performances in a host of domains. They could not if there were no representation against which to do so and, of course, if they were not intrinsically motivated to do so, at least some of the time. That they do have representations and are actively engaged in using them to learn is part of what we mean when we say young children use their principles in the pursuit of skill at counting. Additionally, we mean that procedural competence makes it possible for children to do this since it provides a mechanism for generating feedback internally.

As we will see, when the procedures a child puts into practice reflect the constraints of conceptual competence, the output of these procedures can serve as evidence for the learning of new principles. The development of this argument is facilitated by the consideration of a concrete case. Since this case emerged in one set of our studies of how failures in utilization and procedural competence mask conceptual competence, we turn next to the matter of evidence. We will end with a discussion of how young children could learn about the ordinal principle of counting.

EVIDENCE

Conflicting Interpretations

Gelman (1982) and Greeno et al. (1984) cite several lines of evidence for the view that young children possess implicit knowledge of the counting principles. However, a common feature of this evidence is that children are not perfect and the younger they are the more they err. That young children's performance is variable within and across tasks is highlighted by critics of the idea that principles guide the acquisition of procedural skill. The view is that there is little reason to grant principled understanding if there is a variety of conditions under which young children are not competent (Briars & Siegler, 1984).

Associations-first/principles-later accounts of early number abilities handle performance variability by simply granting to young children fewer and weaker rotely learned components of the counting procedure than to older children. It should now be clear that variable performance can also be handled by the some-principles-first view. In fact, it is predicted, given the Greeno et al. (1984) analysis of competence. By way of a brief reminder, even if young children have complete conceptual competence, there is no guarantee they will display it in their behavior. This is because conceptual competence does not consist of recipes for procedures. It defines the class of acceptable procedures, but these must be generated by procedural competence. Deficits in general problem solving and planning abilities could lead to a failure to use conceptual competence. So could deficits in utilization competence. Finally, problems could arise because children have had little experience coordinating conceptual, procedural, and utilization competencies.

Thus far, then, the two classes of competing theories can account for the same data. One advantage to our analysis is that it provides a tool with which to analyze sources of variability. Some variability may reflect a lack of principled understanding. But this does not mean that all variability should be interpreted in this way. A consideration of the tasks used in the studies at issue points to problems children had with utilization and procedural competence. In the next parts of this section we propose that utilization and procedural competence problems masked conceptual competence in several studies cited against our position. We then present studies designed to test these hypotheses. The section concludes with a summary of recent studies of the constrained counting ("doesn't matter") task developed by Gelman and Gallistel (1978) because the principle-first and skill-first theories make opposite predictions regarding what 3- and 4-year-old children could do on this task.

The One-One Principle:
Error-detection Reconsidered

In their assessments of preschoolers' understanding of the one-one principle, both Briars and Siegler (1984) and Gelman and Meck (1983) included correct but unconventional trials as well as standard-correct and standard-error trials. For example, in both studies, children watched a puppet count a row of alternating red and blue (or green) chips by first counting the red ones and then the blue or green ones. Gelman and Meck labeled these trials pseudoerrors; Briars and Siegler called them unusual correct trials. Gelman and Meck reported an average of 96% correct for their 4-year-old group. The comparable figures from the latter study were 65% and 53%, respectively, for 4- and 5-year-olds. An even greater discrepancy was reported for the 3-year-olds—95% in Gelman and Meck versus 35% in Briars and Siegler. Why the differences on these kinds of trials, given similar results with remaining trial types? We think it is because these trials are ambiguous. Since ambiguity makes demands on one's ability to decide which alternative the experimenter had in mind, it also makes demands on one's utilization competence.

Children and adults alike usually count systematically from left to right or vice versa. Although we need not, doing so helps us keep track of items and honor other constraints placed on procedural competence. Hence, the procedure is likely to be reinforced and become conventional. When we are asked whether a procedure is right or not, there is then the problem of deciding whether to judge on the basis of what is done typically or whether to use some other criterion. If we choose the former, we should say an unconventional trial is wrong. If we set aside the matter of convention and are competent to judge on the basis of principled considerations we might say it is right. Young children typically choose the conventional road unless given a clue to do otherwise (Braine & Rumain, 1983). Therefore, in the Briars and Siegler study, the children may have assumed they were to treat any deviation from standard counting as wrong—especially since they were told that the puppet "knows his numbers." They were also given repeated experience counting a row of objects before every block of testing and hence may have been set to focus on the conventional (see Gelman, Meck & Merkin: Study 4, 1986, for evidence that this happens). Children in the Gelman and Meck (1983) study may have been more flexible because they were told the puppet was "just learning to count" and did not themselves repeatedly count linear arrays throughout the experiment.

Inspection of the Gelman and Meck (1983) transcripts disclosed another hint about the discrepancy and suggests a way to pursue our hypothesis. Children were asked to explain their judgments and were tested in a very interactive mode, which means some trials were tested more than once. This does not seem to be the case for the Briars and Siegler study (personal communication). As a consequence, without planning to, we may have given children a hint about how to approach the difference between conventional and unconventional trials (Vygotsky, 1978).

These arguments focus on the task demands children had to deal with in this seemingly straightforward situation and point to utilization competence as the source of difficulty. They also highlight the potential role of conversational skill and social variables in a child's assessment of ambiguity. If the children did have such problems, Briars' and Siegler's (1984) interpretation of their data as contradicting our position is less compelling.

To assess the above hypothesis, we ran 4- and 5-year-olds (N = 10/group) using an interactive testing procedure in an error detection study demonstrating four kinds of one-one correpondence trials: Correct, Error, Pseudoerror, and Compensation Error. The last involved the puppet's making two compensatory errors, e.g. first double-counting one item and then skipping another. Thus, although the puppet used the same number of tags as there were items, he did not keep the increases equal in both already used subsets.

To do well throughout this task, a child has to infer a procedure that could have generated the display and assess it in terms of the constraints of the counting principles. Thus, clues about how to interpret novel arrays cannot affect success levels unless the children possess the relevant procedural and conceptual competence. Indeed, if the children generally possess these competencies, the effects of an interactive procedure should be limited to those situations that are ambiguous, in this case the Pseudoerror trials. To find out if the effect was so localized, analyses were done twice: once with children's immediate responses and once with their best responses on a trial. In the latter case, a child's immediate response was scored again unless an initial error was followed by a correct response that was justified, for example, "I think it was another one of those okay but silly" trials (in response to a pseudoerror). A child who explained his response could hardly have responded randomly or switched his answer because of a perceived challenge to his initial reply.

After the error detection phase, children were probed in further ways, including a request to assume the role of the experimenter and generate correct and incorrect trials.

Each child was tested with sets of five and seven trinkets, in that order. There were eight trials per set size, two for each of the trial types. On Correct trials, the puppet counted a linear array from beginning to end. The One-one correspondence error trials involved either skipping or double-counting an item. In the Pseudoerror trials, the puppet either started counting in the middle of the array and then returned to the beginning to count the remaining items or skipped an item in the middle of the array and returned to count it last. In the Compensation-error trials, the final tag used in the count list was the same as the cardinal value of the set; however, two errors that cancelled each other were made during each trial—on one trial one item was skipped and a subsequent one was double-counted, and on the other trial the puppet counted a nonexistent item on the table and then skipped another item in the array. Instructions were as given in Gelman and Meck (1983), and ended with the children being told that they had to wait until the puppet had finished before deciding whether the trial was correct or not. An attempt was made to elicit an explanation for each judgment. Where it seemed a child's interest was lagging, the testing was broken up over two days.

Error Detection Results.   Figure 2.1 shows the overall percentage of correct responses for both the Immediate and Best response analyses. As in previous experiments, children were flawless in judging Correct trials on their first encounter with them. Likewise, they did very well on the remaining 12 error trials. Four-year-olds got a mean of 9.3 of their immediate responses correct; 5-year-olds scored a mean of 10.5 correct. On the best-trial analysis, the respective means for the two age groups were 11 and 11.4. Since so many children achieved perfect scores, we could not do an overall analysis of variance.

The age difference for the Immediate-response data from the three kinds of error trials is reliable as assessed by a 1-tail independent t-test ($t(18) = 2.78$; $p = .006$). The Best-response difference is not statistically significant ($t(18) = 1.447$; $p = .08$). For the younger group, the differences between Immediate-response and Best-response scores on their error trials were significant for both set sizes (correlated t's for 1-tail tests with $df = 9$ were 2.21 and 2.24, $p = .03$ and .01, for set sizes of 5 and 7, respectively). These differences were not

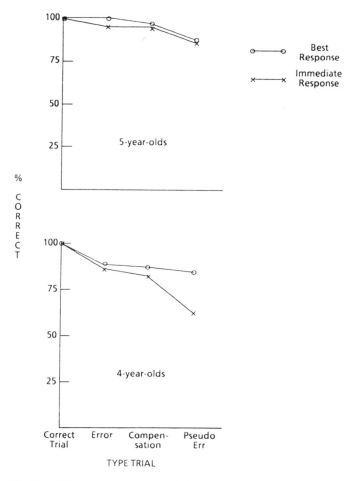

FIG. 2.1. Children's percent correct judgments of a puppet's counting sequences. Immediate-response scores are just that. Best-response scores take into account a child's ability to explain a correct judgment after an initial error.

reliable for the older children. As shown in Fig. 2.1, these analyses reveal that the effect of interactive testing was localized in the 4-year-olds' pseudoerror trial data, a conclusion that was confirmed by analyses of individuals' data as well.

Error Generation. The final phases of the experiment had children play the role of experimenter. We thought if children knew the difference between error trials and correct trials, they might be able to generate both and do so appropriately. They did. Nine (of 10) and 8 (of 10) children in the younger and older groups produced both error and correct trials. Four of the children in each age

44

group even produced order-irrelevant correct trials, a kind of trial they had not seen during testing. Five children (three and two, in the young and old groups) introduced errors in the count list, another novel error). Otherwise error trials were like the skip, double-count, and compensation (rare) trials the children had seen.

Summary.   We proposed that utilization factors contributed to the discrepancy between the results reported by Briars and Siegler (1984) and by Gelman and Meck (1983). The fact that pseudoerror trials are ambiguous led us to predict that children would benefit more from a second chance with a pseudoerror than with a more standard error or correct trial. The results support the proposal that variability in performance may reflect utilization as opposed to conceptual competence deficits. A similar conclusion holds for the task used by Baroody (1984) to assess children's understanding of the order-irrelevance principle. As we will see, subtle variations in question types can lead children to do either very well or very poorly.

Order-Irrelevance and Cardinality:
A Follow-up of Baroody (1984)

Inasmuch as children in the foregoing study judged pseudoerror trials correct and sometimes gave accounts of why, one might conclude they understood the order-irrelevance principle. Baroody (1984) cautions against this assumption, preferring instead to conclude that children can be indifferent to the order in which items in an array are tagged and yet not assume that two different orders yield the same cardinal value. If this is so, Baroody is correct in saying that children do not understand the order-irrelevance principle.

Baroody's conclusion is based on the following task. Children were shown a row of eight items and asked first to count left to right and then to indicate the cardinal value of the set. Then, while the experimenter pointed to the rightmost item, they were asked, "Could you make this number one?" Children typically answered yes. Then the experimenter covered the array and said, "We got N [where N stood for the child's cardinal response] by counting this way [Experimenter points to initial way]. What do you think we would get counting the other way?" The large majority of 5-year-olds (representing a rural sample) responded with some value other than N. Most 6-year-olds were correct.

Gelman et al. (1986, Study 1) replicated the Baroody result with a group ($N = 12$) of 4-year-old urban children. (An initial pilot study with 5-year-olds yielded too few errors). They also compared this group of children with two others of twelve each on Count and Altered-Question.

Gelman et al. hypothesized that the younger children took the Baroody (1984) instructions for the second half of the trial as a challenge to their first answer, thereby implying they should change it. Since the children had but one counting trial and could have been unsure of their answer to start, this possibility is especially salient. Donaldson (1978) provides several demonstrations of how communication factors lead the very young to change their answers, apparently because they lack confidence or the ability to assess correctly the real intent of an ambiguous message. Braine and Rumain (1983) offer a related reason for why young children might had misinterpreted the second question in the Baroody study. They note that young children do not spontaneously adopt an analytic (as opposed to an ordinary) comprehension mode of language processing. But use of this mode would help them decide that the experimenter did not intend to challenge their initial response. All these considerations help clarify the way utilization variables can influence the performance of young children. They also highlight the need to be especially sensitive to the role of instructions in the design of studies with young children.

Design and Experimental Features.   To test our hypothesis, a second group of children (Count) were first given three chances to count the array. Another group (Altered Question) started out like those in the Baroody condition. Then (again like Baroody) the experimenter pointed to the last item and said, "Can you start counting with N?" When the array was covered, she continued and asked, "How many will be there?" or "What will you get?" Note the absence of a focus on what answer the children had given initially. Such a contrast might serve the sociolinguistic function of a challenge or an instruction to hedge (Labov & Fanshel, 1976). Since preschool children respond to and produce linguistic variations of this sort (Shatz, 1983), we reasoned that despite the seeming minor variation between the instructions in the Altered-Question and Baroody conditions, children would interpret our instructions differently from Baroody's.

Following Baroody's important suggestion, we ran all of the children on two subsequent tests: a Trick order-irrelevance test, and an Error-detection cardinal test. These tasks provide a way of deciding whether a test of the order-irrelevance principle is valid.

For the Trick task, a puppet started by correctly counting the number of items in a row and then answering a "How many?" question. Then the puppet introduced a surreptitious double-count error on a second trial and answered the cardinal question with a value of $N + 1$. To be scored as correct, the children had to infer the puppet had made an error. Otherwise, the puppet should have answered N, just as he did on the preceding round.

The Error-detection task included six correct and twelve incorrect trials. The incorrect trials were of two forms: on one kind, the puppet counted correctly but then gave the wrong answer to the "How many?" question at the end of the trial; on the other, the puppet made a one-one error, for example, a double-count, and then reponded to the "How many" question by repeating the final tag used given the error (in this example $N + 1$ was offered).

Findings.   The results are straightforward. Only one child (of 12) in the Baroody condition was correct; all others changed the value of the cardinal number they gave the second time. Half the children in the Count group changed their answer; half did not. In contrast, there was little tendency for those in the Altered Question group to change their answers. Ten out of twelve did not, and most gave lucid accounts of why not. Consider G. J. (53 months), who said there were eight to start and then said there would be eight should there be a second count.

> Because that way [the first way] there was 8 and there's no way you can try and change numbers. (Why not?) Watch. [S counts.] (How come you knew there would be 8?) Because I knew that . . . (But you knew even before you counted them. How did you? . . . How could you change the number? What would you have to do?) You would have to put more things on the table or take things away.

Our interpretation of the effects of language in the Baroody condition is buttressed by the fact that children in all three conditions did well on their subsequent tasks. Nine of the children in the Baroody replication condition passed the Trick trial; so did 10 in each of the other two conditions. Finally, all groups did well on the Error-detection trials. The average number correct (immediate) responses on the 12 error trials were 10.3, 11.0 and 10.75 for the Baroody, Count, and Altered-Question groups. Although children did find the one-one trials the hardest, they got 82% (immediate response) correct. And no fewer than seven children in each group got five out of six of their trials like this correct (chance $p \leq .03$ by a binomial expansion). Further, when in this phase of the experiment, 28 of the 36 subjects made explicit reference at least once to the fact that the resulting count sequence, the cardinal number, or both were wrong on such trials. In fact, 21 of these children corrected the puppet. Finally, it turns out that the experimenter sometimes challenged children and suggested that the trial was right as long as the puppet repeated the last tag used in the second count list. For example, on a set size of 11, the experimenter said, "But he counted six and he said the six." One child came back with, "No. He had to go 1, 2, 3, 4, 5, 6, 7. And that's seven." Thirteen of the 16 who were challenged responded similarly.

Discussion.   The results of this experiment lead to the conclusion that children may fail tasks designed to tap their understanding of the order-irrelevance and cardinal principles because of problems in the domain of utilization competence. It is well known that young children are sensitive to variations in the social context in a way that older children are not. Whether one talks about their being more dependent on a supporting social context, less able to stand back and reinterpret communication messages, or more likely to misinterpret instructions, the theme is clear. This is a general issue and not restricted to the domain of number (cf. Braine & Rumain, 1983; Brown & Reeve, in press; Donaldson, 1978). The generality of the phenomenom strengthens our argument that utilization factors influence the generation and assessment of procedures.

One might accept our conclusion regarding 4-year-olds in the Gelman et al. (1986) study and still maintain that matters are different for younger children. For this reason Gelman et al. ran a study of 3-year-olds (Study 2), comparing children in the Baroody condition and those in an Experimental condition. The latter combined features of the Count and Altered-Question conditions used earlier with the 4-year-olds. This was done on the assumption that younger children would be even more in need of instructions that induced confidence and did not challenge them. Two to three months after testing in these conditions, a Trick and Error-detection phase was administered in both groups.

As before, children in the Baroody condition changed their answers more often than those in the Experimental group. Likewise, both groups did well on the Trick and Error-detection tasks. Thus, we can conclude that the argument outlined earlier applies as well for a group of children with an average age of three and a half years.

It is not just utilization factors that are highlighted by these findings. Consider the fact that children did well on both the trick trials and the one-one error-detection trials. Fuson and Hall (1983) have argued that young children's tendency to repeat the last tag they recite when counting is consistent with their conclusion that young children lack the cardinal principle, for they can do this while following the simple rule "Repeat the last number you heard." If so, children could not have succeeded on the follow-up tasks. Instead they should have said the puppet who did repeat the last tag he used was correct on the trick and the one-one error trials. Since they did not, they must have used cardinal representations built up on previous trials and compared the values they expected with those rendered by the puppet. We conclude that they made use of the cardinal principle—as one hopes they did, given how well they performed in the Altered Question condition. (Parenthetically, this means these tasks can be used to sort children on standard counting tasks into those who repeat the last tag they use—simple repeaters—and those who are applying the cardinal principle.)

If young children do have implicit knowledge of the cardinal principle, why would they ever resort simply to repeating the last tag they hear or say and ignore whether a puppet's or their own application of the counting procedure was correct? (Fuson & Hall, 1983). Perhaps they would if task conditions suggested they should keep separate their tagging and cardinal response goals. This could happen if children were first asked to count and allowed to do so and then asked to answer the "How many" question—just as they were in Ginsburg and Russell (1981) and the study cited by Fuson and Hall (1983). In the Gelman et al. (in press) tasks, children were encouraged to wait before answering until all components of the counting performance were complete. In other words, the task setting encouraged their integration of the various goals and subgoals involved in the assignment of the cardinal value of a set. If our account is correct, then the child's problem lies in the realms of both procedural and utilization competence. A failure to maintain a number-relevant goal could indicate a fragile coupling between conceptual and procedural competence, a limit on the side of procedural competence, or a failure to render a correct interpretation of the task. These are nontrivial' developmental problems and may even reflect what Baroody and Ginsburg (this volume) call "weak schemata." But they cannot be ascribed entirely to the lack of a principled understanding—not in view of the findings of the present experiment.[4]

Order-Irrelevance: Constrained Counting

Return to the Briars and Siegler (1984) account of 3- and 4-year-olds' trouble with pseudoerror trials. This is that the younger the children, the more likely they know but a few conventional counting acts, ones they have had ample opportunity to observe and learn by rote. If so children of this age should not be able to generate novel ways of counting, which is exactly what children must do in order to pass the Gelman and Gallistel (1978) constrained counting task. In this task, children cannot succeed if they think linear arrays can be counted only from one end to the other. The reader is referred to Fig. 2.2 as an aid to the following description of why this is so.

After a child first counted a five-item array, she was asked to show a puppet some tricks. The first trick was to count while making the object in the second position (the "baby") be the "one." If the child succeeded on this trial, she was then asked to make the baby be the "two," the "three," the "four," the "five," and finally the "six." Each row of Fig. 2.2 schematizes a heterogeneous set of trinkets. The X inside a circle indicates to which object the labeling constraint applies. The order in which objects were tagged, as well as which numeral was used as a tag, is illustrated by the flow of arrows. The value in the right hand column indicates which tag the child was asked to use to designate the object marked with an X. To be scored as correct on a problem

---

[4]Baroody and Ginsburg (personal communication) suggest that less mature children might lack the order-irrelevance principle and think that the set size of a display changes as a function of the order in which they tag items. We have no data to rule out this possibility. However, when so few children fail a test, perhaps an appeal to measurement error is appropriate. Further, we draw attention to the fact that tasks like ours and Baroody's require children to reason about the consequence of a previous act vis-à-vis future acts. Following Braine and Rumain (1983) it seems reasonable that success on this class of tasks requires an analytic mode of thought. Therefore, children who do succeed can be said to have accessed implicit knowledge about counting. In other words, they may have demonstrated a beginning *explicit* understanding of the order-irrelevance principle, a conjecture supported by their ability both to explain their predictions and to reject a request to make a particular object the x + 1th tag in the "doesn't matter" experiments described later.

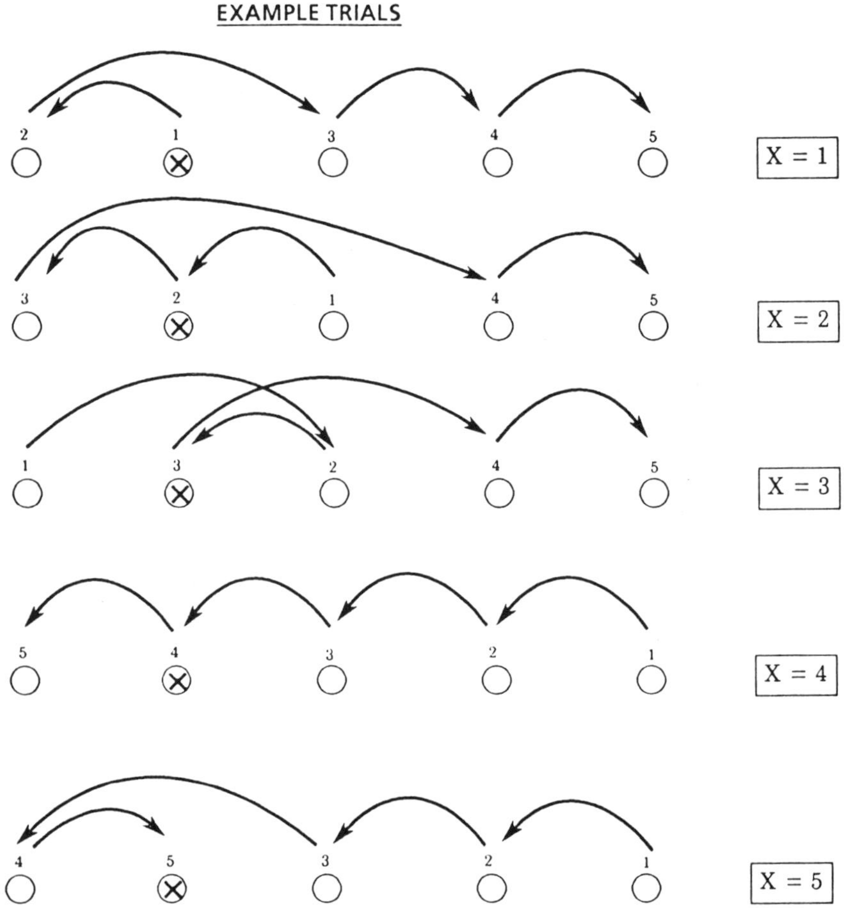

EXAMPLE TRIALS

FIG. 2.2. Schematic representation of the first half of the Gelman and Gallistel (1978) "doesn't matter" test of the order-irrelevance principle.

block, a child had to get all but the last trial right. The $N + 1$ responses were scored separately.

Children have to count in nonstandard ways in order to pass this task. Only 12% and 44% of the 3- and 4-year-olds did pass. Does this mean that the children lacked the ability to generate novel counting solutions? The answer is no. Gelman et al. (1986; Studies 3 and 4) provide evidence that the utilization and procedural demands of a five-item display interfered with 3- and 4-year-olds' ability to generate novel and strategic solutions. When the same aged children started with a three-item problem of the same form, they did very well on both the regular and $N + 1$ trials. They also were able to transfer to four-item and five-item problems.

50

Smith and Greeno (1984) have shown that all but one of the solutions in Fig. 2.2 can be modeled by upgrading the procedural and utilization components of the Greeno et al. (1984) computer model. The conceptual competence is left intact, thereby providing yet another demonstration that the constrained counting task places special demands on utilization and procedural competence, ones that can mask conceptual competence.

LEARNING NEW PRINCIPLES: OR WHY CONCEPTUAL, PROCEDURAL, AND UTILIZATION COMPETENCE INTERACT

All solutions but that shown in line 4 of Fig. 2.2 are examples of what Gelman et al. (1986) called Skip-around solutions. The exception, that for the X = 4 trial, is an example of the Correspondence-Capitalize solutions used by almost all children. These, as well as the Correspondence-Create solutions shown in Figs. 2.3 and 2.4, cannot be generated by the Smith and Greeno (1984) version of the counting model for a reason that is especially interesting. To do so, the model would have to add to conceptual competence schemata representing the ordinal counting principle, something we are not willing to place in the set of initial

STRATEGY   EXAMPLE SOLUTIONS

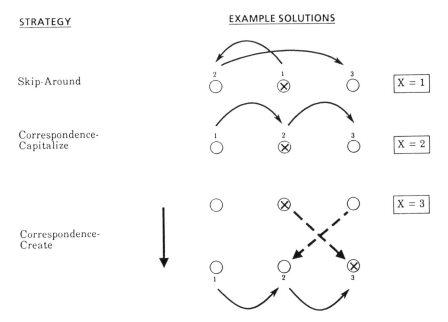

FIG. 2.3.   Examples of strategies children used in the Gelman, Meck and Merkin "doesn't matter" 3-item problems. Dotted lines show the way children moved items.

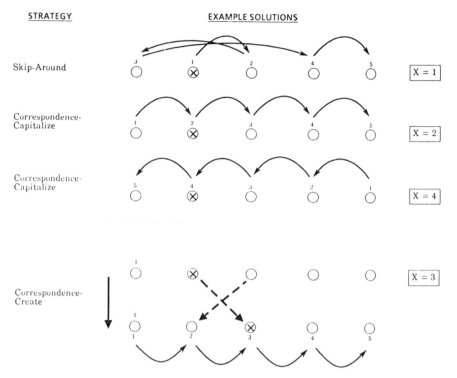

FIG. 2.4. Examples of strategies children used in the Gelman, Meck and Merkin "doesn't matter" 5-item problems.

principles young children bring to the task of learning to count. Otherwise, the children must learn a principle or component of a principle not covered in our account of initial conceptual competence. The Greeno et al. (1984) model fails to generate these strategies then because it lacks the additional requisite conceptual competence.

Why assume the children had this additional competence? How could they have learned it? The first question is answered by a more careful look at the strategies the children invented.

The children who used the Correspondence-Capitalize strategies, did so almost invariably after using a Skip-around solution. They did this only on those trials where the ordinal position of the target item in the display and the particular count word it was supposed to be tagged with would be in correspondence if the child started to count at one end or the other. Thus, after using a Skip solution for a request to make X = 1 when X was in the second position, children typically started at one end of the array and counted to the other end when asked to make X = 2. Rather than continue to use the Skip strategy, they moved to a smooth left-to-right (or vice versa) count. More telling were those cases where, for a five-item array, children switched sides and counted right to left for an X = 4 request. It seems unlikely that children would do this if they had not recognized the correspondence between the ordinal position of the number word in their count list and the serial position of the fourth object from the right.

Both 3- and 4-year olds used the Correspondence-Capitalize strategies. The older children went one step further. They used Correspondence-Create strategies like those shown in Figs. 2.3 and 2.4 and did so by moving items around to establish a correspondence between the serial position of the targeted items and the ordinal value of the number word they were to use as a tag. We were surprised that the children used either of these strategies, let alone the more complex of the two. To do so, they already had to have some knowledge of the ordinal meaning of the count words and the relation of these to the serial order of items in a linear display. In other words, they had to have some knowledge of the ordinal counting principle—a principle that is not part of the competence we originally granted very young children.

In the introduction we said that we could provide an account of how children could learn the ordinal principle—if allowed the assumption that they already have some principles to start. Although the counting principles we have discussed indicate that the order in which items are counted can be haphazard, most actual count sequences are not. There is good reason for this, one dictated by the procedural and utilization demands placed on the child.

Recall that the principles require children to keep separate items they have already counted from those they will yet have to count. Therefore children should prefer plans that maximize the likelihood of honoring this constraint. Plans to count systematically from one end of a row to the other do just this. Interestingly, task settings which present such linear displays are also easier to evaluate than those which involve circular or disorderly displays. For in the latter cases, plans must be generated which marks both the beginning and end of the display. For disorderly displays, children must also come up with a way to keep track of those items already tagged. These considerations of how procedural and utilization competence interact with conceptual competence converge on the fact that the best way to meet the constraints of the one-one principle is to generate plans which yield linear arrays and then proceed smoothly from beginning to end. This means that children will be reinforced (either through their own or someone else's monitoring efforts) for counting this way—even if it is not required by the counting principles. And some thought about the matter suggests this may be a very good thing. For the effect of it is that children repeatedly create environments that are structurally isomorphic to a component of their conceptual competence, and thereby set the stage for learning to extend what they already know. In Piagetian (1976, 1978) terms, by following the linear order in the environment as they recite the numerals in order, children generate logical experiences, which can lead to the development of new structures. Utilization factors that influence the choice of procedures interact with the constraints of conceptual competence to produce a procedure that in turn sets up a potential learning experience. In other words, what seemed at first a procedural nicety turns out to be much more. Competent procedures, that is, ones that are tied to conceptual competence, generate opportunities to learn principles the child does not know. In the present case, the procedure for insuring a proper application of the counting principles provides the basis for the realization that the numbers may also be used to represent position in a nonnumerical ordering— this could then be the beginning of the ordinal use of number words.

In this discussion of learning, procedural competence plays a central role. It generates experiences that make it possible to enlarge the domain of conceptual competence. But note how closely tied procedural competence must be to some conceptual competence for our account to go through. If young children did not make use of the stable order principle, they would not be in a position to recognize the correspondence between numerical and linear order. Further, if there were no reason for children to use procedures that allow this—if the procedures were not generated in response to the constraints of the counting principles already available to the child—children could not contrast the cases where order is irrelevant and where it is relevant. By granting the child certain basic principles for obtaining numerical representations, we also provide an account of how new representational principles may be acquired. If we deny children any principles at all, we deny them the very tools they need to assimilate structured information. For they have no representation against which to assess whether they have encountered something that is related to what they already know. It is for this reason that we conclude that conceptual competence must interact with utilization and procedural competence if learning is to continue.

CONCLUSION

In this chapter we developed the thesis that some counting principles constitute the conceptual competence young children use to select from their environment numerically relevant information, to build procedures for generating count sequences, and to gain skill at counting. We showed that the fact that young children are variable in their ability to succeed on counting tasks can be explained by both a principle-first and principle-after account of early numerical skill. In doing so we developed the theme that counting competence is made up of conceptual, procedural, and utilization competence. A major consequence of this analysis of competence is that it provides a way of showing how procedural competence can lead to the development of new principles of conceptual competence.

Ours is a theory of how number knowledge can start to expand in the domain of counting. Because it depends on the assumption that children start with some components of conceptual competence, one might conclude it does not apply to the learning of more complex kinds of arthimetic—let alone higher mathematics. But we think there is a generalization to be drawn. In our account of how new principled knowledge is acquired, procedural competence leads to learning if it reflects some existing conceptual understanding. When procedures honor the constraints of what is understood, a major condition for learning is met. This is because the procedures, in response to the constraints of a setting, sometimes create environments that present structured inputs, inputs which serve as fuel for the induction of a concept which is related to ones already known. If we are correct, then one problem facing mathematics instructors is to figure out how to get students to use procedures that do reflect at least a bit of conceptual competence on their part. Carpenter's discussion of arithmetic and Schoenfeld's of geometry (this volume), are examples of this approach to pedagogy.

ACKNOWLEDGMENTS

The research reported here was supported by NSF grant BNS8004881 to Rochel Gelman, who wrote this version of the chapter while a Fellow at the Center for Advanced Study in the Behavioral Sciences. Fellowship support came from an NIHHCD Senior Fellowship to her as well as funds to the Center from the Alfred P. Sloan and MaCarthur Foundations. Extensive discussions with Jim Greeno influenced all aspects of the work. Some arguments were shaped by discussions with Ann Brown, Sue Carey, and Frank Keil, who (with Rochel Gelman) worked at the Center on a project on the nature of structural constraints on cognitive development. We also thank Lincoln Moses for statistical advice and Arthur Baroody, Ann Brown, Jim Greeno, Jim Hiebert, Ellen Markman and Alan Schoenfeld for especially helpful comments on an earlier draft of this paper.

REFERENCES

Bartlett, E. J. (1977). The acquisition of the meaning of color terms: A study of lexical development. R. Campbell & P. Smith (Eds.), *Recent Advances in the psychology of Language, IVa* (pp. 89–108). New York: Plenum Press.

Baroody, A. J. (1984). More precisely defining and measuring the order-irrelevance principle. *Journal of Experimental Child Psychology. 38*, 33–41.

Botman, H. (1981). *Cardinal and ordinal number skills in preschool children.* Unpublished manuscript, Duke University.

Bornstein, M. H. (1985). Colour naming versus shape naming. *Journal of Child Language, 12*, 387–93.

Braine, M. D. S. & Rumain, B. (1983). Logical reasoning. In J. H. Flavell & E. M. Markman (Eds.), *Handbook of Child psychology: Cognitive Development* (vol. 3) (pp. 263–340). New York: Wiley.

Briars, D. J., & Siegler, R. S. (1984). A featural analysis of preschoolers' counting knowledge. *Developmental Psychology, 20*, 607–18.

Brown, A. L., Bransford, J., Ferrara, R., & Campione, J. (1983). Learning, remembering and understanding. In J. H. Flavell & E. M. Markman (Eds.), *Handbook of Child psychology: Cognitive Development* (vol. 3) (pp. 77–166). New York: Wiley.

Brown, A. L., & Reeve, R. A. (in press). Bandwidths of competence: The role of supportive contexts in learning and development. In L. S. Liben & D. H. Feldman (Eds.), *Development and learning: Conflict or congruence.* Hillsdale, NJ: Lawrence Erlbaum Associates.

Brown, R. (1973). *A first language: The early stages.* Cambridge, MA: Harvard University Press.

Bruner, J. S. (1973). Organization of early skilled action. *Child Development, 44,* 1–11.

Case, R. (1984). The process of stage transition: A Neo-Piagetian view. In R. J. Sternberg (Ed.), *Mechanisms of cognitive development* (pp. 19–45). San Francisco: W. H. Freeman.

Carpenter, T. P., Moser, J. M., & Romberg, T. A. (Eds.). (1982). *Addition and subtraction: A cognitive perspective.* Hillsdale, NJ: Lawrence Erlbaum Associates.

Chomsky, N. (1957). *Syntactic structures.* The Hague: Mouton.

Clark, H. H., & Clark, E. V. (1977). *Psychology and language: An introduction to psycholinguistics.* New York: Harcourt Brace Jovanovich.

Cooper, R. G., Campbell, R. L., & Safady, R. S. (1985, April). *Infants' development of an understanding of numerical equality and inequality.* Paper presented at meeting of the Society for Research in Child Development, Toronto.

DeLoache, J. S. (1984). On where, oh where: memory-based searching by very young children. In C. Sophian (Ed.), *Origins of cognitive skills* (pp. 57–80). Hillsdale, NJ: Lawrence Erlbaum Associates.

Donaldson, M. (1978). *Children's minds.* New York: Norton.

Evans, D., & Gelman, R. (1985). *An initial understanding of infinity.* Unpublished manuscript, University of Pennsylvania.

Fuson, K. C. (1982). An analysis of the counting-on solution procedure in addition. In T. P. Carpenter, & J. M. Moser & T. A. Romberg (Eds.), *Addition and subtraction: A cognitive perspective* (pp. 67–81). Hillsdale, NJ: Lawrence Erlbaum Associates.

Fuson, K. C., & Hall, J. W. (1983). The acquisition of early number word meanings: A conceptual analysis and review (pp. 49–107). In H. P. Ginsburg (Ed.), *The development of mathematical thinking.* New York: Academic Press.

Fuson, K. C., Richards, J., & Briars, D. J. (1982). The acquisition and elaboration of the number word sequence. In C. J. Brainerd (Ed.), *Children's logical and mathematical cognition* (pp. 33–92). New York: Springer-Verlag.

Gelman, R. (1982). Basic numerical abilities. In R. J. Sternberg (Ed.), *Advances in the psychology of intelligence.* Vol. 1 (pp. 181–205). Hillsdale, NJ: Lawrence Erlbaum Associates.

Gelman, R., & Gallistel, C. R. (1978). *The child's understanding of number.* Cambridge, MA: Harvard University Press.

Gelman, R., & Meck, E. (1983). Preschoolers' counting: Principle before skill. *Cognition. 13,* 343–59.

Gelman, R., Meck, E., & Merkin, S. (1986). Young children's numerical competence. *Cognitive Development, 1,* 1–29.

Ginsburg, H. P., & Russell, R. L. (1981). Social class and racial influences on early mathematical thinking. *Monographs of the Society for Reserach in Child Development. 46*(6, Serial No. 193).

Ginsburg, H. P. (Ed.). (1983). *The development of mathematical thinking.* New York: Academic Press.

Greeno, J. G., Riley, M. S., & Gelman, R. (1984). Conceptual competence and children's counting. *Cognitive Psychology, 16,* 94–134.

Inhelder, B., & Piaget, J. (1964). *The growth of logical thinking.* New York: Norton.

Labov, W., & Fanshel, D. (1976). *Therapeutic discourse: Psychotherapy of conversations.* New York: Academic Press.

Landau, B., & Gleitman, L. R. (1985). *Language and experience: Evidence from the blind child.* Cambridge, MA: Harvard University Press.

Markman, E. M. (1984). The acquisition and hierarchical organization of categories by children, 371–406. In C. Sophian (Ed.), *Origins of cognitive skill* (pp. 371–406). Hillsdale, NJ: Lawrence Erlbaum Associates.

Markman, E. M., & Hutchinson, J. E. (1984). Children's sensitivity of constraints on word meaning: Taxonomic vs. thematic relations. *Cognitive Psychology, 16*, 1–27.

Piaget, J. (1976). *The grasp of consciousness: Action and concept in the young child.* Cambridge, MA: Harvard University Press.

Piaget, J. (1978). *Success and understanding.* Cambridge, MA: Harvard University Press.

Premack, D. (1976). *Intelligence in ape and man.* New York: Wiley.

Quine, W. V. O. (1960). *Word and object.* Cambridge, MA: MIT Press.

Rice, M. (1980). *Cognition to language: Categories, word meanings and training.* Baltimore, Md.: University Park Press.

Ross, J. R. (1967). *Constraints on variables in syntax.* Unpublished doctoral dissertation, MIT.

Saxe, G. B., Guberman, S. R., & Gearhart, M., (1984). The social organization of early number development. In B. Rogoff & J. Wertsch (Eds.). *Children's learning in the "Zone of proximal development"* (pp. 19–30). San Francisco: Jossey-Bass.

Schaeffer, B., Eggleston, V. H. & Scott, J. L. (1974). Number development on young children. *Cognitive Psychology, 6*, 357–79.

Shatz, M. (1978). The relationship between cognitive processes and the development of communication skills. In C. B. Keasey (Ed.) *Nebraska Symposium on Motivation.* (Vol. 26) (pp. 1–42). Lincoln: University of Nebraska Press.

Shatz, M. (1983). Communication. In J. H. Flavell & E. M. Markman (Eds.), *Handbook of Child psychology. Cognitive Development* (vol. 3), (pp. 13–889). New York: Wiley.

Siegler, R. S. & Shrager, J. (1984). Strategy choices in addition: How do children know what to do? In C. Sophian (Ed.), *Origins of cognitive skills* (pp. 229–294). Hillsdale NJ: Lawrence Erlbaum Associates.

Smith, D. A., & Greeno, J. G. (1984). *Implicit understanding and competence: A theoretical analysis of procedural and utilization competence.* Unpublished manuscript. Learning, Research and Development Center, University of Pittsburgh.

Smith, L. B., & Kemler, D. G. (1978). Levels of experienced dimensionality in children and adults. *Cognitive Psychology, 10*, 502–32.

Sophian, C. (Ed.). (1984). *Origins of cognitive skill.* Hillsdale, NJ: Lawrence Erlbaum Associates.

Spelke, E. S. (1982). Perceptual knowledge of objects in infancy. In J. Mehler, M. Garrett, & E. Walker (Eds.), *Perspectives on mental representations.* pp. 409–431. Hillsdale, NJ: Lawrence Erlbaum Associates.

Starkey, P. D., Spelke, E. S., & Gelman, R. (in press). Numerical abstraction by human infants. *Cognition.*

Vygotsky, L. S. (1978). *Mind in society: The development of higher psychological processes.* (M. Cole, V. John-Steiner, S. Scribner & E. Souberman, Eds. and Trans.). Cambridge, MA: Harvard University Press.

Waxman, S., & Gelman, R. (1986). *Preschoolers' use of superordinate relations in classification. Cognitive Development, 1*, 139–159.

Wilkinson, A. C. (1984). Children's partial knowledge of the cognitive skill fo counting. *Cognitive psychology, 16*, 28–64.

Children's Mastery of Written Numerals and the Construction of Basic Number Concepts

H. Sinclair
A. Sinclair
University of Geneva

At all ages, and many times a day, human beings successfully perform acts without being aware of underlying principles: children swim without understanding flotation; cooks make mayonnaise without understanding emulsification. Conversely, physicists may study the action of steel sliding on ice without being able to skate.

We are not usually bothered by the gap between knowing-how-to and scientific knowledge. In everday life, knowing-how-to is seen as useful, normal and learnable, and scientific knowledge is felt to be a matter for the expert. Yet the distinction between knowing-how-to and some kind of more general "understanding" is not altogether clear even in the situations just referred to. Whoever knows how to make mayonnaise not only knows the correct order of manipulation and its desired result (starting with the egg yolk, beating it, then adding oil while beating), but also about quantities (start with all the egg yolk one intends to use, then add oil little by little), and about temperature (all ingredients should be at room temperature).

It is intriguing that such a distinction as that between knowing-how-to and understanding has in recent years become the theme of many interesting discussions of mathematics and especially the teaching of mathematics, as if in this field the distinction is particularly clear or particularly useful. It is true that in mathematics the debate has a long history. It is also true that one does not have to spend much time in elementary classrooms to see examples of "something going wrong," of "lack of understanding," even at the level of simple arithmetic. Obviously, "something wrong" is noticed mainly when mistakes are made. Some mistakes are simply the result of inattention or sloppiness and do not reveal lack of understanding or of procedural skill. At other times, the mistake seems to be "real," but the child's thinking remains opaque and the misconception cannot be pinned down. However, there are many instances where the teacher/researcher feels that he understands where the child went wrong.

Children often make mistakes in sums that demand borrowing or carrying. They are also often incapable of solving so-called word-problems, choosing, for instance, to multiply rather than to divide. Closer scrutiny often reveals that the borrowing or carrying mistakes correspond to specific patterns (i.e. children make up their own "procedures"). Similarly, in word-problems children also appear to follow rules of their own making: ignoring the "words," for example, they inspect the numerals and subtract if the first is bigger than the second. Subtle experimentation may reveal deep-seated difficulties even in the absence of mistakes: M. Kamii and C. Kamii showed that many third and fourth graders who carry out the borrowing and carrying procedures correctly do not understand place-value; for example, they do not understand that both the 3 and the 4 in 34 have a specific relation to the numerical totality (C. Kamii, 1985, p. 55–63). Similarly, the seemingly unequivocal arithmetical signs, $+$, $-$, $\times$, $\div$ and $=$ are often interpreted by the child very differently from the adult (cf. Erlwanger & Bélanger, 1983).

In all the foregoing examples the symbol system is involved (often in written form, but similar difficulties can be found when only the oral equivalent is used): the children's procedures are faulty, because a principle such as place-value has not been mastered; or their procedures are correctly carried out, but the system is not understood; or both procedures and system are mastered, but an inappropriate procedure is chosen for solving a problem.

At first sight, many of these instances can be explained by either a lack of understanding or a lack of procedural knowledge. Moreover, some of the children's behavior resembles adult behavior that is considered perfectly understandable and acceptable. Most adults have no way of finding the square root of 622521 (with paper and pencil only) other than by trial and error: they lack procedural knowledge but not the concept of "square root." Conversely, in the adult community it is widely accepted that as long as certain routines are carried out correcly, there is no need for mathematical understanding of the procedure. (Statistics is most often used in this way in the social sciences.)

Despite the parallelisms, there are important differences between the mathematical difficulties of elementary schoolchildren and those of well-educated adults.

It is true that from a certain level upwards (grade three would be our guess), some children may be considered to lack procedural knowledge only: for example, those who understand what division is about and have mastered the characteristics of the symbol system, but who do not "know how to do it" when the numbers are beyond a certain size. Other children seem to lack conceptual knowledge: for example, those who do not understand place-value but do certain sums correctly, and those who do not know what procedure to apply. In elementary school clear-cut lack of procedural knowledge seems to be rare; it certainly becomes more frequent as students progress to more complex mathematics instruction. Lack of conceptual knowledge, even in the examples we have just given, seems to be heterogeneous and difficult to determine in any precise way. Moreover, at the very beginning of school arithmetic, matters are even more complex.

First, at that level, many mistakes in procedure appear to be due not to a lack of procedural knowledge, but to a lack of conceptualization of the symbol system and its principles, such as place-value or the number zero. The conceptual content of our symbol system seems to be severely underestimated in school. Why this should be so can only be guessed. Maybe the routines have become so automatic for adults that they seem to be just that—routines. Maybe the reason lies deeper. The most brilliant mathematicians of classical antiquity remained imprisoned in their symbol systems and had to rely on material devices such as the abacus. Curiously enough, as mentioned by Hogben (1936, p. 293) one of the earliest books on the new Arabic system to be written in English is called "Craft of Nombrynge" (A.D. 1300). Craft? Was there already then a tendency to separate craft, or skill, from knowledge, or understanding? Was there a tendency to deny new conceptual content to a symbol system that came from a different culture?

Second, it is not clear what kind of conceptualization is needed for choosing the appropriate mathematical procedure to solve a word-problem (or possibly, a practical problem in daily life). Is there something that can be called a concept of addition, subtraction, multiplication outside a symbol system (not necessarily our own)? What are the developmental links between augmenting a quantity or combining two quantities, taking away something from a quantity, taking some quantity several times, partitioning a quantity into several equal quantities on the one hand and addition, subtraction, multiplication and division on the other?

These issues have led to the study of "informal arithmetic" (e.g. Baroody & Ginsburg, this volume) and "intuitive understanding in mathematics" (e.g. Herscovics & Bergeron, 1984). The conclusions of such research are usually convergent in the sense that the relation between meaning and mechanistic knowledge or understanding and knowledge of procedures (or other dichotomies) is found to be extremely complex, and that many questions remain unanswered. Baroody and Ginsburg touch on the problem of the connection between "count meanings" and "cardinal meanings" (i.e. the ability to appreciate that, for example, the cardinal term 5 in 5 + 3 predicts or is equivalent to the outcome of counting a set of five objects). In their discussion of the child's construction of multiplication, Bergeron and Herscovics (1983) conclude:

> The word "times" is used very early by the child in the process of counting actions
> as for instance in skipping rope. And the counting of the number of equivalent sets
> may only represent a counting of actions. It is only when the focus shifts from

actions to the equivalent sets produced by such actions and that these equivalent sets are perceived as parts of a whole that we can truly refer to a multiplicative situation. . . . Of course we do not know how this shift from actions to equivalent sets occurs. We do not even know how the child constructs equivalent sets. (pp. 199–204)

These authors end their paper with the all-too-true remark that the design of experimental situations and the construction of probing but nonleading questions are exceedingly difficult.

Research on informal or intuitive arithmetic seems highly relevant to the debate on procedural and conceptual knowledge. As far as we know, it has only been carried out in our own cultural environment. It could, of course, also be undertaken in different cultures having different numerical symbol systems (spoken, and possibly also written).

The value of a theoretical distinction such as procedural versus conceptual knowledge often depends on its epistemological context. Distinctions that are natural and necessary for certain theories of knowledge may be less so for another theory. They may, however, raise new problems and incite researchers with a different epistemological view to re-examine their premises and data. Therefore, we keep the conceptual-procedural distinction in mind while describing the main aspects of the development of numerical ideas during the preschool years (roughly between the ages of $2\frac{1}{2}$ and 6) as we see it. It is during this period that the foundations of later modes of mathematical reasoning are laid, and the child becomes actively interested (in our culture) in at least one aspect of the numerical symbol system, that is, spoken and written numerals. We give a brief sketch of a constructivist, Piagetian approach to the early development of number concepts on the one hand, and of the beginnings of the child's construction of the written number system on the other hand.

THE DEVELOPMENT OF NUMBER CONCEPTS

According to Piaget (see Piaget & Inhelder, 1969), knowledge stems from actions: actions on things, and interaction with people. From birth, human beings begin to make sense of their surroundings and actually construct the world they live in by organizing their actions. These actions are creative in the sense that they transform rather than uncover reality. The term *action* is taken in a broad sense, not merely as the manipulation of objects: looking at something from different angles by turning one's head and attracting somebody's attention by crying also have this creative aspect. Actions that are repeated engender what Piaget calls "schemes"—abstract patterns characterized by what is repeatable and generalizable in the action, which for effective performance has constantly to be adjusted to the practical situation. From the preverbal period onwards, these abstract action patterns become coordinated and combined, presenting general forms of coordination (order of movements, embedding of a subscheme in a larger scheme, establishment of correspondences, etc.). As such, they are powerful heuristics.

These deep-seated, general forms of coordination provide the basis for all further knowledge within a context of social interaction, which itself shows a similar development of interpersonal coordinations and without which no human knowledge is possible.

Piaget makes a distinction between two kinds of knowledge. For understanding flotation, for example, knowledge needs to be derived, at least in part, from the properties of the objects themselves: wooden objects do not behave like metal ones. By contrast, in order to come to understand one-to-one correspondence or other mapping operations, one has to introduce some kind of order into the objects being handled, and knowledge is derived from the actions, the particular properties of the objects being irrelevant (as long as they keep their discreteness—drops of water would not do). This is why such actions become interiorized and handling becomes unnecessary: the subject knows that deductive operations cannot be proved wrong by contradictory physical experience. This is also, according to Piaget, why logico-mathematical knowledge becomes progressively "purified" ("formal"), whereas physical experience is always a sort of mixture. To be able to experiment and to understand the outcome of experiments, logico-mathematical knowledge is necessary, if only to organize the experimental activity in such a way that something about the properties of the objects can indeed be discovered.

The young child cannot do without actual experience when logico-mathematical knowledge is in its beginnings. Only when interiorized actions begin to form a system (however restricted) do deductions and inferences without empirical verification become possible.

In the domain of number, an important milestone is reached when a system is constructed that leads to elementary number conservation: the realization that the equality of quantity of two collections of objects put in one-to-one correspondence and judged equal does not change when one of the collections is spaced out and the optical correspondence destroyed. Conservation becomes intellectually necessary to the point where 7- or 8-year-olds find the traditional questions foolish and will proffer an argument only if the experimenter tells them, for example, that younger children think that there is more in one of the rows and asks them how they would explain the problem to a child of 4 or 5.

Piaget's epistemological analysis of number concepts can be found in several of his works (e.g., Beth & Piaget, 1961) and explains elementary number conservation as the reciprocal assimilation of schemes of ordering and inclusion (relations and classes). This does not mean that he sees number as reducible to logic; number constitutes a specific construction, a *sui generis* synthesis of logical notions in which the idea of one-to-one correspondence plays an important part. The roots of this construction reach far back into infancy. Organizing behavior in the form of gathering together (quasi) identical objects, of seriating and of constructing one-to-one correspondences has been observed in infants at the age of about 24 months (Sinclair, Rayna, Stambak, & Verba, 1982). In one of the experimental situations, the infants were seated on the floor in front of a collection of six open cubes (of different sizes), six sticks (different sizes) and six balls of modelling clay (also of different sizes) placed randomly and were encouraged to play with the objects. From 12 months onwards, a favorite action was to put as many objects as possible into the biggest cube; between 12 and 16 months, an iterative action whereby one of the sticks is pointed into several cubes, or even all the cubes successively, was frequently observed. By 24 months, all the children constructed one-to-one correspondences between the balls of clay or the sticks on the one hand and the cubes on the other: usually each ball or stick was placed into each cube, but sometimes a ball was too big for a particular cube, and sometimes a stick was too long, so that it toppled out. This did not bother the children; they simply put the stick or ball next to the cube—*correspondence* was their goal, not the act of putting into. At the same age, the children also made three collections, gathering all the sticks together putting them down somewhere, gathering all the balls together, and gathering all the cubes (the collections were often placed to the left of the left leg, in between the legs, and to the right of the right leg). They also nested the six cubes together. That these three kinds of organizing behavior appear at the same time (often during the same observational session) supports the hypothesis that they are destined to develop into a coherent system that will engender fundamental concepts. In the child's mind, the actions clearly belong together and are carried out with great attention and interest, without any suggestion or modeling by the adult observer. At the age of two, however, there is no indication that they form a coordinated system, nor that they are a means of solving problems: the actions are, so to speak, their own reward.

At this level of development, the action patterns cannot yet be inserted into "a system of conditions or consequences" (Piaget & Garcia, 1983, p. 199). Such a system seems to imply something more than a network of relations: it would allow a certain mode of reasoning to be chosen as applicable, and it would permit deductions and inferences. Comparing different repeatable actions (which may sometimes give the same result), or comparing different results of the same action, leads the subject (child or adult) to think about "Why?" rather than "How?" Often this implies that a series of actions becomes an object of thinking rather than a means for obtaining an effect or succeeding in a way of reasoning. This process has been called "thematisation" by Piaget (1983); it constitutes a special case of reflexive abstraction.

At the level of the 2-year old subjects, there is no distinction possible between procedural and conceptual knowledge. The observed repeatable actions are considered to form the building blocks of a protosystem that already comprises the idea of several types of actions' being coordinated and providing various ways of organizing a collection of objects. One cannot ask these children questions that would give psychologists further insight into the protosystem; all one can do is observe how the children act—and, of course, they can act only sequentially. These observations lead to the idea that (to the child) repeating interesting actions and their coordination with other actions go hand in hand with the construction of a conceptual system. They also reinforce the importance of the distinction between logico-mathematical and physical concepts. The difference between the establishment of a series of actions that give a desired result and reflecting on why this is so appears more appropriate in the construction of the latter than in the construction of logico-mathematical concepts, where the focus of attention is always on the actions and their coordinations (and not on object properties).

From this point of view, counting is also a sequential activity, though, evidently, more culturebound than establishing one-to-one correspondences. Indeed, several researchers have objected that Piaget's analysis of number concepts (Inhelder & Piaget, 1959; Piaget & Szeminska, 1941) does not take into account the contribution of counting activities (e.g. Droz & Paschoud, 1981; Gelman & Gallistel, 1978; Gréco & Morf, 1962) and that it is therefore psychologically incomplete. Indeed, in the Piagetian studies, task situations and questions were chosen to direct the children *away* from counting (possibly not to cloud the picture of conceptual development by the introduction of a culture-bound element). However, children in our cultures are certainly very interested in counting from the age of $2\frac{1}{2}$ or 3, and they do so spontaneously. Counting, too, seems to be an activity that is its own reward, though, obviously, learning the series of counting numbers is partly the result of cultural pressure and adult modeling and approval. Moreover, when children begin to use a few conventional number words, they do so meaningfully (see Droz & Paschoud, 1981; Gelman & Gallistel, 1978): they know that counting has to do with the question "How many?" and they have constructed certain rudiments of addition and subtraction. No doubt their already well-established schemes of collecting, ordering, and creating one-to-one correspondences allow them to assimilate count words meaningfully, but that does not exclude an eventual constructive role of the counting activity itself.

Gréco, one of Piaget's collaborators, carried out a lengthy series of experiments (Gréco & Morf, 1962) that throw light on this problem, starting from observations of the curious behavior of some children who did not succeed the conservation task. When children had constructed a one-to-one correspondence between two rows of, say, seven counters, they were often quite capable of counting "their" row (for example, the top row of red counters) correctly. Then, when the experimenter spaced out "his" row (the bottom row of blue counters), extending it to the right but leaving the first counter on the left below the first counter of the top row, and asked the child how many there were in the bottom row without actually counting them, the child would often immediately say "seven". "Seven and seven, so are there just as many blue ones here as red ones there?" "Yes," the child would answer, "But there is one more here, look, that one" (pointing to the last one in the bottom row). Such (to the adult) incomprehensible contradictions can take many forms and may persist for a long time. They led Gréco to make a distinction between *quotity,* arrived at by counting, and *quantity,* a judgment of comparison between two physically present collections given in answer to questions such as "Just as many? Or more? Or less?". This distinction makes it possible to explain the paradoxical behaviors referred to earlier and to make counting part of progress towards conservation.

For young children, to compare two quantities means to compare two collections or classes with a certain configuration in space; their inferences about "more" or "less" are bound to the spatial extension. Counting, by contrast, exploits and generates one-to-one correspondences and is an action on these spatialized real quantities. As such, it leads to different inferences, initially still incompatible with the inferences drawn from the spatial extensions. A new coordination takes place subsequently, in which the counting activity, which transforms physical reality into arithmetical reality, and the one-to-one correspondence generated during the comparison and implied in counting lead to a new mathematical concept—numerical invariance. At this point, the inferential system no longer produces contradictory judgments, and neither the counting activity nor that of reestablishing a correspondence needs to be applied to the situation of the elementary conservation of number task.

An interesting parallel to Gréco's distinction between quotity and quantity is to be found in Baroody and Ginsburg's chapter in this volume. Discussing the fact that children often exhibit an "order-indifferent adding scheme," the authors note that "two numbers can be combined in any order to produce correct—though not necessarily the same—answers. . . . addend order can affect outcome" (p. 83). Research by Inhelder, Blanchet, Sinclair & Piaget (1975) showed that if children are not asked to count, but asked only if there are the same number of counters in two boxes, one in which the experimenter first put two and then four counters, and another in which he first put four and then two counters, their answer is an unequivocal yes. Our explanation for these apparent contradictions is the same as Gréco's: the child's conceptual schemes are not yet assimilated into one inferential system; they remain isolated and dependent on the task either one or another preoperation is invoked.

In this type of constructivist framework, actions form action-schemes; schemes become combined and coordinated; systems are built up that render certain actions and verifications superfluous and certain inferences and deductions necessary. Activities, as well as modes of reasoning, continue to change their status as they form ever more general and abstract systems.

From this point of view, counting is not strictly procedural knowledge. It is a special activity that is coordinated with other actions to become part of a conceptual system. At the same time, counting in the conventional manner and being able to write and read numerals also constitute prerequisites and sources for the mastery of arithmetical procedures at a higher level.

At the ages we are concerned with in this chapter, counting does not yet bear any of the marks of our decimal system, with zero and place value. Until the early school years, number concepts (and, no doubt, the meaning of the counting numbers) are limited to certain relations between integers and, at first, to a small series of the latter (see "the slow arithmetization of number", Gréco, Grize, & Papert, 1960, p. 23–24). Later, counting activities will be assimilated into a larger system exhibiting such properties as connexivity (Gréco & Morf, 1963) and recursivity (Gréco, Inhelder, Matalon, & Piaget, 1963). How these more complex properties are assimilated into the conceptual and the symbolic system is an as yet unresolved question.

THE BEGINNING OF THE CHILD'S CONSTRUCTION OF THE WRITTEN NUMBER SYSTEM

Our symbol system constitutes for children an object of knowledge which they gradually conceptualize and which they can use meaningfully only at their level of conceptualization. Though Piaget was not interested in the child's mastery of symbols, we believe it can also be studied in the frame of his constructivist theory and that such studies contribute to a deeper understanding of the development of mathematical competence. In the remainder of this chapter we give some examples of children's ideas about written numerals in the early preschool years.

In recent years, several researchers and theorists have shown that children begin to learn about our written symbol systems (numerals and letters) well before they enter school. Using these notational systems appropriately and correctly is the result of a slow development, beginning at age 3 (if not before), during which children reconstruct and come to understand the notational systems that surround them (e.g., Allardice, 1977; Clay, 1975; Ferreiro & Teberosky, 1982; Sinclair & Sinclair, 1984).

Two aspects of written notation are important: (a) the child's understanding of or ideas about the abundant written numerical material in the environment and the comments others make about this material; and (b) the personal production of these or other symbols when a written notational task is to be performed. At early ages, the child's interpretation of written numerals on the one hand and the production of numerical notation on the other may reflect understanding of written symbols and of number concepts in different ways.

Concerning the first-mentioned aspect, we should note that children see few examples of the computational use of written numbers (receipts from grocery stores are perhaps the one exception), and only a small proportion of the numerals seen represent cardinalities (generally, prices). In the environment, there are many ordinalities (elevator buttons for example), identifying labels (bus numbers, telephone numbers, etc.), and a wealth of numerals that refer to measurements of various kinds (dates, sizes, weights, speeds, scores, etc.). These numerals generally inform (describe), although some of them have a prescriptive function (speed limits, for example), and others appear useful only for search procedures or reference (page numbers, house numbers, etc.). Environmental use of numerals is in marked contrast to the written numerical material children are presented with in school, where all numerals represent cardinalities and where their use is restricted to more or less relevant or interesting (but generally artificial) computations. Numerals surround children from the moment they isolate them from the mass of graphic material around them; it is this material that children work on to construct their early understanding of the written numeral system.

We should not forget that our decimal system (with place value and symbols such as $+$, $-$, $=$) is a recent construction. There is nothing "natural" or "obvious" about it, as the history of numerical notations cogently shows (see Guitel, 1975). Research has shown (Sastre & Moreno, 1976) that school children construct or invent notational procedures even when they are familiar with our system and handle it correctly in arithmetical tasks.

Interpretation of Numerals

Sixty-five children aged 3 to 6 (Sinclair & Sinclair, 1984) were asked about the meaning of ten examples of numerical environmental print (such as bus numbers, numbers on the T-shirts of runners, car license plates, price tags, etc.). It seems clear that children are working on two complementary aspects of these environmental symbols: their form and their meaning.

Form. Children describe the numeral 22 on the front of a bus in such ways as: "two of the same," "two numbers, alike," "numbers, not letters," "those things like what you write," "oh, those are twos," "two," etc.—verbal descriptions (which may be perfectly correct) of the numeral(s). In these responses, the children made no attempt to discuss the meaning or use of the numeral. Such responses are not surprising: clearly, children *want* to learn to distinguish numerals and to "name" these different shapes correctly. (We never encountered denominations that were idiosyncratic, although they might have been incorrect, as in "S" for 5, "six" for 9, etc.) Indeed, this labeling aspect is the one probably most explicitly "taught" by adults in the environment, but we should not forget that there is nothing numerical about learning "correct" (but arbitrary) names for particular (arbitrary) written shapes.

More surprising, children describing written numerals are also concerned with the *quantity* of shapes that are aligned one after the other, and the variety of these shapes. (Similar concerns are noted in studies on alphabetical writing; see Ferreiro & Teberosky, 1982). Often, the 3- and 4-year-olds count, or attempted to count, the numerals shown to them, as if numerals are simply "for counting" (as some of them say themselves), or as if that is how one "reads them." Older children (aged 5 and 6) often say how many there are. Children until the age of 7 often remark on the fact that numerals following one another are similar, when this is the case (generally speaking, they prefer variety; variety seems to make for "better" numbers). Considerations of color, size, neatness, or iconic resemblance to objects of the numerals seldom come up. From the age of three, children believe such aspects are irrelevant. Written numerals are thus seen as particular entities that have particular properties of shape and position (they are always "read" in a linear direction, one following the other, whether from right to left or left to right) and that may combine in various ways. Conceptual work on the form of written numerals is thus from a very early age oriented towards finding a *system*.

Independent of difficult problems that will be encountered at later ages (like place value, the nature and status of the zero, and the difficulty of decimal points and other marks) various stumbling blocks appear in the search for a system: the link between sound (spoken numeral) and shape (written numeral) is very different from that of the alphabet (which children are reflecting on concurrently); the combinations encountered are quite different from those observed in written language (usually shorter and "more isolated," and often only one shape); and some shapes pose particular problems (1, 5 and 0, which are similar to letters). Finally, the "reading aloud," "description," or "naming" of written numerals is rife with inconsistencies (ordinals, cardinals, powers of the base, traces of nondecimal systems, arbitrary conventions, etc.).

Attempting to attribute consistency and meaning to what are arbitrary conventions, children construct some very curious ideas, even about something as simple as the shapes of our numerals: for example, eight is three and three (to write eight one makes the shape of three twice), different languages (many of our Genevan subjects are bilingual) have "different" written numerals, but the differences are so minute that they are difficult to detect (they think that differences in sound must be reflected in the written form); one cannot write zero because one cannot read it (i.e. it is nothing and therefore meaningless); numerals are always "big" or always "small" (no capital form exists), and the like.

Responses that describe, name, or discuss the numerals presented as entities in themselves, with no particular meaningful link to the context in which they appear (on a bus, for example), diminish with age in our simple task. They constitute about 30% of meaningful responses of the 3-year-olds, and 14% of all responses at age 6. Six-year-olds generally (70% of responses) answer by explaining what the numeral *means*.

Meaning.   For the numeral 22 on a bus, different types of responses clearly relate the numeral's meaning to the context in which it appears. For example: "for the people who go on the bus," "for the driver to look at," "it means it's a bus, not a truck,'' ''to tell which one it is, if it's the one you want to take,'' ''to see where it goes, which one it is,'' ''the price of the bus,'' ''for telling that it goes two different ways,'' ''so that it stops at the right stops.'' Some of these responses attribute a global function to the numeral and link it to its context in a loose way (''for the driver to look at,'' ''for the people . . .''). In other responses, however, the numeral provides information of a specific nature, and the information transmitted (in the bus item and in other items) deals with *quantity* (''price of the bus''), *order, classification or grouping* (''to tell which one it is''), or *one to one correspondence* (''so that it stops at the right stops''), all common functions of written numerals in the environment. A large proportion (55%) of the responses given by 5- and 6-year-old children were of this specific type.

Clearly, young children possess a wealth of information and knowledge about the communicative function of numerals. Although their ideas are often nonspecific—without being incorrect or strange—(for example ''for the people . . .''), when their responses were more precise, they specify the type of information that is indeed transmitted by numerals in the environment, even when the response may be called ''incorrect'' from an adult point of view (''price of the bus''). In fact, a large proportion of their responses resemble the responses of adult city-dwellers when we questioned them about the meaning of numerals penciled on eggs (they guessed the numbers might represent the size or grade of the egg, specify the hen who laid it, the date on which it was laid, etc.).

These ideas and the knowledge they are based on are relatively independent of the knowledge the child may have of specific number shapes and their ''names.'' Often the child simply cannot ''read'' or ''name'' the numerals presented or does not do so because it is considered unimportant. Children occasionally describe or name the numeral correctly but will not draw the correct conclusion from the description. An example is buttons in an elevator: ''It's a four. It says where you want to go, to which floor in the building''. ''And if you push here [the experimenter points to the 4 on the picture], to which floor will you go?'' ''Don't know!'' We were struck by the fact that in this and in many of their other responses children showed us that for them the numerals specified one particular possibility or instance (one or another entity, quantity, order, place, speed, etc.) among many possibilities, which is exactly what environmental numbers do. (The functions of environmental alphabetic print are quite different.) Not being able to determine precisely *which* possibility is meant is not seen by them as a difficulty.

Learning the written symbol system is thus composed of work on the form of the symbols, the rules for their combination and use, linking them to their verbal counterparts, and integrating and coordinating information provided by other people on the function and meaning of particular environmental numerals.

Production

When asked to represent, with pencil and paper, the numerosity of small sets (one to eight) of identical objects placed on the table in front of them, children from the age of 3 to 6 will use a variety of nonconventional notational procedures. The children were asked to note (or mark, or write, following the child's terminology) "what was on the table"; the experimenter did not explicitly mention "how many" (Sinclair, Siegrist & Sinclair, 1983). Only a few 5-year-olds but all 6-year-olds (who also used other types of notation) represented such arrays with a single written numeral, such as 6 for a collection of six small stars. By far the most common system of notation is one in which each object is represented by one graphic mark: crosses, sticks, letters, mock letters (shapes that resemble our letters in their composition of curved and straight lines, or shapes that are very similar to our letters) or numerals. Many 3-year-olds use the one-to-one correspondence principle with success: almost all 4-year-olds do so also; many 5-year-olds and a few 6-year-olds use this type of notation. For a display of five pencils, many of the responses, all based on the one-to-one correspondence principle, can be represented as follows:

11111, or XXXXX (the same tally mark being used for displays of chips, etc.)
□□□□□ (and 00000 for displays of round chips or balls)
AIUOP (and different combination of letters, such as POU used for displays of three other objects)
AAAAA (with the use of YYYY for a display of four chips, RR for a display of two balls, etc.)
55555 (used by some children for displays of any five objects)
12345 (also used by some children for displays of any five objects)

Cursive writing, or mixtures of letters and numbers, did not appear, and conventional numeral shapes were used in only three ways, the two just described and the cardinal standing alone (5), and were always correct in the cardinality of the display and the ordering of the numerals. (see Sinclair, Siegrist & Sinclair, 1983; see also Hughes, 1982, who notes some of the same behaviors).

Children who used 55555 or 12345 for displays with cardinality of five sometimes discovered that the four first numerals written are "useless" (they do not correspond to their verbal description, which is generally "five houses"), and go on to write the cardinal alone. A few others would not accept this possibility even when it was suggested to them. One child explained that it was only in this way that he could add: count the total number of shapes, write the result, which is then in one-to-one correspondence with the two terms—22 "and" 22 is 4444.

Children who did use the cardinal alone often proposed an alternative notational form, that is, the numeral written with letters, usually incorrectly (DE for *deux,* TRO for *trois,* etc.), as if for them it was no longer important to use a specific type of notation but merely somehow to symbolize the cardinality of the set.

The results of the interpretation task may be summed up as follows: In any representational system, meaning can be expressed only through form, and young children work on both aspects when attempting to "crack the code" of the material they see around them. The work they carry out is conceptual in nature and draws heavily on knowledge that concerns objects and actions in the real world, but is socially mediated, that is, transmitted to the child, by other children and adults. It may be that the importance of this kind of knowledge and the child's attempts to piece it together has been underestimated; researchers have concentrated on universals, individually constructed numerical reasoning, such as number conservation, and, more recently, on spoken numerals. To our mind, trying to understand the written number system activates conceptual schemes similar to those at work in the construction of the number concepts themselves. Although initially these schemes are separate, gradually they lead to their reciprocal assimilation.

The results of the production tasks show that early, invented notational systems (particularly one-to-one correspondences) are heavily dependent on the conceptual grasp of the domain to be represented. Clearly, one-to-one correspondences are a powerful heuristic. Iterative actions (pointing at or touching each object) and their verbal counterparts (counting—one tag to each object) showing that each object is an individual but that they all belong "together" are also applied to the domain of written representation. The use of these strategies may be encouraged by the child's perception of the discrete nature of print, but it is worth noting that the strategy embodies the fundamental aspects of any coding system: one entity must be made both to *stand for* and to *correspond to* another entity (in this case, an object).

Some few children perfectly familiar with our number shapes, their "names," and their ordering felt the necessity to write one shape for one object (as in 12345 for 5 stars) or to write down the counting numerals used for that display, depending on the interpretation one makes. Here, the children's efforts to integrate their knowledge of the written symbol system and their view of mathematical reality are particularly clear. We may speculate that it is only when children have understood cardinality that they will write 5 to represent a display of five objects.

It should be emphasized that the children's notations never showed an erroneous use of nonassimilated aspects of our numerals. For example, no child ever noted something like 66 or 145 for a collection of four objects. All their notations appear to be the result of constructing environmental information into different and limited but coherent systems made to fit the children's nascent number concepts.

One could, no doubt, consider a certain number of the behaviors we are discussing in this paper to be "procedures." For example, counting, as the children used it in Gréco's experiment (leading them to say things like "There are seven and seven, but here there is one more") seems like the result of a faulty counting procedure used without a conceptual background, because the correct inference (equality) is not drawn (Gréco & Morf, 1962). However, as we have said, we view this use of counting as the symptom of an as yet limited inferential field. Similarly, the fact that children always interpret and produce numerals in a linear manner might be considered a procedure (in this case, the same procedure as that used by adults). However, it certainly also indicates a conceptual link between a spatial representation and the number-after and number-before relationship. This is no mean conceptual feat!

In other words, either one admits such highly complex relations between conceptual and procedural knowledge that they become indissociable, or, as we prefer, one decides that the distinction is not applicable to the period during which children construct concepts and collate information on their own, without receiving any specific formal instruction, and in many respects build up a numerical world of their own, which is often incompatible with what they are presented with once formal education starts.

ACKNOWLEDGMENTS

The research reported here was supported by a grant from the Fonds National Suisse de la Recherche Scientifique, No. 1.368-0.81. The authors would like to thank D. Mello and F. Siegrist for their help in the collection of data. The authors also express their thanks to the staff of the kindergartens for their cooperation.

REFERENCES

Allardice, B. (1977). The development of written representations for some mathematical concepts. *Journal of Children's Mathematical Behavior, 1(4),* 135–148.

Beth, E. W., & Piaget, J. (1961). *Epistémologie mathématique et psychologie,* PUF, Paris.

Bergeron, J. C., & Herscovics, N. (1983). Models of multiplication based on the concept of ratio. *Proceedings of the Seventh International Conference on the Psychology of Mathematics Education, Rehovot, Israel,* 199–205.

Clay, M. M. (1975). *What did I write? Beginning writing behavior.* Auckland, NZ: Heinemann.

Droz, R., & Paschoud, J. (1981). Le comptage et la procédure "(+1) itéré" dans l'exploration intuitive de l'addition. *Revue suisse de psychologie, 40(3),* 219–237.

Erlwanger, S., & Bélanger, M. (1983). Interpretations of the equal sign among elementary school children. *Proceedings of the Fifth Annual Meeting of the North American Chapter of the International Group for the Psychology of Mathematics Education,* vol. 1, 250–259, Montreal.

Ferreiro, E., & Teberosky, A. (1982). *Literacy before schooling.* London: Heinemann.

Gelman, R., & Gallistel, C. R. (1978). *The child's understanding of number.* Cambridge, MA: Harvard University Press.

Gréco, P., Grize, J. B., Papert, S., & Piaget, J. (1960). *Problèmes de la construction du nombre.* Paris: PUF (Presses Universitaires de France).

Gréco, P., Inhelder, B., Matalon, B., & Piaget, J. (1963). *La formation des raisonnements récurrentiels,* Paris: PUF.

Gréco, P. & Morf, A. (1962). *Structures numériques élémentaires.* Paris: PUF.

Guitel, G. (1975). *Histoire comparée des numérations écrites.* Paris: Flammarion.

Herscovics, N., & Bergeron, J. C. (1984). A constructivist vs. a formalist approach in the teaching of mathematics. *Proceedings of the Eighth International Conference on the Psychology of Mathematics Education,* Sydney.

Hogben, L. (1936). *Mathematics for the million.* London: Allen & Unwin.

Hughes, M. (1982). Rappresentazione grafica spontanea del numero nei bambini: Alcuni risultati preliminari. *Eta Evolutiva, 12,* 5–10.

Inhelder, B., Blanchet, A., Sinclair, A., & Piaget, J. (1975). Relations entre les conservations d'ensembles d'éléments discrets et celles des quantités continues. *Année psychologique, 75,* 23–60.

Inhelder, B., & Piaget, J. (1959). *La genèse des structures logiques élémentaires.* Neuchâtel & Paris: Delachaux & Niestlé.

Kamii, C. K. (1985). *Young children reinvent arithmetic.* New York: Teachers College Press. Columbia University.

Piaget, J., & Inhelder, B. (1969). The gaps in empiricism. In Koestler, A., & Smythies, J. R., (eds.) *Beyond reductionism.* Boston: Beacon Press.

Piaget, J., & Garcia, R. (1983). *Psychogenèse et histoire des sciences.* Paris: Flammarion.

Piaget, J., & Szeminska, A. (1941). *La genèse du nombre chez l'enfant.* Neuchâtel & Paris: Delachaux & Niestlé.

Sastre, G., & Moreno, M. (1976). Représentation graphique de la quantité. *Bulletin de psychologie de l'Université de Paris, 30,* 346–355.

Sinclair, A., Siegrist, F., & Sinclair, H. (1983). Young children's ideas about the written number system. In D. Rogers & J. Sloboda (eds.), *The acquisition of symbolic skills.* New York: Plenum Press.

Sinclair, A., & Sinclair, H. (1984). Preschool children's interpretation of written numbers. *Human Learning, 3.* 173–184.

Sinclair, H., Rayna, S., Stambak, M., & Verba, M. (1982). *Les bébés et les choses,* Paris: PUF.

4

The Relationship Between Initial Meaningful and Mechanical Knowledge of Arithmetic

Arthur J. Baroody
University of Rochester

Herbert P. Ginsburg
Teachers College, Columbia University

Especially in recent years, much has been learned about children's informal (largely self-invented, counting-based) arithmetic. It is clear that children's informal arithmetic is an important basis for learning formal (school-taught, symbolic) arithmetic (e.g., Baroody, 1986; Brownell, 1935; Ginsburg, 1982; Hiebert, 1984). In this chapter, we examine arithmetic routines that develop either without formal instruction or during the first years of formal schooling. We discuss, in turn, (a) informal addition procedures, (b) automatic production of the basic arithmetic combinations, and (c) (counterproductive) routines for coping with school-assigned arithmetic.

More specifically, we focus on both the meaningful and the more mechanical knowledge that may underlie basic arithmetic routines. Our aim is to examine what can be inferred about the relationships between early meaningful and mechanical knowledge of arithmetic. We equate meaningful knowledge with semantic knowledge—with implicit or explicit knowledge of concepts or principles. We define mechanical knowledge as knowledge of facts (specific associations) and procedural knowledge (rules and algorithms).[1]

---

[1]A distinction between meaningful and mechanical knowledge is not always easy to discern. Consider the automatic routine of responding N to $N + 0 = ?$ ($0 + N = ?$) problems, such as $2 + 0 = ?$ or $9 + 0 = ?$. A child might rotely learn to respond to "$N + 0 = ?$" problems by simply repeating the non-zero number. Here the child just follows a routine (uses an $N + 0 = N$ rule) to produce an answer. In contrast, another child may assimilate the formal arithmetic sentence into the informal understanding that adding nothing to a set does not change the set (informal identity principle) and realize that all such symbolic problems will have an answer of N (Baroody, 1985a). Here the child's routine is directed by a meaningful principle.

Moreover, a distinction between meaningful and mechanical knowledge is not always clear. Consider the "number-fact" $5 + 5 = 10$. A child might rotely memorize "$5 + 5 = 10$" without any

Our basic premise is that what can be inferred from arithmetic routines about underlying knowledge is often less clear than it seems. This theme runs through each of three major sections of the chapter. First, even with informal addition, the relationships among computational procedures, meaningful knowledge, and mechanical knowledge may be more complex than expected. Nonconceptual factors, such as the drive to reduce memory load, may be as important as, or more important than, conceptual factors in the invention or choice of informal procedures. Second, in the formal domain, the basis of automatic "number-fact" production may be more complicated than is commonly assumed. Automatic number-combination knowledge has usually been attributed to one form of mechanical knowledge (factual knowledge). However, other forms of mechanical knowledge (procedural knowledge, such as rules or invented procedures) *and* semantic knowledge may also play a role. Third, because of the constraints and beliefs imposed by formal education, many children may resort to mechanical routines that are divorced from or disguise their understanding of mathematics. In each of three sections, we note inferences about the underlying knowledge of routines that may be incomplete or incorrect and attempt to delineate additional or alternative explanations. We conclude the chapter by pointing out how the development of early arithmetic knowledge fits into a schema theory of knowledge acquisition outlined by R. C. Anderson (1984).

INFORMAL ARITHMETIC

Unexpected Complexity

The Case of Counting.   Recent research suggests an intimate relationship between early meaningful and mechanical knowledge of mathematics. In the domain of counting development, Gelman (Gelman & Gallistel, 1978; Gelman & Meck, 1983) proposes that some principles develop very early and direct the development of counting procedures. For example, Gelman and Gallistel (1978) argue that important aspects of children's counting behavior imply and are guided by an order-irrelevance principle (an understanding that the order in which elements of a set are tagged does not affect the cardinal designation of the

---

real understanding of what the arithmetic sentence means. In this case, $5 + 5 = 10$ is just an arbitrary association and clearly an example of mechanical knowledge. In contrast, a child might count the five fingers on each hand and discover that there are a total of 10. In other contexts, such as with dice, the child notes that 5 and 5 also make 10 and, as a result, abstracts a meaningful relationship (Brownell, 1935). In this case, the distinction between meaningful knowledge (a relationship) and mechanical knowledge (a factual association) is not clearcut. For the sake of this discussion, we will refer to a number combination such as $5 + 5 = 10$—whether acquired by rote or meaningful learning—as mechanical knowledge *if* we are implying that such knowledge is stored as a *specific* numerical association in a direct (S → R) fact retrieval network.

set). In particular, they note that their subjects were indifferent to the order of items when the preschoolers enumerated sets. Indeed, many were willing to designate any item in a set as "one" and count sets in different ways. Moreover, their subjects could even explain that assigning counting tags was an arbitrary process. Can such behaviors, however, be taken as evidence of an underlying order-irrelevance principle? Is it really necessary to posit a guiding principle to explain such counting behaviors? To what extent are young children's counting behavior, in particular, and mathematical behavior, in general, principle driven?

Even the relationship between meaningful and mechanical knowledge of counting does not seem to be uncomplicated. In contrast to Gelman's view of principle-driven counting development, preschoolers apparently first learn to use numbers mechanically and only gradually construct an understanding of number and counting (e.g., Baroody & Ginsburg, 1984; Fuson & Hall, 1983; von Glasersfeld, 1982; Wagner & Walters, 1982). Increased understanding then leads to procedural advances and more sophisticated application of procedures. These, in turn, may lead to further conceptual insights, and so forth.

Take, for instance, a willingness to disregard order when assigning counting tags. A child might assign tags to elements of a set in different orders and even explain that tag assignment is an arbitrary process but *not* realize that different count orders yield the same cardinal designation (Baroody, 1984d). It seems that procedural knowledge concerning tagging may be based on a developmentally less advanced order-indifferent tagging rule (count tags from the number sequence do not have to be assigned to set elements in a fixed order). Unlike an order-irrelevance *principle,* an order-indifferent tagging *rule* does not necessarily imply that differently ordered counts of a set will produce the same cardinal value (cf. Gelman & Gallistel, 1978). Some research (Baroody, 1984d; Briars & Siegler, 1984; Fuson & Hall, 1983) suggests that an order-indifferent tagging rule develops prior to an order-irrelevance principle.

Indeed, an order-indifferent tagging rule is probably a necessary condition for the development of an order-irrelevance principle. It does not seem likely that such a principle is innate or somehow deduced from more elementary counting principles. Rather, it seems likely that the principle is induced from counting experience, a routine directed by more basic conceptual *and* procedural counting knowledge. Specifically, to discover that differently ordered counts of a set do not affect the outcome, children must first be willing to count sets in different orders (see examples cited by Baroody & Mason, 1985; Piaget, 1964).

Gelman and Meck (this volume) clearly and elegantly demonstrate that previous research (e.g., Baroody, 1984d) appears to have underestimated order-irrelevance competence. However, the basic issues remain open: Is it important to distinguish between an order-indifferent tagging rule and an order-irrelevance principle? Does the rule precede the principle developmentally?

In brief, although the relationship between meaningful and mechanical knowledge of counting is a close one, it is a complex one. Indeed, children's early mathematical behaviors sometimes seem more sophisticated than, or even at odds with, their conceptions. Sinclair and Sinclair (this volume) describe a number of logically inconsistent phenomena, such as the difference between making quotity and quantity judgments. As we will see, the same seems to hold true for children's informal arithmetic.

Early Arithmetic Development. Gradually, children extend their counting skills to the task of calculation. At first, a child may see that if one block is added to one already present, the result is "two," and that one added to two makes "three," and so on (Baroody & White, 1983; Ginsburg & Baroody, 1983; von Glasersfeld, 1982). There is only a thin line between counting and incrementing and decrementing by one. Even before they enter school, children discover that counting can be used to solve simple arithmetic ($N + 1$ and $N - 1$) problems, such as "three candies and one more" or "five dolls, take away one" (e.g., Court, 1920; Fuson & Hall, 1983; Ginsburg, 1982; Resnick, 1983; Resnick & Ford, 1981; Starkey & Gelman, 1982).

With experience, children learn to add and subtract one without concrete objects. By the time they enter first grade, most children have sufficient facility with number-after and number-before relationships to mentally compute $N + 1$ up to at least $5 + 1$ and $N - 1$ up to at least $5 - 1$ (Fuson, Richards, & Briars, 1982). Some evidence indicates that this simple mental arithmetic is guided by a fundamental understanding of addition and subtraction: Addition is an incrementing process; subtraction is a decrementing process, and the addition of an item can be undone by the removal of an element and vice versa (Brush, 1978; Gelman, 1972, 1977; Starkey & Gelman, 1982).

Likewise, before they learn the "number facts," children solve $M + N$ or $M - N$ (where M and $N \neq 1$) and $1 + N$ by relying on informal procedures that, at least initially, require the aid of countable objects (e.g., Carpenter & Moser, 1982, 1984; Fuson, 1982; Resnick, 1983; Siegler & Shrager, 1984; Steffe, von Glasersfeld, Richards, & Cobb, 1983). Children's initial concrete and mental computing procedures directly model the semantic structure of addition and subtraction word problems—the actions or relationships described in the problems (Carpenter, this volume; Carpenter & Moser, 1983). At this point, there appears to be an intimate connection between young children's meaningful and mechanical knowledge. Their solution procedures appear to be directed by and reflect conceptual knowledge. When scrutinized, however, the relationship between young children's conception of addition and their solution procedures is not always clearcut. The following discussion details some of the complexities.

Children's Initial Conception of Addition. What conception of addition do young children have? Addition can be defined as a binary operation that involves the union of two sets. For example, $4 + 2$ represents combining the cardinal number four and the cardinal number two *or* combining the cardinal number two and the cardinal number four. (This binary operation is commutative—that is, the order of the terms makes no difference to the outcome. Therefore, the expression 4 + 2 is equivalent to 2 + 4). However, it has been argued that, psychologically, young children initially view addition as a change of state—making an existing set larger (e.g., Baroody & Ginsburg, 1983; Weaver, 1982). In Weaver's terms, they treat addition as a unary operation. For instance, young children probably interpret and often read 4 + 2 as "four and then two *more*" and 2 + 4 as "two and then four *more*." That is, they probably view 4 + 2 and 2 + 4 as *different* problems. Moreover, because they cannot foresee that the outcomes will be the same, children first view 4 + 2 and 2 + 4 as nonequivalent (Baroody & Gannon, 1984). On the face of it, it seems reasonable to assume that children initially have a unary view of addition but, as we will see, the empirical support is equivocal.

The Case of Concrete Addition

Assuming that children do begin with the unary conception of addition, to what extent does this conceptual knowledge guide their informal addition procedures? To solve problems more complicated than $N + 1$, children first use concrete counting-all (CCA): Count out a number of objects or fingers to represent one term, do the same for the other term, and then count all the real entities to find the sum. Actually, this procedure could be used to model *either* a binary or a unary conception of addition. However, if a unary rather than a binary conception of addition is guiding the solution process, we would expect children to respect the order of the addends. That is, a child with a unary conception should represent the existing set (augend) first and then the amount added (the addend). (Once the sets are represented or joined, the order-irrelevance principle applies, and the sum count might be done in any order.) However, some evidence (e.g., Capenter & Moser, 1982) indicates that children do not always respect addend order when executing CCA.

One explanation is that a CCA procedure does not necessarily imply a unary concept. In other words, CCA might be employed by children with more advanced conceptions of addition as well as those with a basic unary view (Cobb, 1985b). Baroody and Gannon (1984) note that, though not the rule, a few of their subjects who relied on CCA did appear to appreciate commutativity. Thus, it seems that a basic CCA procedure is used by some children with a developmentally more advanced (a more binary-like) conception of addition. (Whether or not knowledge of commutativity actually accounts for those instances in which children disregard order in representing the addends remains to be investigated.)

Another explanation is that nonconceptual factors may (occasionally) prevent direct modeling of the unary schema. Performance factors, such as forgetting or not paying attention to the order of the addends, may account for momentary lapses in respecting addend order. The discrepancy is simply another example of the need to distinguish between competence and performance (see Gelman & Meck, this volume). A child might also disregard addend order for the sake of convenience. Thus, utilization competence does not necessarily reflect conceptual competence (Gelman & Meck, this volume; Greeno, Riley, & Gelman, 1984). For example, a child may have a representation of the second addend readily available and dispense with that representation before turning to the task of creating a representation of the first addend. Consider the child who can automatically make finger representations of 1, 2, and 5 but still has to count out three or four fingers. Given a problem such as "3 + 5," the child might "choose" to display the finger pattern for five before turning attention to counting out three fingers. Thus, illogically to adults, the addend order is disregarded even though $3 + 5 = ?$ and $5 + 3 = ?$ are considered different and nonequivalent. As we see later, there is an analogous, labor-saving but paradoxical situation with mentally computing sums.

Moreover, if young children hold a unary conception, they should have more success with *change* problems (e.g., Al has 2 marbles, and he buys 4 more. How many does he have now?) than with *combine* problems (e.g., Al has 2 marbles, and Sam has 4. How many marbles do the boys have altogether?), because change problems more directly reflect a unary understanding of addition (Briars & Larkin, 1984). Combine problems, in turn, should be easier than symbolic problems, such as $2 + 4$, because young children may be unfamiliar with the written representations of mathematical concepts (Allardice, 1977; Sinclair & Sinclair, this volume). Thus, combine problems are more likely than abstract problems to engage a child's unary schema. Although some evidence (e.g., Ginsburg, 1982) suggests that word problems are easier than symbolic problems, existing research (e.g., Carpenter, Hiebert, & Moser, 1983; Carpenter & Moser, 1983; Lindvall & Ibarra, 1979; Riley, Greeno, & Heller, 1983; Steffe, 1968; Steffe & Johnson, 1971) does not consistently show that change problems are easier than combine problems for kindergarten and first-grade children.

Because of young children's unary view, it may be that, initially, change problems are more readily comprehended and solvable than combine problems. However, because of the similarity of the problems, children may then readily assimilate combine-type problems to their unary schema. Briars and Larkin (1984) argue that the typical wording of combine problems may provide an implicit action cue. That is, the word "altogether" or subset words followed by a superset word cue a "join action" and the child's unary schema.

Other problem-solving data are consistent with the hypothesis of an initial unary schema. Children have considerably greater difficulty with missing-augend problems ($? + B = C$) than with missing-addend problems ($A + ? = C$) (e.g., Carpenter, this volume; Hiebert, 1982; Riley et al., 1983). Modeling a problem in which the initial state is missing is quite difficult if a child is tied to a unary view of addition. With a binary view, the child has the flexibility to model a missing-augend problem as a more easily solvable missing-addend problem.

Thus flexibility in solving addition word problems may reflect domain-specific conceptual development: The addition of the relatively sophisticated and abstract binary view *may* make solving ? + B = C problems more probable.

In summary, one would expect that children's initial informal algorithm (CCA—concrete counting-all) would reflect their initial conception of addition. If this is a unary conception, children should consistently represent the first term (augend) before the second term (addend). However, CCA users do not always respect addend order. It may be that the basic CCA procedure is used by children with more advanced conceptions of addition as well as by those with a basic unary view. Furthermore, a basic unary view may not be translated faithfully into a procedure because of nonconceptual factors, such as inattentiveness or convenience. One would also expect that children would be more successful on change problems than on combine problems because the former directly reflect a unary view. Though this might be the case initially, the equal difficulty often found may be due to the similarity of the problems and the process of generalizing assimilation. In any case, children may have more difficulty with ? + B = C problems than with A + ? = C problems because a unary conception prevents them from translating the former (missing-augend) problems into the more easily modeled missing-addend format. These matters clearly require more systematic investigation, especially with children just beginning to add.

The Case of Mental Addition

When we examine informal mental solutions for $N + M/M + N$, the relationship between a unary concept and informal procedures is clearer, at least initially. The most basic mental addition procedure is *counting-all starting with the first addend* (CAF) (e.g., 2 + 4: "1, 2; 3[is one more], 4[is two more], 5[is three more] 6[is four more]—six") (Baroody, 1984a, in press-a; Baroody & Gannon, 1984). CAF is a fairly sophisticated invention because it does not directly model the whole concrete counting-all process, and it entails enumerating the addend *as* the child counts on from the augend (a simultaneous keeping-track process) (Baroody & Gannon, 1983; Carpenter & Moser, 1983). *Counting-on from the first addend* (COF) shortcuts the CAF procedure by starting with the cardinal term of the first addend (e.g., 2 + 4: "2; 3[+1], 4[+2], 5[+3], 6[+4]—six"), but it does not reduce the number of steps in the keeping-track process (Baroody & Gannon, 1984). Both CAF and COF entail a four-step keeping-track process. This cognitively demanding process can be minimized by starting with the larger term. One strategy that accomplishes this end is *counting-all starting with the larger term* (CAL) (Baroody, 1984a). CAL entails beginning with "one," counting up to the larger cardinal term, and then counting-on from there while the smaller term is enumerated (e.g., 2 + 4: "1, 2, 3, 4; 5[+1], 6[+2]—six"). For 2 + 4, note that the keeping-track process is reduced to only two steps. *Counting-on from the larger term* (COL) short-cuts CAL by starting with the larger cardinal term. Hence it is the most economical informal mental-addition procedure (e.g., 2 + 4: "4; 5[+1], 6[+2]—six"). Thus, unlike the case of CCA, disregarding addend order can save considerable effort when calculating sums mentally.

There are some data on the developmental sequence of these mental-addition procedures. Mentally counting-all precedes counting-on (Groen & Resnick, 1977; Ilg & Ames, 1951), and COF appears to precede COL (Carpenter & Moser, 1984; Ilg & Ames, 1951). Research subsequent to the discovery of CAL indicates that CCA tends to be followed by CAF, CAF tends to be followed by CAL, and COF tends to be experimented with only briefly, if at all, before COL is adopted (Baroody, in press-a; Baroody & Gannon, 1984). In brief, empirical investigations indicate that initially children tend to use CAF or COF before relying on CAL or COL; initial mental procedures tend to honor addend order and model a unary conception of addition. Assuming children initially view addition as unary, this suggests a close link between children's first mental procedures and their conceptual knowledge. Later, they invent more flexible procedures that disregard addend order; these seem more consistent with a binary than a unary view.

Commutativity

What accounts for the development of more flexible informal addition procedures? Does the invention of procedures that disregard addend order indicate a change in children's underlying conceptualization of addition? More specifically, does the invention of CAL or COL imply an understanding of commutativity and a binary conception of addition?

The invention of an addition procedure that disregards addend order (COL) has been equated with an understanding of commutativity (e.g., Groen & Resnick, 1977; Resnick & Ford, 1981). Several models (Briars & Larkin, 1984; Riley et al., 1983) hypothesize a direct link among the development of conceptual sophistication (flexible mental representation ability), commutativity, and COL (a procedure that does not directly represent the problem). In this view, knowledge of commutativity is considered a necessary condition for the invention of more flexible addition procedures.

However, some empirical work (Baroody, 1982, in press-a; Baroody & Gannon, 1984) indicates that children who invent CAL or COL do not necessarily realize that, say, 5 + 3 and 3 + 5 will produce the same sums.[2] Consider the example of Case (Baroody & Gannon, 1984). During the second of three sessions, Case switched from relying on CAF to using CAL. For 3 + 6, for instance, he counted "1, 2, 3" as he tapped the card. He stopped and com-

---

[2]The research cited used symbolic problems that may have underestimated children's conceptual competence. It may be that children would demonstrate an understanding of commutativity earlier if problems were concretely represented (see Sinclair & Sinclair, this volume).

mented, "I'll count to 6, I guess: 1, 2, 3, 4, 5, 6 [pause], 7, 8, 9." Whether consciously or not, Case must have anticipated the difficulty of a six-step keeping-track process and readjusted his approach to the problem. During Sessions 1 and 2, he was also given a comparison task in which he had to judge whether two problem sentences, one written above the other, would add up to the same thing or something different. Case indicated that commuted items (6 + 2 and 2 + 6 and 5 + 4 and 4 + 5) were "*almost* the same but different." Because of his unusual response and the possibility that he was responding to the similarities and differences of the addends rather than the sums, the interviewer asked a follow-up probe. After Case had responded "different" to the pair 2 + 7 and 7 + 2, the experimenter asked Case to compute 7 + 2. After Case counted and responded correctly, the interviewer asked how much 2 + 7 was. Apparently unaware of the equivalence of the problems, Case again responded by counting. In the third session, Case was given another, somewhat different, comparison task but still appeared unsure about the equivalence of commuted pairs. Given 4 + 6 and asked if it would add up to the same thing as 6 + 4 or something different, he shook his head to indicate no. Thus, without concern for the outcome of the operation, children may search for ways to save cognitive effort. Starting with the larger addend accomplishes this end (Baroody, 1982; Resnick & Neches, 1984).

It appears, then, that young children may hold contradictory notions about the effects of addend order (Baroody & Gannon, 1984). Initially, because of their unary conception of addition, children may assume that addend order makes a difference in the definition of the problem and thus in the sum. A child is especially likely to invoke this "misconception" when commuted pairs are juxtaposed, as in the comparison tasks used by Baroody and Gannon (1984). On the other hand, some children also appear to have a primitive notion of commutativity. Protocommutativity, or what might be termed an "order-indifferent *adding* scheme," implies that two numbers can be combined in any order to produce correct—though not necessarily the same—answers (Baroody, Ginsburg, & Waxman, 1983). That is, like knowledge of commutativity, protocommutativity implies that addend order does not constrain the order in which the addends are operated. Unlike commutativity, protocommutativity allows that addend order can affect outcome. This logical impasse is probably due to the influence of nonconceptual factors and the lack of reflection on the part of young children. That is, in the service of economy and because they fail to consider the logical relationship between method and outcome, children are willing to disregard addend order without believing that, say, 3 + 5 and 5 + 3 add to the same sum. Thus, it appears that the invention of CAL or COL necessarily implies only protocommutativity—not commutativity.

Eventually, a child's logically inconsistent views about the role of addend order can be resolved by focusing on the outcome of addition—by discovering the commutative property of addition (Baroody & Gannon, 1984). Some evidence (Baroody, 1982; Baroody & Gannon, 1984) suggests that some young children readily abstract this principle from their computational efforts with commuted pairs. Other evidence (e.g., Baroody et al., 1983) indicates that the principle is widely known as early as first grade, before formal instruction on the topic. From their computational experience, then, children may adopt the view that it does not matter whether you start with two blocks and add three more or start with three blocks and add two more *because the result is the same*. Note that the preceding statement implies only a unary conception of addition (Weaver, 1982). An understanding that addend order does not affect the outcome of addition (an understanding of commutativity) can be abstracted empirically before the development of a binary conception of addition and is not necessarily *linked* with it (Baroody & Gannon, 1984).

To recapitulate, although it seems obvious that procedures that disregard addend order imply commutativity, the development of these informal procedures and concepts apparently are not necessarily linked (Baroody, 1985c). Children may invent CAL or COL—may add numbers in either order—because they believe they will get a *correct* (though not necessarily the *same*) answer. So what looks like a procedure driven by a sophisticated concept may be a procedure invented to reduce cognitive demand and reflecting an incomplete concept of addition. That is, the general cognitive tendency to achieve economical processing (Gibson, 1969)—a nonconceptual factor—may account for the invention of CAL or COL (Baroody, 1985c). Commutativity, it appears, may be noticed separately—either before or after the invention of CAL or COL—by detecting regularities in computational effort and outcome. Here we seem to have a case where application of procedures leads to a conceptual breakthrough rather than vice versa.

The Invention of Counting-on

The drive for cognitive economy may also account for the development of counting-on procedures (COF or COL). Counting-all involves redundancy. Consider 5-year-old Felicia, who while playing an addition game rolled dice showing five dots and three dots. Like many children her age, she automatically recognized (subitized) the number patterns as "five" and "three." Though she recognized and announced the cardinal value of the first addend, Felicia did not begin with five and count on three ("5; 6, 7, 8—8"). Instead, she began with ("1, 2, 3, 4, 5; 6, 7, 8—8"). Apparently, the young girl did not realize that *within a sum count*, the count of the first addend could be abbreviated and that the cardinal term of the first addend could be the starting point for a sum count (e.g., Fuson, 1982, 1985; Secada, Fuson, & Hall, 1983).[3]

---

[3]Typical of children her age, Felicia did understand that a number like five is simultaneously a cardinal number and a count number. That is, she could connect a cardinal meaning with a count meaning: Five is the cardinal designation of the set *and*, if the set were counted, five would be the

During the course of their computational efforts, children may realize that counting out the first (larger) addend is redundant with simply stating the cardinal term of the first (larger addend) (Fuson, 1982; Resnick & Neches, 1984). This discovery is especially likely with sets that are automatically recognized, either kinesthetically through finger patterns or visually through subitizing (Baroody, in press-b). For instance, given a dice roll of five and three dots, a child might readily recognize "five plus three," count the dots of the first die, note that the outcome of the count is the same as the subitized value, and conclude that it is safe and easier to start with the cardinal term of the first addend.

The issue of cognitive economy may also account for why COF is a brief and infrequent transitional step and why children do not adopt COL sooner (e.g., Carpenter & Moser, 1982). Once they begin to use mental procedures (CAF), many children quickly adopt CAL because disregarding the addend order minimizes the cognitively demanding keeping-track process (Baroody, in press-a; Baroody & Gannon, 1984). It is not likely a child would abandon CAL for COF, a procedure that involves more effort by working memory. Once children reach the stage of counting-on, they probably tend to use a strategy that minimizes the keeping-track process: COL (Baroody & Gannon, 1984). Moreover, given that the number of steps in the keeping-track process is the same for CAL and COL, there is only a small savings of effort to be gained by adopting COL (at least for most of the problems a young child encounters). In effect, CAL may be sufficiently economical to account for the relatively long delay in adopting COL.

In brief, to count on, children need to recognize that the count of the first addend can be abbreviated and that the cardinal term for the first addend can serve as the starting point for a sum count. Pattern recognition may be an important means by which children realize that generating the count for the first (larger) addend is redundant to stating the cardinal designation of the first (larger) addend. In effect, the natural tendency to economize effort may be the driving force behind the adoption of COF or COL. The factor of cognitive economy also helps to explain why CAL is a common and enduring transitional strategy before COL, but COF is not.

Factors Affecting Choice of Addition Procedure

As with the *development* of informal addition procedures, strategy *choice* or the flexible use of procedures may reflect nonconceptual as well as conceptual factors. Consider the following examples.

---

count tag assigned to the last item (Fuson & Hall, 1983). Because the girl understood the cardinal-count connection, she could, for example, produce (count out) a specified number of objects (Baroody & Mason, 1984; Fuson, 1982). Felicia, however, failed to see the cardinal-count connection in the more complex (two-set) context of addition (K. C. Fuson, personal communication, June 27, 1985). That is, within a sum count, she failed to realize that the cardinal-count connection allows one to abbreviate the count production of the first addend.

Semantic Structure.   There is good reason to believe that semantic knowledge can guide choice of procedures. Various studies (e.g., Carpenter, Hiebert, & Moser, 1981) have found that the semantic structure of addition word problems influences children's solution strategies. For example, in the results obtained by DeCorte and Verschaffel (1984), combine problems that imply a binary conception of addition ("Pete has 3 apples. Ann has 7 apples. How many apples do Pete and Ann have altogether?") were typically solved by COL. In contrast, change problems that imply a unary conception of addition ("Pete had 3 apples. Ann gave him 5 *more*. How many apples does Pete have now?") typically induced children to use COF. It may be that children more directly linked unary-worded problems with their unary conception of addition and so modeled this view, whereas the binary-worded problems were only weakly linked to their underlying unary conception of addition and solved by the least taxing method. On the other hand, some children may have supplemented a unary conception of addition with a binary view. Though such statements as $2 + 3 = 5$ and $3 + 2 = 5$ are mathematically equivalent, Kaput (1979) notes that psychologically they imply different meanings even for adults. It does not seem likely that a binary conception ever entirely *replaces* a unary view. Rather, a child's conception of addition probably expands to incorporate a formally more correct binary view. The different semantic structures tap into different underlying conceptions, and this accounts for the differences in solution procedures.

Cognitive Economy.   The choice of addition procedure, however, does not always reflect conceptual understanding (Cobb, 1985b). Other cognitive factors, such as the need to reduce the load on working memory, may play a key role in the choice of procedures. This may account for some of the inconsistency in procedure choice typically observed by researchers (e.g., Carpenter & Moser, 1984). For example, some children use the CAL procedure selectively (Baroody, 1984a). Case, for instance, used his newly invented CAL procedure with the problems $2 + 6 = ?$, $2 + 8 = ?$, and $3 + 6 = ?$ but continued to use CAF with problems such as $2 + 4 = ?$ and $4 + 5 = ?$ that required a less involved keeping-track process (Baroody & Gannon, 1984). Similarly, once children acquire counting-on, they do not appear to use COL exclusively. Again, this makes some sense if we examine the cognitive demands of different problems. Baroody (1983b) notes that COF was used most frequently with near doubles such as $2 + 3$ and $3 + 4$, where minimizing the keeping-track process matters the least (and where picking the larger term is relatively demanding). Also, given the readily available finger model for five, it is not surprising that COF might be used with $1 + 5$, $2 + 5$, $3 + 5$, and $4 + 5$.

Problem Size.   Problem size effects also indicate that nonconceptual factors, such as the drive for cognitive economy, affect children's choice of procedures. Carpenter and Moser (1982) found that most children who relied on CCA to solve small-number problems were unable to solve large-number problems with sums in the teens. However, some children switched to a mental counting-on procedure for larger problems (e.g., 15 + 4: "*15;* 16[+1], 17[+2], 18[+3], 19[+4]—nineteen").

A similar kind of flexibility was found in a case study of a preschooler (Baroody, 1984a). For small problems, Felicia would use concrete or mental counting-all. For problems with a two-digit addend, she switched to a COL or COL-like procedure (e.g., 4 + 22: "23, 24, 25, 26—twenty-six" or "20, 21, 22; 23, 24, 25, 26—twenty-six"). Two pieces of evidence suggest that the switch to a counting-on strategy was basically an invention of necessity—a shortcut induced by larger problems. First, with problems in the thirties, she tended to count on from the *decade* rather than the specified addend (e.g., "32 + 6: "31, 32, 33, 34, 35, 36"). Such systematic errors make sense if we assume that the construction of the more efficient procedure is not directly tied to conceptual knowledge but influenced by the need for cognitive economy (Carpenter, this volume). Second, though both small and large problems appeared meaningful to her (i.e., it did not appear that she mechanically used an addition procedure to operate on numbers), this preschooler resisted using COL with smaller problems. Indeed, over the course of the case study (more than a year), Felicia seemed to consider the counting-on procedure as inappropriate when applied to small problems (Baroody & Mason, 1985).

Likewise, John invented counting-on to cope with larger problems and then abandoned the procedure as soon as one-digit problems were reintroduced (Baroody, 1983d). John relied on CAF to compute the sums of 4 + 5 = ?, 5 + 2 = ?, 2 + 6 = ?, and 7 + 3 = ?. When confronted with teen problems, he switched to a counting-on procedure. For example, for 3 + 17 = ?, he began computing from one: "1, 2, 3; 4 is 1, 5 is 2, 6 is 3, 7 is 4, 8 is 5 [pause] 1, 2, 3; 4 is 1, 5 is 2. No. I think I'll start with 17, that'll be easier: 17, 18 is 1, 19 is 2, 20 is 3!" John continued to use this counting-on procedure for four problems involving an addend in the 20s and four with an addend in the 30s. Curiously, when small addition problems were again administered at the end of the session, the child switched to a CAL procedure. That is, he again counted from "one" but then counted up to the cardinal value of the larger addend. Apparently his experience with larger problems was not sufficient to induce him to adopt COL as a general addition strategy, but it did help him to discover that dealing with the larger addend first saves labor. This is consistent with other data (Baroody, in press-a; Baroody & Gannon, 1983) that suggest that CAL is adopted readily but that consistent use of COL requires a relatively large amount of addition experience.

Why children count-on with larger problems but fail to do so with smaller problems is not entirely clear. It does not seem likely that a more sophisticated conception underlies their more advanced procedures for dealing with larger combinations. It would be more plausible to argue that, for some children, large problems are so abstract and meaningless that they use whatever works to produce an answer. For small, meaningful problems, they use their familiar, more conceptually based strategy. In effect, conceptual disengagement frees the child to use a more efficient, "experimental" strategy with larger problems. For other children for whom both small and large problems are meaningful, counting from one may be just a well-ingrained habit that the child is forced to abandon temporarily with larger problems. Whether or not the larger problem is meaningful to the child, it seems plausible that a driving force behind the switch to a more advanced procedure for larger problems is the factor of cognitive economy.

Summary

Though young children's conceptual knowledge of arithmetic no doubt informs their informal solution processes, it would not be safe to conclude that the nature of children's informal procedures clearly reflects their conceptual level. Though it is not clear why, young children do not always respect addend order when executing concrete counting-all—as might be expected if a unary conception of addition were directly guiding their actions. The assumption of a unary view does not explain why change and combine problems often appear to be equally difficult but does help to explain why missing-augend problems are more difficult than missing-addend problems. Young children's initial mental procedures for $M + N$ and $N + M$ problems do respect addend order and are consistent with a unary view. The development of more advanced informal procedures or the choice among procedures appears to be influenced heavily by a drive for cognitive economy. Consideration of this factor makes it clear (a) why it is important to distinguish between concrete and mental counting-all and between CAF and CAL; (b) why children who do not necessarily appreciate commutativity invent addition algorithms that disregard addend order (CAL or COL); (c) why children invent counting-on procedures; (d) why CAL is a popular and enduring transitional step to COL and COF is not; (e) why children tend to prefer mental addition strategies that disregard addend order but sometimes fall back on those that do not; and (f) why some children resort to more advanced mental strategies only with larger problems.

BASIC NUMBER COMBINATIONS

There is more to the learning, mental representation, and efficient production of the basic number combinations than is commonly assumed. Consider a child who is shown the flash card $2 + 6$ and automatically responds "eight." How did that bit of knowledge get into long-term memory (LTM)? How is this basic bit of arithmetic knowledge stored in and obtained from LTM? According to the prevalent view, the answers are obvious. The child now "just knows" this fact because of repeated exposure and practice. The child has a storehouse of specific numerical associations (e.g., 2 + 6 ↔ 8) from which he or she "retrieves the number fact." In brief, it is commonly assumed that mastery of the single-digit combinations entails only factual knowledge, only one type of mechanical knowledge. We argue, though, that an explanation of the learning, representation, and efficient production of basic number combinations must include various types of knowledge, including conceptual knowledge, and is integrally tied to the development and representation of general mathematical knowledge.

Associative-Learning Models

According to the prevalent view of mental arithmetic development, children gradually replace *slow* reconstructive processes (counting-based procedures) with an efficient reproductive process (fact retrieval) (e.g., Ashcraft, 1982; Ilg & Ames, 1951; Resnick & Ford, 1981). Associative-learning models (e.g., Ashcraft, 1985a; Siegler & Shrager, 1984) posit that learning the basic combinations entails gradually strengthening problem-answer bonds by means of practice. Some associative-learning models (Rabinowitz, 1985; Thorndike, 1922) do allow for a facilitating effect from previously learned or related combinations. Even so, the mainstay for initially establishing and then cementing an association between a problem and answer is practice. Thus, the sequence of fact acquisition is determined largely by practice frequency. For example, a problem such as 2 + 6 might not be mastered as quickly as 6 + 2 because of a lower frequency of exposure.

In time, a child builds up a storehouse of number facts—specific numerical associations such as "2 + 6 = 8." In a manner of speaking, the child fills in a mental arithmetic table (Ashcraft & Battaglia, 1978). Fig. 4.1 illustrates the arithmetic-table analogy for the mental representation of basic addition facts. The time needed to produce a particular fact is determined in part by the mental "distance" traversed during a memory search (i.e., the time needed to find the intersection of the two addends in the table). The table stretches out to reflect addend size effects (the geometric increase in reaction time required to produce sums as addend-size increases) (Ashcraft, 1982). When presented the stimulus 2 + 6, the child accesses his or her mental arithmetic table and retrieves the value stored in the 2, 6 cell or node. Thus efficient production of basic number combinations is attributed solely to reproductive processes. Reconstructive processes, which involve tapping procedural and conceptual knowledge, are relegated to a backup role—used only if a fact is not known or something such as fatigue prevents retrieval of a fact.

The associative network of basic facts in adult LTM is usually viewed as separate from and not directly involving procedural and conceptual knowledge. Campbell and Graham (1985) label this *autonomous* fact-retrieval system the "arithmecon." Within the arithmecon, each basic fact has a distinct location or node. Note that in Fig. 4.1, for example, the answers for 2 + 6 and 6 + 2 are

AUGEND

ADDEND	0	1	2	3	4	5	6	7	8	9
0	0	1	2	3	4	5	6	7	8	9
1	1	2	3	4	5	6	7	8	9	10
2	2	3	4	5	6	7	8	9	10	11
3	3	4	5	6	7	8	9	10	11	12
4	4	5	6	7	8	9	10	11	12	13
5	5	6	7	8	9	10	11	12	13	14
6	6	7	8	9	10	11	12	13	14	15
7	7	8	9	10	11	12	13	14	15	16
8	8	9	10	11	12	13	14	15	16	17
9	9	10	11	12	13	14	15	16	17	18

FIG. 4.1. Arithmetic-table model of the mental representation of the basic addition combinations.

stored in separate cells of the mental arithmetic table. The recall of $2 + 6 = 8$ and $6 + 2 = 8$ are psychologically unrelated events—unaffected by knowledge of commutativity stored in semantic memory.

An Alternative Model

In contrast to associative-learning models, an alternative model (Baroody, 1983c, 1984e, 1985a, 1985b; Baroody & Ginsburg, 1982) suggests that procedural and conceptual knowledge are integral aspects of the learning, representation, and efficient production of the *basic* number combinations. The alternative model posits that children do not learn the basic number combinations separately as specific numerical associations (as hundreds of feats of memory) but as a system of interrelated experiences (Olander, 1931). It suggests, moreover, that the mental representation of the basic number combinations entails relations as well as facts. Thus, the efficient production of basic combinations involves automatic propositional processes as well as the retrieval of data.

Semantic models that incorporate both facts and relations (data and processes) have been proposed by some information-processing theorists (e.g., Norman & Rumelhart, 1975) to account for the development, memory, and use of language and other cognitive skills. Similarly, semantic models have been proposed to account for the development of mathematical knowledge (e.g., see Greeno, 1978; Resnick & Ford, 1981). Such semantic models propose that knowledge can be thought of as a structural framework. A child's structural framework guides the interpretation and acquisition of new information. As a child learns relations, knowledge structures become increasingly interconnected, and this integration permits more efficient problem solving. As existing knowledge is used and becomes more automatic (routine), it can serve as the data for the next, more complex level of knowledge and problem solving (Anderson, 1982). Might not a semantic model provide a reasonable account for *basic* number-combination mastery?

Number-Combination Learning. General arithmetic knowledge can provide the structural framework for organizing and learning an otherwise large array of new information. For example, it is not necessary to memorize each of the 100 single-digit addition combinations because, except for the 10 ties, half are related to the other half by the principle of commutativity (e.g., Folsom, 1975). Knowledge of this principle, which is acquired early (Baroody & Gannon, 1984; Baroody et al., 1983), might enable a child to learn both $2 + 6 = 8$ and $6 + 2 = 8$, even if the first combination was practiced considerably less than the second.

As general mathematical knowledge becomes more extensive, integrated, and automatic, number-combination facility should grow correspondingly. As children internalize mathematical relationships, they have a broader base for learning the basic number combinations. Indeed, some research (e.g., Brownell &

Chazal, 1935; Steinberg, 1985; Thornton, 1978) indicates that meaningful instruction, such as teaching children "thinking strategies," is more effective than drill in facilitating the learning, retention, and transfer of basic combinations (Suydam & Weaver, 1975). Moreover, as existing number-combination knowledge is used and becomes more routine, it can serve as the data (basis) for processing harder number combinations. Practice, then, is important to the extent that it provides an opportunity to discover new relationships and routinizes known facts and relationships so that they can be used to process harder problems.

This model explains why there seems to be a psychological relationship between mastery of the basic addition combinations and learning basic subtraction combinations (e.g., Baroody et al., 1983; Buckingham, 1927; Knight & Behrens, 1928; Smith, 1921). Addition and subtraction are related to each other by the complement principle: Subtracting a part (an addend) from a whole (the sum) yields the other part (addend) (e.g., $6 + 2/2 + 6 = 8$ and $8 - 6 = 2$ or $8 - 2 = 6$). During their efforts to compute differences, children are more likely to discover this important relationship if they can readily call to mind the addition counterparts. After the connection is discovered, automatic addition combinations, such as $6 + 2/2 + 6 = 8$, can serve as the data for efficiently generating the answer to subtraction problems, such as $8 - 6 = ?$ and $8 - 2 = ?$.

In contrast to associative-learning models, then, the alternative model proposes that knowledge of relationships permits children to learn combination "partners" and "families," which obviates extensive practice of each combination. Thus, though practice may play a role in discovering relationships and routinizing knowledge, the development of basic number-combination facility basically depends on internalizing mathematical relationships—on the growth of the structural network underlying general mathematical knowledge.

Acquisition Order.   The alternative model suggests that the order of number-combination mastery is more directly linked to the development of general mathematical knowledge than to practice frequency. Empirical evidence (e.g., Olander, 1931; Thiele, 1938; Wheeler, 1939) suggests that the amount of practice is not predictive of mastery. To account for differences in the relative difficulty of combinations, the alternative model notes that the relationships that underlie different families of combinations vary in the ease with which they can be learned and used.

More obvious and less intricate relationships should be learned early, learned by practically all children, and processed relatively quickly. For example, the $N + 0$ and $0 + N$ family combinations can be generated by the easily internalized and implemented $N + 0/0 + N = N$ relationship (Baroody, 1985a). This may explain why the $N + 0$ ($0 + N$) combinations are the most rapidly generated addition combinations (see Svenson, 1975, Fig. 2)—even among children just beginning school (see Groen & Parkman, 1972, Fig. 2). Likewise, the $N \times 0$ ($0 \times N$), $N \times 1$ ($1 \times N$), $N - 0$, and $N - N$ combinations can be generated by relatively discernible and straightforward relationships ($N \times 0 = 0$, $N \times 1 = N$, $N - 0 = N$ and $N - N = 0$, respectively). This may explain, for example, the relative quickness of the $N - 0$ and $N - N$ subtraction combinations as early as the second grade (Woods, Resnick, & Groen, 1975, Fig. 1).

Other relationships are less apparent but, once learned, should generate combinations automatically because of their ease of implementation. For example, it may take children some time to recognize the regularity that when number-sequence pairs are involved in a subtraction combination, the difference is always one (e.g., $5 - 4 = 1$, $6 - 5 = 1$, $7 - 6 = 1$). Once the relationship is noted, however, difference-of-one combinations should become quite automatic.

The learning and processing of some relationships may be relatively involved. For example, use of the complement principle to generate subtraction combinations should be a relatively late development—perhaps not achieved by all children. This regularity is not highly salient to children, and its efficient use must await the development of a repertoire of at least fairly automatic addition combinations (part-part-whole associations) (Baroody et al., 1983; Siegler, in press). In brief, the relative difficulty and hence the acquisition order of number combinations may be largely determined by the salience and complexity of the relationship underlying various number-combination families rather than by practice frequency as proposed by association-learning models.

Mental Representation and Processing of Number Combinations. The alternative model proposes that internalized relationships are a central aspect of the structural network underlying the basic number combinations. For example, knowledge of commutativity permits $2 + 6 = 8$ and $6 + 2 = 8$ to be stored in associative memory as a *single* part-part-whole combination: 2, 6, 8. Thus, the alternative model suggests that the representation of the basic number combinations is like that of knowledge in general (as depicted by semantic models): It involves both facts *and* relationships (Baroody, 1984e, 1985a).

The alternative model stipulates that the efficient production of combination involves reconstructive as well as reproductive processes. For instance, producing the sums of $2 + 6$ and $6 + 2$ entails tapping both semantic knowledge (the proposition that specifies that addend order is irrelevant: commutativity) and factual knowledge (the associated whole of 2 and 6: 8).

The relations component of the structural network is instrumental in processing stored data. Because any two terms of a triple can also be associated with another term, the relations component of the structural network specify which triple must be accessed. For example, although 2 and 6 may share an affinity with 8 ($2 + 6/6 + 2 = 8$), they may also be associated with 4 ($2 + 4/4 + 2 = 6$). Likewise, 2 and 8 can be linked to 10 ($2 + 8/8 + 2 = 10$). Given the problem $6 + 2 = ?$, the "plus" specifies increment—thus discounting the triple 2, 4, 6. The 2, 6, 8 triple is accessed and 8 is advanced as the sum. Given the problem $8 - 2 = ?$, the "minus" specifies decrement—thus discounting the triple 2, 8, 10. Again the 2, 6, 8 triple is accessed, and this time 6 is advanced as the difference.

In the case of a problem such as 2 + ? = 8, the relational concept of equals would specify a search for a missing part smaller than 8. Thus, the triple 2, 8, 10 would be discounted in favor of the triple 2, 6, 8, and 6 would be advanced as the missing addend.

Therefore, unlike most associative-learning models, which posit data nodes only (e.g., Ashcraft, 1982; Rabinowitz, 1985; Siegler & Shrager, 1984), the alternative model proposes that the mental representation of the basic number combinations entails *both* facts and relations. Moreover, unlike associative models that attribute efficient production exclusively to reproductive processes of factual knowledge, the alternative model stipulates that reconstructive processes that reflect relations are involved as well.

An Integrated Structural Framework.   The alternative model assumes that the representation of the basic number combination is integral to the structural framework that underlies number and general arithmetic knowledge. The representation of the number sequence has been described as a "mental number line" that, with development, embodies an increasing number of relationships (Resnick, 1983). That of the typical child just beginning school includes numbers positioned in a string with each position linked by a number-after (N-after) relationship and a directional marker that specifies that the later position is "more." This mental number line can be used for such purposes as magnitude comparisons—e.g., to judge that 9 is more than 1 or 8. Gradually children internalize new numerical relationships, such as even numbers, that expand the child's representation of number (Miller & Gelman, 1983).

The alternative model posits that basic number-combination knowledge builds on knowledge of the number sequence and is incorporated as another element in the gradual expansion of number representation. For example, at some point, children seem to discover that N-after relationships apply to $N + 1$ problems (and later to both $N + 1$ and $1 + N$ problems). Once children discover the connection between the number-after relationship and adding one more (an $N + 1$ principle), the well-learned number sequence provides a ready means for representing and efficiently processing $N + 1$ combinations. Moreover, an $N + 1$ principle is an important elaboration of the existing representation of the number sequence. It specifies that the number after in the sequence is not only more but *one* more and that this relationship holds for the entire sequence. Later, as children practice computing the sums of problems such as 2 + 6 = ? and 6 + 2 = ?, part-part-whole associations become an ingrained aspect of their mental number line, just as even numbers come to share a special affinity. Thus the structural network that underlies number and general arithmetic knowledge not only serves to assimilate the basic number combinations but is enriched by the basic combinations it incorporates.

In recent years, there has been a growing acceptance of the view that procedural and conceptual knowledge play a role in the recall of number facts. For example, Miller, Perlmutter, and Keating (1984) hypothesize that accessibility (the ease of recalling a combination) may vary because of the availability of redundant information, such as the rule that the product of two odd numbers will itself be odd. Campbell and Graham (1985) attributed a lower error rate for the $N \times 5/5 \times N$ family to a rule that states, if a times problem contains 5, the product must end in 5 or 0—rendering implausible many of the products that would be associated with other operands.

However, the alternative model proposes that procedural and conceptual knowledge plays a more direct role in generating basic number combinations than simply *facilitating* the recall of stored facts or *checking* the plausibility of factual recall. Because it assumes that factual, conceptual, and procedural knowledge form an integrated unit, the alternative model asserts that data and propositional processes interact to *create answers* efficiently. Ashcraft (1983) now allows that internalized relationships may account for the efficient production of zero and one combinations. This makes sense given the essentially infinite number of zero and one combinations an adult can efficiently generate.[4] The alternative model goes a step further and suggests that reproductive and reconstructive processes are intertwined for a broad range of number combinations (Baroody, 1984e, 1985a).

Therefore, unlike associative-learning models that hypothesize an arithmecon, the alternative model proposes that the mental representation of the basic number combinations incorporates facts and relations integral to the structural framework underlying all mathematical knowledge. The efficient production of basic number combinations involves more than extracting data from an autonomous fact-retrieval system but involves engaging the data and propositional processes of an integrated structural network.

A Comparison with Siegler's Model

To illustrate the fundamental differences with associative-learning models, we turn now to a comparison of the alternative model and Siegler's (e.g., Siegler & Shrager, 1984). Siegler (e.g., Siegler & Robinson, 1982) has advanced an asso-

---

[4]A pure retrieval model would have to posit an infinite number of stored associations—infinite zero and one rows and columns in the mental arithmetic table. Arguing that the zero and one problems are special cases, Ashcraft (1983) avoids this improbable position. However, Ashcraft (1985b) also posits different mechanisms (a network-retrieval process) for single-digit combinations, including basic zero and one combinations, and (an algorithmic process involving successive retrievals) for larger combinations. This position implies that basic zero and one combinations are stored as specific numerical associations. R. S. Siegler (personal communication, May 18, 1984) avoids this apparent contradiction by positing that single-digit zero and one combinations are generated by factual retrieval, and larger zero and one combinations are generated from rules. However, taking the position that basic zero and one combinations are learned as specific associations does not explain how a child can—by exposure to a few $N + 0 = N$ combinations—rather suddenly start to automatically produce a range of $N + 0 = N$ combinations (Baroody, 1985a).

ciative-learning model that explains how informal computational efforts lead to automatic fact retrieval. According to Siegler's model, each problem is associated with various answers. The probability of retrieving a particular answer is proportional to the strength of the association between that answer and the problem. Siegler and Shrager (1984) argue that the formation of distributions of associations for adding are initially influenced by a child's prior knowledge of the counting string. Thus, when a problem like 2 + 4 is first presented to a child, it triggers an association with the counting string, and the child in most cases simply advances to the number after the second addend in the count string ("5"). The response produces a mental trace, that is, helps form a bond between the problem and the (incorrect) response. The corrective mechanism in this model is the child's (informal) computational efforts. As the child uses informal algorithms to compute the sum correctly, the bond between the problem and the correct sum is gradually strengthened. Eventually the correct answer is produced so frequently that the association between the problem and the correct sum becomes preemptively strong.

The alternative model of mental arithmetic development differs from Siegler's in four key respects. First, the alternative model contends that before they can automatically produce the number combinations, children do not retrieve sums from a repertoire of stored associations but construct estimates from their knowledge of arithmetic and the number sequence (Baroody, 1985b). For ascending problems (e.g., 2 + 4, 3 + 5) and ties (e.g., 2 + 2, 5 + 5), at least, the computer simulation of Siegler's model implies that a child's initial estimates for any given problem will include the whole range of known numbers and that, except for the counting-string associates, all the known numbers are equally likely to be given as initial estimates. Later, computing errors make certain responses more probable than others. For example, the common off-by-one computing error should tend to give 7 a disproportionate associative strength for 3 + 5 or 5 + 3.

The alternative model contends that young children manufacture estimates by using strategies that are based on existing conceptual and procedural knowledge and that operate on the stored number string. As their knowledge of addition evolves, children should become capable of more sophisticated mental arithmetic. Children at different levels of development should produce qualitatively different kinds of estimates. Moreover, the estimation errors of individual children should form a characteristic pattern that in nature and range may not be directly related to their computational efforts.

Existing evidence suggests that initial estimates do not range more or less evenly over all known numbers. Instead, inexperienced adders simply tend to repeat an addend (Baroody, 1985b; Ilg & Ames, 1951). Such a response bias enables a child who has little or no understanding of addition at least to manufacture some answer. More experienced adders honor the addition-as-incrementing concept by using strategies that add one to an addend. A relatively unsophisticated version involves adding one to the first or perhaps the second addend. A more advanced version, which reflects the understanding that the whole must be larger than either part, is an increment-the-larger addend-by-one strategy. A very sophisticated child takes for granted that one problems such as $7 + 1$ or $1 + 7$ and non-one problems such as $7 + 3$ and $3 + 7$ cannot produce the same sum. This can lead a child to use an increment-the-larger-by-several strategy for $N + M/M + N$ problems while still responding to $N + 1/1 + N$ problems with an increment-by-one approach (Baroody, 1983b).

Some evidence suggests that the pattern and frequency of estimation errors cannot be attributed to the frequency of children's computational errors. For example, Baroody (1985b) found that among his kindergarten subjects a popular strategy for $N + M/M + N$ problems such as $4 + 8$ and $8 + 5$ was to state a number in the teens—especially a teen that incorporated one of the addends (e.g., for $5 + 8$: "15" or "18"). The high relative frequency of such responses could not be attributed to frequent computing errors; it is unlikely that 15 or 18 are common computational errors for $5 + 8$. In brief, early estimation errors appear to be "more an error of method than an error of answer" (Ilg & Ames, 1951, p. 10).

Second, the alternative model contends that semantic and procedural knowledge are used to manufacture estimates regardless of problem type. Siegler and Shrager (1984) found that their subjects did not respond with counting-string associates nearly as often to descending problems, such as $4 + 2$, as they did to ascending problems, such as $2 + 4$, or ties, such as $4 + 4$. To account for these results, they hypothesize the introduction of a reasoning process. In Siegler and Shrager's words: "The last addend in an addition problem may always activate its immediate successor as a potential answer. However, other knowledge that preschoolers have, namely that answers to addition problems should be at least as great as the larger addend, may prevent them from stating counting-string associates as answers on descending-series problems" (p. 265). In the case $4 + 2$, for instance, the child would not say 3 as an answer because semantic knowledge disqualifies numbers equal to or less than 4. The model does not explain why semantic knowledge is not also used to disqualify answers of, say, 4 or less for $2 + 4$ or $4 + 4$.

According to the alternative model, a child should tend to use the same strategy for ascending problems and ties as well as descending problems. That is, depending on the level of development, the child will seize on one of the addends, add one to the last addend, add one to the larger addend, or add several to the larger added for all three types of problems. Thus, the alternative model explains why some children will generally give impossible estimates (answers equal to or less than the larger addend) regardless of problem type, others may give impossible sums for descending problems only, and some will give very few or no impossible estimates (Baroody, 1985b). It also helps to account for the fact that when Siegler and Shrager (1984) tallied their data across subjects, about one quarter of the responses to descending problems were impossible estimates: A portion of their sample may have relied on relatively unsophisticated estimation strategies.

Third, the alternative model posits a more parsimonious use of cognitive resources than does the associative-learning model (Baroody, 1985b). According to the associative-learning model (e.g., Siegler & Shrager, 1984), before a child learns a basic number fact (before the distribution of associations becomes peaked), a problem is associated with numerous responses. Indeed, the model assumes that incorrect computing strengthens the associations between a problem and incorrect responses. If for the sake of argument we grant that each basic addition combination is associated with only five responses, this would mean that a child has stored in LTM 500 mostly incorrect, specific numerical associations. Later, mastery of all basic number combinations implies storing just over 300 specific numerical associations. Though this is not beyond the child's capabilities (Ashcraft, 1985b), it does not seem to be the most economical use of resources.

The alternative model requires less to be stored in LTM. When presented a problem, the child draws upon already existing resources (extant knowledge of arithmetic and the number sequence). The child can quickly manufacture an answer without having stored in LTM numerous problem-sum associations. Though computed results may have an impact on LTM either incidentally or through conscious effort, the alternative model does not assume that every computational effort—whether correct or incorrect—leaves a lasting trace in LTM (Baroody, 1985b). After the basic number combinations are mastered, stored relationships permit many fewer specific numerical associations to be stored (Baroody, 1983c).

Fourth, the alternative model allows for qualitative as well as quantitative change in the development of children's mental arithmetic. The model of Siegler and Shrager (1984) posits only one process to account for development: practice. Computing or other experiences that involve stating an answer build up the associative strength of responses incrementally. In effect, mastering the basic combination entails only quantitative change: the gradual strengthening of bonds.

According to the alternative model, the discovery or learning of relationships can give a child the relatively sudden capacity to respond automatically to a whole range (family) of combinations. In effect, insights can produce gestalt-type learning of basic combinations. Thus, unlike associative-learning models that posit a gradual strengthening of individual problem-answer associations, the alternative model allows for qualitative change that is not necessarily related to the amount of practice. In other words, a child's *most probable response (estimate) might evolve* in ways that are *independent of the child's previous response history ("distribution of associations")*.

In fact, Baroody (1985b) found that after 8 weeks of training, pretest "distributions of associations'' did not provide a good indication of posttest responses for *nonpracticed* problems. For example, seven kindergartners, who consistently responded incorrectly to zero combinations such as $0 + 6$ and $8 + 0$ on the pretest, efficiently responded to nonpracticed zero problems on the posttest. These children also efficiently responded to unfamiliar three-term zero problems (e.g., $0 + 0 + 2$, $4 + 0 + 0$). None of these children simply stated the larger addend when presented $1 + N/N + 1$ or $M + N/N + M$ problems (e.g., respond "7" to $1 + 7$ or $3 + 7$), which would have indicated a response bias. Apparently, these children learned a general rule that was discriminately applied to problems for which a specific association had not been strengthened through practice.

In brief, it appears that early arithmetic estimates are manufactured by strategies based on procedural and conceptual knowledge rather than simply retrieved from a network of associations built up through practice. In comparison to an associative-learning model, the alternative model better accounts for children's error patterns, provides a more consistent account of children's use of semantic knowledge, entails a more parsimonious use of cognitive resources, and allows for qualitative as well as quantitative changes.

Summary

The complexity of the relationships between children's meaningful and mechanical knowledge is illustrated in a striking fashion by the learning, representation, and efficient production of basic number combinations. This is a domain in which one would expect to find operating only one type of mechanical knowledge: factual knowledge. However, a closer look suggests that the learning of the number combinations is not simply a process of forming and strengthening bonds between specific problems and answers but an outgrowth of mathematical development in general. For example, the order of combination acquisition may be affected more by the salience and complexity of relationships that underlie combination families than by practice frequency. The mental representation of the basic number combinations may not only involve facts but relationships as well. Efficient production of the basic number combinations may not simply be a process of retrieving a specific numerical association from an autonomous fact-retrieval system but a process of engaging propositions and data stored in a unified network of mathematical knowledge.

THE EFFECTS OF SCHOOLING

The effects of schooling often make it even more difficult to discern the relationship between conceptual and more mechanical knowledge. Sometimes children use school mathematics mechanically because they do not have the concepts necessary to understand the formalisms. However, sometimes they do so because formalisms are not connected with their conceptual knowledge (e.g., Ginsburg, 1982; Hiebert, 1984). Chapters in this volume by Silver, Schoenfeld, and Hiebert and Wearne detail how mechanistic some students' mathematical behavior becomes after years of instruction. In this section, we speculate about the origins of mechanistic behavior and why such behavior makes it difficult to gauge young children's conceptual knowledge.

The National Assessment of Educational Progress (NAEP) (1983) suggests that American schools are relatively successful in teaching skills but less successful in encouraging conceptual learning and competencies that require understanding (Carpenter, Matthews, Lindquist, & Silver, 1984). Furthermore, the NAEP data indicate that in many cases instruction does not teach children how to solve problems (Silver & Thompson, 1984). We suspect that the structure of primary school mathematics instruction can work against the development and use of conceptual knowledge (e.g., Brownell, 1935; Romberg, 1984).

The nature of primary mathematics education may cause children to learn and use mathematics mechanically. Often the design and practice of primary mathematics instruction does not sufficiently take into account the nature of children's mathematical learning—the importance of informal knowledge and the tremendous individual differences among children (Baroody, in press-b). Because instruction usually introduces formal symbolism too quickly and requires children to learn in a lockstep manner, most children resort to memorization, some fail to learn, and nearly all develop misleading beliefs. Not only does formal schooling tend to foster mechanical learning of mathematics, it fosters the mechanical use of mathematics. Because of the misleading beliefs engendered by formal instruction, children may fail to use the conceptual knowledge they do possess (e.g., Schoenfeld, 1985). In effect, formal schooling may not encourage thinking and problem solving but blind procedure following and answer producing (Holt, 1964).

Mechanical Learning of Mathematics

Absorption (associative) theories of learning (e.g., Thorndike, 1922) have provided the dominant model for how to teach arithmetic (Romberg, 1982). According to this view, the basis of learning is the internalization of facts (associations), and this is best accomplished by means of didactic instruction and drill. Thus, children are expected to learn the basic number facts (simple associations between two digits and a response), arithmetic rules such as commutativity (complexes of associations), and arithmetic algorithms (sequences of habits) by means of imitation and repetition. Informal approaches are not considered important vehicles for mastering the basic skills. Indeed, informal approaches often are viewed as hindrances. For example, the use of counting algorithms (e.g., counting-on to solve 2 + 4: "4, 5 is 1 more, 6 is 2 more—so the sum is 6") or derived facts (e.g., using a known fact to reason out 3 + 4: "3 and 3 is 6 and 4 is one more than 3 so the answer is 7") are seen as attempts to evade the real work of "memorizing" the number facts (e.g., see Smith, 1921, pp. 764–765; Wheeler, 1939, p. 311). Even today, most instruction only briefly uses physical models to introduce arithmetic and then quickly jumps to drilling the number facts and arithmetic algorithms—not acknowledging the need for an extended period of informal figuring (Carpenter & Moser, 1984). Too frequently, the results of ignoring or discouraging children's informal arithmetic are deficiencies in basic skills or concepts, misconceptions, and debilitating beliefs that affect children for the rest of their school days and beyond.

Educationally, encouragement of children's informal mathematics is crucial. Cognitive research (e.g., Baroody, 1984c; Baroody & Ginsburg, 1983; Behr, Erlwanger, & Nichols, 1980) indicates that regardless of how instruction introduces mathematical skills, symbols, and concepts, children tend to interpret and deal with school mathematics in terms of their informal mathematics (Hiebert, 1984). Children often use informal procedures that make sense in terms of their informal concepts rather than adopt procedures taught in school for which they do not have an adequate conceptual understanding (Ginsburg, 1982). For example, despite the emphasis in primary school on memorizing the basic addition and subtraction facts, children typically rely on informal counting strategies to do basic arithmetic because initially that is more meaningful (e.g., Brownell, 1935). Through their experience with informal mathematics, children learn mathematical (e.g., identity and commutativity) relationships in a meaningful manner.

Moreover, informal mathematics is a foundation for learning formal mathematics. It is important for children to learn formal mathematics because it is in many ways a more powerful tool than informal mathematics. For example, informal calculational procedures are fine as long as the child has to deal only with small quantities. To solve problems involving large quantities, it is much more efficient and less taxing on memory to use written symbols and arithmetic algorithms. However, if formal instruction fails to build upon or connect with informal knowledge, children may have to rely on rote memorization and mechanical use of the new material.

Most children—including those with low academic achievement—already know a good deal of informal mathematics (Baroody, 1983a; Baroody & Ginsburg, 1984; Baroody & Snyder, 1983; Russell & Ginsburg, 1984). When informal strengths are exploited, it not only increases the likelihood of successful school learning but often helps children to feel more confident about their mathematical ability (Baroody, 1983a, 1986). On the other hand, some children have deficiencies in informal concepts or skills that may lead to learning difficulties in school (e.g., Baroody, 1984b, 1984c). Children enter school with important individual differences in informal mathematics and hence readiness to learn formal mathematics. When such deficiencies are not identified and remedied, the result too often is mechanical learning or failure.

Mechanical Use of Mathematics

Children's beliefs about mathematics, school, and themselves can critically affect their mathematical behavior (e.g., Baroody, 1983a, 1986; Cobb, 1985a; Erlwanger, 1973; Reyes, 1984; Schoenfeld, 1985, this volume; Tobias, 1978). Too often, children learn misleading beliefs that interfere with using the conceptual knowledge at their disposal. For example, Baroody et al. (1983) gave first-, second-, and third-grade children a sequence of problems $6 + 7$, $6 + 8$, $6 + 9 \ldots 6 + 15$ to see if they would shortcut their computational efforts by simply adding one to the previously figured sum. Surprisingly, the *second-graders* used the $N + 1$ shortcut far more frequently than either the first- or third-graders. In a similar vein, Bisanz, LeFevre, Scott, and Champion (1984) found that 6-year-olds (and adults) tended to use an inverse principle to solve such problems as $5 + 3 - 3 = ?$ (i.e., recognized that, in effect, the $+3$ and -3 cancelled each other) while 9-year-olds tended laboriously to compute the answers (e.g., computed the sum of $5 + 3$ and then the answer for $8 - 3$). How can such curvilinear results be explained? It seems unlikely that children learn a $1 + N$ progression principle or an inverse principle and then later forget it. Apparently, something is interfering with the use of previously learned principles. One plausible explanation is that the older children believe that when given an arithmetic problem, they are supposed to calculate—not look for patterns or relationships. Indeed, Baroody et al. (1983) note that one girl felt that not calculating was tantamount to cheating: "I cheated on that one. I looked at the [previously computed sum]" (p. 168) (see Cobb, 1985a). In short, beliefs that are sometimes encouraged by schooling can distort children's views of mathematics, interfere with their use of conceptual knowledge, and induce an overreliance on mechanical knowledge.

Because misleading beliefs can induce children to approach mathematics mechanically, it is possible to draw incorrect conclusions about their conceptual knowledge—to impute knowledge deficiencies where none exist. One case in point may be children's "small-from-large bug" (Baroody, 1985c). Given a problem such as $23 - 17 = ?$ or $3 - 7 = ?$, many young children answer 14 and 4, respectively. Such answers have been taken as evidence that children overgeneralize the principle of commutativity to subtraction (e.g., see Resnick, 1983). To answer $23 - 17 = ?$ correctly, the child would either have to know the borrowing algorithm (perhaps only implicitly) or use an informal counting strategy. However, young children may not know the borrowing algorithm. Moreover, many may believe that the use of informal counting strategies is "bad" or "stupid"—an attitude too frequently promoted by parents and teachers. As a result, young children are left in a bind. They can make an estimate, but "guessing" is usually discouraged in school. They can choose not to respond, but this is a sure sign of low intelligence. Or they can manufacture an answer by subtracting 1 from 2 and 3 from 7. This at least has the virtue of yielding some answer (Holt,

1964), and it follows the teacher's mandate to "always subtract the smaller term from the larger." For the problem $3 - 7 = ?$ a correct response of -4 is not likely because most young children do not know about negative numbers. From a young child's point of view, a solution may not seem possible. However, children are not typically trained to respond: "An answer is not possible." Indeed, because children are usually trained to believe that there must be a correct answer (cf. Holt, 1964), they may override their intuition that an answer is impossible and manufacture an answer. Misleading beliefs may affect what Gelman and Meck (this volume) term "utilization competence." In brief, the small-from-large "bug" may be the result of misleading beliefs that are fostered by schooling—not sound evidence that children really think that subtraction, like addition, is commutative.

CONCLUSION

In this final section, we attempt to interpret the chapter content in terms of a general cognitive framework, a schema theory of knowledge, as summarized by Anderson (1984): "A schema is an abstract structure of information. It is abstract in the sense that it summarizes information about many particular cases. A schema is structured in the sense that it represents the relationships among components" (p. 5). Much about the development of meaningful and mechanical knowledge underlying early mathematical routines, in general, and basic arithmetic routines, in particular, seems to fit Anderson's description of a schema theory of comprehension (Baroody & Mason, 1985).

Anderson (1984) argues that ordinary comprehension can be better accounted for by positing weak rather than strong schemata. A strong schema implies that comprehension is principle driven and that predictions can be derived. A weak schema implies that comprehension is precedent driven and that predictions are not so much derived as looked up. Weak schemata include generalizations local in scope and treated with caution. Weak schemata entail low standards for internal consistency and provide an uncertain basis for a priori reasoning.

Applied to the development of mathematical thinking, the weak versus strong schema distinction should be thought of as a continuum rather than a dichotomy. Progress in various domains of mathematics appears to take a similar course. Initial cognitive structures, which emerge from concrete activities and are based on global perceptions, can be characterized as intuitive or infralogical (e.g., Lunkenbein, 1985). This unanalyzed, impressionistic knowledge is quite context bound and unsystematic. Thus reasoning is idiosyncratic and prototypical. In time, the child begins to abstract and formulate the properties and relations of a domain, but not as a coherent system. Such knowledge may be of limited generality and logically inconsistent. Reasoning is still more descriptive than truly deductive. Advanced development entails recognizing and defining precise properties and logical relations. Because knowledge is organized into an axiomatic system, the child is capable of seeing logical implications and reasoning deductively. For a few, mathematical knowledge is taken a step further. Properties and relations are formally defined in terms of abstract symbols. These can be used to build a self-contained system of deductions of increasing complexity (Davis & Hersh, 1981). Thus schemata can range from weak (intuitive or infralogical) to relatively weak (principled but unsystematic) to relatively strong (principled and systematic) to strong (principles formally defined).

This continuum model is consistent with the argument that the development of mathematical principles need not be an all-or-nothing phenomenon (Greeno et al., 1984). Greeno, Riley, and Gelman (1984) point out that competence for a principle may be distributed among several schemata, and so a child may develop some aspects of competence but not others. Initially, knowledge of a principle may be incomplete, context bound, and applied with hesitation—better characterized as a relatively weak schema. The integration of weak or relatively weak schemata can produce a stronger or a relatively strong schema and hence a more accurate understanding of mathematical principles.

Much of children's initial counting and informal arithmetic knowledge might aptly be described as a weak or relatively weak schema. Consider first an order-indifferent tagging rule. This aspect of procedural knowledge concerning counting is a prime example of a weak schema. It is a generalization inconsistently applied and of limited scope. Young children are willing to tag sets in some orders but not all possible orders. For example, Mierkiewicz and Siegler (1980) found that reversing the count direction is more acceptable to 3-, 4-, and 5-year-olds than recounting from a mid-item. Moreover, the rule provides an uncertain basis for a priori reasoning. For example, young children are initially uncertain about predicting the outcome of reversing the direction of their count. Only after empirical investigation do they formulate an order-irrelevance "principle," which initially may be of limited scope (a relatively weak schema). In brief, counting behavior may, especially at first, be guided by weak rather than relatively strong schemata—may be more precedent driven than principle driven.

Likewise, especially at first, informal arithmetic routines may be guided by weak or relatively weak schemata (Baroody & Mason, 1985). Consider the child who denies the commutativity of addition but disregards addend order and uses CAL or COL to compute the sum for 2 + 4. If the child's behavior were guided by a relatively strong schema, the child would not act as if order both makes and does not make a difference. A weak or relatively weak schema tolerates such a logically inconsistent scenario because there is either no or an insufficient precedent to disallow the labor-saving maneuver. When asked if 2 + 4 and 4 + 2 will add up to the same thing, the child responds "No" or "I don't know" because the relatively weak schema contains only a limited number of precedents that provide either an incorrect or uncertain basis for making a prediction.[5]

Weak or relatively weak schemata may account for other labor-saving maneuvers that, in the absence of conceptual advances, appear to be logically inconsistent. Children may use an advanced addition procedure with large problems and then fall back on a less advanced procedure for smaller problems, because a relatively weak schema entails low standards for internal consistency. The child does what works with larger (perhaps less familiar) problems and then returns to the well-precedented procedure for dealing with smaller problems.

Anderson (1984) notes that "the term schema is an apt one for characterizing knowledge, because the essence of knowledge is structure. Knowledge is not a 'basket of facts' " (p. 5). We have argued that knowledge of the basic number combinations is not simply a "basket of facts," as is commonly assumed. Meaningful and procedural knowledge embody structure and may be central to the learning, representation, and automatic generation of number combinations.

Anderson (1984) argues that "nothing about the schools' regimen would be expected to disturb 'weak' views of knowledge; indeed, it is likely to reinforce them . . . Poor students' beliefs about knowledge do not lead them to suppose that consistent interpretations of events are generally possible, or even desirable. For the poor student, knowledge *is* a 'basket of facts' " (p. 10). We suspect that Anderson's observation applies to all but a few, exceptional mathematical students. For most children, school mathematics involves the mechanical learning and mechanical use of facts—adaptations to a system that are unencumbered by the demands of consistency or even common sense.

For much informal mathematics, weak or relatively weak schemata evolve into relatively strong schemata. For much of formal mathematics, weak or relatively weak schemata remain weak. Two important factors that account for this difference are time and practical need. Because young children have numerous opportunities to use and reflect upon their counting activities and because counting activities are an important part of everyday life, the semantic and procedural knowledge underlying counting behavior gradually increases and becomes more interconnected. Eventually, children do come to understand an order-irrelevance principle. This advance involves the integration of a new insight and previous counting knowledge (Gelman & Gallistel, 1978). Moreover, this knowledge is

---

[5]There may be few or no precedents for same-sum commuted pairs. In comparison, the child may have numerous precedents of different-looking problems producing different sums. Children are often surprised to find that different-looking problems—both noncommuted (e.g., 4 + 4, 5 + 3, 6 + 2) and commuted (e.g., 5 + 3 and 3 + 5)—can add up to same thing. Moreover, because a weak schema has low standards of internal consistency, a child may begin to use CAL or COL with $N + 1$ and $1 + N$ before such strategies are used with $N + M$ and $M + N$ (Baroody, 1983b).

applied consistently and can provide the basis for confident a priori predictions. Indeed, we could characterize the knowledge as obvious and automatic. The child may even be able to explain the principle. Likewise, children eventually abstract the commutativity principle that reconciles their unary conception of addition (different addend orders imply different problems) with their procedures that disregard addend order.[6] Again, this principle can be characterized as a relatively strong schema because children tend to be logical, consistent, and confident in its application.

The development of number-combination mastery may depend in part on the development and integration of semantic and procedural knowledge. The abstraction and linking up of knowledge may take a considerable period of time. For children who see no practical need to attend to the structure of the arithmetic combinations, mastery of the basic combinations may present a tremendous hurdle. When children do discover structure, the formation or elaboration of a schema may be sudden. Such a schema may be strengthened with verification (the accumulation of precedents) and may, sooner or later, be used automatically and confidently to generate solutions to new as well as familiar problems. The development and strengthening of schemata may account, in part, for the order in which a child masters the number combinations.

For most of the formal mathematics to which they are exposed, children are not given either the time or the incentive to develop stronger schemata. Indeed, the structure of formal instruction can provide powerful disincentives for such development. The practices of primary mathematics instruction can help create beliefs that prevent children from searching for structure and reflecting about their mathematical experiences (Baroody, in press-b). The challenge that confronts our educational establishment is to learn to help children develop stronger schemata rather than encourage the maintenance or acquisition of weak ones. It is the familiar question: How do we encourage children to be thinkers as well as fact storers?

---

[6]Baroody and Mason (1985) report the case of a mentally retarded boy who routinely disregarded addend order to solve $N + 0 = ?$ and $0 + N = ?$ problems automatically. That is, the child had a schema representing the knowledge: When addition involves zero, the other addend remains unchanged. Thus when given the written problem $0 + 4 =$ ___, the child orally responded quickly and correctly and then recorded the sum. When $4 + 0 =$ ___ was presented to the child immediately below the previous number sentence, the child thought for several minutes and finally answered: "Zero." What caused the child to hesitate and then abandon his zero schema? Given a unary conception of addition and no understanding of commutativity, the juxtaposition of the commuted trials probably led the boy to believe that two different problems must have different sums (Baroody & Gannon, 1984). In other words, the task forced a conflict between his zero schema and unary addition schema. In this particular case, the stronger schema (a unary concept of addition) won out. The insight of commutativity may later resolve the conflict between the schemata and strengthen both.

ACKNOWLEDGMENTS

Preparation of this chapter was supported by Grants Numbered HD 16757-02 and HD 16757-03 from NICHD (NIH). Thanks to Karen Fuson, Rochel Gelman, Cathleen A. Mason, Robert Siegler and especially James Hiebert for their helpful comments in preparing this chapter. The opinions expressed in the chapter are solely those of the authors' and do not necessarily reflect the position or endorsement of those mentioned above.

REFERENCES

Allardice, B. (1977). The development of written representations for some mathematical concepts. *Journal of Children's Mathematical Behavior, 1,* 135–148.

Anderson, J. R. (1982). Acquisition of cognitive skill. *Psychological Review, 89,* 369–406.

Anderson, R. C. (1984). Some reflections on the acquisition of knowledge. *Educational Researcher, 13*(9), 5–10.

Ashcraft, M. H. (1982). The development of mental arithmetic: A chronometric approach. *Developmental Review, 2,* 213–236.

Ashcraft, M. H. (1983). Procedural knowledge versus fact retrieval in mental arithmetic: A reply to Baroody. *Developmental Review, 3,* 231–235.

Ashcraft, M. H. (1985a, April). *Children's mental arithmetic: Toward a model of retrieval and problem solving.* Paper presented at the biennial meeting of the Society for Research in Child Development, Toronto.

Ashcraft, M. H. (1985b). Is it that far-fetched that some of us remember our arithmetic facts? *Journal for Research in Mathematics Education, 16,* 99–105.

Ashcraft, M. H., & Battaglia, J. (1978). Cognitive arithmetic: Evidence for retrieval and decision processes in mental addition. *Journal of Experimental Psychology: Human Learning and Memory, 4,* 527–538.

Baroody, A. J. (1982). Are discovering commutativity and more economical addition strategies related? *Problem Solving, 4*(12), 1–2.

Baroody, A. J. (1983a, April). *The case of Adam: A specific evaluation of a math learning disability.* Paper presented at the meeting of the American Educational Research Association, Montreal.

Baroody, A. J. (1983b). The development of children's informal addition. In J. C. Bergeron & N. Herscovics (Eds.), *Proceedings of the Fifth Annual Meeting of the North American Chapter of the International Group for the Psychology of Mathematics Education,* (Vol. 1, pp. 222–229). Montreal: Université de Montréal, Faculté des Sciences de l'Education.

Baroody, A. J. (1983c). The development of procedural knowledge: An alternative explanation for chronometric trends of mental arithmetic. *Developmental Review, 3,* 225–230.

Baroody, A. J. (1983d). *Problem size effects on addition and commutativity performance.* Unpublished manuscript.

Baroody, A. J. (1984a). The case of Felicia: A young child's strategies for reducing memory demands during mental addition. *Cognition and Instruction, 1,* 109–116.

Baroody, A. J. (1984b). Children's difficulties in subtraction: Some causes and cures. *Arithmetic Teacher, 32*(3), 14–19.

Baroody, A. J. (1984c). Children's difficulties in subtraction: Some causes and questions. *Journal for Research in Mathematics Education, 15,* 203–213.

Baroody, A. J. (1984d). More precisely defining and measuring the order-irrelevance principle. *Journal of Experimental Child Psychology, 38,* 33–41.

Baroody, A. J. (1984e). A re-examination of mental arithmetic models and data: A reply to Ashcraft. *Developmental Review, 4,* 148–156.

Baroody, A. J. (1985a). Mastery of the basic number combinations: Internalization of relationships or facts? *Journal for Research in Mathematics Education, 16,* 83–98.

Baroody, A. J. (1985b, April). *Mental addition protostrategies: Retrieval or problem solving?* Paper presented at the biennial meeting of the Society for Research in Child Development, Toronto.

Baroody, A. J. (1985c). Pitfalls in equating informal arithmetic procedures with specific mathematical conceptions. *Journal for Research in Mathematics Education, 16,* 233–236.

Baroody, A. J. (1986). The value of informal approaches to mathematics instruction and remediation. *Arithmetic Teacher, 33*(5), 14–18.

Baroody, A. J. (in press-a). The development of counting strategies for single-digit addition. *Journal for Research in Mathematics Education.*

Baroody, A. J. (in press-b). *Learning basic mathematics.* New York: Teachers College Press.

Baroody, A. J., & Gannon, K. (1983, April). *The use of economical mental addition strategies by young children.* Paper presented at the annual meeting of the American Educational Research Association, Montreal.

Baroody, A. J., & Gannon, K. (1984). The development of the commutativity principle and economical addition strategies. *Cognition and Instruction, 1,* 321–339.

Baroody, A. J., & Ginsburg, H. P. (1982). Generating number combinations: Rote process or problem solving? *Problem Solving, 4*(12), 3–4.

Baroody, A. J., & Ginsburg, H. P. (1983). The effects of instruction on children's concept of "equals." *Elementary School Journal, 84,* 199–212.

Baroody, A. J., & Ginsburg, H. P. (1984, April). *TMR and EMR children's ability to learn counting skills and principles.* Paper presented at the annual meeting of the American Educational Research Association, New Orleans.

Baroody, A. J., Ginsburg, H. P., & Waxman, B. (1983). Children's use of mathematical structure. *Journal for Research in Mathematics Education, 14,* 156–168.

Baroody, A. J., & Mason, C. A. (1984). The case of Brian: An additional explanation for production deficiencies. In J. Moser (Ed.), *Proceedings of the Sixth Annual Meeting of the North American Chapter of the International Group for the Psychology of Mathematics Education* (pp. 2–8). Madison: Wisconsin Center for Educational Research.

Baroody, A. J., & Mason, C. A. (1985, April). *Early arithmetic thinking processes.* Paper presented at the annual meeting of the National Council of Teachers of Mathematics, San Antonio.

Baroody, A. J., & Snyder, P. (1983). A cognitive analysis of basic arithmetic abilities of TMR children. *Education and Training of the Mentally Retarded, 18,* 253–259.

Baroody, A. J., & White, M. (1983). The development of counting skills and number conservation. *Child Study Journal, 13,* 95–105.

Behr, M. J., Erlwanger, S., & Nichols, E. (1980). How children view the equals sign. *Mathematics Teaching, 92,* 13–15.

Bisanz, J., Lefevre, J., Scott, C., & Champion, M. A. (1984, April). *Developmental changes in the use of heuristics in simple arithmetic problems.* Paper presented at the annual meeting of the American Educational Research Association, New Orleans.

Briars, D. J., & Larkin, J. H. (1984). An integrated model of skills in solving elementary word problems. *Cognition and Instruction, 1,* 245–296.

Briars, D., & Siegler, R. S. (1984). A featural analysis of preschoolers' counting knowledge. *Developmental Psychology, 20,* 607–618.

Brownell, W. A. (1935). Psychological considerations in the learning and the teaching of arithmetic. *The teaching of arithmetic* (Tenth Yearbook, National Council of Teachers of Mathematics pp. 1–31). New York: Bureau of Publications, Teachers College, Columbia University.

Brownell, W. A., & Chazal, C. (1935). The effects of premature drill in third-grade arithmetic. *Journal of Educational Research, 29,* 17–28.

Brush, L. (1978). Preschool children's knowledge of addition and subtraction. *Journal for Research in Mathematics Education, 9*, 44–54.

Buckingham, B. R. (1927). Teaching addition and subtraction facts together or separately. *Educational Research Bulletin, 6*, 228–229, 240–242.

Campbell, J. I. D., & Graham, D. J. (1985). Mental multiplication skill: Structure, process, and acquisition. *Canadian Journal of Psychology, 39*, 338–362.

Carpenter, T. P., Hiebert, J., & Moser, J. M. (1981). Problem structure and first grade children's initial solution processes for simple addition and subtraction problems. *Journal for Research in Mathematics Education, 12*, 27–39.

Carpenter, T. P., Hiebert, J., & Moser, J. M. (1983). The effect of instruction on children's solutions of addition and subtraction word problems. *Educational Studies in Mathematics, 14*, 55–72.

Carpenter, T. P., Matthews, W., Lindquist, M. M., & Silver, E. A. (1984). Achievement in mathematics: Results from the National Assessment. *The Elementary School Journal, 84*, 485–495.

Carpenter, T. P., & Moser, J. M. (1982). The development of addition and subtraction problem-solving skills. In T. P. Carpenter, J. M. Moser, & T. A. Romberg (Eds.), *Addition and subtraction: A cognitive perspective* (pp. 9–24). Hillsdale, NJ: Lawrence Erlbaum Associates.

Carpenter, T. P., & Moser, J. M. (1983). The acquisition of addition and subtraction concepts. In R. Lesh & M. Landau (Eds.), *Acquisition of mathematical concepts and processes* (pp. 7–44). New York: Academic Press.

Carpenter, T. P., & Moser, J. M. (1984). The acquisition of addition and subtraction concepts in grades one through three. *Journal for Research in Mathematics Education, 15*, 179–202.

Cobb, P. (1985a). Two children's anticipations, beliefs, and motivations. *Educational Studies in Mathematics, 16*, 111–126.

Cobb, P. (1985b). A reaction to three early number papers. *Journal for Research in Mathematics Education, 16*, 141–145.

Court, S. R. A. (1920). Numbers, time, and space in the first five years of a child's life. *Pedagogical Seminary, 27*, 71–89.

Davis, P. J., & Hersh, R. (1981). *The mathematical experience.* Boston: Houghton Mifflin.

DeCorte, E., & Verschaffel, L. (1984). First graders' solution strategies of addition and subtraction word problems. In J. M. Moser (Ed.), *Proceedings of the Sixth Annual Meeting of the North American Chapter of the International Group for the Psychology of Mathematics Education* (pp. 15–20). Madison: Wisconsin Center for Educational Research.

Erlwanger, S. H. (1973). Benny's concept of rules and answers in IPI mathematics. *Journal of Children's Mathematical Behavior, 1*, 7–26.

Folsom, M. (1975). Operations on whole numbers. In J. N. Payne (Ed.), *Mathematics learning in early childhood.* (37th Yearbook of the National Council of Teachers of Mathematics, pp. 162–190). Reston, VA: NCTM.

Fuson, K. C. (1982). An analysis of the counting-on solution procedure in addition. In T. P. Carpenter, J. M. Moser, & T. A. Romberg (Eds.), *Addition and subtraction: A cognitive perspective* (pp. 67–82). Hillsdale, NJ: Lawrence Erlbaum Associates.

Fuson, K. C. (1985, March). *Teaching an efficient method of addition.* Paper presented at the annual meeting of the American Educational Research Association, Chicago.

Fuson, K. C., & Hall, J. W. (1983). The acquisition of early number word meanings: A conceptual analysis and review. In H. P. Ginsburg (Ed.), *The development of mathematical thinking* (pp. 49–107). New York: Academic Press.

Fuson, K. C., Richards, J., & Briars, D. J. (1982). The acquisition and elaboration of the number word sequence. In C. J. Brainerd (Ed.), *Children's logical and mathematical cognition: Progress in cognitive development* (pp. 33–92). New York: Springer-Verlag.

Gelman, R. (1972). Logical capacity of very young children: Number invariance rules. *Child Development, 43*, 75–90.

Gelman, R. (1977). How young children reason about small numbers. In N. J. Castellan, D. B. Pisoni, & G. R. Potts (Eds.), *Cognitive Theory* (Vol. 2, pp. 219–238). Hillsdale, NJ: Lawrence Erlbaum Associates.

Gelman, R., & Gallistel, C. R. (1978). *The child's understanding of number.* Cambridge, MA: Harvard University Press.

Gelman, R., & Meck, E. (1983). Preschoolers' counting: Principles before skill. *Cognition, 13,* 343–359.

Gibson, E. J. (1969). *Principles of perceptual learning and development.* Englewood Cliffs, NJ: Prentice-Hall.

Ginsburg, H. P. (1982). *Children's arithmetic.* Austin, TX: Pro-Ed.

Ginsburg, H. P., & Baroody, A. J. (1983). *The test of early mathematics ability.* Austin, TX: Pro-Ed.

Greeno, J. G. (1978). Understanding and procedural knowledge in mathematics education. *Educational Psychologist, 12,* 262–283.

Greeno, J. G., Riley, M. S., & Gelman, R. (1984). Conceptual competence and children's counting. *Cognitive Psychology, 16,* 94–143.

Groen, G. J., & Parkman, J. M. (1972). A chronometric analysis of simple addition. *Psychological Review, 79,* 329–343.

Groen, G. J., & Resnick, L. B. (1977). Can preschool children invent addition algorithms? *Journal of Educational Psychology, 69,* 645–652.

Hiebert, J. (1982). The position of the unknown set in children's solutions of verbal arithmetic problems. *Journal for Research in Mathematics Education, 13,* 341–349.

Hiebert, J. (1984). Children's mathematics learning: The struggle to link form and understanding. *The Elementary School Journal, 84,* 497–513.

Holt, J. (1964). *How children fail.* New York: Delta.

Ilg, F., & Ames, L. B. (1951). Developmental trends in arithmetic. *The Journal of Genetic Psychology, 79,* 3–28.

Kaput, J. J. (1979). Mathematics learning: Roots of epistemological status. In J. Lochhead and J. Clement (Eds.), *Cognitive process instruction* (pp. 289–304). Philadelphia: Franklin Institute Press.

Knight, F. B., & Behrens, M. S. (1928). *The learning of the 100 addition combinations and the 100 subtraction combinations.* New York: Longmans, Green.

Lindvall, C. M., & Ibarra, C. G. (1979, April). *The relationship of mode of presentation and of school/community differences to the ability of kindergarten children to comprehend simple story problems.* Paper presented at the annual meeting of the American Educational Research Association, Boston.

Lunkenbein, D. (1985, April). *Cognitive structures underlying processes and conceptions in geometry.* Paper presented at the research presession of the annual meeting of the National Council of Teachers of Mathematics, San Antonio, TX.

Mierkiewicz, D., & Siegler, R. S. (1980, August). *Preschoolers' abilities to recognize counting errors.* Paper presented at the Fourth International Conference for the Psychology of Mathematics Education, Berkeley, CA.

Miller, K., & Gelman, R. (1983). The child's representation of number: A multidimensional scaling analysis. *Child Development, 54,* 1470–1479.

Miller, K., Perlmutter, M., & Keating, D. (1984). Cognitive arithmetic: Comparison of operations. *Journal of Experimental Psychology: Learning, Memory, and Cognition, 10,* 46–60.

National Assessment of Educational Progress (1983). *The third national mathematics assessment: Results, trends, and issues.* Denver: Education Commission of the States.

Norman, D. D., & Rumelhart, D. E. (1975). *Explorations in cognition.* San Francisco: W. H. Freeman.

Olander, H. T. (1931). Transfer of learning in simple addition and subtraction. II. *Elementary School Journal, 31,* 427–437.

Piaget, J. (1964). Development and learning. In R. E. Ripple & V. N. Rockcastle (Eds.), *Piaget rediscovered* (pp. 7–20). Ithaca, NY: Cornell University Press.

Rabinowitz, M. (1985, April). *A representation of simple addition knowledge and related processing characteristics.* Paper presented at the biennial meeting of the Society for Research in Child Development, Toronto.

Resnick, L. B. (1983). A developmental theory of number understanding. In H. P. Ginsburg (Ed.), *The development of mathematical thinking* (pp. 109–151). New York: Academic Press.

Resnick, L. B., & Ford, W. W. (1981). *The psychology of mathematics for instruction.* Hillsdale, NJ: Lawrence Erlbaum Associates.

Resnick, L. B., & Neches, R. (1984). Factors affecting individual differences in learning ability. In R. J. Sternberg (Ed.), *Advances in the psychology of human intelligence* (Vol. 2, pp. 275–323). Hillsdale, NJ: Lawrence Erlbaum Associates.

Reyes, L. H. (1984). Affective variables and mathematics education. *The Elementary School Journal, 84,* 558–581.

Riley, M. S., Greeno, J. G., & Heller, J. I. (1983). Development of children's problem-solving ability in arithmetic. In H. P. Ginsburg (Ed.), *The development of mathematical thinking* (pp. 153–200). New York: Academic Press.

Romberg, T. A. (1982). An emerging paradigm for research on addition and subtraction skills. In T. P. Carpenter, J. M. Moser, & T. A. Romberg (Eds.), *Addition and subtraction: A cognitive perspective,* (pp. 1–7). Hillsdale, NJ: Lawrence Erlbaum Associates.

Romberg, T. A. (1984, April). *School mathematics: Options for the 1990s. Chairman's Report of a Conference* (U.S. Department of Education, Office of Educational Research and Improvement, National Council of Teachers of Mathematics, Wisconsin Center for Educational Research). Madison, WI. (December 5–8, 1983).

Russell, R., & Ginsburg, H. P. (1984). Cognitive analysis of children's mathematical difficulties. *Cognition and Instruction, 1,* 217–244.

Schoenfeld, A. H. (in press). *Mathematical problem solving.* New York: Academic Press.

Secada, W. G., Fuson, K. C., & Hall, J. (1983). The transition from counting-all to counting-on in addition. *Journal for Research in Mathematics Education, 14,* 47–57.

Siegler, R. S. (in press). Strategy choices in subtraction. In J. Sloboda & D. Rogers (Eds.), *Cognitive process in mathematics.* Fair Lawn, NJ: Oxford University Press.

Siegler, R. S., & Robinson, M. (1982). The development of numerical understandings. In H. W. Reese & L. P. Lipsitt (Eds.), *Advances in child development and behavior,* Vol. I. (pp. 241–312). New York: Academic Press.

Siegler, R. S., & Shrager, J. (1984). Strategy choices in addition: How do children know what to do? In C. Sophian (Ed.), *Origins of cognitive skills* (pp. 229–293). Hillsdale, NJ: Lawrence Erlbaum Associates.

Silver, E. A., & Thompson, A. G. (1984). Research perspective on problem solving in elementary school mathematics. *Elementary School Journal, 84,* 529–545.

Smith, J. H. (1921). Arithmetic combinations. *Elementary School Journal,* June, 762–770.

Starkey, P., & Gelman, R. (1982). The development of addition and subtraction abilities prior to formal schooling in arithmetic. In T. P. Carpenter, J. M. Moser, & T. A. Romberg (Eds.), *Addition and subtraction: A cognitive perspective* (pp. 99–116). Hillsdale, NJ: Lawrence Erlbaum Associates.

Steffe, L. P. (1968). The relationship of conservation of numerousness to problem-solving abilities of first-grade children. *Arithmetic Teacher, 16*(1), 47–52.

Steffe, L. P., & Johnson, D. C. (1971). Problem-solving performances of first-grade children. *Journal for Research in Mathematics Education, 2,* 50–64.

Steffe, L. P., von Glasersfeld, E., Richards, J., & Cobb, P. (1983). *Children's counting types.* New York: Praeger.

Steinberg, R. M. (1985). Instruction on derived facts strategies in addition and subtraction. *Journal for Research in Mathematics Education, 16,* 337–355.

Suydam, M., & Weaver, J. F. (1975). Research on mathematics learning. In J. N. Payne (Ed.), *Mathematics learning in early childhood* (37th Yearbook of the National Council of Teachers of Mathematics, pp. 43–67). Reston, VA: NCTM.

Svenson, O. (1975). Analyses of time required by children for simple additions. *Acta Psychologica, 35,* 289–302.

Thiele, C. (1938). *The contribution of generalization to the learning of the addition facts.* New York: Bureau of Publications, Teachers College, Columbia University.

Thorndike, E. L. (1922). *The psychology of arithmetic.* New York: Macmillan.

Thornton, C. A. (1978). Emphasizing thinking strategies in basic fact instruction. *Journal for Research in Mathematics Education, 9,* 214–227.

Tobias, S. (1978). *Overcoming math anxiety.* New York: Norton.

von Glasersfeld, E. (1982). Subitizing: The role of figural patterns in the development of numerical concepts. *Archives de Psychologie, 50,* 191–218.

Wagner, S., & Walters, J. (1982). A longitudinal analysis of early number concepts: From numbers to number. In G. Forman (Ed.), *Action and thought* (pp. 137–161). New York: Academic Press.

Weaver, J. F. (1982). Interpretations of number operations and symbolic representations of addition and subtraction. In T. P. Carpenter, J. M. Moser, & T. A. Romberg (Eds.), *Addition and subtraction: A cognitive perspective* (pp. 60–66). Hillsdale, NJ: Lawrence Erlbaum Associates.

Wheeler, L. R. (1939). A comparative study of the difficulty of the 100 addition combinations. *Journal of Genetic Psychology, 54,* 295–312.

Woods, S. S., Resnick, L. B., & Groen, G. J. (1975). An experimental test of five process models for subtraction. *Journal of Educational Psychology, 67,* 17–21.

5 Conceptual Knowledge as a Foundation for Procedural Knowledge

Thomas P. Carpenter
University of Wisconsin

Conceptual and procedural knowledge are difficult to define precisely. For a working definition, this chapter utilizes the distinctions between conceptual and procedural knowledge proposed by Hiebert and LeFevre (this volume): Procedural knowledge is characterized as step-by-step procedures executed in a specific sequence; conceptual knowledge involves a rich network of relationships between pieces of information, which permits flexibility in accessing and using the information. According to Hiebert and Lefevre, "Perhaps the biggest difference between procedural knowledge and conceptual knowledge is that the primary relationship in procedural knowledge is 'after,' which is used to sequence subprocedures and superprocedures linearly. In contrast, conceptual knowledge is saturated with relationships of many kinds" (p. 8).

These distinctions between conceptual and procedural knowledge provide a framework for examining the relationship between the two kinds of knowledge as young children's ability to represent and solve certain basic problems in arithmetic develops.

PROCEDURAL AND CONCEPTUAL KNOWLEDGE IN YOUNG CHILDREN

Initial Problem-Solving Abilities

Children enter school with highly developed informal systems of arithmetic (Fuson & Hall, 1983; Gelman & Gallistel, 1978; Ginsburg, 1977). Much of the research in this area has investigated how children use this informal knowledge in problem solving (Carpenter, 1985; Carpenter & Moser, 1983; Riley, Greeno, & Heller, 1983). Contrary to popular notions, young children are relatively successful at analyzing and solving simple word problems. Before receiving formal instruction in addition and subtraction, most young children invent informal modeling and counting strategies to solve basic addition and subtraction problems (Carpenter, Hiebert, & Moser, 1981; Carpenter & Moser, 1983, 1984). The informal solution procedures invented have a clear relationship to the structure of the problems solved. Most young children directly model quantities described in a problem, perform actions on those models, and enumerate sets to determine an answer. Table 5.1 includes a set of problems that provide different interpretations of addition and subtraction and consequently are solved in different ways. To solve each of the problems in Table 5.1, young children generally attempt to represent the problem directly. For the first problem, they construct a set of 5 objects, add 8 objects, and count the number of objects in the resulting set. To solve the second problem, they make a set of 13 objects and remove 5. The answer is found by counting the number of objects remaining. The third problem is solved by constructing a set of 5 objects, adding more objects until there are a total of 13 objects, and counting the number of objects added. The fifth problem is solved by matching two sets and counting the unmatched elements. Most young children have difficulty solving the fourth problem because the initial quantity is the unknown, and consequently the problem cannot be readily modeled.

The problem-solving analysis that children naturally apply to simple word problems reflects a better model of problem-solving than many of the superficial tricks for solving word problems that often are taught. Solution procedures appear to be linked to conceptual knowledge. They are based on reliable, accurate representations of the problems. The representations are formed from the semantics of the problem rather than from superficial features like key words. Children's structural analysis allows them to distinguish between problems that are similar in context and wording. Several of the problems in Table 5.1 describe the same action and use the same key words denoting joining or separating

TABLE 5.1
Basic Word Problem Types

1. Sally has 5 candies. She bought 8 more candies. How many candies does she have altogether?
2. Sally had 13 candies. She ate 5 of them. How many candies does she have left?
3. Sally has 5 candies. How many more candies does she have to buy to have 13 candies altogether.
4. Sally had some candies. She ate 5 of them. Now she has 8 candies left. How many candies did she have to start with?
5. Sally has 5 candies. Tom has 13 candies. How many more candies does Tom have than Sally?

actions, but each is solved differently. Furthermore, children justify their solutions by referring to semantic features of the problem. In short, the solution procedures have meaning for the children, and the meaning corresponds to an acceptable adult interpretation of the problem. But the conceptual knowledge upon which young children's procedures are based is limited. Consequently, the procedures lack flexibility. Most young children below the middle of first grade can only represent and solve problems by directly modeling the action or relationships in the problem. Their solutions for a given problem must follow a specified sequence corresponding to the action in the problem. They cannot reverse the action in a problem to undo a particular sequence. For example, they do not recognize that the fourth problem in Table 5.1 is equivalent to putting 5 candies back with the 8 from which they were taken, because that sequence of action does not follow the action sequence in the problem.

Advances in Problem-Solving Abilities

The development to more advanced levels of problem solving is characterized by an increase in flexibility. This increase in flexibility is made possible by an increasingly rich conceptual base, more efficient procedures, and the maintenance of links between them. It is driven by an expanding network of relationships between problems, procedures for solving problems, and arithmetic operations. The flexibility is manifested in the choice of procedures for solving problems and in the nature of the strategies chosen. Children become more flexible in choosing procedures to solve different problems, and the strategies themselves become more flexible.

Older children are not limited to procedures that directly match problem structure. They can use a variety of procedures to solve the same problem and can solve problems that cannot easily be modeled. They recognize that different procedures are equivalent and can be used to solve the same problem and that different problems are equivalent and can be solved with the same procedure. In other words, they have a more integrated network of relationships between problems and strategies, which makes possible a unified concept of addition and subtraction rather than isolated sets of problems and procedures. One model of the conceptual knowledge underlying this unified conception hypothesizes that relationships between problems are established through a part–whole schema (Riley, Greeno, & Heller, 1983). The action or relationships in a problem are analyzed in terms of whether the given problem includes the two parts that make up the whole or the whole and one of the parts. This allows children to partition the different problem types into two major classes of equivalent problems, which can be solved using the same procedures.

As children gain flexibility in the choice of procedures, the procedures themselves also become more flexible. Older children do not have to represent each quantity described in a problem with a set of objects. For example, to solve the first problem in Tabel 5.1, older children generally recognize that it is unnecessary to represent the first set. They find the answer by starting to count at 5 and counting on 8 more units. This involves a significant advancement in the flexibility in counting. It is necessary not only to count from 5 to 13, but also to keep track of the number of steps in the counting sequence. This requires a double counting process in which the numbers in the counting sequence themselves become units to be counted. A more efficient version of counting on involves counting on from the larger number. This strategy, which appears to be based on at least a tacit understanding of the principle of commutativity, is similar to the counting-on strategy described earlier except that the order of the addends is reversed so that the count begins with the larger number. This results in fewer steps in the counting sequence.

Counting strategies also can be used to solve subtraction problems. A counting strategy that corresponds to the action in problem 3 is similar to the counting-on strategy used to solve addition problems. The child again counts from 5 to 13, but in this case the number of steps in the counting sequence is the answer. A backward counting sequence in which a child counts backward 5 units from 13 can be used to represent and solve problem 2. It is more difficult, however, to count backwards than to count forwards. Because older children are more flexible in their choice of solution and are not limited to solutions that directly model problem structure, many of them would use the same forward counting sequence to solve all three subtraction problems (problems 2, 3, and 5) in Table 5.1. In fact, some research suggests that at least for certain problems, children will choose whichever strategy provides the most efficient solution (Groen & Poll, 1973; Woods, Resnick, & Groen, 1975). For example, finding $11 - 2$ would require fewer steps to count back, whereas finding $11 - 9$ requires fewer steps to count up from 9 to 11.

The key to children's flexibility in choosing procedures to solve word problems appears to rest on an understanding of relationships between different types of problems. The ability to use relationships between number facts plays a role in the transition from counting strategies to knowledge of number facts. Children initially learn certain number combinations earlier than they do others; and before they have completely mastered their addition tables, some children use a small set of memorized facts to derive solutions for addition and subtraction problems involving other number combinations (Carpenter & Moser, 1984). These solutions usually are based on doubles or numbers whose sum is 10. For example, to solve a problem representing $6 + 8 = ?$, a child might respond that "$6 + 6 = 12$ and $6 + 8$ is just two more than 12." In an example involving the operation $4 + 7 = ?$, a solution might involve the following analysis: "$4 + 6 = 10$ and $4 + 7$ is just 1 more than 10."

Derived facts also are used for subtraction problems. Derived subtraction facts often are based on relationships between addition and subtraction. For example, the solution to $14 - 8$, may be found as follows: "Seven and 7 is 14; 8

is 1 more than 7; so the answer is 6." This is consistent with many of the explanations given for subtraction facts learned at a recall level. Children's explanations frequently suggest that the number combinations they call on to solve a subtraction problem are addition facts. For example, to explain how they know the answer to 13 − 7, many children respond that they just know that 7 + 6 = 13 (Carpenter & Moser, 1984).

Although derived facts seem to require a great deal of insight about numerical relations, they are not used by only a handful of bright students. In a 3-year longitudinal study of children in grades one to three, children were interviewed three times a year to ascertain the solutions they used to solve a variety of addition and subtraction problems (Carpenter & Moser, 1984). More than 80% of the children in the study used derived facts at some time during the 3 years, and 40% used derived facts as their primary strategy for at least one interview during this period. The high frequency of derived fact use suggests that many children recognize important relationships between number facts and between arithmetic operations.

Connections Between Conceptual and Procedural Knowledge

Given that children become more flexible in their choice of procedures for solving problems and that this flexibility appears to be based on some understanding of relations between problems, the question remains how procedures are linked to conceptual knowledge to make this flexibility possible. Three different models have been proposed to describe the relationship between conceptual and procedural knowledge in the development of children's abilities to solve addition and subtraction problems. The first model hypothesizes that advances in procedural knowledge are driven by broad advances in conceptual knowledge. The second proposes that advances in conceptual knowledge are neither necessary nor sufficient to account for all advances in procedural knowledge. The third model concurs with the first that advances in procedural skills are linked to conceptual knowledge but proposes that the connections are more limited than suggested by the first model.

Riley, Greeno, and Heller (1983) have developed a computer simulation model of the knowledge required to solve addition and subtraction problems that characterize development in terms of broadly based advances in conceptual knowledge. A significant feature of their model is that it distinguishes between problem schemata and action schemata, which roughly correspond to conceptual knowledge and procedural knowledge, respectively. Problem schemata are used to represent problems as semantic networks that specify the relations between elements in the problems. Action schemata are organized into different levels. The most basic level includes schemata for making sets, adding elements to sets, removing elements from sets, counting sets, and so on. There are also more global action schemata, composed of the basic schemata. These schemata correspond to the procedures for solving addition and subtraction word problems just described.

Riley and her associates (1983) identify three basic levels of knowledge involved in problem solving. The levels differ in the ways in which knowledge is represented and quantitative information manipulated. More advanced levels are characterized both by more elaborated representations and by more sophisticated procedures. In other words, development is characterized by advances in both conceptual and procedural knowledge. At the first level, children are limited to external representations of problems using physical objects. They can solve only problems that can be modeled directly, like the first and second problems in Table 5.1. But even their direct modeling capabilities are limited. They cannot solve the third problem in Table 5.1 because they do not fully understand set-subset relations. If they attempt to model the third problem, they make a set of 5 objects and add objects to it until there are a total of 13 objects. But because they do not understand that an element can simultaneously be a member of a set and a member of a subset, they are unable to anticipate the necessity to separate the elements added to the set from the original 5 elements in the set. As a consequence, once they have constructed the set of 13 objects, they have no way to reconstruct the answer. The major advance of level 2 over level 1 is that it includes conceptual knowledge of simple set-subset relationships. This allows children at level 2 to keep track of all the elements in the problem. Children at this level can solve the third problem in Table 5.1 by modeling the action in the problem, but they are limited to direct modeling solutions and are unable to solve the fourth problem because the initial quantity is unknown and therefore cannot be easily represented. Level 1 and level 2 children are limited to direct representations of problem structure. Level 3 includes a schema for representing part–whole relations that allows children to proceed in a top–down direction to construct a representation of the relationships among all the pieces of information in the problem before solving it. This frees children from relying on solutions that directly represent the action in a problem so that they can solve all types of addition and subtraction problems using any appropriate strategy.

In essence, the development from level 1 through level 3 is characterized by an increasingly sophisticated ability to represent relationships within and between problems. The transition from level 1 to level 2 is characterized by the growth of the ability to represent relationships within problems. The transition to level 3 is marked by the ability to represent problems such that relationships between different types of problems are understood. Thus, the development of more advanced problem-solving procedures depends on the major development of conceptual knowledge.

Briars and Larkin (1984) have designed a similar model of the development of problem-solving skills, although it differs from the model of Riley et al. (1983) in some fundamental ways. Briars and Larkin do not as clearly specify distinctions between conceptual and procedural knowledge as Riley and her associates, and they hypothesize a somewhat different specification of the conceptual knowledge available at level 3. But the models agree on many essential features. They both propose the same three basic levels, and development though the levels in both models is characterized by broad advances in conceptual knowledge and the linking of procedures to this conceptual knowledge.

Baroody and Ginsburg (this volume) provide a different picture of advances in children's ability to solve addition and subtraction. They argue that the development of procedures used to solve addition and subtraction problems is not always governed by the development of conceptual knowledge, even in cases in which procedures appear to be based directly on conceptual knowledge. They argue that the connection between procedural and conceptual knowledge is extremely complex and that in many cases the development of conceptual knowledge is neither necessary nor sufficient to ensure the acquisition of related procedures. A key to their argument is that it is inappropriate to infer that because a child can use certain procedural routines, the child has acquired the related conceptual knowledge. They propose that construction of more advanced routines is motivated as much by an attempt to reduce cognitive processing demands of tasks as by the acquisition of underlying conceptual knowledge. In fact, the application of certain procedures may lead to conceptual knowledge rather than vice versa, as children note regularities in applying the procedures.

There is ample evidence that the development of conceptual knowledge alone does not drive the acquisition of procedures for solving addition and subtraction problems (Baroody & Ginsburg, this volume; Carpenter & Moser, 1984). The models proposed by Briars and Larkin (1984) and Riley et al. (1983) are overly parsimonious, and children's behavior is not as orderly as suggested (Carpenter & Moser, 1984). Systematic differences are not accounted for by the models. Children abandon direct modeling solutions for some problems before others. For example, the tedious matching strategy used for problems involving comparisons (Table 5.1, problem 5) is replaced by more efficient counting procedures while children still are consistently modeling directly the action in problems involving simple joining and separating (Table 5.1, problems 1, 2, and 3). The models also do not accurately reflect differences between other, presumably related procedures. For example, the models suggest that the same conceptual knowledge underlies the ability to count on and the ability to solve missing addend problems (Table 5.1, problem 3). There is evidence, however, that before they can count on children solve missing addend problems (Carpenter & Moser, 1984). Conceptual knowledge alone is not sufficient to account for advances in procedural knowledge.

A related question is whether conceptual knowledge is necessary. Baroody and Ginsburg (this volume) argue that it is not, but their claim is more difficult to substantiate. They cite as evidence for their conclusion the fact that children appear to hold contradictory conceptions for related problem situations. For example, children may disregard addend order in solving addition problems but maintain that two addition problems with commuted addends (8 + 5 and 5 + 8) do not have the same answer. This example certainly suggests that children may use solution procedures like counting on from the larger number, which disregards addend order, without understanding the principle of commutativity. However, the issue is what constitutes evidence of commutativity. Clearly, children who do not recognize that 8 + 5 and 5 + 8 have the same answer do not have a complete understanding of commutativity. But children do not immediately apply concepts to all appropriate situations. There is evidence to suggest that some of the more difficult applications of certain principles are those that involve establishing relationships between quantities (Carpenter & Lewis, 1976). Children may have some initial conception of the effect of addend order before they are able to use it to compare two sums. Perhaps it is appropriate to label this conceptual knowledge ''protocommutativity'' (Baroody & Ginsburg, this volume) rather than commutativity; but whatever it is called, it is inappropriate to conclude that it does not provide a valid conceptual basis for the procedural routines used to invert addend order. In other words, it is inappropriate to conclude that conceptual knowledge of some kind is unnecessary for procedural advances in this case.

Certainly children can learn procedures by rote without relating them to any appropriate form of conceptual knowledge, and some invention appears to occur strictly within the context of procedural knowledge (Brown & Burton, 1978; Brown & Van Lehn, 1982; Van Lehn, this volume). However, when invention occurs at a procedural level, it often results in errors. The more advanced procedures that children use to solve addition and subtraction problems are relatively free of the systematic errors described by Brown and his associates. This suggests that the procedures are somehow linked to some level of conceptual knowledge. If children were simply attempting to increase cognitive economy, they presumably would construct more efficient routines that were inappropriate more frequently than they do.

A third perspective on the relationship between conceptual and procedural knowledge is that advances in children's ability to solve addition and subtraction problems are based on conceptual knowledge, but connections between conceptual and procedural knowledge are established gradually and on a piecemeal basis. Conceptual knowledge is not immediately integrated with all related procedures; rather, initially, it is applied locally to individual problems and procedures. The examples cited in the preceeding paragraph illustrate the task specific nature of initial links between conceptual and procedural knowledge.

This conclusion is consistent with more general findings from research on cognitive development (cf. Gelman & Meek, this volume). Piaget (1952) theorized that children's ability to solve a wide variety of problems depended on the development of certain key concepts. But he acknowledged that the concepts were applied in some domains earlier than others, and subsequent research found that there was even more variability in children's performance than initially suspected (Carpenter, 1980). Thus, it is consistent with the findings in other areas that there is less coherence in the application of conceptual knowledge than proposed by Briars and Larkin (1984) and Riley et al. (1983).

Discussion

The relationship between conceptual and procedural knowledge does not appear to be simple. Major advances in conceptual knowledge are difficult to identify, and concepts appear to be applied in local domains before they are broadly generalized. A persistent problem is that conceptual knowledge is difficult to measure directly, and it is often inferred through the observation of particular procedures for which it presumably is a prerequisite. The issue of what performance should be taken as evidence of a child having acquired a particular piece of conceptual knowledge is difficult to resolve, and it may not be productive to argue whether particular conceptual knowledge exists at a given point in time. There is strong evidence, however, that major advances in solving addition and subtraction problems are characterized both by more sophisticated procedures and more elaborated conceptual knowledge, and that both need to be taken into account to understand children's problem-solving processes and to plan for instruction.

Given the lack of flexibility of the initial direct modeling level of solving addition and subtraction problems, it may appear that the initial level is based primarily on procedural knowledge and that advances are characterized by establishing links with conceptual knowledge. Although it is true that the links to conceptual knowledge at the initial level are more limited than at subsequent levels, it would be a mistake to conclude that the direct modeling solutions are strictly procedural. There are significant differences between these processes and rote procedures that are learned as fixed sequences of steps. The initial processes are not automatized into fixed sequences. They are generated anew for each problem by attending to semantic structure.

Distinctions between levels of problem solving reflect differences in how problems are represented and how these representations incorporate different kinds of relations. The initial level is limited to direct representations of problems because children at that level have limited understanding of relations between problems. They are, however, sensitive to relations within problems, and they reflect these relations in their solution procedures. At more advanced levels, children have the conceptual knowledge to establish relations between problems. At the initial level, children can only use information and relations explicitly stated in the problem. At subsequent levels, children begin to incorporate implicit knowledge about relationships that are not explicitly stated in the problem.

There is an important difference between this characterization and other analyses of the distinctions between novice and expert problem solvers (cf. Chi,

Glaser, & Rees, 1982). Although children's problem representations initially are limited to relationships explicitly stated in problems, it appears that for at least certain problem domains, these representations are not based on surface features of the problems, but are accurate representations of the problem's semantic structure.

Procedural and Conceptual Knowledge in Other Content Domains

This general characterization of problem solving likely applies to other domains as well as basic addition and subtraction. The general features are that children, and possibly adults with a limited conceptual knowledge base in a problem domain, initially are limited to direct representations of problems based on data explicitly given in the problems. As they gain a more elaborated network of conceptual knowledge, they are able to construct more sophisticated representations of the problems that include relations not specified explicitly in the problem. Younger children often can learn step-by-step procedures but have difficulty establishing relations among different pieces of data. The development of basic measurement skills appears to follow this general pattern (Carpenter, 1976, 1980; Hiebert, 1981). Young children can learn to perform accurately a number of simple measuring procedures and use the results to make judgments about the magnitudes of quantities. The procedures do not appear to be rote, meaningless routines, but they are limited in important ways. Although young children can measure using single units, initially they are unable to establish relationships between quantities measured with different units. The ability to establish such relationships is a milestone in the development of more advanced measurement skills. The same analysis might be applied to the solution of algebra word problems and to other problem-solving domains in the mathematics curriculum. In other words, if procedures are based on conceptual knowledge, there are limits on the procedures that can be learned initially. Attempts to accelerate the learning of procedural knowledge may result in the procedural knowledge being isolated from the related conceptual knowledge.

Procedural knowledge appears to be connected to conceptual knowledge as skill in solving basic addition and subtraction problems develops. But this is not uniformly the case for other topics in the curriculum. Children acquire simple addition and subtraction concepts without explicit instruction. More complex concepts are not as readily constructed without support. Much of the emphasis in mathematics curricula is on learning procedural skills, and for many children procedures are not consistently based on conceptual knowledge. Connections between conceptual and procedural knowledge play a critical role in solving problems, and the failure to build an adequate conceptual base or to link procedures to concepts generally results in superficial analysis of problem situations. A consequence of the emphasis on procedural knowledge is that for many children, problem solving reduces to simply deciding whether to add, subtract, multiply, or divide whatever numbers are given in a problem (Carpenter, Corbitt, Kepner, Lindquist, & Reys, 1981).

Procedural knowledge has been isolated from related conceptual knowledge in some cases because of a failure to develop the necessary conceptual base and in others because of a failure to link procedures to the conceptual knowledge that has been acquired. For example, early instruction on fractions stresses the development of simple fraction concepts. Children appear to acquire a general idea of the magnitude of fractions. They at least know that $\frac{7}{8}$ of a pie is less than the whole pie. Similarly, they have a reasonable concept of addition. Addition of fractions is a straightforward extension of whole-number addition, and children have a basic understanding of whole-number addition by the first or second grade. Thus, children seem to have the conceptual knowledge necessary to solve the estimation exercise in Table 5.2. However, procedures they have learned for adding fractions seem not to be clearly linked to this conceptual knowledge. Over half of the 13-year-olds in the second mathematics assessment of the National Assessment of Educational Progress (NAEP) chose answers of 19 or 21 as the best estimate of the sum of two fractions less than one (Carpenter, Corbitt, et al., 1981). These students simply added either the numerators or denominators without thinking about how their answer related to their knowledge of fractions and their knowledge of addition. They chose a procedure to apply to numbers given in the problem without relating that procedure to their conceptual knowledge. For fraction multiplication, a somewhat different picture emerges. The procedures for multiplying common fractions are straightforward and easy to learn. The numerators and denominators are simply multiplied. The procedure is

TABLE 5.2
Estimating the Sum of Two
Fractions*

ESTIMATE the answer to $^{12}/_{13} + \frac{7}{8}$. You
will not have time to solve the problem
using paper and pencil.

Responses	Percent Responding	
	Age 13	Age 17
1	7	8
2	24	37
19	28	21
21	27	15
I don't know	14	16

*From National Assessment of Educational Progress (Carpenter, Corbitt, Kepner, Lindquist, & Reys, 1981)

so simple that it easily can be learned without links to conceptual knowledge, and that appears to be the level of most students' learning. Fraction multiplication is not a straightforward extension of the concept of whole number multiplication held by most students, and most of them appear to have little understanding of the meaning of fraction multiplication. As a consequence, they cannot apply the procedure to solve simple problems. For example, over 70% of the 13- and 17-year-olds in the second NAEP mathematics assessment could multiply two common fractions, but only 20% could solve the following word problem (Carpenter et al., 1981):

Jane lives $\frac{2}{3}$ mile from school. When she has walked $\frac{2}{3}$ of the way, how far has she walked?

Instruction in fractions provides a reasonable introduction to simple fraction concepts, but it does not extend these concepts to develop an adequate knowledge base so that procedures like multiplication can be learned with meaning. Even in situations in which the knowledge base is adequate, as with simple fraction addition, procedures are not clearly connected to the conceptual knowledge that the children have acquired.

CONCEPTS, PROCEDURES, AND INSTRUCTION

Designing instruction to establish connections between conceptual and procedural knowledge is not a simple task. The knowledge initially available to a student constrains what the student can learn from instruction in specific and often subtle ways.

A study providing some perspective on this issue investigated how instruction directed at teaching formal procedures for representing different problems is limited by children's initial understanding of relations between them. The study was concerned with children's ability to learn to write number sentences to represent addition and subtraction problems (Carpenter, Bebout, & Moser, 1985). At the time children are first introduced to writing mathematical sentences to solve word problems, their informal modeling and counting strategies make more sense to them than the formal strategies being taught. As a consequence, although most children are able to solve the problems using these informal modeling and counting strategies, they see no connection between their solutions and the number sentences they are asked to write by the teacher (Carpenter et al., 1983). The operations represented by the number sentences that children write are often incorrect and inconsistent with the modeling and counting strategies that they actually use to solve the problem.

The difficulties that children experience in writing number sentences to represent word problems occur because the representations they have available (a + b, a − b) do not always correspond to their informal solutions. For children, a − b represents a separating action which corresponds to their solution of problems like problem 2 in Table 5.1. As a consequence, they have no difficulty writing a number sentence for this type of problem. Problems like the third problem in Table 5.1, however, generally are solved by joining elements to another set and keeping track of the number of elements joined rather than removing elements from a larger set (Carpenter & Moser, 1983). This solution corresponds more closely to the noncanonical number sentence $3 + \square = 8$. This suggests that for young children, noncanonical number sentences may be the most natural representation for certain types of addition and subtraction problems. In other words, children who can solve problems with objects only by direct modeling may be limited to writing number sentences (both canonical and noncanonical) that directly represent the action described in a problem.

For this study, 22 first-grade children and 41 second-grade children were randomly assigned to two instructional groups. Both groups received two 30-minute lessons in writing number sentences to represent basic addition and subtraction word problems. The word problems covered during instruction were limited to problems similar to the first three problems in Table 5.1. One group of students received instruction in writing both canonical and noncanonical number sentences. For problems similar to the third problem in Table 5.3, they were taught to write number sentences of the form $5 + \square = 13$. The other group was shown only how to write canonical number sentences ($8 + 5 = \square$ or $13 - 5 = \square$). They were encouraged to use a part–whole analysis to identify the appropriate number sentences (Riley et al., 1983; Wilson, 1967). On the basis of this analysis, if both parts are given and the whole is the unknown, the operation is addition; if one part and the whole is given, the operation is subtraction. Following instruction, children in both groups were tested on their ability to write number sentences to represent addition and subtraction word problems.

Selected results from the study are summarized in Tables 5.3 and 5.4. The four problems correspond to the first four problems in Table 5.1. Some children attempted to reflect the structure of the problem in their number sentences but did not write complete number sentences with a box to represent the unknown. For example, rather than writing $5 + \square = 7$ or $5 + \boxed{2} = 7$, they wrote $5 + 2 = \boxed{7}$ or $5 + 2 = 7$. These responses were labeled incomplete noncanonical. The other categories of number sentences were appropriate canonical sentences, appropriate noncanonical sentences, and sentences involving a wrong operation. The wrong operation sentences were all canonical ($a + b = \square$ when the appropriate canonical sentence was $a - b = \square$ or vice versa). Almost all children in both canonical and noncanonical groups wrote correct canonical number sentences for the first two problems. For these two problems, the canonical number sentences provide a direct representation. Over 80% of the first graders in the noncanonical group attempted to write a noncanonical number sentence to represent the third problem, and more than 70% attempted to write a noncanonical number sentence

TABLE 5.3
First Grade Children's Symbolic Representations
of Addition and Subtraction Word Problems*

Problem	Corresponding Sentence	Percent Correct	Number Sentence (Percent Responding)			
			Canonical	Noncanonical	Incomplete	Wrong Operation
Noncanonical Group						
1	2 + 4 = ☐	100	100	0	0	0
2	9 − 7 = ☐	100	100	0	0	0
3	5 + ☐ = 7	100	0	45	36	18
4	☐ − 2 = 6	73	0	27	45	27
Canonical Group						
1	2 + 4 = ☐	100	100	0	0	0
2	9 − 7 = ☐	91	91	0	0	9
3	5 + ☐ = 7	36	18	0	18	55
4	☐ − 2 = 6	55	27	0	45	27

*From Carpenter, Bebout, & Moser, 1985

TABLE 5.4
Second Grade Children's Symbolic Representations
of Addition and Subtraction Word Problems*

Problem	Corresponding Sentence	Percent Correct	Number Sentence (Percent Responding)			
			Canonical	Noncanonical	Incomplete	Wrong Operation
Noncanonical Group						
1	5 + 7 = ☐	90	95	0	0	5
2	13 − 8 = ☐	90	95	0	0	5
3	9 + ☐ = 13	100	5	85	0	5
4	☐ − 4 = 7	55	35	35	0	25
Canonical Group						
1	5 + 7 = ☐	95	95	0	0	5
2	13 − 8 = ☐	100	100	0	0	0
3	9 + ☐ = 13	90	76	0	14	10
4	☐ − 4 = 7	62	57	0	10	33

*From Carpenter, Bebout, & Moser, 1985

that directly represented the fourth problem, even though they had received no explicit instruction in representing that type of problem. By contrast, relatively few first graders in the canonical group could write canonical sentences to solve the third or fourth problems. In fact, 45% attempted to directly represent the fourth problem rather than writing a standard canonical number sentence.

Thus, most first graders were limited in the kinds of sentences that they could learn to write. They could learn to represent a variety of problems provided they were taught to write number sentences to represent the action in the problem, but they were not successful in learning to write number sentences that required them to transform the problems. Many of the second graders, on the other hand, were able to learn to write number sentences that required a transformation.

From the age norms provided by other studies (Carpenter & Moser, 1984), it is reasonable to conclude that most children in the first grade would have been at a level in which informal counting and modeling strategies were limited to directly modeling action and relations in problems. Many second graders, however, would have passed into more advanced levels in which they were capable of transforming problems. The results of this study suggest that children at the direct modeling level do not easily learn to represent problems symbolically with number sentences that do not correspond to the action in the problem. At the more advanced levels, children can transform problems to solve them with the most economical counting strategy and can learn to represent them all with canonical number sentences.

Examples can be drawn from other areas that show how learning from instruction reflects fundamental limits of students' knowledge of conceptual relations. A study by Hiebert (1981) investigated how prior knowledge of fundamental quantitative relations affected children's ability to learn formal measurement concepts and skills. An earlier study by Carpenter (1975) had found that understanding the effects of measuring with different units of measure reflected the same quantitative reasoning involved in solving traditional conservation problems. Hiebert found that children who failed traditional conservation tasks could readily learn a number of basic measuring skills, but they were unable to learn to relate measurements made with different units. Children who conserved, on the other hand, were able to learn about the effects of measuring with different units. In other words, children's informal knowledge of quantitative relations directly influenced their ability to learn formal concepts involving parallel relationships, but it did not affect their ability to learn simple step by step procedures.

This perspective may also provide some general insights on the use of manipulative materials to teach basic mathematics concepts. Although manipulative materials appear to have the potential for linking procedural routines in mathematics to conceptual knowledge, it has proved difficult to demonstrate consistently that they are effective in giving conceptual meaning to algorithmic procedures. The most effective technique appears to involve establishing a clear map between paper and pencil algorithms and manipulations of objects (Resnick,

1982); however, even when mappings have been clearly established, instruction has not been uniformly effective (Resnick & Omanson, in press). One possible reason manipulative materials have not been more consistently successful in linking conceptual knowledge with particular procedures is that the manipulations of the physical materials themselves may be based on limited conceptual knowledge. Manipulative materials are often structured so that it is relatively easy to manipulate them to get the correct answer. Children may be able to perform manipulations with objects to get an answer but still be operating at a procedural level with the objects.

Children's understanding of operations with physical objects often is more limited than we realize. Piaget (1952) showed us that children frequently have a different understanding of concrete operations than we do as adults. If a child's manipulations of physical materials are not derived from an operational understanding of the conceptual knowledge underlying the procedures, it is unlikely that experiences with materials will provide a basis for linking formal procedures to underlying conceptual knowledge. For manipulative materials to be effective in relating algorithmic procedures and conceptual knowledge, it seems necessary to ensure that the conceptual knowledge is adequately developed at the concrete level and that relationships between the physical procedures with the materials and the corresponding conceptual knowledge are firmly established.

Designing Instruction to Relate Conceptual and Procedural Knowledge

The foregoing examples illustrate the level of analysis required to design instruction consistent with students' knowledge base. The first example demonstrates that it is not a simple question of whether or not to introduce mathematical symbolism to children at a particular level in the development of addition and subtraction concepts. For young children, certain kinds of symbolism can be connected to their conceptual knowledge but others cannot. The nature of the instruction is also critical.

Mathematics programs developed in the 1960s included noncanonical number sentences. For the most part, this approach met with teachers' resistance, because they found it was difficult to teach the particular approach to noncanonical sentences. At that time, noncanonical sentences were to be solved by relating them to corresponding canonical sentences. Current analyses suggest that such transformations require children to have attained advanced levels for solving addition and subtraction problems (Briars & Larkin, 1984; Riley et al., 1983). However, young children can solve such sentences directly by using the same modeling and counting processes that they use to solve corresponding word problems (Blume, 1981). The results of this study suggest that young children will use noncanonical forms to represent and solve appropriate problems. In other words, both the number sentences and the operations performed on them must be chosen with care to be consistent with children's conceptual knowledge.

There are several alternatives for designing instruction to be consistent with the conceptual knowledge available. One can either limit instruction to procedures that can be related to the existing conceptual knowledge, or one can attempt to enrich the knowledge base to support more advanced procedural knowledge. Thus, one alternative for teaching young children symbolic representation of simple word problems is to teach them to represent problems with both canonical and noncanonical number sentences so that they can represent them when they are still at a direct modeling level. Another alternative is to delay the introduction of symbolism or limit exposure to types of problems that correspond to canonical number sentences until children attain a level at which they can transform problems. On the other hand, one could attempt to accelerate the development of more advanced conceptual knowledge by providing instruction in part whole relations that can be used to transform problems (see Kouba & Moser, 1980).

Goals of Instruction

Procedural knowledge is related to things children do; consequently, it is easier to observe than conceptual knowledge, which often must be inferred from children's procedures. This makes it easier to evaluate procedural knowledge than conceptual knowledge, and it makes deficiencies in procedural knowledge more apparent. The linearity of procedures also is more consistent with traditional instructional sequences than the complex relations involved in networks of conceptual knowledge. These are among the reasons that much of the instruction in mathematics focuses on procedural knowledge.

Learning procedures does not, however, ensure that the related conceptual knowledge has been acquired. This is particularly critical for programs designed to teach procedures that usually are linked to conceptual knowledge. It is sometimes possible to simplify procedures that normally are based on conceptual knowledge to step-by-step procedures. Whereas spontaneous procedures may be taken as evidence that a child has acquired certain conceptual knowledge, it would be a mistake to assume that the instructed procedure reflects the same knowledge. It may be possible to teach children procedures of advanced levels by focusing on the procedures themselves, but this does not ensure that the children have acquired the corresponding conceptual knowledge. For example, teaching children procedures that solve some of the more difficult addition and subtraction problems does not guarantee that they understand part–whole structures or have a clear picture of the relations between different types of problems. This does not mean that such instruction is harmful or that links to conceptual knowledge cannot be established, but it is important to understand the potential distinctions between knowledge that is engendered by such instruction and knowledge that is built on conceptual relations.

How instruction on procedural knowledge is evaluated depends on the role assigned to the procedures in and of themselves. It is a very different issue if the procedures are perceived as important to learn in their own right than if the procedures are important primarily as windows on children's conceptual knowledge. For example, instruction in number facts or algorithms should be regarded very differently from instruction on tasks designed to establish the concept of commutativity. Instruction on transitional procedures like counting on or derived facts may also be viewed differently from instruction designed to teach procedures that represent terminal goals of instruction. For number facts and algorithms, a certain level of automaticity is eventually necessary. It is important that the conceptual knowledge be available so that one can fall back on it to determine whether or how a particular algorithm applies to a new situation and avoid the kinds of "bugs" identified by Brown and his associates (Brown & Burton, 1978; Brown & Van Lehn, 1982; Van Lehn, this volume). But it would be inefficient always to relate algorithms to underlying conceptual knowledge. Efficiency is not the goal, however, with transitional procedures or procedures designed to teach underlying concepts.

Procedural knowledge is important, and we often apply procedures mechanically without thinking about the related conceptual knowledge. There is nothing wrong with efficient, automatized procedures; but students need to recognize the limits of procedures and when to draw upon conceptual knowledge. In the long run, both conceptual knowledge and procedural knowledge are important. Current instruction in mathematics appears to place a greater emphasis on procedural knowledge than on conceptual knowledge. This often results in impoverished conceptual knowledge and tenuous links between the conceptual knowledge that is learned and related to procedural knowledge. One consequence is that children acquire flawed procedural knowledge.

The analysis of the development of addition and subtraction concepts and procedures provides a model of how conceptual and procedural knowledge can be linked. Following this pattern, conceptual knowledge is developed throughout the course of instruction so that the conceptual knowledge becomes enriched and able to support the acquisition of more advanced procedures.

It is an iterative process. Procedures are taught that can be supported by existing conceptual knowledge, and the conceptual knowledge base is extended to provide a basis for developing more advanced concepts. At every point during instruction, procedures are taught that can be connected to existing conceptual knowledge. This is easier said than done. It requires a detailed analysis of the mathematics curriculum and of children's learning of specific topics in the curriculum. It requires that the goals of instruction be analyzed at every stage of instruction and that instruction is designed carefully so that the requisite conceptual knowledge is given a chance to develop and so that procedural knowledge is connected to this conceptual knowledge.

ACKNOWLEDGMENTS

The research reported in this paper was funded by the Wisconsin Center for Education Research which is supported in part by a grant from the National Institute of Education (Grant No. NIE-G-84-0008).

REFERENCES

Blume, G. (1981). *Kindergarten and first-grade children's strategies for solving addition and subtraction missing addend problems in symbolic and verbal problem contexts* (Technical Report No 538). Madison: Wisconsin Center for Education Research.

Briars, D. J., & Larkin, J. G. (1984). An integrated model of skills in solving elementary word problems. *Cognition and Instruction, 1*(3), 245–296.

Brown, J. S., & Burton, R. R. (1978). Diagnostic models for procedural bugs in basic mathematical skills. *Cognitive Science, 2,* 153–192.

Brown, J. S., & VanLehn, K. (1982). Toward a generative theory of "bugs." In T. P. Carpenter, J. M. Moser, & T. A. Romberg (Eds.), *Addition and subtraction: A cognitive perspective* (pp. 117–135). Hillsdale, NJ: Lawrence Erlbaum Associates.

Carpenter, T. P. (1975). Measurement concepts of first- and second-grade students. *Journal for Research in Mathematics Education, 6,* 3–13.

Carpenter, T. P. (1976). Analysis and synthesis of existing research on measurement. In R. A. Lesh (Ed.), *Number and measurement.* Columbus, OH: ERIC.

Carpenter, T. P. (1980). Cognitive development and mathematics learning. In R. Shumway (Ed.), *Research in mathematics education* (pp. 146–206). Reston, VA: National Council of Teachers of Mathematics.

Carpenter, T. P. (1985). Learning to add: An exercise in problem solving. In E. Silver (Ed.), *Teaching and learning mathematical problem solving: Multiple research perspectives.* Philadelphia: Franklin Institute Press.

Carpenter, T. P., Bebout, H. C., & Moser, J. M. (1985). *The representation of basic addition and subtraction word problems.* Paper presented at the annual meeting of the American Educational Research Association, Chicago.

Carpenter, T. P., Corbitt, M. K., Kepner, H. S., Lindquist, M. M., & Reys, R. E. (1981). *Results from the second mathematics assessment of the national assessment of educational progress.* Washington, DC: National Council of Teachers of Mathematics.

Carpenter, T. P., Hiebert, J., & Moser, J. M. (1981). Problem structure and first-grade children's initial solution processes for simple addition and subtraction processes. *Journal for Research in Mathematics Education, 12,* 27–39.

Carpenter, T. P., Hiebert, J., & Moser, J. M. (1983). The effect of instruction on children's solutions of addition and subtraction problems. *Educational Studies in Mathematics, 14,* 52–72.

Carpenter, T. P., & Lewis, R. (1976). The development of the concept of a standard unit of measure in young children. *Journal for Research in Mathematics Education, 7,* 53–58.

Carpenter, T. P., & Moser, J. M. (1983). The acquisition of addition and subtraction concepts. In

R. Lesh & M. Landau (Eds.), *The acquisition of mathematical concepts and processes*. New York: Academic Press.

Carpenter, T. P., & Moser, J. M. (1984). The acquisition of addition and subtraction concepts in grades one through three. *Journal for Research in Mathematics Education, 15,* 179–202.

Chi, M. T. H., Glaser, R., & Rees, E. (1982). Expertise in problem solving. In R. Sternberg (Ed.), *Advances in the psychology of human intelligence* (pp. 7–75). Hillsdale, NJ: Lawrence Erlbaum Associates.

Fuson, K. C., & Hall, J. W. (1983). The acquisition of early number word meanings: A conceptual analysis and review. In H. Ginsburg (Ed.), *The development of mathematical thinking*. New York: Academic Press.

Gelman, R., & Gallistel, C. R. (1978). *The child's understanding of number*. Cambridge, MA: Harvard University Press.

Ginsburg, H. (1977). *Children's arithmetic: The learning process*. New York: Van Nostrand.

Groen, G. J., & Poll, M. (1973). Subtraction and the solution of open sentence problems. *Journal of Experimental Child Psychology, 16,* 292–302.

Hiebert, J. (1981). Cognitive development and learning linear measurement. *Journal for Research in Mathematics Education, 12,* 197–211.

Kouba, V. L., & Moser, J. M. (1980). *Development and validation of curriculum units related to two-digit addition and subtraction algorithms*. Madison: Wisconsin Center for Education Research.

National Advisory Committee on Mathematical Education (1975). *Overview and analysis of school mathematics, grades K-12*. Washington, DC: Conference Board of the Mathematical Sciences.

Piaget, J. (1952). *The child's conception of number*. London: Routeledge & Kegan Paul.

Resnick, L. B. (1982). Syntax and semantics in learning to subtract. In T. P. Carpenter, J. M. Moser, & T. A. Romberg (Eds.), *Addition and subtraction: A cognitive perspective* (pp. 136–155). Hillsdale, NJ: Lawrence Erlbaum Associates.

Resnick, L. B., & Omanson, S. F. (in press). Learning to understand arithmetic. In R. Glaser (Ed.), *Advances in instructional psychology* (Vol. 3). Hillsdale, NJ: Lawrence Erlbaum Associates.

Riley, M. S., Greeno, J. G., & Heller, J. I. (1983). Development of children's problem-solving ability in arithmetic. In H. P. Ginsburg (Ed.), *The development of mathematical thinking* (pp. 153–200). New York: Academic Press.

Wilson, J. W. (1967). The role of structure in verbal problem solving. *Arithmetic Teacher, 14,* 486–497.

Woods, S. S., Resnick, L. B., & Groen, G. J. (1975). An experimental test of five process models for subtraction. *Journal of Educational Psychology, 1,* 17–21.

6

Arithmetic Procedures are Induced from Examples

Kurt VanLehn
Carnegie-Mellon University

Suppose one asked some concerned adults, for example, parents, how multi-column subtraction is learned in school. Their explanation would probably run something like this: The teacher tells the students how to perform the algorithm, then sets them to solving practice exercises. Perhaps the practice causes some students to realize that they hadn't quite understood what the teacher meant. Or perhaps the teacher notices that certain students are following the wrong procedure. In either case, the teacher helps the students by telling them in more detail about the algorithm, probably by adapting the explanation to the particular exercises that the students are working on. *Telling* dominates both the initial instruction and the subsequent teacher-student interactions, according to this folk model of arithmetic acquisition. Winston (1978) dubbed this model "learning by being told."

The evidence to be presented below suggests that learning-by-being-told is an inaccurate model of the kind of arithmetic learning that actually occurs in classrooms. Rather, arithmetic is learned by induction—the generalization and integration of examples. An "example" of a procedure is an execution of it. When teachers work a subtraction exercise on the blackboard, their writing actions constitute an example of the subtraction procedure. Although some inductive learning may occur while passively observing the teacher work problems, most inductive learning probably occurs in the midst of problem solving. For instance, a student may try to solve a practice exercise, get stuck, and seek help from the textbook, the teacher, or a classmate. With this help, the student determines what writing actions to perform next and thereby continues toward a solution of the exercise. Learning occurs when the student generalizes these actions and incorporates them into his or her procedure. The writing actions are an example of a

133

subprocedure that the student needs to learn. The student's generalization of that example yields a subprocedure, although it may not be the correct subprocedure. This hypothetical incident illustrates how inductive learning can occur in the midst of problem solving. The defining characteristic of induction of arithmetic procedure is that learning is based on *generalization of writing actions*, regardless of whether those actions are acquired by actively soliciting help or by passively observing an exercise being solved.

The folk model of arithmetic learning holds that verbal explanations provide information from which students learn procedures. Although verbal explanations certainly dominate the instruction, the evidence presented below suggests that the examples that inevitably accompany such explanations are doing the pedagogical work. However, the examples don't do all the work. The verbal explanations are crucial for indicating to the students the particular kind of induction to perform on the examples. The verbal explanations indicate what aspects of the examples to generalize and how to integrate them. That is, verbal explanations have an indirect effect. They function as if they tell the student *how to induce the arithmetic procedure* despite the fact that their literal content is about how to perform the procedure. This view of arithmetic learning will be called the induction hypothesis.

Clearly, the induction hypothesis would be false if it were tested in a fine-grained way. During the hundreds of classroom hours that a student spends learning the multicolumn arithmetic algorithms, there are, no doubt, many episodes where the student suddenly grasps a new aspect of an algorithm, and yet there is no example in sight. Because examples are a prerequisite for induction, such episodes would be outright contradictions of the induction hypothesis, if the hypothesis were to be taken as a statement about the second-by-second learning process. Such a fine-grained interpretation is not the intended one. An explanation of the intended interpretation requires that a little background on the research project be presented first.

The research project began with the "buggy" studies of Brown and Burton (1978). It is well known that arithmetic students make a large variety of systematic errors (Buswell, 1926; Brueckner, 1930; Brownell, 1941; Roberts, 1968; Lankford, 1972; Cox, 1975; Ashlock, 1976). Brown and Burton used the metaphor of bugs in computer programs in developing a precise, detailed formalism for describing systematic errors. The basic idea is that a student's errors can be accurately reproduced by taking a formal representation of the correct algorithm and making one or more small perturbations to it, such as deleting a rule. The perturbations are called bugs. A systematic error is represented by a correct procedure for the skill plus a list of one or more bugs. Bugs describe systematic errors with unprecedented precision. If a student makes no unintentional mistakes (e.g., $7 - 2 = 4$), then the student's answers will exactly match the buggy algorithm's answers, digit for digit.

Burton (1982) developed an automated data analysis program, called Debuggy. Using it, data from thousands of students learning subtraction were analyzed, and 76 different kinds of bugs were observed (VanLehn, 1982). Similar studies discovered 68 bugs in addition of fractions (Shaw et al., 1982), several dozen bugs in linear equation solving (Sleeman, 1984), and 57 bugs in addition and subtraction of signed numbers (Tatsuoka & Baillie, 1982).

It is important to stress that bugs are only a notation for systematic errors and not an explanation. The connotations of "bugs" in the computer-programming sense do not necessarily apply. In particular, bugs in human procedures are unstable. They appear and disappear over short periods of time, often with no intervening instruction, and sometimes even in the middle of a testing session (VanLehn, 1982). Often, one bug is replaced by another, a phenomenon called bug migration.

Collecting bugs leads inevitably to wondering why those bugs exist. There are an infinite number of possible bugs; why do students only acquire certain of these? One way to answer such questions is to develop a generative theory of bugs. Such a theory should generate (predict) exactly which bugs will occur and which bugs won't. The way that it generates a bug constitutes an explanation for the bugs' existence.

Repair theory (Brown & VanLehn, 1980) was our first version of a generative theory of bugs. The basic idea of repair theory is that students don't simply halt when they reach an impasse while following a procedure, as a computer would. Rather, they apply certain metalevel problem solving operations, called repairs, that change their interpretation of the procedure in such a way that they can continue. As an illustration, suppose that a student who has not yet learned about borrowing from zero encounters the problem $305 - 109$. When the student trys to decrement the top digit in the tens column, as his incomplete procedure says he should, he finds that it is a zero and can't be decremented. He is at an impasse (see **a** below).

$$
\begin{array}{lllll}
\text{a.} & 30^15 & \text{b.} & 30^15 & \text{c.} & \overset{2}{\cancel{3}}0^15 \\
 & -10\ 9 & & -10\ 9 & & -10\ 9 \\
\hline
 & & & 20\ 6 & & 10\ 6 \\
\end{array}
$$

(The small numbers represent the student's scratch marks.) Several repairs could potentially be applied here. A simple one is just to skip an action when the preconditions are violated. In this case, the repair would result in omitting the decrement half of borrowing (see *b* above). If the student does this on every problem that requires borrowing from zero, then he or she will appear to have a systematic error, a bug called Stops-Borrow-At-Zero. (The appendix lists the observed subtraction bugs, with a short description of each.) If the student chooses a different repair, such as relocating the stuck action, then a different bug would be generated. Problem *c* above exhibits Borrow-Across-Zero, a bug where the decrement has been moved leftward. The impasse/repair mechanism can explain many bugs as coming from the same underlying incomplete procedure. Such underlying procedures are called *core procedures*.

Repair theory can also explain bug migrations. Suppose a student has the same core procedure throughout a testing session, but instead of repairing every occurrence of an impasse with the same repair, he or she makes different repairs. This would make it appear as if the student were exhibiting different bugs on different problems, or maybe even on different columns within the same problem. For instance, if the hypothetical student mentioned above chooses the first repair for some impasses and the second repair for others, then it will appear that there is a bug migration between Stops-Borrow-At-Zero and Borrow-Across-Zero. Even though the core procedure is stable, there is instability in what appears on the surface to be the student's procedure. The *surface procedure,* which exists only in the eye of the observer and not in the mind of the student, changes from one buggy procedure to another.

If one stipulates just the right set of core procedures, then repair theory can generate a large set of observed bugs. The set of bugs is larger than the set of core procedures, so repair theory is not a vaccuous theory. Originally, the set of core procedures was discovered by trial and error. In a sense, we "observed" those core procedures in the subject population. Something is needed to explain why exactly that set of core procedures is observed in the subject population. A generative theory of core procedures is needed. Such a theory has been developed (VanLehn, 1983). It is the topic of this chapter.

As the example above makes clear, some core procedures are a direct result of the fact that diagnostic tests are administered to students who have not yet completed the subtraction curriculum, and therefore have not yet been taught the entire algorithm. The incompleteness in their training causes their core procedure to lack some of the subprocedures that a correct, complete procedure would have. This incompleteness shows up as bugs on the diagnostic test. Testing beyond training explains why some core procedures have missing subprocedures.

Other core procedures, however, are not easily explained as missing subprocedures. Instead, some of the subprocedures have wrong information in them. The following is a simple example. In the correct subtraction procedure, the student should borrow when $T < B$ in a column, where T and B are the top and bottom digits, respectively, in the column. The bug N-N-Causes-Borrow performs a borrow when $T \leq B$ (see below).

$$
\begin{array}{r}
6 \\
7^1 5 \\
-2\ 5 \\
\hline
410
\end{array}
$$

Apparently, students with this bug have overgeneralized the condition for when to borrow. Their core procedure is complete, but incorrect.

To sum up, there are a variety of core procedures. Some seem quite naturally to be the result of testing beyond training, whereas others seem to be the result of learning processes that have gone awry. The research project is to find a learning theory that generates (predicts) the core procedures that are found in the subject population.

Because the learning theory should actually construct the core procedures, a computational learning model is needed. It should take in something that represents the classroom experiences that the students have. Using that input, it should construct some knowledge structures that represent the core procedures that students acquire from those experiences. Researchers in Artificial Intelligence (AI) have built such computational models of learning (Cohen & Feigenbaum, 1983). There are models of skill acquisition based on induction (Biermann, 1972), analogy (Carbonell, 1983), learning-by-being-told (Badre, 1972), planning and debugging (Sussman, 1976), practice (Mitchell, Utgoff, & Banerji, 1983), and other techniques.

In general, these researchers make no attempt to empirically test their model's psychological validity, but there are exceptions. Perhaps the most thorough validation is Anderson's study of the acquisition of skill in geometry theorem proving and Lisp programming (Anderson 1983; Anderson, Greeno, Kline, & Neves, 1981; Anderson, Farrell, & Saurers; 1984). In Anderson's studies, the main data are protocols of students solving problems, with a textbook and a tutor beside them. Their comments and actions are coded and presented to the learning model. When the model is successful, it simulates the students' learning behavior accurately at a second-by-second level of detail. Despite the fact that learning such complex skills requires hundreds of hours of learning and practice, the protocols cover only two or three hours of an individual student's education. That is, of course, inevitable. It is impossible to record, analyze, and simulate the whole of a student's education. Consequently, significant extrapolation beyond the data is needed in order to claim that the observed samples of the learning process characterize the whole of the students' education.

Rather than taking a small sample of the students' education and analyzing it in great detail, the present research takes the whole of the students' education and analyzes it at a higher level of detail. The essential information in the students' experiences is abstracted and presented in an ideal form to the learning model. The key question is, what should this essential information be? This question is intimately related to the question of what the learning process is. If the learning process is inductive, as claimed earlier, then examples are the essential information to abstract from the curriculum and present to the learning model. If the learning process is learning-by-being-told, then the teacher's verbal explanations are the essential information. Either way, the objective is to find some learning process and its associated abstraction of the curriculum such that (1) the whole curriculum can be presented to the learning model, and (2) the learning model accurately predicts the core procedures that the students acquire. In short, the desired learning theory is a generative theory of core procedures (and hence bugs) that models learning over the whole curriculum.

This, then, is the interpretation under which the induction hypothesis seems true. Induction is more accurate than learning-by-being-told as a whole-curriculum, generative theory of bugs. This claim creates an interesting tension. How can induction be such a good model when the curriculum is viewed as a whole, and such a mediocre model when instruction is viewed on a second-by-second level? The research required to resolve the tension is just beginning. Some speculative explanations are offered in the last section of the chapter.

The body of the chapter is devoted to explicating and supporting the induction hypothesis. Three hypotheses will be defined and contrasted: the induction hypothesis, learning-by-being-told, and a third hypothesis—learning from analogies to familiar procedures. The familiar procedures used in arithmetic classrooms are usually ones for manipulating concrete numerals (e.g., coins, Dienes blocks, poker chips, Montessori rods, etc.). Analogy is included as a third hypothesis even though it is not particularly plausible as a stand-alone learning process. Much goes on in the classroom that does not involve drawing analogies to familiar procedures. However, it is plausible that analogy might go on in combination with induction or learning-by-being-told. That is, we might find that some bugs can be explained by analogy, and the rest can be explained by either induction or learning-by-being-told. Analogy may be of special interest in the context of this book, for it seems to engender (more so than either induction or learning-by-being-told) conceptual knowledge of arithmetic, as opposed to procedural knowledge.

At any rate, the first task is to clarify these three hypotheses. In the process, the role of the conceptual/procedural distinction, as it applies in this context, will also become clear. To this end, it is helpful to begin by making an assumption about the kind of knowledge that students acquire from the arithmetic curriculum.

SCHEMATIC vs. TELEOLOGICAL KNOWLEDGE

The assumption is that student's knowledge about procedures is schematic but not teleological. To define these terms, *schematic* and *teleological,* it is helpful to relate them to more familiar terms. (Fig. 6.1 is a road map of the terms to be discussed.) Computer programmers generally describe a procedure in three ways (N.B., the term "procedure" is being used temporarily to mean some very abstract, neutral idea about systematic actions):

- *Program:* A program is a schematic description of actions. It is schematic, because one must say what its inputs are before one can tell exactly what actions it will perform. That is, a program must be instantiated, by giving it inputs, before it becomes a complete description of a chronological sequence of actions.

- *Action sequences:* Executing a program produces an action sequence. In principle, one could describe a procedure as a set of action sequences. This is analogous to specifying a mathematical function as a set of tuples (e.g., n! as $\{< 0,1 >, < 1,1 >, < 2,2 >, < 3,6 >, < 4,24 >, \ldots\}$).

- *Specifications:* Specifications say what a program ought to do. Often they are informally presented in documents that circulate among the programmers and market researchers on a product development team. Sometimes specifications are written in a formal language so that one can prove that a program meets them.

There are names for the processes of transforming information about the procedure from one level to another. *Programming* is the transformation of a specification into a program. *Execution, interpretation* and *running* are names for the transformation of a program into an action sequence. There are also names for static, structural representations of these transformations. A *trace* is a structural representation of the relationship between a program and a particular execution of it. A *procedural net* (Sacerdoti, 1977), a *derivation* (Carbonell, 1983) and a *planning net* (VanLehn & Brown, 1980) are all formal representations of the relationship between a specification and a program. Actually, these three terms are just a few of the formalisms being used in an ongoing area of investigation. Rich (1981) has concentrated almost exclusively on developing a formalism describing the relationship between a specification and a program. In his representation system, both the specification and the program are *plans*—the surface plan (program) is just a structural refinement of the other. Rather than seeming to commit to one or another of these various formalisms, the neutral term *teleology* will be used. Thus, the teleology of a certain program is information relating the program and its parts to their intended purposes (i.e., to the specification).

Because teleology may be an unfamiliar term, it is worth a moment to sketch its meaning. The teleology of a procedure relates the schematic structure (pro-

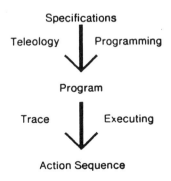

FIG. 6.1. Three levels of description for a ''procedure.'' Names for the processes of converting from higher levels to lower levels are on the right. Names for conversion structures are on the left.

gram) of the procedure to its goals and other design considerations. The teleology might include, for instance, a goal-subgoal hierarchy. It might indicate which goals serve multiple purposes, and what those purposes are. It might indicate which goals are crucially ordered, and which goals can be executed in parallel. If the program has iterations or recursions, it indicates the relationship between the goals of the iteration body (or recursion step) and the goal of the iteration (recursion) as a whole. In general, the procedure's teleology explicates the *design* behind the procedure.

A procedure for making gravy serves well as an illustration of the difference between teleological and schematic knowledge. A novice cook often has the only schematic knowledge (a program) for the gravy recipe—which ingredients to add in which order. The expert cook will realize that the order is crucial in some cases, but arbitrary in others. The expert also knows the purposes of various parts of the recipe. For instance, the expert understands a certain sequence of steps as making a flour-based thickener. Knowing the goal, the expert can substitute a cornstarch-based thickener for the flour-based one. More generally, knowing the teleology of a procedure allows its user to adapt the procedure to special circumstances (e.g., running out of flour). It also allows the user to debug the procedure. For instance, if the gravy comes out lumpy, the expert cook can infer that something went wrong with the thickener. Knowing which steps of the recipe make the thickener, the cook can discover that the bug is that the flour-fat mixture (the roux) wasn't cooked long enough. The purpose of cooking the roux is to emulsify the flour. Because the sauce was lumpy, this purpose wasn't achieved. By knowing the purposes of the parts of the procedure, people are able to debug, extend, optimize, and adapt their procedures. These added capabilities, beyond merely following (executing) a procedure, can be used to test for a teleological understanding.

It is an empirical question whether the students' knowledge level corresponds to the schematic level (i.e., a program for the procedure) or the teleological level. The assumption made here is that their knowledge is schematic. This is a rather uncontroversial assumption. In fact, much research in arithmetic begins with the assumption that current instruction gives students only a schematic (or procedural) knowledge of arithmetic, then seeks some new instructional methods that will give them a teleological (conceptual) knowledge of the skill. Although the assumption of schematic knowledge is uncontroversial, it might be worth discussing it a little further in order to illustrate how one might detect teleological knowledge if one succeeded in teaching it.

One hallmark of expert cooks, and others who have a teleological knowledge of procedures, is their ability to debug and extend the procedures when necessary. Gelman and her colleagues (Gelman & Gallistel, 1978; Greeno, Riley, & Gelman, 1984) used tests based on debugging and extending procedures in order to determine whether children possess the teleology for counting. Adapting their techniques, I tested five adults for possession of teleology for addition and subtraction. All subjects were competent at arithmetic. None were computer programmers. The subjects were given nine tasks. Each task added some extra constraint to the ordinary procedure, thereby forcing the subject to redesign part of the procedure in order to bring it back into conformance with its goals. A simple task, for example, was adding left to right. A more complex task was inventing the equal additions method of borrowing (i.e., the borrow of 53 − 26 is performed by adding one to the 2 rather than decrementing the 5).

The results were equivocal. One subject was unable to do any of the tasks. The rest were able to do some but not all of the tasks. The experiment served only to eliminate the extremes: Adults don't seem to possess a complete, easily used teleology, but neither are they totally incapable of constructing it (or perhaps recalling it). Further experiments of this kind may provide more definitive results. In particular, it would be interesting to find out if adults were constructing the teleology of the procedure, or whether they already knew it. At any rate, it's clear that not all adults possess operative teleology for their arithmetic procedures, and moreover, some adults seem to possess only schematic knowledge of arithmetic.

Adults found the teleology test so difficult that I was unwilling to subject young children to it. However, there is some indirect evidence that students acquire very little teleology. It concerns the way students react to impasses. Consider the decrement-zero impasse discussed earlier. The hypothetical student hasn't yet learned how to borrow from zero although borrowing from non-zero numbers is quite familiar. Given the problem

$$\begin{array}{r} 604 \\ -217 \\ \hline \end{array}$$

the student starts to borrow, attempts to decrement the zero, and reaches an impasse. If the student understands the teleology of borrowing, then the student understands that borrowing from the hundreds would be an appropriate way to fix the impasse. That is, the teleology of non-zero borrowing allows it to be easily extended to cover borrowing from zero. Although some students may react to the decrement-zero impasse this way, many do not. They repair instead. Because students do not make teleologically appropriate responses to impasses, it appears that they did not acquire much teleology (or if they did, they are unwilling to use it—in which case it's a moot point whether they have it or not).

THREE WAYS THAT ARITHMETIC COULD BE LEARNED

Given the assumption that students' knowledge of arithmetic procedures is schematic, we can more accurately address the issue of how they acquire that knowledge. The tripartite distinction between specifications, programs, and actions sequences will be used again. If the goal is to construct a description of the procedure at a schematic (program) level, there are four possible routes (see Fig. 6.2):

1. From specification to program: A kind of learning by discovery.
2. From examples (action sequences) to programs: induction.
3. From some other schematic description, either
   a. another familiar program: learning by analogy, or
   b. a natural language presentation of the program: learning-by-being-told.

The first possibility is not particularly plausible in the domain of arithmetic. The teleology of arithmetic is very complex, and the curriculum would have to modified radically in order to teach it. VanLehn and Brown (1980) present a complete teleology for addition, and discuss how it could be taught. This form of learning will not be considered further here. However, the remaining three forms of learning—induction, analogy, and learning-by-being-told—are exactly the three hypotheses to be discussed.

The best way to compare these three hypotheses would be to develop three complete generative theories, one for each hypothesis, then see which theory is better according to the usual scientific criteria. In fact, only the induction hypothesis has such a theory behind it (VanLehn, 1983). The theory is quite rigorously formulated. There are 31 main hypotheses. The induction hypothesis is one of them. The other 30 hypotheses concern the form of the knowledge representation, the mechanisms for impasses and repairs, and the details of the inductive learning process. From the standpoint of supporting the induction hypothesis, this degree of rigor presents some problems. First, the empirical adequacy of the theory depends on all the hypotheses and not just the induction hypothesis. Thus, if the theory fails to generate a certain bug, this does not necessarily mean that the bug can not be acquired by induction. It could be that some other hypotheses in the theory are wrong, and they should shoulder the blame for the theory's

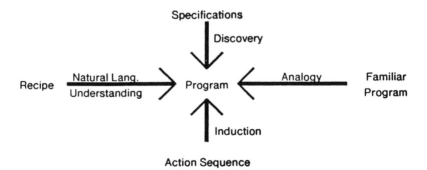

FIG. 6.2.   Ways to acquire a program level of description.

inability to predict the bug. This problem of assigning blame to hypotheses can be solved, but it takes a very careful analysis of the relationships among the hypotheses and the data. That analysis has been undertaken, but it is too lengthy to present here (see (VanLehn, 1983)). Instead, two informal analyses of the the theory's empirical adequacy will be presented.

The first analysis will be a conservative evaluation of the induction hypothesis. It will present exactly the bugs the theory can generate in the task domain of subtraction. It will turn out that the theory can generate 33% of the observed bugs. This conservative evaluation confounds the effects of the induction hypothesis with the other 30 hypotheses. In order to pick their effects apart somewhat, the derivations of a few of the bugs will be presented. The relationship of the induction hypothesis to these bugs is typical of its relationship to other, similar bugs.

The second analysis will be a liberal estimate of the generative power of the induction hypothesis. It is meant to indicate how many bugs the induction hypothesis could generate if the other hypotheses in the theory were relaxed or discarded. Essentially, it is an estimate of the generative power of the best possible inductive learning theory. It will be shown that 85% of the observed bugs can be generated.

Following these two analyses, there will be a discussion of the two competing hypotheses, learning by analogy and learning-by-being-told. Because no generative theories have been developed for these hypotheses, their empirical predictions will be derived informally. It will be shown that they are not as productive as the induction hypothesis.

THE CONSERVATIVE EVALUATION OF THE INDUCTION HYPOTHESIS

First, some background. The bug data to be presented were collected from 1147 subtraction students in grades 2 through 5. The collection and analyses of these data are detailed in VanLehn (1982). The learning model used to generate the theory's predictions is the one documented in VanLehn (1983). The model has changed since then, and its predictions have improved. However, the figures from that publication are used because it presents a detailed account of how they were generated.

The overall adequacy of the theory is displayed in Fig. 6.3. There are 76 observed bugs. The theory generates 49 bugs, 25 of which are observed. These 25 bugs are confirmed predictions. Seventeen of the predicted bugs are plausible, but have not yet been observed. Perhaps if another thousand students were examined, some of these would be found. However, 7 of the predicted bugs are so strange that it is extremely doubtful that they would ever be observed. These bugs should not be generated by the theory. Of the observed bugs, 51 are not generated by the theory. This is not as damning an inditement of the theory as the 7 implausible bugs. It could be that other bug-generating processes are at work, and they are responsible for some of the 51 bugs. When those processes are discovered, they can be added to the theory, converting some of the 51 bugs to confirmed predictions. However, the generation of the 7 implausible bugs can't be fixed by adding another bug-generating process to the theory. They indicate problems with the present theory that need rectification.

In developing the theory, it was often the case that one could increase the number of confirmed predictions but only at the expense of increasing the number of implausible predictions. In the case of this theory, such choices were always made in favor of reducing the number of implausible predictions. If these choices had been made the other way, then many of the 51 unaccounted for bugs would be accounted for. The liberal evaluation, which will be presented in the next section, indicates roughly how many of the 51 bugs could be converted to confirmed predictions if the theory were liberalized.

The numbers presented above are difficult to understand without some point of reference. Two such points are provided by earlier generative theories of subtraction bugs. An early version of repair theory is documented in Brown and VanLehn (1980). Its empirical adequacy can be compared with the present theory's. Clearly, this theory will do better since it includes the ideas of its predecessor. Another generative theory of subtraction bugs was developed by Richard Young and Tim O'Shea (1981). They constructed a production system for subtraction such that deleting certain of its rules (or adding other rules, in some cases) would generate observed bugs. They showed that these mutations of the production system could generate many of the bugs described in the original Buggy report (Brown & Burton, 1978).

A chart comparing the results of the three theories is presented as Table 6.1. Observed bugs that no theory generates are not listed, nor are bugs that have not

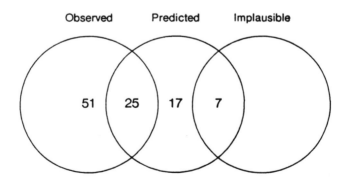

FIG. 6.3. A Venn Diagram showing relationships and size of the sets of observed and predicted bugs.

TABLE 6.1
Comparison of Observed Bugs Generated by Three Theories:
Y&O = Young and O'Shea; B&V = Brown & VanLehn;
Cur. = current theory

Y&O	B&V	Cur.	Occurs	Bug
		√	6	Always-Borrow-Left
		√	1	Blank-Instead-of-Borrow
		√	7	Borrow-Across-Second-Zero
√	√	√	41	Borrow-Across-Zero
		√	4	Borrow-Don't-Decrement-Unless-Bottom-Smaller
		√	2	Borrow-From-One-Is-Nine
		√	1	Borrow-From-One-Is-Ten
√	√	√	14	Borrow-From-Zero
√			1	Borrow-From-All-Zero
	√	√	2	Borrow-From-Zero-Is-Ten
	√	√	18	Borrow-No-Decrement
		√	6	Borrow-No-Decrement-Except-Last
		√	1	Borrow-Treat-One-As-Zero
	√		1	Can't-Subtract
		√	1	Doesn't-Borrow-Except-Last
√			15	Diff-0$-$N=0
√			43	Diff-0$-$N=N
√			1	Diff-N$-$N=N
√			6	Diff-N$-$0=0
		√	7	Don't-Decrement-Zero
		√	4	Forget-Borrow-Over-Blanks
		√	2	N$-$N-Causes-Borrow
		√	1	Only-Do-Units
	√	√	5	Quit-When-Bottom-Blank
	√		4	Stutter-Subtract
√	√	√	115	Smaller-From-Larger
		√	3	Smaller-From-Larger-Except-Last
	√	√	5	Smaller-From-Larger-Instead-of-Borrow-From-Zero
		√	7	Smaller-From-Larger-Instead-of-Borrow-Unless-Bottom-Smaller
		√	3	Stops-Borrow-At-Multiple-Zero
√	√	√	64	Stops-Borrow-At-Zero
	√	√	1	Top-Instead-of-Borrow-From-Zero
√	√		5	Zero-Instead-of-Borrow
10	12	25		totals

been observed. Brown and VanLehn (1980) count bugs differently than they are counted here. (See VanLehn 1983, pg. 68, for details). The chart shows that the present theory generates more bugs, which is not surprising since it embeds many of the earlier theories' ideas. What is perhaps a little surprising is that there are a few bugs that they generate and it does not. These bugs deserve a closer look.

Young and O'Shea's model generates a class of bugs that they call *pattern errors*. Four bugs were included in this class:

Diff-0 − N = N If the top of a column is 0, write the bottom as the answer.

Diff-0 − N = 0 If the top of a column is 0, write zero as the answer.

Diff-N − 0 = 0 If the bottom of a column is 0, write the zero as the answer.

Diff-N − N = N If the top and bottom are equal, write one of them as the answer.

Young and O'Shea derive all four bugs the same way. Each bug is represented by a production rule, and the rule is simply added to the production system that models the student's behavior. Phrased differently, they derive the bugs formally by stipulating them, then explain the stipulation informally. Their explanations are:

> From his earlier work on addition, the child may well have learned two rules sensitive to zero, NZN and ZNN [two rules that mean N + 0 = N and 0 + N = N]. Included in a production system for subtraction, the first, NZN, will do no harm, but rule ZNN will give rise to errors of the "0 − N = N" type. Similar rules would account for the other zero-pattern errors. If the child remembers from addition just that zero is a special case, and that if a zero is present then one copies down as the answer one of the numbers given, then he may well have rules such as NZZ or ZNZ [the rules for the bugs Diff-N − 0 = 0 and Diff-0 − N = 0]. . . . .Rule NNN [the rule for the bug Diff-N − N = N] covers the cases where a child asked for the difference between a digit and itself writes down that same digit. It is clearly another instance of a "pattern" rule. (Young & O'Shea, 1981, pg. 163).

The informal explanations, especially the one for Diff-0 − N = N, are plausible. (Note, by the way, that some of these explanations crucially involve induction.) To treat them fully, one would have to explain why *only* the zero rules are transferred from additions, and not the other addition rules.

The point is that one can have as much empirical adequacy as one wishes if the theory is not required to explain its stipulations in a rigorous, formal manner. The present theory could generate the same pattern bugs as Young and O'Shea's model simply by making the appropriate modifications to the core procedures and reiterating their informal derivation (or tell any other story that seems right intuitively). This would not be an explanation of the bugs, but only a restatement of the data embroidered by interesting speculation. This approach does not yield a theory with explanatory value. In short, there is a tradeoff between empirical adequacy and explanatory adequacy. If the model does not itself construct the appropriate knowledge representations, then it is the theorist and not the theory that is doing the explaining. The theory per se has little explanatory value, even though it might cover the data quite well. The present theory aims first for explanatory adequacy, even if that means sacrificing empirical adequacy.

With the foregoing background information in hand, we can return to discussing the induction hypothesis. Induction is generalization from examples. Almost always, there are many possible concepts consistent with a given set of examples. Some will be more general than the target concept, and some will be more specific. If the learner is not somehow given extra information about which of the consistent concepts is the target concept, then there is a strong chance that the learner will guess wrong, and pick either an overgeneralized or overspecialized concept instead. If human students are learning inductively, then there should be many bugs that are the result of overgeneralization or overspecialization.

In order to demonstrate the influence of the induction hypothesis, the bugs generated by the theory will be divided into several groups, and characteristic bugs from each group will be discussed.

The first group consists of bugs generated by overgeneralization of the conditions that determine whether or not to perform a subprocedure. A prototypical case is the bug N-N-Causes-Borrow, which was mentioned earlier. The proper test for when to borrow is $T < B$, where T is the top digit of a column and B is the bottom digit. The bug borrows when $T \leq B$. This makes sense given the induction hypothesis. The student sees many columns, some with $T > B$ and some with $T < B$. The student induces that the $T < B$ columns trigger borrowing, and the $T > B$ columns don't. However, the student must see a $T = B$ column in order to induce that $T = B$ columns don't trigger borrowing. Such problem types are rare in the textbooks used by the students in our subtraction study, and they never occupy a lesson of their own. Nowhere in the teacher's guides are $T = B$ columns pointed out as deserving special mention. So it is plausible to assume that sudents never notice that $T = B$ columns do not require borrowing. Unless a $T = B$ column is examined, the student doesn't know whether the borrowing predicate is $T \leq B$ or $T < B$. The students who guess $T \leq B$ show up in the data as having the bug $N - N$-Causes-Borrow, and the students who guess $T < B$ will show up as having the correct test for borrowing. Both kinds of performance have been observed.

A similar explanation works for the bug Borrow-Treat-One-As-Zero. The proper test for when to borrow across zero is $T = 0$ (see problem A, below). However, students with this bug will perform the subprocedure when $T = 1$ or $T = 0$ (see problem b).

$$a. \quad \begin{array}{r} {\scriptstyle 2\,9} \\ \cancel{3\cancel{0}}{}^{1}5 \\ -10\ 9 \\ \hline 19\ 6 \end{array} \qquad b. \quad \begin{array}{r} {\scriptstyle 2\,9} \\ \cancel{3}\cancel{1}{}^{1}5 \\ -10\ 9 \\ \hline 19\ 6 \end{array}$$

Perhaps the student thinks that 1 and 0 are special numbers (which they are, for they are the identity elements of the field), and that "*T* is a Special Number" is the appropriate test condition for when to perform the borrow-from-zero subprocedure. The bug can be explained by the induction hypothesis and the fact that problems like *b* are rare among the textbooks' examples. Two other bugs in this class of overgeneralized test condition bugs are Borrow-From-One-Is-Nine and Borrow-From-One-Is-Ten.

The preceding group of bugs illustrated that the test conditions can be overgeneralized. One would also expect overspecialization, if the induction hypothesis is correct. The next group of bugs result from overspecialization of test conditions. (These bugs were not generated by the version of the theory discussed earlier, and do not appear in Table 6.1. They are generated by the learning model in its present form.) The following is a classic case of a bug generated by overspecialization of a test condition. In the textbooks in our study, borrowing is introduced in two-column problems. This means that the borrow originates in the units column. Some students who are tested at this point in the curriculum believe that borrowing can only be triggered in the units column (see problem *a*, below). This is inductively correct, because they have not yet seen examples that contradict their overspecialized idea about when to borrow.

$$a. \quad \begin{array}{r} {\scriptstyle 5} \\ 65\cancel{6}{}^{1}5 \\ -191\ 9 \\ \hline 544\ 6 \end{array} \qquad b. \quad \begin{array}{r} {\scriptstyle 5\ \ 2} \\ \cancel{6}{}^{1}5\cancel{3}{}^{1}5 \\ -1\ 98\ 9 \\ \hline 4\ 66\ 6 \end{array} \qquad c. \quad \begin{array}{r} {\scriptstyle 6\!1\,5} \\ \cancel{7}\ \cancel{6}{}^{1}5 \\ -1\ 9\ 8 \\ \hline 5\ 6\ 7 \end{array} \qquad d. \quad \begin{array}{r} {\scriptstyle 2} \\ 5\cancel{3}{}^{1}5 \\ -11\ 9 \\ \hline 41\ 6 \end{array}$$

A similar story explains the bug shown in problem *b*. This bug, Smaller-From-Larger-When-Borrowed-From, borrows in any $T < B$ column, except those where the top digit in the column has been scratched out already, as in the tens column of problem *b*. The textbooks delay teaching about adjacent borrowing (e.g., problem *c*) until well after isolated borrowing has been taught (e.g., problem *d*). Consequently, a student who is tested between these two lessons cannot yet have seen a $T < B$ column with the top digit scratched out, and therefore cannot know whether to borrow or not. In short, for both these bugs, the students have an overspecialized concept of when to borrow because certain examples haven't yet been presented to them. Two other bugs, $X - N = 0$-After-Borrow and $X - N = N$-After-Borrow, have nearly identical derivations.

Another four bugs are generated by overspecialized tests of when to perform borrowing across zero. They are: Borrow-Across-Zero-Over-Zero, Borrow-Across-Zero-Over-Blank, Don't-Decrement-Zero-Over-Zero, and Don't-Decrement-Zero-Over-Blank.

So far, the bugs discussed have concerned *when* to borrow. The next group of bugs concerns a different kind of procedural knowledge, *how* to borrow. Students with the bug Always-Borrow-Left borrow from the leftmost column in the problem no matter which column triggers the borrowing. Problem *a* below shows the correct placement of borrow's decrement. Problem *b* shows the bug's placement.

$$
a. \quad \begin{array}{r} \overset{5}{3\overset{1}{6}5} \\ -10\ 9 \\ \hline 25\ 6 \end{array} \qquad b. \quad \begin{array}{r} \overset{2}{3}6^{1}5 \\ -10\ 9 \\ \hline 16\ 6 \end{array} \qquad c. \quad \begin{array}{r} \overset{5}{6}^{1}5 \\ -1\ 9 \\ \hline 4\ 6 \end{array}
$$

The explanation begins with the fact that borrowing is introduced using only two-column problems, such as problem *c* above. Multi-column problems, such as *a*, are not used. Consequently, the student has insufficient information to unambiguously induce where to place borrow's decrement. The correct placement is in the left-adjacent column, as in *a*. However, two-column examples are also consistent with decrementing the leftmost column, as in *b*. Once again, the induction hypothesis provides the key for explaining how a bug is acquired. Other bugs in this group are Forget-Borrow-Over-Blanks, Only-Do-Units, Borrow-Don't-Decrement-Unless-Bottom-Smaller, Smaller-From-Larger-Unless-Bottom-Smaller. Doesn't-Borrow-Except-Last, and Smaller-From-Larger-Except-Last.

The other bugs generated by the theory stem from core procedures that are incomplete, rather than misinduced. Examples of bugs in this group are Stops-Borrow-At-Zero and Borrow-Across-Zero, which were described in the introduction. The bugs in this group are consistent with the induction hypothesis. Indeed, the inductive learning model constructs their core procedures from the initial few lessons of the lesson sequence. However, these bugs also would be consistent with any form of learning that could derive a correct (albeit incomplete) procedure from an initial segment of the lesson sequence. So the bugs in this group confirm the induction hypothesis, but don't differentiate it from other hypotheses.

This completes the conservative analysis of the empirical adequacy of the induction hypothesis. It was shown that overgeneralization and overspecialization could account for many bugs. On a deeper level, there are three ultimate causes for the bugs. (1) Many bugs are generated by testing subskills that haven't been taught yet. Stops-Borrow-At Zero is a good illustration of this. (2) Certain critical examples are missing from the curriculum or under-emphasized. The bug N -- N-Causes-Borrow is a clear case of this. If the critical examples were added to the curriculum and emphasized, such bugs might not occur. (3) Certain examples that should be grouped into the same lesson are separated into two lessons, and a diagnostic test is administered in between them. The bug Always-Borrow-Left is a good illustration of this. If the two lessons were merged or placed close together, this bug may not occur. In short, all three causes for bugs can be cured by modifying the curriculum and the testing policies—or so it seems. These are suspiciously crisp predictions. I suspect that there will be some surprises if one tries to eliminate bugs by changing instruction in the indicated ways.

A LIBERAL EVALUATION OF THE INDUCTION
HYPOTHESIS

As mentioned earlier, the theory generates only 33% of the observed subtraction bugs. It does not, for instance, generate the bug Diff-0 − N = N. This bug could be explained as an overgeneralization of the correct subtraction rule that N − 0 = N. The current theory could in fact generate the bug by overgeneralization, but only if the rule N − 0 = N is taught in a separate lesson, which it is not in the textbook series used by the subjects. Similarly, other bugs could be induced if the theory were tested less rigorously than it was, or if the various ancillary hypotheses of the theory were relaxed. This section estimates the best possible empirical adequacy that a theory based on induction could have. It will be, of course, be a rough estimate.

The estimate is based on the following, admittedly weak, line of reasoning. (The weakness of this kind of reasoning, by the way, is exactly why one must build theories.) If a bug is induced from examples, then there ought to be some way to describe it in terms of the visual and numerical features that examples have. For instance, the bug Diff-0 − N = N can be described by a rule "If T = 0, then write B in the answer," where T and B are the top and bottom digits in a column. The feature T = 0 is a visual-numerical feature. On the other hand, if a bug is not acquired by induction, then it might be difficult to describe it with simple rules composed of visual-numerical features. For instance, the bug Borrow-Unit-Difference seems to be acquired noninductively. In a correct borrow, the student adds ten to T and decrements the next digit over by one. Borrow-Unit-Difference calculates how much needs to be added to T in order to make T equal B, then it decrements the next digit over by that amount:

$$
\begin{array}{r}
4\,9 \\
8\,\cancel{5} \\
-1\,9 \\
\hline
2\,1
\end{array}
$$

Teachers who use coins, Dienes blocks, or other concrete numerals to teach subtraction will recognize this bug almost immediately. In a monetary representation, the problem above is "You have 8 dimes and 5 pennies. What do you have left if you give me one dime and 9 pennies?" There is a bank, consisting of piles of dimes and pennies, that the student may use to make change. Many students, seeing that they need to hand out 9 pennies, will take exactly four pennies from the bank. That's all they need to make 9. However, they know that they must make change fairly, so they hand in four dimes. They have got almost everything right and they are doing a fine job of means-ends analysis problem solving, except that they have one constraint wrong: They think that dimes and pennies are worth the same amount in this context. So their concrete procedure has a small bug in it. To put it differently, when Borrow-Unit-Difference is represented as problem-solving with concrete numerals, it has a succinct, accurate representation as the substitution of an incorrect constraint for the correct one. However, there is no such succinct representation when the bug is represented as a procedure for manipulating written numerals. In particular, it can not easily be represented as a condition-action rule using simple visual-numerical features.

When a bug is learned by processes other than induction, such as the analogy process that evidently underlies this bug's acquisition, it will be difficult to represent as condition-action rules over a vocabulary of simple visual-numerical features. Consequently, the ease of description of a bug in these terms can be used as a weak test for whether it can be generated by an inductive theory.

At the end of this chapter all 78 currently observed subtraction bugs are listed. (Two bugs have been discovered since the empirical results of Fig. 6.3 were calculated.) The list demonstrates that 66 of these (i.e., 85%) can be easily represented as condition-action perturbations to a correct procedure. The set of visual-numerical features used in these perturbations are listed in Table 6.2.

Of the observed subtraction bugs, 12 could not be represented in a simple way with visual-numerical features. These bugs are potentially disconfirming to the induction hypothesis. Let's examine them. Of the 12 bugs, 5 have relatively simple explanations. One of them, Borrow-Unit-Difference, has been discussed already. It seems to have been acquired by analogy from concrete manipulative procedures. One bug, Add-Instead-Of-Sub, seems to result from confusing addition with subtraction. Simple-Problem-Stutter-Subtract seems to be a confusion between multiplication and subtraction. When the bottom row of the subtraction problem has a single digit in it, the student uses a pattern of calculation similar to multiplication: the single digit is subtracted from each digit in the top row. Stutter-Subtract is generated by the theory from an incomplete procedure, one that doesn't know how to handle columns with a blank in the bottom. Don't-Write-Zero seems to be due to overgeneralization of a special kind. Somewhere in the curriculum (there is no lesson for it), teachers instruct students to omit writing a zero if the zero will be the leftmost digit in the answer. That is, younger students answer as in a, below, and older students answer as in b:

$$
a. \quad
\begin{array}{r}
\overset{2}{\cancel{3}}^{1}5 \\
-2\ 9 \\
\hline
0\ 6
\end{array}
\qquad
b. \quad
\begin{array}{r}
\overset{2}{\cancel{3}}^{1}5 \\
-2\ 9 \\
\hline
6
\end{array}
\qquad
c. \quad
\begin{array}{r}
339 \\
-237 \\
\hline
1\ 2
\end{array}
$$

Apparently, the bug Don't-Write-Zero, whose work is shown in c, is an overgeneralization of the prohibition against writing leading zeros. So this bug actu-

TABLE 6.2
The Visual-Numerical Features

B=#	The bottom digit in the column is blank.
B=0	The bottom digit in the column is zero.
BORROWED	A borrow has taken place already.
DECR'ED	The top digit in the column has been decremented.
DECR'ED/BOT	The bottom digit in the column has been decremented.
IN/LAST/COLUMN	The current column is the leftmost one.
IN/NEXT/TO/LAST/COLUMN	The current column is the penultimate one.
NEXT/B=#	The bottom digit in the next column to the left is blank.
NEXT/T=0	The top digit in the next column left is zero.
NEXT/T=00	The top two digits in the next two columns to the left are zero.
NEXT/T=1	The top digit in the next column left is one.
T≤B	The top digit is less than or equal to the bottom digit.
T<B	The top digit is strictly less than the bottom digit.
T>B	The top digit is strictly greater than the bottom digit.
T=B	The top digit is equal to the bottom digit.
T=B/ORGINALLY	T=B in the original column, before decrementing occurred.
T−#	The top digit in the column is blank.
T=0	The top digit in the column is zero.
T=00	The top digit in the column and the next one to its left are zero.
T=1	The top digit in the column is one.
T=1V0	The top digit is a one or a zero.
T=9	The top digit is nine.

ally supports the induction hypothesis, even though it can't be simply expressed in the given feature vocabulary.

Of the 12 bugs, the remaining 7 baffle me. If the reader has explanations for any of the these bugs, I would appreciate hearing about them.

At any rate, if appears that, whatever the noninductive learning processes are, they generate only a few bugs each. Induction, on the other hand, seems able to handle, in principle, 85% of the bugs. This 85% includes all the most commonly occurring bugs, as the appendix documents.

This completes the informal, liberal analysis of the empirical adequacy of the induction hypothesis. Perhaps the evidential relationships are a little weak, but the data side strongly with the induction hypothesis. The remaining two sections discuss the competing hypotheses, learning by analogy and learning by being told.

LEARNING BY ANALOGY

Learning by analogy is the mapping of knowledge from one domain over to the target domain, where it is applied to solve problems. Analogies are used in the early grades to teach base-10 numeration. Students are drilled on the mapping between written numerals and various concrete representations of numbers, such as collections of coins, Diennes blocks, Montessori rods, and so forth. This is a mapping between two kinds of numerals, and not two procedures. Later, this internumeral mapping is drawn on in teaching carrying and borrowing. For example, a known procedure for making change—trading a dime for ten pennies—is mapped into the borrowing procedure of written subtraction. Many textbooks and teachers' manuals advocate this method of teaching by analogy. Although it is not clear how much this technique is actually used in the classroom, it warrants our attention as one possible hypothesis about how students learn procedures. Indeed, one piece of evidence for the analogy hypothesis, the bug Borrow-Unit-Difference, has been discussed already. However, it is only one bug, and only one subject in our 1147-student sample had it.

Presumably, once an analogy has transferred some knowledge, it is still available for use later to transfer more knowledge about the procedure. In some cases, this predicts significant student competence. For instance, if the students learned simple borrowing via the analogy, then it's quite plausible that when confronted with more complex borrowing problems, such as

$$\begin{array}{r} 607 \\ -238 \\ \hline \end{array}$$

(assuming the student hasn't yet been taught how to solve such borrow across zero problems), the student could solve the problem in the concrete domain by trading a dollar for nine dimes and ten pennies, then map back into the written domain, thus producing the correct solution. Indeed, the analogies used in instruction may have been designed so that these productive extensions of the base analogy are encouraged.

But this is a much more productive understanding of borrowing than most students achieve. As discussed earlier, when most students discover that it is impossible to decrement the zero, they repair. These students do not use analogies to familiar procedures (e.g., making change). If the students had learned their procedures via analogy, one would have to make ad hoc stipulations to explain why they no longer use that analogy after they have learned the procedure. It's more plausible that they simply didn't utilize the analogy in the first place. Loosely speaking, learning by analogy is too good. It predicts that students would fix impasses by constructing a correct extension to their current procedure. That is, they would *debug* instead of repair. Because many students have repair-generated bugs, another explanation would be needed for how these students acquired their procedures. At the very least, analogy cannot be the only kind of learning going on, if it happens much at all.

Carbonell (1983) makes a telling argument about analogies between procedures. His ARIES program was unable to form analogies between certain procedures when all it had was the program (schematic) representations. However, Carbonell found that analogies could be forged when the procedures were described teleologically (i.e., in Carbonell's terminology, the analogy is between *derivations* of procedures). Suppose one stretches Carbonell's results a little and claims that knowing the teleology (derivation) of procedures is *necessary* for procedural analogy. (Carbonnell claims only sufficiency, if that.) Because most math students are ignorant of the teleology of their procedures, as discussed earlier, one can conclude that students did not acquire their procedures via analogy.

How is it that teachers can present material that is specifically designed to encourage learning procedures by analogy, and yet their students show few signs of doing so? Winston's research (Winston, 1979) yields a speculative answer. It indicates that the most computationally expensive part of analogy can be discovering how best to match the parts of the two sides of the analogy. To solve electrical problems given hydraulic knowledge, one must match voltage, electrical current, and resistance to one each of water pressure, current, and pipe size. There are six possible matchings, and only one matching is correct. The number of possible matchings rises exponentially with the number of parts. For a similar analogy, a best match must be selected from 11! or 40-million possible matches. The matching problem of analogy is a version of a NP-complete problem: finding the maximal common subgraph of two digraphs (Hayes-Roth & McDermott, 1978). Hence, it is doubtful that a faster solution than an exponential one exists. Even if the matching algorithm were implemented on a connection machine (i.e., a computer that is like a neural net in that it uses millions of small processors arranged in a network instead of a single powerful processor, as conventional computers use), it seems that the combinatorics would not decrease radically (D. Christman, personal communication).

If computational complexity can be equated with cognitive difficulty, Winston's work predicts that students may find it difficult to draw an analogy unless either it is a very simple one (i.e., few parts) or they are given some help in finding the matching. Resnick (1982) has produced some experimental evidence supporting this prediction. Resnick interviewed students who were taught addition and subtraction in school, using the usual analogies between concrete and written numerals. She discovered that some students had mastered both the numeral analogy and the arithmetic procedures in the concrete domain, and yet they could not make a connection between the concrete procedures and the written ones. Resnick went on to demonstrate that students could easily make the mapping between the two procedures provided that the steps of the two procedures were explicitly paired. The students were walked through the concrete procedure in parallel with the written one. A step in one was immediately followed by the corresponding step in the other.[1] If we assume the conjecture from above, that combinatorial explosions in mapping equates with difficulty for humans making analogies, and we assume that "parts" of procedures roughly

---

[1]Although Resnick's technique makes learning by analogy easier, it does not guarantee that such learning will occur. In recent work, Resnick found that the instruction was effective only half the time (Resnick & Omanson, in press).

correspond to steps, then Resnick's finding makes perfect sense. The procedures are currently presented in school in a nonparallel mode. This forces students to solve the matching problem, and most seem unable to do so. Consequently, the analogy does little good. Only when the instruction helps the students make the matching, as it did in Resnick's experiment, does the analogy actually succeed in transferring knowledge about one procedure to the other. In short, analogy could become a major learning technique, but current instructional practices must be changed to do so.

There is anecdotal evidence that analogy is common, but it is analogy of a very different kind. In tutoring, I have watched students flip through the textbook to locate a worked problem that is similar to the one they are currently trying to solve. They then draw a mapping of some kind between the worked problem and their problem that enables them to solve their problem. Anderson et al. report the same behavior for students solving geometry problems (Anderson, Greeno, Kline, Neves, 1981) and Lisp problems (Anderson, Farrell, & Saurers, 1984). Although the usage could be disputed, Anderson et al. use "analogy" to refer to this kind of example-exercise mapping. It differs significantly from the kind of analogy discussed earlier. The abstraction that is common to the two problem solutions is exactly the schematic knowledge (program) of the procedure. In the analogy between making change and borrowing, the common abstraction lay much deeper, somewhere in the teleology (conceptual basis) of the procedure. To state it differently, the example-exercise analogy maps two action sequences of a procedure together, thus illustrating the procedure's schematic structure (program). The other analogy maps two distinct procedures together in order to illustrate a common teleology.

The former mapping, between two instances of a schematic object, is nearly identical to induction. In both cases, the most specific common generalization of the two instances is calculated. Winston also points out the equivalence of generalization and analogy in such circumstances (Winston, 1979). Although I have not investigated example-exercise analogy in detail, I expect it to behave indistinguishably from learning by generalizing examples.

To summarize, one form of analogy (if it could be called that) is indistinguishable from induction. The other form of analogy seems necessarily to involve the teleology of procedures. Because students show little evidence of teleology, it is safe to assume that analogic learning is not common in classrooms, perhaps because current instructional practices aren't encouraging it in quite the right way.

LEARNING BY BEING TOLD

One framework for acquiring a procedure involves following a set of natural language instructions until the procedure is committed to memory. This framework for explaining learning is called *learning by being told* (Winston, 1978). It views the central problem of learning as one of natural language understanding. There are possible several sources for the natural language "recipes." One is the teacher, who explains the algorithm while presenting it. Another source is the textbook. Because students spend most of their time doing seatwork, when their major source of recipes is the textbook, let's begin by examining what the textbooks say. The key issue is whether the textbooks describe the procedure in enough detail. If they do, then all the students need to do is understand the language, and they will be able to perform the procedure.

Manuals of procedures are ubiquitous in adult life. Examples are cookbooks, user guides, repair shop manuals, and office procedure manuals. In using procedure manuals, adults sometimes learn the procedures described therein, and cease to use the manuals. So learning by being told is probably quite common among adults. The content of procedure manuals can be taken as a model for how good a natural language description has to be if it is to be effective in teaching the procedure.

Open any arithmetic text, and one immediately sees that it is not much like a cookbook or an auto repair manual. There is very little text; the books are mostly practice exercises and worked examples. The reason is obvious. Because students in the primary grades are just beginning to read, they could make little use of an elaborate written procedure.

Badre (1972) built an AI program that reads the prose and examples of a fourth grade arithmetic textbook in order to learn procedures for multicolumn addition and subtraction. Badre sought in vain for simple, concise statements of arithmetic procedures that he could use as input to his natural language understanding program. He comments:

> During the preliminary work of problem definition, we looked for a textbook that would explain arithmetic operations as a clearly stated set of rules. The extensive efforts in this search led to the following, somewhat surprising result: nowadays, young American grade-school children are never told how to perform addition or subtraction in a general way. They are supposed to infer the general algorithms from examples. Thus actual texts are usually composed of a series of short illustrated stories.' Each story describes an example of the execution of the addition or the subtraction algorithms. (Badre, 1972, pg. 1–2)

Despite the fact that Badre's program "reads" the textbook's "stories" in order to obtain a description of the examples, the role of reading in its learning is minimal. The heart of the program is generalization of examples. In particular, the program employs only a few heuristics that use the book's prose to disambiguate choices left open by generalization.

Although textbooks don't seem to have the right sort of language to make learning-by-being-told work, perhaps the teachers supply it. It is infeasible to find out everything that teachers say in classrooms over the years that arithmetic is taught. However, one way to test this hypothesis is to make a plausible assumption about what teachers might give as an explanation, and see whether that makes any useful predictions. Suppose that the teacher is describing borrowing for the first time. As mentioned earlier, borrowing is invariably introduced with two-column problems, such as problem *a*.

$$
a. \quad
\begin{array}{r}
\overset{5}{\cancel{6}}{}^{1}5 \\
-1\ 9 \\
\hline
4\ 6
\end{array}
\qquad
b. \quad
\begin{array}{r}
\overset{2}{3}\cancel{6}{}^{1}5 \\
-10\ 9 \\
\hline
46\ 6
\end{array}
$$

Under the induction hypothesis, this causes Always-Borrow-Left, as in *b*. Let's see what kind of prediction is produced by assuming that learning is dominated by natural language understanding.

In problems like *a*, "tens column" is probably the most common noun-phrase used to describe the place to decrement from. Under the natural language hypothesis, "tens column" would be how students would describe to themselves where to do the decrement. This predicts that if they are given borrowing problems with more than two-columns, then they would always decrement the ten column, as in *c* and *d* below:

$$
c. \quad
\begin{array}{r}
\overset{5}{1}{}^{1}5\cancel{6}5 \\
-\quad 910 \\
\hline
1\ 655
\end{array}
\qquad
d. \quad
\begin{array}{r}
3{}^{1}\overset{15}{\cancel{6}}\ 5 \\
-1\ 9\ 0 \\
\hline
2\ 6\ 5
\end{array}
$$

This kind of problem solving has never been observed, and in the opinion of the project's diagnosticians and teachers, it never will. The natural language hypothesis is making an implausible prediction. Perhaps the hypothesis can be salvaged. In problem *c*, the student decrements a column that has already been answered. Perhaps the student would somehow appreciate that this won't have any effect on the answer, and thus not do it. However, this salvage attempt won't work for problem *d*. The decremented column is not yet answered at the time it is decremented.

These brief examples illustrate the kinds of trouble that a naive approach to natural language understanding as the source of procedure knowledge falls into. The basic problem is that natural language is terribly imprecise. The examples add the precision that the language lacks. But attending to the examples brings us back to the induction hypothesis.

SUMMARY

This chapter presented two hypotheses. The first hypothesis, a rather uncontroversial one, is that the knowledge that students acquire is schematic/procedural (at the level of a program) rather than teleologic/conceptual (at the level of the design for a program). Both descriptive levels are logically sufficient to describe a procedure. However, if students possessed the teleology of their procedures, most impasses could be fixed by deriving a correct procedure (i.e., students would debug instead of repair). At least some students, the ones with bugs, must be lacking such teleological knowledge. Also, there is experimental evidence that some adults have no teleology for their arithmetic procedures. They either never learned it or they forgot it while somehow retaining the schematic level (program) for the procedure. All in all, it is more parsimonious to assume that students learn just the schematic level descriptions for their procedures. This implies that students' knowledge can be formalized by something like Lisp procedure or production systems. It is not necessary to use more powerful formalisms such as planning nets (VanLehn & Brown, 1980), planning calculi (Rich, 1981) or procedural nets (Sacerdoti, 1977).

The second hypothesis is that students learn inductively. They generalize examples. There are several less plausible ways that procedures could be learned: (1) Learning-by-being-told explains procedure acquisition as the conversion of an external natural language information source, e.g., from a procedural manual, into a cognitive representation of the procedure. Learning from written procedures is implausible in this domain because young students don't read well. If spoken natural language were the source of procedure descriptions, some bugs would be predicted that should not be, for they have never occurred. (2) Learning-by-analogy is used in current mathematical curricula, but in ways that would produce an overly teleological understanding of the procedural skills. If students really understood the analogies, they wouldn't develop the bugs that they do.

Of the various ways to learn procedures, only induction seems both to fit the facts of classroom life and to account for the schematic (program) level of knowledge that students appear to employ. Most importantly, the induction hypothesis can account for many bugs, ranging from 33% to 85% of the observed bugs, depending on how rigorously one tests the hypothesis.

Most of the evidence supporting the induction hypothesis came from bug data. This invites a counter-hypothesis that runs as follows: Students who learn by induction acquire bugs, whereas students who learn by being told acquire a correct procedure. However, induction is perfectly adequate for acquiring a correct procedure. In all cases where induction leads to bugs, there is an alternative path that leads to a correct procedure. Because the examples aren't rich enough to tell the student which path is correct, some will guess wrong, and end up with bugs. The others will guess correctly, and end up with a correct procedure. The induction hypothesis can't help predicting that some students acquire correct procedures. It would require extremely ad hoc stipulations to block that prediction.

An advocate of the counter-hypothesis might suggest a modified version of it: Students who learn by induction acquire either bugs or a correct procedure, whereas students who learn by being told acquire a correct procedure. The implausibility of this hypothesis should be obvious. Why is learning-by-being-told so perfect that no bugs are ever acquired? It was shown in the preceding section that when one assumes that learning-by-being-told is less than perfect, then the kinds of bugs that are produced are quite implausible. To block these bugs would require, I suppose, some rather ad hoc stipulations.

In short, we are left in a classic Occam's razor situation. One mechanism, induction, suffices to account for most of the data. Another mechanism, although intuitively plausible, accounts for only one datum: the acquisition of the correct procedure, and it must be constrained in ad hoc ways in order to do so. We can choose to believe that one empirically adequate mechanism, induction, is present. Or we can choose to believe that induction is accompanied by a second mechanism that adds nothing to the empirical coverage and may even hurt it. Occam's razor counsels us to choose the former, simpler theory.

CONCLUDING REMARKS

Induction works well as the foundation of a whole-curriculum, generative theory of bugs. However, it seems inconsistent with a fine-grained, second-by-second account of classroom learning. There is just too much natural language being used in the classroom for induction per se to accurately characterize the student's learning processes. This section contains a few speculations about what all that natural language is doing, and what the relationship of the induction hypothesis is to fine-grained, daily classroom life.

As a form of inference, induction is incomplete. In order to be useful, induction must be constrained by predilections or biases. For instance, a common bias is to prefer the *simplest* concept that is consistent with the examples. Several of the 31 hypotheses of the present theory concern the inductive biases that arithmetic students seem to have. Another prerequisite for induction is a vocabulary of primitive features with which to describe the examples. In arithmetic, the primitives used by students seem to be mostly visual and numerical (see Table 6.2). The present theory has no account for why students use exactly those primitives. It also has no account for why they hold the inductive biases that they do. There are certainly other primitives and biases that they could use, and don't. For instance, $T < B$, $T = B$ and $T > B$ are all salient features to arithmetic students. Yet they don't appear to use $T = B + 1$ or $T = 2 \times B$, relationships that are crucial in counting (Groen & Parkman, 1972; Groen & Resnick, 1977). They use the notions of leftmost column and rightmost column, but not the notion of second-column-from-the-right (i.e., the tens column). They segment problems into columns and rows, but not into diagonals or 2×2 blocks. They use primitive operations for decrementing by one and incrementing by ten, but they don't use tens complement (7 − 3) or doubling. There are infinitely many primitives and biases that students could use, yet they seem to employ only a remarkably small set. Why?

One possibility is that the teacher's explanations somehow indicate which primitives and biases are appropriate for arithmetic. Suppose the teacher says, "You can't take 6 from 3 because it's too large." The phrase "too large" tips the student off that some relationship of relative magnitudes, e.g., $T < B$, is involved, and not, say $T = 2 \times B$. It doesn't say specifically what relationship to use, but it does narrow the set of relevant primitives down. On this view, the role of verbal explanations is to give the students a rough idea of what the procedure is. Induction fills in the details. On this view, the language is absolutely crucial. There are infinitely many numerical relationships that can hold, say, between 3 and 6. The words "too large" narrows it down to a small set. Without the language to indicate the kinds of primitives that induction should use, induction would be impossible.

Some students, when interviewed, seem to have an excellent grasp of subtraction in that they can explain, in words quite similar to those that a teacher might use, how borrowing is done and why. Yet, when they start solving problems, they have borrowing bugs (Resnick, 1982). There is a dramatic decoupling of their verbal competence and their written competence. Children aren't the only ones that show this decoupling. When adults play the Buggy game (Brown & Burton, 1978), they are required to infer a buggy procedure from examples. When they feel that they have discovered the bug, they first type in a verbal description of it, and then take a diagnostic test where they solve the problems using the procedure that they have induced. Quite frequently, the players would pass the test with flying colors, indicating that they really had induced the target procedure. However, their verbal explanations would have little recognizable relationship to the procedure. Brown and Burton (1978, pg. 169) comment on this phenomena, concentrating on the use of language during remediation:

Another important issue concerns the relationship between the language used to describe a student's errors and its effect on what a teacher should do to remediate it. Is the language able to convey to the student what he is doing wrong? Should we expect teachers to be able to use language as the tool for correcting the buggy algorithms of students? Or should we expect teachers only to be able to understand what the bug is and attempt remediation with the student with things like manipulative math tools? The following descriptions of hypotheses given by student teachers, taken from protocols of [the Buggy game], give a good idea of how difficult it is to express procedural ideas in English. The descriptions in parentheses are [the Buggy game's] prestored explanations of the bugs.

"Random errors in carryover." (Carries only when the next column in the top number is blank.)

"If there are less digits on the top than on the bottom she adds columns diagonally." (When the top number has fewer digits than the bottom number, the numbers are left-justified and then added.)

"Does not like zero in the bottom." (Zero subtracted from any number is zero.)

"Child adds first two numbers correctly, then when you need to carry in the second set of digits, child adds numbers carried to bottom row then adds third set of digits diagonally finally carrying over extra digits." (The carry is written in the top number to the left of the column being carried from and is mistaken for another digit in the top number.)

"Sum and carry all columns correctly until get to last column. Then takes furthest left digit in both columns and adds with digit of last carried amount. This is in the sum." (When there are an unequal number of digits in the two numbers, the columns that have a blank are filled with the left-most digit of that number.)

Even when one knows what the bug is in terms of being able to mimic it, how is one going to explain it to the student having problems? Considering the above examples, it is clear that anyone asked to solve a set of problems using these explanations would, no doubt, have real trouble. One can imagine a student's frustration when the teacher offers an explanation of why he is getting problems marked wrong, and the explanation is as confused and unclear as these are.

For that matter, when the correct procedure is described for the first time, could it, too, be coming across so unclearly!

For both children and players of the Buggy game, there is often a huge difference between the procedure that is performed and its verbal description. This is not, I believe, the fault of the individuals, but rather a property of natural language. Natural language is just not well suited for describing procedures. It takes considerable work to generate a good description of a procedure, and even then, ambiguities remain. This is evident not only in the student teachers' descriptions quoted above, but also in the Buggy game's descriptions of bugs, which, although painstakingly fine-tuned, are still easily misunderstood.

On the other hand, the verbal descriptions produced by the players of the Buggy game (and its authors!) probably seem quite clear to the people writing them. Most teachers probably believe that their descriptions of the arithmetic algorithms are quite lucid. Moreover, anyone else *who already knows the algorithm* would probably agree that the teacher's verbal descriptions are clear. Yet, for those who don't know the algorithm yet, viz. the students, the verbal descriptions are vague, muddied, and useless. If this is the true situation, one can easily see how the folk model of arithmetic learning stays alive. It accurately characterizes what the teacher, the parent, and anyone else who already knows arithmetic would "hear" if they visited a classroom. But from the students' point of view, the verbal descriptions are, at worst, just noise, and at best, a hint about what kind of inductive primitives and biases to employ.

APPENDIX

Can Bugs be Expressed Using Only Visual-Numerical Features?

The demonstration consists of presenting, for each bug, a formal representation of the bug that employs only visual-numerical features. This appendix is intended to show that 85% of the observed subtraction bugs can be represented using a only visual and numerical features. This result supports the hypothesis that the bugs are learned from generalizing examples, as described in the text.

The most precise demonstration of the point would employ the bug representation used by Debuggy (Burton, 1982), because Debuggy is the final arbiter of bug existence, as the data are normally analyzed (VanLehn (1982) describes the analysis technique and the particular 1147-student sample used herein). Debuggy is used as the judge of existence because it is more uniform and reliable than human judges (VanLehn, 1982). However, Debuggy uses a rather complicated representation for bugs. The point could be made with Debuggy's representation, but it would be difficult to follow unless one were a proficient Lisp programmer. The representation presented here is much simpler and much easier to understand. However, it cannot be substituted for Debuggy's representation. It's main deficit is that it cannot accurately model multiple, co-occurring bugs. Much of the complications in Debuggy's representation are for handling the interactions of bugs when they are installed together in a procedure. This representation has no such provisions. It could probably be extended to deal with bug combining, but then it would lose some of the simplicity that makes it useful in this context.

The representation consists of two formalisms, one for correct procedures and one for bugs. First, the correct procedures' formalism will be described. A correct procedure represented by an applicative And-Or graph which, by the way, is the representation used by the generative theory of bugs discussed in the text. Table 6.3 shows an And-Or graph for the standard subtraction procedure. It furnishes a concrete illustration for explaining the formalism.

The subprocedures of subtraction, e.g. SUB/COLUMN, BORROW, etc., are represented as nodes. Each node has a definition. The definition indicates the node's arguments. In table A1, all nodes except the first one have a single argument, C, which holds the column that is the current focus of attention. The definition also indicates the node's type, which is either AND or OR. (The first node, SUBTRACTION, is special. It is neither an AND nor an OR. It is not perturbed by the bugs, so its internal structure doesn't matter.)

TABLE 6.3
And-Or Graph for the Standard Subtraction Procedure

```
(DEFINE SUBTRACTION (P)
        (for C from (FIRST/COLUMN P) to (LAST/COLUMN P)
             do (SUB/COLUMN C)))

(DEFINE SUB/COLUMN (C) OR
        (If (T=# C) then (QUIT)
        (If (B=# C) then (SHOW/TOP C)
        (If (T<B C) then (BORROW C)
        (If (TRUE) then (DIFF C)))

(DEFINE BORROW (C) AND
        (REGROUP C)
        (DIFF  C))

(DEFINE REGROUP (C) AND
        (B/FROM (NEXT/COLUMN C))
        (B/INTO  C))

(DEFINE B/INTO (C) OR
        (If (TRUE) then (ADD10 C)))

(DEFINE B/FROM (C) OR
        (If (T=# C) then (QUIT))
        (If (T=0 C) then (BFZ C))
        (If (TRUE) then (DECR C)))

(DEFINE BFZ (C) AND
        (REGROUP C)
        (DECR  C))
```

An AND node's definition has an ordered list of subgoals. They are just like subprocedure calls. They are executed in order. When the last one is finished, the AND itself is finished.

An OR node's definition has an ordered list of if-then rules. If the antecedent (the if-part) of a rule is true, then its consequent (then-part) is executed. The rules are tested in order. The first rule whose antecedent is true runs, and only one rule runs.

The primitive operations are listed in Table 6.4. It lists both the primitive operators employed by bugs as well as correct procedures. Table 6.5 (and also in the text as table 6.2) lists the primitive predicates that are used in the antecedents or rules in correct procedures and bugs.

A bug is represented by list of deletions, insertions, and substitutions. These are to be performed on the standard correct procedure, whose definition was presented earlier. The substitutions convert the standard correct procedure to an alternative, but still correct, procedure for subtraction. The deletions and insertions install the bug. The substitutions are performed first, and the deletions and

TABLE 6.4
Primitive Operators (nodes).
All Take a Column as an Argument.

ADD&TRUNCATE	Adds the column and writes the units digit of the sum in answer.
ADD10	Adds ten to the top digit in the column.
DECR	Decrements the top digit in the column by 1.
DECR/BOT	Decrements the bottom digit in the column by 1.
DIFF	Takes the absolute difference of the digits in the column and writes it in the answer.
INCR	Increments the top digit in the column by 1.
QUIT	Cause the procedure to give up on this problem.
REMEMBER/BORROW	Sets a bit to true, which is read by the predicate BORROWED.
SHOW/BOT	Writes the bottom digit of the column in the answer.
SHOW/ONE	Writes a one in the answer.
SHOW/TOP	Writes the top digit of the column in the answer.
SHOW/ZERO	Writes a zero in the answer.
WRITE10	Changes the top digit of the column to ten.
WRITE8	Changes the top digit of the column to eight.
WRITE9	Changes the top digit of the column to nine.
WRITE9/BOT	Changes the bottom digit of the column to nine.

TABLE 6.5
Primitive Predicates. All Take a column as Argument.

$B = \#$	The bottom digit in the column is blank.
$B = 0$	The bottom digit in the column is zero.
BORROWED	A borrow has taken place already.
DECR'ED	The top digit in the column has been decremented.
DECR'ED/BOT	The bottom digit in the column has been decremented.
IN/LAST/COLUMN	The current column is the leftmost one.
IN/NEXT/TO/LAST/COLUMN	The current column is the penultimate one.
NEXT/$B = \#$	The bottom digit in the next column to the left is blank.
NEXT/$T = 0$	The top digit in the next column left is zero.
NEXT/$T = 00$	The top two digits in the next two columns to the left are zero.
NEXT/$T = 1$	The top digit in the next column left is one.
$T < B$	The top digit is less than or equal to the bottom digit.
$T < B$	The top digit is strictly less than the bottom digit.
$T > B$	The top digit is strictly greater than the bottom digit.
$T = B$	The top digit is equal to the bottom digit.
$T = B$/ORIGINALLY	$T = B$ in the original column, before decrementing occurred.
$T = \#$	The top digit in the column is blank.
$T = 0$	The top digit in the column is zero.
$T = 00$	The top digit in the column and the next one to its left are zero.
$T = 1$	The top digit in the column is one.
$T = 1 v 0$	The top digit is a one or a zero.
$T = 9$	The top digit is nine.

insertions are performed second. They are performed in parallel. Thus, if a bug's description says "Delete rule 1 of node B/FROM; Insert rule XXX in B/FROM after rule 1," then XXX will wind up exactly where rule 1 was because, in both the insertion statement and the deletion statement, the mention of rule 1 of B/FROM refers to the same rule in the correct subprocedure.

The substitutions used in the bugs are all variant of the standard subprocedure, BFZ. BFZ and its variants are listed in Table 6.6. These variants correspond to different ways of ordering the three subgoals that BFZ performs. The last variant, BFZ/2B/FROM is a little unusual, in that it calls 2B/FROM, which is a duplicate copy of B/FROM. Because 2B/FROM is called from a different place than B/FROM, perturbing the rules of 2B/FROM can give different bugs than perturbing the rules of B/FROM.

With these definitions of the representation language behind us, the bugs themselves can be presented. They are listed in two groups. The first group consists of 66 bugs that can be easily represented in this formalism. A short description and an example is provided with each bug in order to explain what it does informally. The formal description, in terms of substitutions, deletions and insertions, follows the informal one. Also, the number of occurrences of the bug is given. There are two numbers. The first is the number of students who had that bug alone, and the second is the number of students who had that bug in combination with some other bug.

TABLE 6.6
BFZ and the Variants that may be
Substituted for it.

```
(DEFINE BFZ (C) AND
    (REGROUP C)
    (DECR C))

(DEFINE BFZ/WRITE9 (C) AND
    (WRITE9 C)
    (B/FROM (NEXT/COLUMN C)))

(DEFINE BFZ/3ACTS (C) AND
    (ADD10 C)
    (B/FROM (NEXT/COLUMN C))
    (DECR C))

(DEFINE BFZ/BF/A10/DECR (C) AND
    (B/FROM (NEXT/COLUMN C))
    (ADD10 C)
    (DECR C))

(DEFINE BFZ/2B/FROM (C) AND
    (ADD10 C)
    (DECR C)
    (2B/FROM (NEXT/COLUMN C)))
```

The second group of bugs listed below consists of 12 bugs that can not be easily represented in this formalism. Only their informal descriptions and occurrence frequencies are listed, of course.

The end result is that of the 78 bugs that have occurred, 66 (85%) can be represented in this formalism. Moreover, almost all the frequently appearing bugs are included among these 66. Since the formalism uses only the numerical and visual features listed in tables A2 and A3, these 66 bugs could be induced from examples.

Bugs that are Easily Represented

0 − N = 0/AFTER/BORROW occurrences: (2 3)
When a column had a 1 which changed to a 0 by a decrement, the student uses 0 − n = 0 in that column. Example: 113 − 28 = 105
Insert the rule
    If (AND (T=0 C) (DECR'ED C))
    then (SHOW/ZERO C)
in the Or node SUB/COLUMN before rule 3.

0 − N = 0/EXCEPT/AFTER/BORROW occurrences: (0 2)
When the top digit in a column is 0, the student writes 0 in the answer, ie. 0 − n = 0, unless the 0 is the result of decrementing a 1 during a borrow operation. Example: 80 − 25 = 60
Insert the rule
    If (AND (T=0 C) (NOT (DECR'ED C)))
    then (SHOW/ZERO C)
in the Or node SUB/COLUMN before rule 3.

0 − N = N/AFTER/BORROW occurrences: (1 6)
When a column had a 1 which was changed by a borrow to a 0, the student used 0 − n = n in that column. Example: 113 − 28 = 125
Insert the rule
    If (AND (T=0 C) (DECR'ED C))
    then (SHOW/BOT C)
in the Or node SUB/COLUMN before rule 3.

0 − N = N/EXCEPT/AFTER/BORROW occurrences: (4 7)
When the top digit in a column is 0, the student writes the bottom digit in the answer, ie. 0 − n = n, unless the 0 is the result of decrementing a 1 during a borrow operation. Example: 80 − 25 = 65
Insert the rule
    If (AND (T=0 C) (NOT (DECR'ED C)))
    then (SHOW/BOT C)
in the Or node SUB/COLUMN before rule 3.

1 − 1 = 0/AFTER/BORROW occurrences: (1 7)
When a column starts with a 1 on top and a 1 on the bottom and is then borrowed from, the student writes 0 in the answer for this column. Example: 113 − 18 = 105
Insert the rule
    If (AND (T=0 C) (DECR'ED C) (T=B/ORIGINALLY C))
    then (SHOW/ZERO C)
in the Or node SUB/COLUMN before rule 3.

1 − 1 = 1/AFTER/BORROW occurrences: (0 2)
If a column starts with a 1 in both the top and the bottom, and is borrowed from, the student writes 1 as the answer in the 1 over 1 column. Example: 113 − 18 = 115
Insert the rule
    If (AND (T=0 C) (DECR'ED C) (T=B/ORIGINALLY C))
        then (SHOW/BOT C)
in the Or node SUB/COLUMN before rule 3.

ALWAYS/BORROW/LEFT occurrences: (6 0)
The student always subtracts all borrows from the left-most digit in the top number. Example: 602 − 137 = 375
Delete subgoal 1 from the And node REGROUP.
Delete rule 2 from the Or node B/FROM.
Insert subgoal (B/FROM (LAST/COLUMN))
in And node REGROUP before subgoal 1.
Insert the rule
    If (T=0 C)
        then (QUIT)
in the Or node B/FROM before rule 2.

BLANK/INSTEADOF/BORROW occurrences: (0 1)
The student leaves a blank in the answer for any column which requires borrowing. Example: 208 − 113 = 15
Delete rule 3 from the Or node SUB/COLUMN.
Insert the rule
    If (T<B C)
        then (NO/OP)
in the Or node SUB/COLUMN before rule 3.

BORROW/ACROSS/SECOND/ZERO occurrences: (2 5)
Borrows from the rightmost zero by changing it to nine, but the second and following zeros are skipped over. Example: 1003 − 358 = 45
Substitute BFZ/2B/FROM for the node BFZ.
Delete rule 2 from the Or node 2B/FROM.
Insert the rule
    If (T=0 C)
        then (2B/FROM (NEXT/COLUMN C))
in the Or node 2B/FROM before rule 2.

BORROW/ACROSS/ZERO occurrences: (13 29)
When the student needs to borrow from a column whose top digit is 0, he skips that column and borrows from the next one. Example: 303 − 78 = 135
Delete rule 2 from the Or node B/FROM.
Insert the rule
    If (T=0 C)
        then (B/FROM (NEXT/COLUMN C))
in the Or node B/FROM before rule 2.

BORROW/ACROSS/ZERO/OVER/BLANK occurrences: (0 10)
When borrowing from a column which has 0 on top and a blank in the bottom, the student skips to the next column. Example: 103 − 8 = 5
Insert the rule
    If (AND (T=0 C) (B=# C))
        then (B/FROM (NEXT/COLUMN C))
in the Or node B/FROM before rule 2.

BORROW/ACROSS/ZERO/OVER/ZERO occurrences: (1 14)
When borrowing, the student skips columns which have zero on both the top and the bottom. Example: 303 − 208 = 5
Insert the rule
    If (AND (T=0 C) (B=0 C))
    then (B/FROM (NEXT/COLUMN C))
in the Or node B/FROM before rule 2.

BORROW/DIFF/0 − N = N & SMALL − LARGE = 0 occurrences: (4 0)
The student doesn't know how to borrow. If the top digit in a column is 0, the student writes the bottom digit in the answer (i.e. 0 − N = N). If the top digit is smaller than the bottom digit, then 0 is written in the answer. Example: 204 − 119 = 110
Delete rule 3 from the Or node SUB/COLUMN.
Insert the rule
    If (T=0 C)
    then (SHOW/BOT C)
in the Or node SUB/COLUMN before rule 3.
Insert the rule
    If (T<B C)
    then (SHOW/ZERO C)
in the Or node SUB/COLUMN after rule 3.

BORROW/DON'T/DECREMENT/TOP/SMALLER occurrences: (2 1)
When borrowing, the student will only decrement the top number in the next column if it is greater than or equal to the bottom number in that column. Example: 563 − 388 = 185
Insert the rule
    If (T<B C)
    then (NO/OP)
in the Or node B/FROM before rule 2.

BORROW/DON'T/DECREMENT/UNLESS/BOTTOM/SMALLER occurrences: (2 2)
When borrowing, the student will not decrement the top digit in the next column to the left unless the bottom digit in that column is smaller than the top. Example: 563 − 388 = 185
Insert the rule
    If (T<B C)
    then (NO/OP)
in the Or node B/FROM before rule 2.

BORROW/FROM/ALL/ZERO occurrences: (1 0)
When borrowing from 0, the student writes 9, but does not continue borrowing from the column to the left of the 0. If there are two 0's in a row in the top number, both are changed to 9's. Example: 203 − 98 = 205
Insert the rule
    If (AND (T=0 C) (NOT (NEXT/T=0 C)))
    then (WRITE9 C)
in the Or node B/FROM before rule 2.

BORROW/FROM/BOTTOM/INSTEADOF/ZERO occurrences: (0 1)
When borrowing from a column with 0 on top, the student borrows from the bottom digit instead of the 0 on top. In all other cases the student borrows correctly. Example: 203 − 158 = 65
Insert the rule
    If (AND (T=0 C) (NOT (B=# C)) (NOT (B=0 C)))
    then (DECR/BOT C)

in the Or node B/FROM after rule 1.
Insert the rule
    If (AND (T=0 C) (NOT (B=# C)) (B=0 C))
    then (WRITE9/BOT C) (B/FROM (NEXT/COLUMN C))
in the Or node B/FROM before rule 2.

BORROW/FROM/ONE/IS/NINE occurrences: (0 2)
When borrowing from a column which has a 1 on top, the student treats the 1 as if it were
a 10. Example 113 − 58 = 145
Insert the rule
    If (T=1 C)
    then (WRITE9 C)
in the Or node B/FROM before rule 2.

BORROW/FROM/ONE/IS/TEN occurrences: (0 1)
The student writes 10 when he/she borrows from a column with a 1 in the top digit.
Example: 913 − 78 = 935
Insert the rule
    If (T=1 C)
    then (WRITE10 C)
in the Or node B/FROM before rule 2.

BORROW/FROM/ZERO occurrences: (10 4)
When borrowing from a column whose top digit is 0, the student writes 9, but does not
continue borrowing from the column to the left of the 0. Example: 103 − 45 = 158
Insert the rule
    If (T=0 C)
    then (WRITE9 C)
in the Or node B/FROM before rule 2.

BORROW/FROM/ZERO&LEFT/TEN/OK occurrences: (1 1)
The student changes 0 to 9 without further borrowing unless the 0 is part of a 10 in the left
part of the top number. Example: 803 − 508 = 395
Insert the rule
    If (AND (T=0 C) (NOT (NEXT/T=1 C)))
    then (WRITE9 C)
in the Or node B/FROM before rule 2.

BORROW/FROM/ZERO/IS/TEN occurrences: (1 1)
When borrowing from a column with a zero on top, the student changes the zero to a ten.
Example: 800 − 168 = 742
Insert the rule
    If (T=0 C)
    then (WRITE10 C)
in the Or node B/FROM before rule 2.

BORROW/INTO/ONE = TEN occurrences: (0 5)
When borrowing into a column whose top digit is 1, the student gets 10 instead of 11.
Example: 321 − 89 = 221
Insert the rule
    If (T=1 C)
    then (WRITE10 C)
in the Or node B/INTO before rule 1.

BORROW/NO/DECREMENT occurrences: (10 8)
When the student needs to borrow, he/she adds 10 to the top digit of the current column without subtracting 1 from the top digit of the next column. Example: $143 - 28 = 125$
Delete subgoal 1 from the And node REGROUP.

BORROW/NO/DECREMENT/EXCEPT/LAST occurrences: (4 2)
When borrowing, the student does not decrement the top digit unless he/she is working in the leftmost column. Example: $313 - 228 = 95$
Insert the rule
    If (NOT (IN/LAST/COLUMN C))
    then (NO/OP)
in the Or node B/FROM before rule 2.

BORROW/ONCE/THEN/SMALLER/FROM/LARGER occurrences: (0 12)
The student subtracts the smaller digit from the larger in all columns after the first borrow.
Example: $133 - 38 = 115$
Delete rule 3 from the Or node SUB/COLUMN.
Insert the rule
    If (AND (T<B C) (NOT (BORROWED)))
    then (BORROW C) (REMEMBER/BORROW)
in the Or node SUB/COLUMN before rule 3.

BORROW/ONLY/ONCE occurrences: (0 1)
The student will only borrow once per problem. After that he/she will add ten to the top number if it is smaller but will not borrow one from the next column to the left. Example: $1250 - 1088 = 262$
Insert the rule
    If (BORROWED)
    then (NO/OP)
in the Or node B/FROM before rule 2.
Insert subgoal (REMEMBER/BORROW)
in And node BORROW after subgoal 2.

BORROW/SKIP/EQUAL occurrences: (0 4)
When borrowing, the student skips over columns in which the top digit and the bottom digit are the same and borrows from the next column.
Example: $293 - 198 = 5$
Insert the rule
    If (T=B C)
    then (B/FROM (NEXT/COLUMN C))
in the Or node B/FROM before rule 2.

BORROW/TREAT/ONE/AS/ZERO occurrences: (0 1)
When borrowing from a column that has 1 on top, the student writes 9 and continues to borrow. That is he/she treats 1 as if it were 0 because he/she doesn't like to make more 0's in the top number. Example: $313 - 158 = 145$
Substitute BFZ/WRITE9 for the node BFZ.
Delete rule 2 from the Or node B/FROM.
Insert the rule
    If (T=1v0 C)
    then (BFZ C)
in the Or node B/FROM before rule 2.

CAN'T/SUBTRACT occurrences: (1 0)
The student doesn't know how to subtract at all. Example: $1003 - 87 = \#$

Insert the rule
    If (TRUE)
    then (QUIT)
in the Or node SUB/COLUMN before rule 1.

DECREMENT/ALL/ON/MULTIPLE/ZERO occurrences: (3 3)
When borrowing into a column which has a 0 on top from a column which has a 0, the student gets uses 9 instead of 10 for the top number. Example: $400 - 199 = 200$
Substitute BFZ/WRITE9 for the node BFZ.
Insert the rule
    If (AND (T=0 C) (T=0/ORIGINALLY (NEXT/COLUMN C)))
    Then (WRITE9 C)
in the Or node B/INTO before rule 1.

DECREMENT/LEFTMOST/ZERO/ONLY occurrences: (1 0)
When borrowing from two or more zeros in the top number, the student decrements the leftmost zero but leaves all the rest as 10 and does not decrement the column to the left of the zeros. Example: $1003 - 958 = 1055$
Substitute BFZ/3ACTS for the node BFZ.
Delete subgoal 3 from the And node BFZ.
Insert the rule
    If (AND (T=0 C) (NOT (NEXT/T=0 C)))
    then (WRITE 9C)
in the Or node B/FROM before rule 2.

DECREMENT/ONE/TO/ELEVEN occurrences: (0 1)
When borrowing from a column which has a one on top, the student writes 11. He/she will also continue borrowing from the next column if there is one. Example: $613 - 238 = 385$
Substitute BFZ/3ACTS for the node BFZ.
Delete subgoal 3 from the And node BFZ.
Delete rule 2 from the Or node B/FROM.
Delete rule 1 from the Or node B/FROM.
Insert the rule
    If (T=1v0 C)
    then (BFZ C)
in the Or node B/FROM before rule 2.
Insert subgoal (If (T=0/ORIGINALLY C) then (DECR C))
in And node BFZ before subgoal 3.
Insert the rule
    If (T=# C)
    then (NO/OP)
in the Or node B/FROM befor rule 1.

DECREMENT/TOP/LEQ/IS/EIGHT occurrences: (1 1)
When borrowing from a column in which the top is less than or equal to the bottom, the top digit is changed to an 8.0 Example: $283 - 198 = 95$
Insert the rule
    If (AND (NOT (B=# C)) (T<B C))
    then (WRITE8 C)
in the Or node B/FROM before rule 2.

DIFF/0 − N = 0 occurrences: (0 10)
Whenever the top digit in a column is 0, the student writes 0 in the answer, i.e. $0 - N = 0$. Example: $140 - 21 = 120$

Insert the rule
> If (T=0 C)
> then (SHOW/ZERO C)

in the Or node SUB/COLUMN before rule 3.

DIFF/0 − N = 0 & N − 0 = 0 occurrences: (0 3)
The student writes 0 in the answer when either the top or the bottom digit is 0. Example: 308 − 293 = 105
Insert the rule
> If (OR (T=0 C) (B=0 C))
> then (SHOW/ZERO C)

in the Or node SUB/COLUMN before rule 3.

DIFF/0 − N = N occurrences: (1 37)
Whenever the top digit in a column is 0, the student writes the bottom digit in the answer, i.e. 0 − N = N. Example: 140 − 21 = 121
Insert the rule
> If (T=0 C)
> then (SHOW/BOT C)

in the Or node SUB/COLUMN after rule 2.

DIFF/0 − N = N & N − 0 = 0 occurrences: (1 0)
The student gets 0 when subtracting 0 from anything and also gets N taken from 0 is N. Example: 302 − 192 = 290
Insert the rule
> If (OR (T=0 C) (B=0 C))
> then (SHOW/BOT C)

in the Or node SUB/COLUMN before rule 3.

DIFF/0 − N = N/WHEN/BORROW/FROM/ZERO occurrences: (0 2)
The student writes n in the answer when subtracting n from 0 if he/she would have to borrow from a column which contains a 0 in top. Example: 1003 − 892 = 291
Insert the rule
> If (T=00 C)
> then (SHOW/BOT C)

in the Or node SUB/COLUMN before rule 3.

DIFF/N − 0 = 0 occurrences: (0 2)
Whenever the bottom digit in a column is 0, the student writes 0 in the answer, i.e. N − 0 = 0. Example: 403 − 208 = 105
Insert the rule
> If (B=0 C)
> then (SHOW/BOT C)

in the Or node SUB/COLUMN before rule 3.

DIFF/N − N = N occurrences: (0 1)
Whenever the top digit in a column is the same as the bottom digit, the student writes that digit as the answer for that column, i.e. N − N = N. Example: 235 − 134 = 131
Insert the rule
> If (T=B C)
> then (SHOW/TOP C)

in the Or node SUB/COLUMN before rule 3.

DOESN'T/BORROW/EXCEPT/LAST occurrences: (0 1)
Quits instead of borrowing, unless the borrow is from the last column. Example: 345 − 120 = 225

Insert the rule
    If (NOT (IN/LAST/COLUMN C))
    then (QUIT)
in the Or node B/FROM before rule 2.

DON'T/DECREMENT/ZERO occurrences: (3 4)
When borrowing from a column in which the top digit is 0, the student rewrites the 0 as 10 by borrowing from the next column to the left but forgets to change 10 to 9 when he/she adds 10 to the column which originally needed the borrow. Example: $603 - 138 = 475$
Substitute BFZ/3ACTS for the node BFZ.
Delete subgoal 3 from the And node BFZ.

DON'T/DECREMENT/ZERO/OVER/BLANK occurrences: (4 2)
When borrowing, the student will not decrement a zero when it is above a blank. Example: $103 - 8 = 105$
Insert the rule
    If (AND (T=0 C) (B=# C))
    then (NO/OP)
in the Or node B/FROM before rule 2.

DON'T/DECREMENT/ZERO/UNTIL/BOTTOM/BLANK occurrences: (0 1)
The student forgets to change 10 to 9 after borrowing from a column which had a 0 on top. The exception is when 0 is part of the leftmost part of the top number then 1 is decremented correctly. Example: $304 - 259 = 55$
Substitute BFZ/3ACTS for the node BFZ.
Delete subgoal 3 from the AND node BFZ.
Insert subgoal (If (B=# C) then (DECR C))
in And node BFZ before subgoal 3.

DOUBLE/DECREMENT/ONE occurrences: (1 2)
When borrowing from a column with a 1 in the top, the student changes the 1 to a 9 and continues borrowing to the left. Example: $313 - 128 = 175$
Substitute BFZ/WRITE9 for the node BFZ.
Insert the rule
    If (AND (T=1 C) (NOT (NEXT/B=# C)))
    then (BFZ C)
in the Or node B/FROM before rule 2.

FORGET/BORROW/OVER/BLANKS occurrences: (1 3)
The student borrows correctly except he/she doesn't take 1 from the top digits that are over blanks. Example: $143 - 88 = 155$
Insert the rule
    If (B=# C)
    then (NO/OP)
in the Or node B/FROM before rule 2.

IGNORE/LEFTMOST/ONE/OVER/BLANK occurrences: (0 6)
The student ignores the leftmost digit in the top number if it is a one and has a blank under it. Example: $188 - 33 = 55$
Insert the rule
    If (AND (B=# C) (T=1 C) (IN/LAST/COLUMN C))
    then (QUIT)
in the Or node SUB/COLUMN before rule 2.

N − N/AFTER/BORROW/CAUSES/BORROW occurrences: (0 2)
When a column has the same number in both the top and the bottom and the digit has been

decremented by a borrow to be the same as the bottom digit, the student borrows from the next column even though they don't really need to. Example: $1073 - 168 = 8105$
Insert the rule
    If (AND (T=B C) (DECR'ED C) (NOT (IN/LAST/COLUMN C)))
    then (BORROW C)
in the Or node SUB/COLUMN before rule 3.

N − N/CAUSES/BORROW occurrences: (1 0)
When a column has the same number on the top and bottom, the next column is decremented and 0 is written in the answer. Example: $288 - 83 = 1105$
Insert the rule
    If (AND (T=B C) (NOT (IN/LAST/COLUMN C)))
    then (BORROW C)
in the Or node SUB/COLUMN before rule 3.

N − N = 1/AFTER/BORROW occurrences: (1 3)
The student gets 1 when subtracting n from n in a column which has been borrowed from. That is, the student knows that he/she doesn't need to borrow to subtract n from n, but he feels he must do something with the borrow, so he writes it in the answer. Example: $354 - 159 = 215$
Insert the rule
    If (AND (T=B/ORIGINALLY C) (DECR'ED C))
    then (SHOW/ONE C)
in the Or node SUB/COLUMN before rule 3.

ONLY/DO/UNITS occurrences: (0 1)
Student only does the units column. Example: $78 - 52 = 6$
Insert the rule
    IF (NOT (IN/FIRST/COLUMN C))
    then (QUIT)
in the Or node SUB/COLUMN before rule 2.

QUIT/WHEN/BOTTOM/BLANK occurrences: (0 5)
The student stops working the problem as soon as the bottom number runs out. Example: $178 - 59 = 19$
Delete rule 2 from the Or node SUB/COLUMN.
Insert the rule
    If (B=# C)
    then (QUIT)
in the Or node SUB/COLUMN before rule 2.

SMALLER/FROM/LARGER occurrences: (103 12)
The student subtracts the smaller digit in a column from the larger digit regardless of which is on top. Example: $253 - 118 = 145$
Delete rule 3 from the Or node SUB/COLUMN.

SMALLER/FROM/LARGER/EXCEPT/LAST occurrences: (0 3)
Student only borrows when decr is in the last column. Takes absolute difference until then. Example: $313 - 228 = 95$
Delete rule 3 from the Or node SUB/COLUMN.
Insert the rule
    If (AND (T<B C) (IN/NEXT/TO/LAST/COLUMN C))
    then (BORROW C)
in the Or node SUB/COLUMN before rule 3.

SMALLER/FROM/LARGER/INSTEAD/OF/BORROW/FROM/ZERO   occurrences: (0 5)
Instead of borrowing from a column which has a 0 in the top, the student subtracts the smaller digit from the larger. Example: $101 - 56 = 55$
Delete rule 3 from the Or node SUB/COLUMN.
Insert the rule
    If (AND (T<B C) (NOT (NEXT/T=0 C)))
    then (BORROW C)
in the Or node SUB/COLUMN before rule 3.

SMALLER/FROM/LARGER/INSTEADOF/BORROW/UNLESS/BOTTOM/SMALLER
occ.: (2 5)
The student takes the absolute different instead of borrowing unless the borrow would decrement a digit that is strictly greater than the digit beneath it. Example: $300 - 39 = 339$
Insert the rule
    If (AND (T<B C) (OR (NEXT/B=# C) (T<B (NEXT/COLUMN C))))
    then (DIFF C)
in the Or node SUB/COLUMN before rule 3.

SMALLER/FROM/LARGER/WHEN/BORROWED/FROM occurrences: (0 7)
The student subtracts the smaller digit from the larger in any column that has been borrowed from. Example: $133 - 38 = 115$
Delete rule 3 from the Or node SUB/COLUMN.
Insert the rule
    If (AND (T<B C) (NOT (DECR'ED C)))
    then (BORROW C)
in the Or node SUB/COLUMN before rule 3.

STOPS/BORROW/AT/MULTIPLE/ZERO occurrences: (2 1)
The student doesn't borrow from two zeros in a row. He/she will just add ten to the column that needs it without decrementing anything. Example: $1003 - 358 = 655$
Insert the rule
    If (T=00 C)
    then (NO/OP)
in the Or node B/FROM before rule 2.

STOPS/BORROW/AT/ZERO occurrences: (34 30)
The student borrows from zero incorrectly. He/she doesn't subtract 1 from the 0 (though he adds 10 correctly to the top digit of the current column). Example: $203 - 178 = 35$
Delete rule 2 from the Or node B/FROM.

SUB/ONE/OVER/BLANK occurrences: (0 2)
The student subtracts one from the top number in any column with a blank in the bottom. Example: $343 - 28 = 215$
Delete rule 2 from the Or node SUB/COLUMN.
Insert the rule
    If (B=# C)
    then (DECR C) (SHOW/TOP C)
in the Or node SUB/COLUMN before rule 2.

TOP/INSTEAD/OF/BORROW/FROM/ZERO occurrences: (0 1)
The student doesn't know how to borrow from zero. When such a borrow is required, the

student just writes the top number of the column instead. Example: $300 - 39 = 270$
Insert the rule
>If (AND (T<B C) (NEXT/T=0 C))
>then (SHOW/TOP C)

in the Or node SUB/COLUMN before rule 3.

TREAT/TOP/ZERO/AS/TEN occurrences: (0 1)
The student treats zeros in the top number as if they were ten. Example: $109 - 81 = 128$
Insert the rule
>If (AND (T<B C) (T=0 C))
>then (ADD10 C) (DIFF C)

in the Or node SUB/COLUMN before rule 3.

X − N = 0/AFTER/BORROW occurrences: (0 1)
In any column except the leftmost one that has been borrowed from, the student writes 0 in the answer. The leftmost column is done correctly. Example: $313 - 98 = 305$
Insert the rule
>If (AND (DECR'ED C) (NOT (IN/LAST/COLUMN C)))
>then (SHOW/ZERO C)

in the Or node SUB/COLUMN before rule 3.

X − N = N/AFTER/BORROW occurrences: (0 1)
In any column that has been borrowed from, the student writes the bottom number in the answer. Example: $313 - 98 = 395$
Insert the rule
>If (DECR'ED C)
>then (SHOW/BOT C)

in the Or node SUB/COLUMN before rule 3.

ZERO/INSTEADOF/BORROW occurrences: (1 0)
The student writes a 0 in any column in which borrowing is needed. Example: $140 - 28 = 120$
Delete rule 3 from the Or node SUB/COLUMN.
Insert the rule
>If (T<B C)
>then (SHOW/ZERO C)

in the Or node SUB/COLUMN before rule 3.

Bugs That are not Easily Represented

ADD/INSTEADOF/SUB occurrences: (1 0)
The student adds instead of subtracts. Example $118 - 5 = 123$

ADD/LR/DECREMENT/ANSWER/CARRY/TO/RIGHT occurrences: (1 0)
The student is adding from left to right, decrementing every column except the rightmost and carrying into every column except the leftmost. Example: $411 - 215 = 527$

BORROW/ACROSS/TOP/SMALLER/DECREMENTING/TO occurrences: (2 0)
When decrementing a column in which the top is smaller than the bottom, 0 the student adds ten to the top digit, decrements the column being borrowed into and borrows from the next column to the left. Also the student skips any column which has a zero over a zero or a blank in the borrowing process. Example: $183 - 95 = 97$

BORROW/ONLY/FROM/TOP/SMALLER occurrences: (1 3)
The student will try to borrow only from those columns in which the top digit is smaller

than the bottom digit. If he can't find one, then borrowing is done properly. Example:
9283 − 3566 = 5627

BORROW/UNIT/DIFF occurrences: (0 1)
When the student needs to borrow, he borrows the difference between the bottom digit
and the top digit of the current column. Example: 86 − 29 = 30

DECREMENT/MULTIPLE/ZEROS/BY/NUMBER/TO/LEFT occurrences: (1 1)
When borrowing from more than one zero in a row, the student decrements each zero by
the number of columns to the left that had to be scanned to find a nonzero digit to
decrement. Example: 8002 − 1714 = 6278

DECREMENT/MULTIPLE/ZEROS/BY/NUMBER/TO/RIGHT occurrences: (3 1)
When borrowing from more than one zero in a row, the student decrements each zero by
the number of columns to its right that are borrowed from. Example: 8002 − 1714 = 6188

DON'T/WRITE/ZERO occurrences: (1 3)
The student does not write zero in the answer; he/she just leaves a blank. Example: 24 −
14 = 1

SIMPLE/PROBLEM/STUTTER/SUBTRACT occurrences: (1 0)
When the bottom number is only one digit and the top number is at least three digits, the
bottom number is subtracted from every column. Example: 348 − 2 = 126

STUTTER/SUBTRACT occurrences: (2 0)
When there are blanks in the bottom number, the student subtracts the leftmost digit of the
bottom number from every column that has a blank. Example: 4369 − 22 = 2147

SUB/BOTTOM/FROM/TOP occurrences: (1 0)
The student always subtracts the top digit from the bottom number. If the bottom number
is smaller, he decrements the top digit and adds ten to the bottom first. If the bottom digit
is zero, however, he writes the top digit in the answer. If the top digit is one greater than
the bottom, he writes 9. Example : 4723 − 3065 = 9742

SUB/COPY/LEAST/BOTTOM/MOST/TOP occurrences: (1 0)
The student makes the answer by taking the most significant digits of the top and the least
significant digits from the bottom number. Example: 648 − 231 = 631

ACKNOWLEDGMENTS

John Seely Brown has contributed substantially to this research, although he may not
agree with all its conclusions. This research was supported by the Personnel and Training
Research Programs, Psychological Sciences Division, Office of Naval Research, under
Contract No. N00014-82C-0067, Contract Authority Identification No. NR667-477. Re-
production in whole or in part is permitted for any purpose of the United States Govern-
ment. Approved for public release; distribution unlimited.

REFERENCES

Anderson, J. R. (1983). *The Architecture of Cognition*. Cambridge, MA: Harvard.
Anderson, J. R., Farrell, R., & Saurers, R. (1984). Learning to program in LISP. *Cognitive
Science, 8*, 87–129.

Anderson, J. R., Greeno, J., Kline, P. J. & Neves, D. M. (1981). Acquisition of problem solving skill. In J. R. Anderson (Ed.), *Cognitive skills and their acquisition*. Hillsdale, NJ: Erlbaum.

Ashlock, R. B. (1976). *Error patterns in computation*. Columbus, OH: Bell and Howell.

Badre, N. A. (1972). *Computer learning from English text*. Berkeley, CA: University of California at Berkeley, Electronic Research Laboratory. ERL-M372.

Biermann, A. W. (1972). On the inference of turing machines from sample computations. *Artificial Intelligence, 10*, 181–198.

Brown, J. S. & Burton, R. B. (1978). Diagnostic models for procedural bugs in basic mathematical skills. *Cognitive Science, 2*, 155–192.

Brown, J. S. & VanLehn, K. (1980). Repair Theory: A generative theory of bugs in procedural skills. *Cognitive Science, 4*, 379–426.

Brownell, W. A. (1941). The evaluation of learning in arithmetic. In *Arithmetic in general education*. Washington, DC: Council of Teachers of Mathematics.

Brueckner, L. J. (1930). *Diagnostic and remedial teaching in arithmetic*. Philadelphia, PA: Winston.

Burton, R. R. (1982). Debuggy: Diagnosis of errors in basic mathematical skills. In D. H. Sleeman & J. S. Brown (Eds.), *Intelligent Tutoring Systems*. New York: Academic.

Buswell, G. T. (1926). *Diagnostic studies in arithmetic*. Chicago, IL: University of Chicago Press.

Carbonell, J. G. (1983). Derivational analogy in problem solving and knowledge acquisition. In R. S. Michalski (Ed.), *Proceedings of the International Machine Learning Workshop*. Urbana, IL: University of Illinois.

Cohen, P. R. & Feigenbaum, E. A. (1983). *The Handbook of Artificial Intelligence*. Los Altos, CA: William Kaufmann.

Cox, L. S. (1975). Diagnosing and remediating systematic errors in addition and subtraction computation. *The Arithmetic Teacher, 22*, 151–157.

Gelman, R. & Gallistel, C. R. (1978). *The child's understanding of number*. Cambridge, MA: Harvard University Press.

Greeno, J. G., Riley, M. S. & Gelman, R. (1984). Conceptual competence and children's counting. *Cognitive Psychology, 16*, 94–143.

Groen, G. J. & Parkman, J. M. (1972). A chronometric analysis of simple addition. *Psychological Review, 79*, 329–343.

Groen, G. J. & Resnick, L. B. (1977). Can preschool children invent addition algorithms? *Journal of Educational Psychology, 69*, 645–652.

Hayes-Roth, F. & McDermott, J. (1978). An interference matching technique for inducing abstractions. *Communications of the ACM, 21*, 401–411.

Lankford, F. G. (1972). *Some computational strategies of seventh grade pupils*. Charlottesville, VA: University of Virginia. ERIC document.

Mitchell, T. M., Utgoff, P. E. & Banerji, R. B. (1983). Learning problem-solving heuristics by experimentation. In R. S. Michalski, T. M. Mitchell & J. Carbonell (Eds.), *Machine Learning*. Palo Alto, CA: Tioga Press.

Resnick, L. (1982). Syntax and semantics in learning to subtract. In T. Carpeter, J. Moser & T. Romberg (Ed.), *Addition and Subtraction: A cognitive perspective*. Hillsdale, NJ: Erlbaum.

Resnick, L. B. & Omanson, S. F. (in press). Learning to understand arithmetic. In R. Glaser (Ed.), *Advances in Instructional Psychology*. Hillsdale, NJ: Erlbaum.

Rich, C. (1981). *Inspection methods in programming* (Tech. Rep. AI-TR-604). Massachusetts Institute of Technology, Artificial Intelligence Laboratory. Cambridge, MA.

Roberts, G. H. (1968). The failure strategies of third grade arithmetic pupils. *The Arithmetic Teacher, 15*, 442–446.

Sacerdoti, E. (1977). *A structure for plans and behavior*. New York: Elsevier North-Holland.

Shaw, D. J., Standiford, S. N., Klein, M. F. & Tatsuoka, K. K. (1982). *Error analysis of fraction arithmetic-selected case studies* (Tech. Report 82-2-NIE). University of Illinois. Computer-based Education Research Laboratory.

Sleeman, D. H. (1984). Basic algebra revised: A study with 14-year olds. *International Journal of Man-Machine Studies*.

Sussman, G. J. (1976). *A computational model of skill acquisition*. New York: Springer Verlag.

Tatsuoka, K. K. & Baillie, R. (1982). *Rule space, the product space of two score components in signed-number subtraction: an approach to dealing with inconsistent use of erroneous rules* (Tech. Report 82-3-ONR). University of Illinois, Computer-based Education Research Laboratory. Urbana, IL.

VanLehn, K. (1982). Bugs are not enough: Empirical studies of bugs, impasses and repairs in procedural skills. *The Journal of Mathematical Behavior, 3*(2), 3–71.

VanLehn, K. (1983). *Felicity conditions for human skill acquisition: Validating an AI-based theory* (Tech. Report CIS-21). Xerox Palo Alto Research Center.

VanLehn, K. & Brown, J. S. (1980). Planning Nets: A representation for formalizing analogies and semantic models of procedural skills. In R. E. Snow, P. A. Federico & W. E. Montague (Ed.), *Aptitude, Learning and Instruction: Cognitive Process Analyses*. Hillsdale, NJ: Erlbaum.

Winston, P. H. (1978). Learning by creating transfer frames. *Artificial Intelligence, 10*, 147–172.

Winston, P. H. (1979). *Learning by understanding analogies* (Tech. Report AI-TR-520). Massachusetts Institute of Technology, Artificial Intelligence Laboratory. Cambridge, MA.

Young, R. M. & O'Shea, T. (1981). Errors in children's subtraction. *Cognitive Science, 5*, 153–177.

7

Using Conceptual and Procedural Knowledge: A Focus on Relationships

Edward A. Silver
San Diego State University

In the opening chapter of this book, Hiebert and Lefevre propose definitions of procedural and conceptual knowledge. Their analysis is thoughtful, and they offer some insights into possible distinctions between procedural and conceptual knowledge. Although these distinctions may sometimes be useful for the purposes of discussion, it is my contention in this chapter that it is the *relationships* among, and not the distinctions between, elements of procedural and conceptual knowledge that ought to be of primary interest. I argue that the distinctions between conceptual and procedural knowledge do not constitute sharp, impenetrable barriers and present some examples illustrating the powerful and complex interrelationships among elements of a person's conceptual and procedural knowledge. The argument is based on the premise that although we can think of the distinctions between static elements of one's procedural or conceptual knowledge base, when knowledge is used dynamically to solve a problem or perform some nontrivial task, it is the *relationships* that become of primary importance.

   This chapter is divided into three sections. The first contains a discussion of the complexity of the relationship between conceptual and procedural knowledge and a consideration of the issue of the dependence of one type of knowledge on the other. In particular, it will be seen that concepts sometimes appear to undergird procedural knowledge, yet at other times the opposite appears to be true. A focus on the *use* of knowledge to solve problems can lead to insights into the fundamental ubiquity of relationships between procedural and conceptual knowledge, thereby relieving us of the obligation to debate the distinctions between the two kinds of knowledge.

The next two sections each present a detailed case study of the relationship between procedural and conceptual knowledge in a specific mathematical setting. Each setting is itself an instance of a larger target area for the study of relationships between conceptual and procedural knowledge. The first target is the set of common procedural errors that are especially resistant to instructional intervention. These systematic procedural errors are likely to be associated with flawed conceptual knowledge or missing linkages between procedural and conceptual knowledge. Several examples are considered, and one example involving rational number addition is discussed in detail.

The second suggested target is the set of mathematical problem-solving tasks that involve understanding or interpretation. The understanding and interpretation processes that are used in solving mathematical problems involve the creation of procedural/conceptual knowledge linkages. An example involving division problems with remainders is discussed in detail.

CONCEPTS, PROCEDURES, AND PROBLEM SOLVING

It has been traditional in mathematics education and psychology to treat problem solving, concept knowledge, and algorithm knowledge as distinct topics. In fact, in compilations of research, those three topics have usually been discussed in separate chapters. For example, the reference volume, *Research in Mathematics Education* (Shumway, 1980), contains separate chapters with the headings "Skill Learning," "Concept and Principle Learning," and "Research on Mathematical Problem Solving." Its subdivision of topics is not very different from that used in the classic volume, *The Learning of Mathematics: Its Theory and Practice* (Fehr, 1953), which also has separate chapters on "Formation of Concepts" and "Problem Solving in Mathematics," as well as more than one dealing with skill proficiency.

It could be argued that modern cognitive research has simultaneously sharpened the focus on these three kinds of knowledge and cognitive activity and blurred the lines of distinction among them. One of the reasons for this interesting consequence of modern cognitive research is that the research has often focused on detailed analyses of problem solving and nontrivial task performance in complex knowledge domains. Problem solving in reasonably complex knowledge domains clearly involves the application of several kinds of knowledge, including elements of both procedural and conceptual knowledge. Therefore, mathematical problems can and do provide a convenient vehicle for the study of conceptual and procedural knowledge, and especially for the linkages between and among the various components of a person's knowledge in a given domain.

A major theme of this chapter is the complexity and depth of the relationships among elements of a conceptual and procedural knowledge, especially in problem-solving situations. The intertwining of procedural and conceptual knowledge is evident even when that knowledge is being applied to apparently simple tasks. In this section we examine the relationship between procedural and conceptual knowledge from both theoretical and empirical perspectives. Our major conclusion is that pure forms of either type of knowledge are seldom, if ever, exhibited and that it is the relationship between the knowledge types that gives one's knowledge the power of application in a wide variety of settings.

CONCEPTS VERSUS PROCEDURES

An examination of the traditional distinctions between concepts and procedures discloses an interesting and unexpected way in which these two knowledge types are related. In canonical experiments on concept attainment, subjects were given a large number of examples and nonexamples of a given concept. The criterion used consistently across these studies to determine when a subject had attained the concept was the reliable identification of and distinction between examples and nonexamples. For example, subjects were said to have attained the concept of "equilateral triangle" when they could both recognize numerous examples of equilateral triangles, regardless of orientation or length of sides, and recognize that nontriangles and isosceles or scalene triangles were not examples of equilateral triangles. It could be argued, then, that the hallmark of concept attainment was the knowledge of a *procedure* to distinguish between examples and nonexamples of the concept.

To examine further the nexus of relationships among elements of one's procedural and conceptual knowledge consider, for example, knowledge of the concept "equilateral triangle." It is clear that knowledge of this elementary concept is related to knowledge of other concepts, such as "triangle," "isosceles triangle," "polygon," and "regular polygon." But it is equally clear that knowledge of this concept is also related to knowledge of *procedures* for constructing triangles, measuring the magnitude of sides and angles, and computing perimeter and area. Thus, in tasks requiring one to engage the concept of an equilateral triangle, there is a very high probability that one will also be engaging related conceptual and procedural knowledge. The exercise of purely conceptual knowledge may occur, if at all, only in carefully designed experiments run by clever researchers.

An argument parallel to the one just given for conceptual knowledge could be constructed for procedural knowledge. Consider, for example, knowledge of addition. When one learns to perform addition procedures in some number system, knowledge of the procedure is almost certainly related to conceptual knowledge about the nature of combining objects, the objects being combined, and adding in other systems or settings. Furthermore, knowledge of this procedure is influenced in the future when other procedures are learned for subtracting or multiplying the objects, because these new procedures relate to and generalize knowledge of the addition procedure.

The argument advanced here is not that there are no distinctions to be made between elements of one's knowledge base, or that one cannot more reasonably label some of those elements ''concepts'' and others ''procedures.'' Rather, the argument is that the two types of knowledge often, and almost always in any reasonably complex or otherwise interesting segment of human cognitive behavior, are inextricably linked. If the argument is valid, then it becomes more fruitful for us to study the linkages among elements of conceptual and procedural knowledge than to try to clarify the distinctions.

A Conceptual Basis for Procedures

For many years, researchers and practitioners at all educational levels have been fascinated by the systematic procedural errors made by students. The observation of procedural flaws that appear to be associated with conceptual deficiencies has led some to conclude that procedural knowledge must rest on a foundation of conceptual knowledge. William Brownell (1928, 1935) and other proponents of ''meaningful'' learning and teaching of arithmetic (e.g. Byers & Herscovics, 1977; Skemp, 1978) have suggested that a thorough understanding of computational procedures cannot be obtained without a solid conceptual basis. In support of this argument, popular educational folklore is replete with tales of children who can demonstrate apparent mastery of arithmetic procedures without having more than a very limited understanding of either the procedures and why they work or the objects upon which the procedure operates. Furthermore, there is no shortage of anecdotal reports from teachers concerned about students who can perform the procedures but who cannot apply them to novel problems or situations.

These observations have led some to conclude that procedural knowledge must rest on a conceptual knowledge base; in other words, that one of the purposes of conceptual knowledge is to form a support system for procedural knowledge. It should be reasonably clear, however, that one can demonstrate procedural fluency without conceptual knowledge. Human beings, and other animals as well, can be trained to respond to certain auditory stimuli, even if they have little knowledge of how the stimuli are generated, theories of tone or pitch, or the psychological theories underlying the experiment. In a more common setting, many people learn the complex procedures for operating motorized vehicles without any apparent understanding of gear/shift ratios or principles of internal combustion, or even knowledge of the stochastic models governing traffic flow. Furthermore, people can learn to perform complex procedures that operate on nonsense words or abstract symbols with no semantic reference system. It is clear that procedural fluency does not have to rest on a conceptual knowledge base.

Rather than arguing that procedural knowledge must rest on a conceptual base, it might be more reasonable and appropriate to observe that procedural knowledge can be quite limited unless it is connected to a conceptual knowledge base. For example, a person who knows how to prepare a meal only by following explicit cookbook directions is left almost helpless when a needed ingredient is unavailable or when the cookbook fails to be explicit about all the details; the person is unlikely to modify a recipe according to taste or to create other recipes based on one found in the cookbook. But when the person's procedural knowledge of cooking is enriched with conceptual information about the nature of spices, the role of various ingredients in the cooking process, and so on, then the person is likely to be able to apply the knowledge to novel situations.

Richard Skemp (1978) has distinguished between "instrumental" and "relational" understanding. By instrumental understanding, he refers to the rote performance of a procedure, whereas, relational understanding refers to the performance of the procedure with understanding. Relational understanding is characterized by a knowledge base for the procedure that is connected to a rich supply of knowledge about related procedures and concepts. Skemp has argued that students who possess relational understanding will be better able to transfer their knowledge to new tasks and situations and will be better able to solve novel problems. Evidence to support this hypothesis has frequently come from consideration of the contrapositive. In other words, as noted earlier, many students have procedural competence but are able neither to transfer their procedural knowledge to new situations nor to solve novel problems. When we examine their knowledge, we observe that they have only instrumental understanding of the procedures. From this evidence we conclude that a relational understanding of the procedure would lead to better transfer and wider application of the procedural knowledge.

A Procedural Basis for Concepts

In the last section we argued that conceptual knowledge is neither necessary nor sufficient for procedural knowledge. Now let us consider a less common but also plausible proposal, namely, that conceptual knowledge is based on procedural knowledge. As noted earlier, one's knowledge of the concept "equilateral triangle" can be thought of as depending on a procedure for distinguishing between examples and non-examples. At a somewhat higher conceptual level, it could be argued that one's concept of addition rests on one's knowledge of procedures for adding in various contexts.

To explore this contention, let us consider the concept of "related problems." My dissertation study (Silver, 1977, 1979) and some follow-up research (Silver,

1981) dealt with students' perceptions of problem similarity, particularly the bases on which junior high school students decide that two problems are or are not mathematically related. In that research, I was especially interested in the relationships among students' perceptions of problem relatedness, their ability to solve the problems, and the information they remembered about the problems and their solutions after a problem-solution episode. Some of the data from these studies can be reanalyzed and interpreted in relation to the issue of conceptual and procedural knowledge. These analyses suggest that studies of students' perceptions of problem relatedness have the potential for increasing our understanding of the complex relationships among elements of a students' conceptual and procedural knowledge bases.

In many ways, the study of perceptions of problem relatedness is a natural area for exploring the relations among procedural and conceptual knowledge. When a person is asked whether or not two problems are mathematically related, the judgment made is likely to be based on procedural knowledge (i.e., two problems are related if the same procedure can be used to solve them), but the judgment is indicative of a possible conceptual organization of problem information (i.e., clusters of problem "types"). Thus, this area of research represents a natural confluence of procedural and conceptual knowledge. It is fairly common in discussions of procedural/conceptual linkages, whether in psychological journals or in the popular pedagogical literature, to describe the dependence of procedural knowledge on conceptual knowledge. This area offers a straightforward example of conceptual knowledge that is apparently dependent on procedural knowledge, that is, the conceptual category of similar problems depends on the procedural knowledge needed for problem solution. But, as we might expect, the apparent dependence in this case is more complicated than it might appear at first glance.

In my research on students' perceptions of problem relatedness, I found that high ability students generally categorized and related problems on the basis of the problems' mathematical structural characteristics (e.g., on the basis of underlying equation structure). One aspect of that categorization, however, that is particularly relevant for the discussion in this paper was the students' ability to distinguish between classes of problems with different structural characteristics, despite the fact that they often did not have distinct techniques available for solving the different classes. For example, many of the high ability students were able to distinguish a class of problems that had an equation structure consisting of two simultaneous linear equations from a class of problems that had a different underlying equation structure consisting of only one complicated linear equation. Yet the students solved both classes of problems by using very similar (in fact, almost identical) trial-and-error procedures. In this instance, it would be difficult to argue that the conceptual categories of related problems for these classes of problems were based on procedural information about how to solve the problem. Thus, even in this setting, the apparent dependence of conceptual knowledge on procedural information is not as obvious as it might have seemed at first.

SYSTEMATIC PROCEDURAL ERRORS

In recent years, the analysis of systematic procedural flaws, or "bugs," has received increased attention. The seminal work of Brown and Burton (1978) on multidigit column subtraction errors suggests that a purely procedural view of procedural bugs can be productive. Nevertheless, neither their analysis nor other analyses inspired by their work has explained the basis for a large percentage of the errors that children make, nor has it directly addressed the remediation of the errors, with reference to the total knowledge base—both conceptual and procedural—that the child possesses or with reference to the total curriculum that is being taught.

The study of "bugs" opens one window from which one can view relationships between procedural and conceptual knowledge. Systematic bugs in procedures can often be traced to flaws in conceptual knowledge or to the lack of conceptual/procedural knowledge linkages. In this section we examine in some detail this contention regarding the relationship between a procedural "bug" and the conceptual support for the error. We begin by considering two examples briefly and then examine in detail an error in rational number addition.

Benny's "Bug"

Erlwanger's (1973) classic study of Benny reminds us that one can "have" procedural competence when it is examined on only a very narrow class of tasks, yet fail to "have" the competence when a broader class of tasks is considered. Benny appeared to have the correct procedure for adding column arrangements of decimal numbers when only one arrangement was given. For example, when asked to find sums in problems like ".2 + .4 = ?" or "2. + 4. = ?," Benny could reliably and accurately answer ".6" and "6," respectively. Yet Benny exhibited a serious bug when alternative arrangements were presented. For example, when asked to find the sum ".2 + 4. = ?", Benny gave the answer ".6."

What can be said about Benny's procedural bug? It is interesting that Benny's procedural bug appears to have conceptual aspects. If his conceptual knowledge of place value and the decimal point were flawed, then it might provide the needed support for the procedural error. On the other hand, if his conceptual knowledge were sound, then the procedural/conceptual knowledge linkages would need to be examined in order to understand the basis for his error.

A LOGO "Bug"

Now let us consider a more contemporary procedural bug, which is common for students studying geometry in connection with LOGO, a graphics-oriented computer language. A very familiar task in LOGO-based courses is writing a program to construct an equilateral triangle. It is common for students, at educational levels ranging from elementary school to college, to err in their first attempt to program the construction of the triangle—even though the task is usually given to students who already "have" the concept of an equilateral triangle. In my experience with college students, they would be able not only to distinguish between examples and nonexamples of equilateral triangles but also to give a correct verbal definition of the concept. The standard erroneous program is the following:

FORWARD 100
RIGHT 60
FORWARD 100
RIGHT 60
FORWARD 100

Although this program appears reasonable at first glance, it does not result in the construction of an equilateral triangle. Most students are surprised to find that the LOGO turtle appears to be drawing part of a regular hexagon rather than all of an equilateral triangle. The difficulty, of course, is that the students' concept of an equilateral triangle is very strongly dependent on knowledge of side length and *interior* angle size, but the correct LOGO procedure depends on side length and *exterior* angle size. For some students, the error is difficult to correct because they do not know how to identify the needed and missing element in their conceptual knowledge. This deficiency in their conceptual knowledge would never have been discovered in standard concept attainment tasks. The conceptual deficiency was uncovered in a setting in which the students were asked to use their conceptual knowledge to construct a procedure needed to solve a problem.

A Rational Number Addition "Bug"

Some errors that students make are easy to eradicate, whereas others persist for many years. The focus of this section of the paper is a particular example of a procedural bug that persisted for many years despite several attempts to correct it. The error may have persisted because of an underlying conceptual network of partially flawed ideas related to the procedure. This conceptual network may have acted as a support system for the error and may have been largely responsible for the persistence and resilience of the error.

The data discussed in this section are drawn from a study of rational number understanding conducted several years ago (Silver, 1983). The study involved about 200 young adults enrolled in community college arithmetic courses or university courses designed for prospective elementary school teachers. The study proceeded in three phases: (a) administering written tests to identify students to participate in follow-up interviews; (b) conducting clinical interviews with selected students to probe the nature of a student's understandings and misunderstandings of rational numbers; and (c) designing appropriate instruction for selected students to assist them in correcting their misunderstandings.

In addition to the problems from the written tests, subjects completed several additional tasks designed to probe their understanding. In some of the tasks, subjects were instructed to close their eyes and to describe what they "see in their mind's eye" when the interviewer said the name of a fraction or a statement about fractions, such as "one third plus one sixth" or "Which is larger, three fifths or five eighths?" Subjects were encouraged to describe the evoked image in as much detail as possible, using pictorial, physical, or verbal descriptions or any combination of these. Subject were then asked to explain fully their responses. On the basis of an individual subject's responses to written test items, other tasks were chosen or designed to probe the underlying conceptual basis of the subject's behavior.

A common error for these students was the so-called freshman error of adding numerators and adding denominators. For example, when asked to find the sum of $\frac{1}{2} + \frac{1}{3}$, these students commonly answered $\frac{2}{5}$ [obtained as $(1+1)/(2+3)$]. Although this error has a great deal of intuitive appeal and is common among students who are first learning the subject, it is striking that the error had persisted for so long with these students, despite many attempts by teachers to eradicate the error. This error is fairly commonly made by children (cf. Carpenter, Coburn, Reys, & Wilson, 1978). The usual explanations for this error seemed inadequate in the face of the fact that for at least 5 school years these young adults had received instruction designed to correct the error.

After conducting interviews with individual students and analyzing their responses to a wide range of fraction-related questions, we realized that the resilience of this error was due in large measure to an underlying conceptual support system that reinforced not only the erroneous answer but also the strategy used to obtain the answer. In particular, the students were characterized by an overdependence on a single mental and physical model for the fraction concept. Almost universally, the students had only one available model for a fraction— the part/whole model expressed as sectors of a circle. That particular model of a fraction is the most heavily taught and illustrated in school mathematics instruction. It is very useful for certain purposes and can be used to illustrate the correct algorithm for addition of fractions. However, for the students in my study, the dominance of this model combined with other elements of their knowledge base (e.g., a static interpretation of fraction addition, lack of distinction between fraction addition and ratio combination situations) to establish a conceptual knowledge base that was in direct support of the error.

For these students, their mental image of the sum of two fractions consisted of two separate images, one for each of the addends; and the sum was found by counting shaded regions and forming the fraction "shaded regions/total number of regions" as one does in the part/whole model. Not only does the final answer correspond to the freshman error, but the procedure is also modeled in their thinking. The students were asked to give an example of a situation in which addition of fractions might occur in everyday life. Seven of the students responded with ratio situations, for which the combination of ratios would not correspond to the sum of fractions. For example, several students gave examples like this one: Suppose you are playing softball and you get 2 hits in 5 times up (that's like $\frac{2}{5}$) and then next time you get 1 hit in 4 times up. What you did altogether is like two-fifths plus one-fourth.

Another aspect of the resilience of the fraction addition error was also evident in that study. One phase of the study involved remediation, using manipulative materials and instructional approaches designed to provide a rich conceptual foundation for fraction operations. The students' addition error was able to resist correction, whereas errors in other areas of fraction manipulation (e.g., equivalence, comparison) were relatively easily corrected. Moreover, some of the students were not troubled by the fact that they could obtain one answer when solving a problem using manipulative materials and a different answer when solving the problem symbolically with paper and pencil. One subject correctly solved the problem, $\frac{1}{4} + \frac{1}{6}$, using fraction bars but gave the answer, $\frac{2}{10}$, for the written problem. When confronted with the discrepancy, she said: ''Well that's the answer when you are working with bars and other is the answer when you are working with numbers.''

Similar evidence of compartmentalized knowledge has been reported in a number of different contexts (e.g., Lawler, 1981). In general, the research into this phenomenon suggests that children learn to segregate school knowledge from real-world knowledge. In the study just cited, it may have been that the work with symbols was viewed as school knowledge, whereas the work with objects was viewed as real. Yet, without some expectation by the students that one should obtain the same answer to the same problem solved in different ways, it is difficult to imagine that the students could be helped in a lasting way by any program of remediation.

It is reasonable to hypothesize that at least part of the reason for the failure of the instructional intervention is that the instructional routines utilized circular and rectangular regions and may have reinforced the conceptual underpinnings of the error. Although the instruction was well designed and had been used effectively with younger students, it was not successful with the older students. It might have been more appropriate and effective to develop alternate instructional routines based on different models for fractions, thereby enriching the conceptual base of the students. In dealing with procedural errors that are resistant to instructional intervention, we would probably be well advised to examine the conceptual basis for the error and to examine the possibility that our instructional procedures may be reinforcing the error rather than eradicating it.

The results of this study suggest that the fraction addition error may be so robust because it has considerable conceptual support in the thinking of the subjects who make the error. It is fairly common (cf. Carpenter et al., 1978) and reasonable to attribute the error, when it is made by young children, to an incorrect generalization of whole number addition. Such an explanation, however, may not be sufficient to explain the error for the subjects in this study. For an error to persist for as many years as this error did for many of the subjects, despite numerous instructional attempts to eradicate it, the error must have considerable conceptual support in subjects' thinking about rational numbers.

The nature of the static, circular region images for statements of fraction addition, together with the dominance of the part–whole interpretation of fractions, may suggest the presence of the needed conceptual support for the error to persist. Moreover, the tendency of many subjects to report ratio situations when asked to produce situations in which addition of fractions would apply also suggests the existence of an underlying conceptual support system that would allow the error to endure, despite well-meaning attempts to correct it.

The addition error was resistant to systematic attempts to use fraction bars or cardboard regions as concrete instruction materials. However, the use of the measuring cup was successful for the subjects with whom it was used. Perhaps the fraction bars and cardboard regions were not successful because they reinforced the dominant image of a fraction that was partly responsible for the error. The measuring cup, on the other hand, provided an alternative model for fractions that enabled the subjects who used it to become more flexible in their thinking about fractions. It is not clear what aspects of the measuring cup image were most helpful to subjects. It is possible that other alternative models would also be effective.

It would be unwise, and probably untrue, to argue that subjects saw the image of two circular regions when they solved a written fraction addition problem, or that they thought of a situation in which such a problem might have arisen. Nevertheless, the images and situations reported by subjects, when asked to do so, suggest that their basic thinking about rational numbers would support the error that they make when adding fractions. It is worth noting that the basic ideas that subjects had about rational numbers were largely correct; however, they were generalized and combined in inappropriate ways.

PROBLEM SOLVING WITH UNDERSTANDING

A major thesis underlying this paper is that mathematical problems are useful vehicles for the study of conceptual and procedural knowledge, since problem solving typically requires the application of both kinds of knowledge. This appears to be especially true when the solver needs to understand the problem situation before a solution can be obtained. Although it is generally aruged that problem solving involves understanding, it is also well known that solvers often proceed without much understanding and that they can often be successful by using procedures that bypass understanding processes. For example, students often decide on the appropriate operation to use in solving a textbook story problem not by understanding the problem situation and acting accordingly, but rather by examining the numbers with respect to the frequency, size, divisibility, and so on (e.g., if there are two numbers and one is very large compared with the other, probably divide; if more than two numbers, probably add). These "rules of thumb" for solving story problems allow the solver to generate answers rapidly with a fairly high success rate. Although the formulation of such rules may involve the application of conceptual knowledge about the algorithms and characteristics of problems that require their use, it is neither that kind of problem nor that kind of behavior that is of primary interest in this section of the paper. The interplay between conceptual and procedural knowledge is even more evident when we consider problems that *require* some level of understanding or interpretation for their solution.

A Problematic Division Problem

Consider the following whole number division problem, which has appeared on the California Assessment Program Mathematics Test at Grade 6:

> The 130 students and teachers from Marie Curie School are going on a picnic. Each school bus holds 50 passengers. How many buses will they need?
>
> a)2   b) 2 R 30   c)$2\frac{3}{5}$ d)3

In 1983, only about 35% of sixth-grade students were able to answer the question correctly. It is surprising that so many of the sixth graders were unable to solve this fairly simple problem. Yet these findings are consistent with those for a related problem administered to a national sample of 13-year-olds on the mathematics portion of the National Assessment of Educational Progress in 1982 (NAEP, 1983). That problem, "An army bus holds 36 soldiers. If 1,128 soldiers are being bused to their training site, how many buses are needed?" was correctly solved by only 24% of the 13-year-olds.

It is interesting to speculate about the causes of difficulty in these problems. It is possible that students do not understand that these are division problems and that they use some other algorithm to find the solution. It is also possible that they cannot perform the necessary arithmetic accurately. On the other hand, it might be that the presence of implicit assumptions and information in the problems is the source of the difficulty. For example, it may be that students do not understand that they are to transport ALL the people on the buses and leave no one behind or that it is acceptable for one of the buses to be only partially full. These factors were examined in a recent study that was conducted with eighth-grade students.

Exploring the Causes of Difficulty.   The study consisted of two phases: the first involved the writing and administration of written test items to a large sample of eighth-grade students; the second phase involved clinical interviews with individual students. In the first phase, special items were written in order to test some of the various explanations for the poor performance, as discussed in the previous section. Each item targeted a specific explanation or combination of explanations. The new items were then included in the pilot testing for the eighth-grade mathematics portion of the California Assessment Program (CAP). The basic problem remained the same as the one given above except that the number of children and teachers was changed to 730. In all, nine multiple-choice variations of the problem and two related problems were written and administered in this part of the study.

The problem variants were designed to examine possible contributing factors in the difficulty of the original problem. On the sixth-grade test, there was a version of the problem in which students were presented with the data and asked which operation (i.e., addition, subtraction, multiplication, or division) would be used to answer the question. Inasmuch as sixth-grade students did very well on that problem (about 80% correct responses), the possibility that the eighth graders did not recognize this problem as a division problem was dismissed and was not examined in this study.

Two factors judged to be likely contributors to problem difficulty were manipulated to create the variants: presence/absence of worked-out computation and explicit/implicit information. In the COMP variants, students were given the problem with the arithmetic worked out in detail. For COMP, they were told that the arithmetic shown was correct and were asked to select the "most sensible" answer to the question. In the EXPLICIT variants, the answer choices were elaborated (EXPLICIT1: "They will need 15 buses. Some of the seats will be empty"; EXPLICIT2: "They will need 14 buses. Some of the children will not go on the picnic"; EXPLICIT3: both EX1 and EX2 information was given) or certain implicit information in the problem was made explicit in the statement of the question (EXPLICIT4: "If *no one* is to be left off the buses, how many buses will they need?"). Thus, the original problem and nine variants of the problem were obtained by crossing COMP/NON-COMP versions and EXPLICIT/IMPLICIT versions of the problem, with the original problem being the NON-COMP & IMPLICIT version.

Each item was administered to approximately 160 different eighth-grade students as part of the pilot testing of the eighth-grade test. Due to the matrix-sampling techniques employed in the CAP test, no student completed more than one variant of the problem. Table 7.1 summarizes the results of the testing.

The results indicate that both the presence of worked-out computation (COMP variants) and the explicit mention of implicit problem information (EXPLICIT variants) positively affect performance, although the mere presence of the worked-out computation (COMP & IMPLICIT) had a relatively modest effect on performance. The combination of worked-out computation and explicit informa-

TABLE 7.1
Number of Students and Percent Correct for Problem Variants

	NON-COMP		COMP	
	N	% Correct	N	% Correct
IMPLICIT	178*	44*	161	53
EXPLICIT1	154	67	160	70
EXPLICIT2	160	51	155	58
EXPLICIT3	177	53	167	55
EXPLICIT4	168	51	159	58

*These are the data for the basic problem.

tion did not make the problem noticeably easier, except when the explicit information related to the correct answer choice (COMP & EXPLICIT1).

The most dramatic effects were noted for the problem variants (COMP & EXPLICIT1 and NON-COMP & EXPLICIT1) in which the correct answer choice was enhanced with implicit information: "They will need 15 buses. Some of the seats will be empty." On these variants, about 70% of the students were able to answer correctly, as opposed to about 45% on the original problem.

How do we interpret the performance of the students on these problems, and what light does their performance shed on the nature of the difficulty with the original problem? The presence of the correct worked-out computation had a mild but not dramatic positive effect on performance. This suggests that most of the students were probably capable of doing the necessary arithmetic. These findings are consistent with NAEP data for the army bus problem, in which some students were given access to a calculator. The calculator group actually performed less well than the noncalculator group on the problem.

The explicit mention of implicit assumptions in the problem also did not have a major effect on performance, except in the case of enhanced information about the correct answer choice. The presence of the explanation "some of the seats will be empty" did have a positive effect on performance. However, the strongest effect for this information was noted in the version in which the correct choice was the only one enhanced. Given students' tendency to choose the most unusual answer choice (e.g., the choice that is much longer than the others), one has to be cautious in asserting that the information given in that choice was the major factor influencing students' selection of that option.

Although the availability of worked-out computation and the explicit mention of implicit information about the problem or answer choices did have a positive effect on performance, only about 50% (and never more than 70%) of the students were able to solve the problem correctly with the available help and clarification. These data suggest that computational difficulties and the involvement of implicit information and assumptions in the problem are not sufficient to explain the poor performance of eighth-grade students on the original problem. We got a more complete picture of the possible roots of the difficulty when we examined performance on the other related items.

In addition to the problem variants just discussed, two other "related" problems were written and administered to the eighth graders. These two problems were designed to determine whether or not the students understood the worked-out computation problem used in some of the variants discussed earlier. The two related problems essentially presented the COMP & IMPLICIT version of the problem but asked a different question. One of the problems asked students to choose the answer option that best expressed the meaning of the number 14 (the quotient) in the division computation; the other asked for the best choice expressing the meaning of the number 30 (the remainder). Only 30% of the students correctly answered the question about the quotient, and 40% correctly answered the question concerning the remainder.

The performance of the students on these two problems was surprisingly poor. In particular, the success rate on these "related" problems was lower than on the basic problem. Especially surprising was the poor performance on the problem asking for an interpretation of the quotient. It was expected that students might have some difficulty interpreting the remainder, but they had an even lower success rate in interpreting the quotient in this situation. These data suggest that the students have a very limited understanding of the division process and the relationships among the symbolic expression of the long division, the components of that symbolic expression, and the semantic features of the problem situation.

The Interviews.   The second phase of this study involved clinical interviews with five eighth-grade students, in which some of the previous problems and some other related problems were solved and discussed. One item included in the interview was a problem variant in which there was no remainder. Each of the students was able to solve this problem correctly, but when presented with questions similar to the "related" problems discussed earlier, only one was able to explain adequately what the quotient and remainder meant in this setting.

In division situations, the dividend represents some quantity that is to be partitioned into shares of equal size. There are two common interpretations of division: partitive and quotitive. In a partitive situation, we know the number of equal shares and need to determine the size of each share. An example of a partitive situation is given in the following problem:

John has 54 marbles to give away. If he gives the same number of marbles to each of his 6 friends, how many marbles will each receive?

On the other hand, in a quotitive situation we know the size of each of the equal shares and we need to determine the number of shares. An example of a quotitive situation is given in the following problem:

John has 54 marbles to give away. If he gives 6 marbles to each friend, to how many friends can he give marbles?

In the interviews, each student was asked to give two examples of real-life division situations. The students had a definite tendency to interpret division situations as partitive. In fact, 9 of the 10 examples given were partitive. This suggests another element of conceptual knowledge that may be influencing performance and understanding relative to this problem.

The data from this study suggest that the explanation of students' errors on the original division problem may involve a complicated nexus of conceptual and procedural knowledge and interrelationships. For example, the data suggest that the students lack a correct procedure for handling the remainders that occur during the calculation. But the data also suggest that the lack of a procedure may be due to a lack of understanding of what a remainder is and how the remainder relates to the problem situation. Moreover, there is evidence that the students also do not understand well the nature of the quotient and its relation to the problem situation.

The data regarding the excessively partitive interpretation of division situations by the students may suggest that there was further difficulty with this problem because it presents a quotitive division situation instead of a partitive one. On the other hand, it may be that the dominance of a partitive view of division is partly responsible for the lack of understanding of the division algorithm—the nature of quotients and remainders—since that algorithm is typically understood, if at all, from a quotitive point of view. For example, students are taught to interpret the indicated division "846 ÷ 9" as the question, "How many 9s are there in 846?" That question represents a quotitive interpretation of division rather than a partitive one. Furthermore, most approaches to the "meaningful" teaching of the division algorithm have been influenced by the classic report by Van Engen and Gibb (1953) and rely on a quotitive interpretation of division. Thus, we see that it is possible that part of the difficulty with the basic problem is the lack of understanding of the decision procedure for handling remainders and quotients in general and that students' lack of understanding may be due, at least in part, to the mismatch between the partitive interpretation of division, which appears to be prominent in their thinking, and the quotitive interpretation, which is dominant both in instruction and in the given problem situation.

It is not possible on the basis of the data presented here to be completely specific about all the factors contributing to the difficulty of the original problem, but the complexity of the interrelationships among elements of relevant knowledge is clear. At this time, further investigations are being planned that should allow for a more complete specification of the relations among the relevant items of knowledge. This analysis could then be used to suggest a possible redesign of instruction in whole number division.

We began this portion of the paper by considering a rather simple division problem that turned out to be quite difficult for sixth- and eighth-grade students to solve. Our analysis of the roots of that difficulty has led us into an intricate web, consisting of strands of conceptual and procedural knowledge. Our journey has suggested that it is indeed reasonable to study relationships among elements of procedural and conceptual knowledge using mathematical problem-solving situations. Moreover, our journey, like the rest of our journeys in this paper, has surely indicated how complex some of those relationships can be.

ACKNOWLEDGMENTS

I am grateful to Art Baroody, Paul Cobb, Tommy Dreyfus, Jim Hiebert, Robert Hunting, Jim Kaput, and David Wheeler for their comments on an earlier draft of this manuscript. Credit for any improvements found in the current version must surely be shared with them, although blame for any new deficiencies must rest solely with the author.

REFERENCES

Brown, J. S., & Burton, R. R. (1978). Diagnostic models for procedural bugs in basic mathematical skills. *Cognitive Science, 2* (2), 155–192.

Brownell, W. A. (1928). *The development of children's number ideas in the primary grades.* Chicago: The University of Chicago.

Brownell, W. A. (1935). Psychological considerations in the learning and the teaching of arithmetic. *The teachings of arithmetic* (Tenth Yearbook of the National Council of Teachers of Mathematics). New York: Teachers College, Columbia University.

Byers, V., & Herscovics, N. (1977). Understanding school mathematics. *Mathematics Teaching, 81,* 24–27.

Carpenter, T., Coburn, T., Reys, R., & Wilson, J. (1978). *Results from the first mathematics assessment of the National Assessment of Educational Progress.* Reston, VA: National Council of Teachers of Mathematics.

Erlwanger, S. H. (1973). Benny's conception of rules and answers in IPI Mathematics. *Journal of Children's Mathematical Behavior, 1,* (2), 7–26.

Fehr, H. (Ed.). (1953). *The learning of mathematics: Its theory and practice.* Washington, DC: National Council of Teachers of Mathematics.

Lawler, R. (1981). The progressive construction of mind. *Cognitive Science, 5,* 1–30.

National Assessment of Educational Progress. (1983). *The third national mathematics assessment: Results, trends and issues.* Denver: Education Commission of the States.

Shumway, R. (Ed.). (1980). *Research in mathematics education.* Reston, VA: National Council of Teachers of Mathematics.

Silver, E. (1977). Student perceptions of relatedness among mathematical word problems. *Dissertation Abstracts International, 39,* 734A-735A. (University Microfilms No. 78-12,015)

Silver, E. (1979). Student perceptions of relatedness among mathematical verbal problems. *Journal for Research in Mathematics Education 10,* 195–210.

Silver, E. (1981). Recall of mathematical problem information: Solving related problems. *Journal for Research in Mathematics Education, 12,* 54–64.

Silver, E. (1983). Probing young adults' thinking about rational numbers. *Focus on Learning Problems in Mathematics, 5,* 105–117.

Skemp, R. (1978). Relational and instrumental understanding. *Arithmetic Teacher, 26,* 9–15.

Van Engen, H. and Gibb, G. (1956). *General mental functions associated with division* (Educational Service Studies No. 2). Cedar Falls: Iowa State Teachers College.

8 Procedures Over Concepts: The Acquisition of Decimal Number Knowledge

James Hiebert
Diana Wearne
University of Delaware

We argue in this chapter that mathematical competence is characterized by connections between conceptual and procedural knowledge. More specifically, we argue that mathematical incompetence often is due to an absence of connections between conceptual and procedural knowledge. We identify several points in the problem-solving process where links between concepts and procedures may be especially critical and consider what happens when such links are not established.

It must be remembered that how concepts and procedures interact is not yet well understood. Although the contributors to this volume lay important pieces into the puzzle, many questions remain. For example, we cannot yet specify how links between concepts and procedures are established, or how to design instruction to create such links. What we can do is present some relevant information on the kind of mathematical behavior that seems to emanate from the absence of critical connections between concepts and procedures.

Although there may be other interpretations of the data, we believe that the weight of the logical arguments, the rational task analyses, and the empirical data converge to the conclusion that poor performance in school mathematics often can be traced to a separation between students' conceptual and procedural knowledge of mathematics. The separation, together with the emphases of ordinary instruction programs (see chapters in this volume by Baroody & Ginsburg, by Carpenter and by Schoenfeld), seems to lead to an overreliance on procedural skill and on syntactic features of the written symbol system. The result is that students' mathematical behavior often consists of looking at surface features of problems and recalling and applying memorized symbol manipulation rules. Mathematically unreasonable answers often are produced, and performance is low across a range of problems, even on those directly instructed and frequently practiced.

To document our claim that many students fail to connect conceptual and procedural knowledge and that the consequences of these failures are damaging, we present performance and interview data on students' work with decimal numbers—numbers that may include digits to the right as well as to the left of the decimal point. The decimal number system comprises the lion's share of the elementary and junior high school mathematics curriculum. By the time students reach high school, they have received many hours of verbal instruction on whole numbers, decimal fractions, and related topics of common fractions. Even more time has been spent practicing the rules for computing, translating between forms, and solving problems with these numbers. Decimal numbers, in other words, is a topic that is familiar and well practiced. Our aim is to present a picture of students' conceptual and procedural knowledge of decimal numbers and to describe the effects of failing to make connections between them.

Definitions of Conceptual and Procedural Knowledge

As illustrated by the varying perspectives in this volume, definitions of conceptual and procedural knowledge in mathematics lack clear consensus. There is some general agreement about certain fundamental features of each type of knowledge but less agreement about the exact location of the boundaries that separate them. Our definition of conceptual and procedural knowledge is consistent with that presented by Hiebert and Lefevre in chapter 1 of this volume. Conceptual knowledge is defined as knowledge of those facts and properties of mathematics that are recognized as being related in some way. Conceptual knowledge is distinguished primarily by relationships between pieces of information. A fact or proposition becomes part of conceptual knowledge only when it is taken in by a larger network through recognizing or constructing relationships between the individual fact and part of a network that already is in place. Many relationships can serve to hook an individual piece of information to a larger system. In mathematics, the metaphor plays an especially important role (Davis, 1984). Often bits of knowledge are fit into place when it is noticed that they are *like* other things that already have been assimilated.

Consider the following example. In second grade, most students are taught the names of the position values of whole numbers (ones, tens, hundreds, etc.). If this knowledge is acquired and stored as isolated pieces of information that provide verbal labels for the value of each position, it does not qualify as conceptual knowledge. However, if the knowledge becomes linked with other numerical information already known, such as counting by tens and hundreds, and grouping objects by ten, then it becomes conceptual. The conceptual network of place value grows as other related bits of knowledge, such as regrouping to add and subtract, are related to earlier ideas.

In contrast, procedural knowledge is characterized by the absence of embedding relationships. For our purposes, procedural knowledge is best thought of in two parts. One part is the knowledge of written symbols in the syntactic system. Symbols are marks on paper that behave in well-defined ways. They are introduced, combined, and moved from one location to another according to syntactic rules. As defined here, procedural knowledge of symbols does not include knowing what the symbol "means," that is, knowing that the symbol represents an external referent. Procedural knowledge, by our definition, is limited to knowledge of how written mathematical symbols behave as part of a syntactic system.

The second part of procedural knowledge is the set of rules and algorithms that are used to solve mathematics problems. These procedures are step-by-step prescriptions for moving from the problem statement to the solution. For most school tasks, the prescriptions come in the form of rules for manipulating symbols. Computation algorithms, for example, are taught as symbol manipulation rules. A distinguishing feature of all procedures is that they are executed in a predetermined linear sequence. Solving problems often involves applying several subprocedures in step-by-step-fashion; the procedure specifies the order in which the subprocedures are executed.

To summarize the definitions, conceptual knowledge is knowledge that is rich in relationships but not rich in techniques for completing tasks. Procedural knowledge is rich in rules and strategies for completing tasks but not rich in relationships. Metaphorically speaking, conceptual knowledge is the semantics of mathematics and procedural knowledge is the syntax.

Overview of Interpretive Framework

In the process of doing mathematics, there are three *sites* where links between conceptual and procedural knowledge take on special importance (Hiebert, 1984). The sites are specified as points in real time during the problem-solving process. From a mathematical point of view, the sites represent three distinguishable phases in solving mathematical problems. They are selected because we believe they represent places where potential links between conceptual and procedural knowledge are especially productive and the absence of links are especially damaging.

Site 1 is the initial point in the problem-solving process, when the problem statement is interpreted. We will limit our discussion to problems that are presented with written symbols, not an overly restrictive limitation for dealing with school mathematics. Site 1, then, is the point at which the symbols of the problem are given some meaning. Two kinds of symbols must be interpreted—numerical symbols (e.g., 3, $\frac{2}{3}$, 1.7) and operational symbols (e.g., +, −). The meanings assigned to the symbols may come from the syntax (from within the store of procedural knowledge), or they may come from connecting the symbols with their conceptual referents. For example, a syntactic meaning of "÷" in the expression $\frac{7}{8} \div \frac{1}{4}$ would connect the symbol with the algorithm "invert and multiply," whereas a semantic meaning would connect the symbol with the intuitive or conceptual notion of "how many fourths are contained in seven-eighths." There are many reasons to believe that connections between symbols and conceptual referents provide the foundation for mathematical competence (see chapter 1, this volume). The importance of Site 1 is reinforced in our interpretive framework by the fact that connections between conceptual and procedural knowledge at Site 1 are essential for establishing connections at the remaining sites.

After the problem has been interpreted, procedures are selected and applied to solve the problem. The execution of procedures is the domain of Site 2. As mentioned earlier, many of the procedures that students are taught in school are rules that prescribe how to manipulate written symbols. Although all the rules are motivated by conceptual considerations, students may not link procedural rules with their conceptual rationales. The absence of such links need not hinder performance as long as procedures are recalled correctly and applied in appropriate contexts. However, as in Site 1, there are good reasons to believe that links at Site 2 between procedures and their conceptual underpinnings contribute to genuine competence.

Site 3 hosts the third point in the problem-solving process, where connections between conceptual and procedural knowledge are especially beneficial. Assuming the procedures have been executed, a response is produced that represents the student's answer to the problem. Conceptual features of the problem situation, while not generating exact answers, do provide some clues about the reasonableness of solutions. For example, the answer to $\frac{7}{8} + \frac{12}{13}$ should be about 2, since each fraction is about 1. Often, conceptual knowledge about the meaning of the symbols and about the operation used to solve the problem can be used to evaluate the reasonableness of the answer. The conceptual knowledge may be knowledge about the mathematical system (as in the previous example) or knowledge about external referents that are represented by the symbols.

The three sites of symbol interpretation, procedural execution, and solution evaluation provide an organizational scheme that allows us to analyze the existence of relationships between conceptual and procedural knowledge in a systematic way. In particular, we believe that the sites provide an interpretive framework that assists in diagnosing the source of many learning problems. We will use the framework to describe students' knowledge of the decimal number system and to assess the consequences of failing to connect concepts and procedures.

To keep the discussion within manageable limits we focus on *computation* with decimal fractions. There are many mathematical processes that could serve as the vehicle for examining relationships between conceptual and procedural knowledge at each of the three sites. Computation processes were chosen in part because they receive a great deal of emphasis during initial instruction on decimal fractions. Soon after being introduced to decimal fractions, students are shown how to compute. They then spend the majority of instructional time practicing computation skills. Thus, decimal computation represents a topic in which upper elementary and junior high school students are well versed.

DECIMAL NUMBER KNOWLEDGE

Information about students' conceptual and procedural knowledge of decimal numbers comes from several sources. Two of the sources are large-scale national surveys, one in the United States (Carpenter, Corbitt, Kepner, Lindquist, & Reys, 1981; National Assessment of Educational Progress(NAEP), 1983) and one in England (Brown, 1981; Hart, 1981). Other sources are individual studies that describe group performance (Carr, 1983; Ekenstam, 1977; Fischbein, Deri, Nello, & Marino, 1985) and individual (Erlwanger, 1975) performance on decimal tasks and that report results of instructional lessons designed to remediate misconceptions (Bell, Swan, & Taylor, 1981). A final source is our recently completed observational project of elementary and junior high school students' knowledge of decimal numbers (Hiebert & Wearne, 1984). Because the results of this project play an important role in our interpretations of conceptual and procedural knowledge relationships, the project itself is described briefly.

Data were collected over a 2-year period from a total of about 700 students in grades four through nine, using written tests and individual interviews. Written tests were given in the fall and spring of each year, and interviews were conducted with a subset of about 100 students several times over the course of the school year. Written tests included items on place value with whole numbers and decimals, decimal computation, verbal problems with decimals, translation between decimal and common fractions, pictorial representations of decimals, and ordering decimals.

Three quasistandardized interviews were developed. The first interview explored students' ability to connect symbolic and concrete representations of decimal fractions. Representations were formed by iterative partitioning—dividing units into tenths, tenths into hundredths, and so on, a process that characterizes the decimal fraction system. Interview 2 extended the work with concrete materials to computation situations. The primary objective was to study the connections students make between written computation procedures and the conceptual rationale that motivates them. Interview 3 was designed to elicit students' rationale for the procedures they apply to written computation problems. Students were presented with selected computation problems and were asked to explain their own solution procedures and to teach the procedures to friends who had missed the instruction lessons.

Connections Between Conceptual
and Procedural Knowledge at Site 1

The description of relationships between conceptual and procedural knowledge at Site 1 is a description of the semantic meanings that students have established for the written symbols. The first step in solving a problem such as .4 × 2.3 is recognizing and assigning some meaning to the symbols .4, ×, and 2.3. Mathematically speaking, the appropriate referents for decimal numerical symbols come both from extending the place value notions from whole numbers and from common fraction ideas of part/whole. Students who have connected the symbols with either referent have created a semantic meaning for decimals. Appropriate referents for the operational symbols also come from extending and refining concepts used in previous contexts. For example, in whole number contexts, "×" represents the idea of creating multiple groups of a particular size. An extended or more general form of this concept is signaled in the illustration above, where "×" refers to taking *part* ($\frac{1}{10}$) of a group. An examination of the meanings students attribute to numeric and operation symbols provides some interesting insights into the complexities of linking conceptual and procedural knowledge.

Connecting Numerical Symbols With Whole Number Concepts.   Extending concepts of whole numbers into referents that are appropriate for decimal fraction symbols is a delicate process. Students must recognize the features of whole numbers that are similar to decimal fractions and those that are unique to whole numbers. Some features of the whole number system (e.g., regrouping by 10) can be imported and hooked to the decimal fraction symbol system, but others (e.g., numbers with more digits are larger) are not appropriate and do not generalize to the decimal fraction system. With some important exceptions, it is the conceptual features that generalize to decimals and the syntactic features that do not. The trick for students is to sort out which are which.

The evidence suggests that many students have trouble selecting the features of whole numbers that can be generalized. They do not easily extend concepts that do apply to decimal fractions, *and* they overextend syntax conventions that do not apply to decimal fractions. Some initial evidence that addresses the first difficulty suggests that students do not automatically import appropriate whole number concepts and link them with decimal symbols. Several items on our written tests asked students to write the whole number represented by a set of sticks pictured as singles, bundles of 10, and bundles of 100. Some items required regrouping before writing the number. Students had not practiced tasks of this kind as part of their textbook curriculum. A parallel series of items, using similar numbers of objects, showed a set of Dienes' (Base 10) Blocks and asked students to write the decimal fraction represented by the blocks. As part of each item, each block size was shown with its assigned value. The large cube had a value of "1," the flat had a value of ".1," and so on. Fifth graders had little trouble writing whole numbers for the sets of sticks. Even the more difficult double regrouping item was answered correctly by 76% of the students. But the link between whole numbers and pictured referents did not extend to decimals. Only 13% of the same group of fifth graders responded correctly to the parallel decimal item. The percentage rises to 36% in seventh grade and to 53% in ninth grade. The grade nine data suggest that after spending several years working with written decimal symbols, about half the students can connect the symbol with a pictured referent, a connection almost all of them can make in the whole number context. Apparently it is not true that students easily extend whole number ideas (e.g., regrouping tens) to the decimal fraction system.

Many students also experience the opposite problem—they overgeneralize features of whole numbers to decimal fractions. In most cases, overgeneralization results from wholesale application of syntax conventions. These cases are easier to identify than those just mentioned because students' error patterns on problems involving decimals often can be generated by the rules students use on whole number problems. The same rule generates correct responses on one class of problems but incorrect responses on the other class. Our confidence in this analysis is bolstered by converging data from many students, along with interview protocols in which students describe their procedures.

Features of the whole-number system that often are inappropriately applied to decimal fractions are captured in students' judgments of magnitude and of the role of zero. To our knowledge, all researchers who report data on ordering decimal fractions (Brown, 1981; Carpenter et al., 1981; Ekenstam, 1977; Grossman, 1983) suggest that many students have trouble judging the relative magnitude of decimal fractions if they have different numbers of digits to the right of the decimal point (e.g., 1.3 and 1.295). Most errors can be accounted for by assuming students ignore the decimal points and treat the numbers as whole numbers. In other words, students assume that the syntax rule "more digits means bigger" that works with whole numbers is true for decimal fractions as well. To get an estimate of the prevalence of this overgeneralization, we asked students to select the largest of .09, .385, .3, and .1814. The percentage of students responding correctly increased from 0% in grade five to 43% in grade nine. The most frequent incorrect response was .1814, with the following percentages of students selecting this response at grades 5, 6, 7, and 9: 89%, 46%, 44%, and 31% respectively.

It is tempting to assume that the process of acquiring magnitude rules is straightforward: students cling to their whole-number strategies until for one reason or another they shift to appropriate decimal strategies. However, this is not so for a number of students. They replace their whole-number strategy with one that is both unique to and inappropriate for decimal numbers. Some students seem to feel that the more digits there are to the right of the decimal, the smaller is the number (see also Resnick & Nesher, 1983). This was evidenced in our project by the steady *increase* in the percentage of students selecting .3 as the largest of the foregoing numbers, from 6% in grade five to 25% in grade nine. Similar percentages chose .065 when asked to identify the smallest of 1.006, .06, .065, and .09.

The rather strange notion that more digits to the right of the decimal means smaller also can be interpreted as an overgeneralization of syntax features, but this time it is decimal fraction features that are overgeneralized. Students learn that digits farther to the right represent smaller magnitudes, and apparently they extend this notion into one that says the entire number is smaller as digits extend farther to the right. Some students seem to employ a number-line model and believe that when digits are added the number is moving away from zero, thereby getting smaller. This meaning of decimal symbols may be transitional between the naive whole-number meaning and the appropriate meaning of decimals. Educationally, however, it is a matter of some concern since it still is the meaning of choice for many entering college freshmen (Grossman, 1983).

A second set of items illustrating the overgeneralization of whole number syntax deals with the role of zero in symbol configurations. It is clear that students' performance on decimal tasks is especially poor when correct answers depend on treating zero appropriately (Carpenter et al., 1981), and it appears that a good deal of students' confusion can be attributed to overgeneralization of the whole-number syntax rules.

A simple syntax convention for whole numbers is that attaching a zero to the right of a whole number increases the number by a factor of 10, whereas placing a zero on the left has no effect. An opposite type of syntax applies to decimal fractions. Many students fail to make this distinction during the first years of decimal instruction. During one of the interviews, we asked a total of 44 fifth, sixth, seventh, and ninth graders to select from a list of numbers those equivalent to .8 and to write some additional equivalent numbers. Two thirds of the fifth graders believed that only numbers with 0 to the left of 8 (on either side of the decimal point) were equivalent. About 20% of the students at the higher grades erred by importing this whole number convention. Another instance of the same overgeneralization occurs when asking for a number ten times as big as a decimal number. Brown (1981) reports that the majority of 12–15-year-old students interviewed placed a 0 to the right of the number for their response. Although this error was less common in our sample, the most frequent error to a written test item "Write a number ten times as big as 437.56" was 437.560.

Our data suggest that as students receive additional instruction, they are less inclined simply to import the whole number syntax conventions for zero. However, their perception of zero remains tied to varieties of other syntax conventions. A common perception is that zero is part of the procedural machinery. Zeros are used in computation when a rule prescribes inserting them as a step in the symbol manipulation process. Zeros are *not* viewed as representations of quantities. This point is illustrated by several interactions in which students describe their paper-and-pencil computation procedures.

A sixth-grade student had just computed 2 + .8 by writing 2.0

$$\begin{array}{r} 2.0 \\ \underline{.8} \\ 2.8 \end{array}$$

Interviewer (I):   Is it Ok to add a zero after the decimal?

Student (S):   Yeah, it says to add zeros [apparently referring to the textbook].

I: Does it change the number?

S: No.

I: Could you add two zeros?

S: No, just one.

I: How do you know how many to add?

S: Say it was 2 and it was .8567, then you would put zeros over the top of the numbers.

For some students, the syntactic notion of restricting the insertion of zeros to "filling the empty spaces" in computation clashes with another rule they learn for decimals: adding zeros on the right does not change the value. The following illustrates a seventh grader's reasoning:

Interviewer (I):   Tell me how you did number three (2 + .8).

Student (S):   There is no decimal point in there so it would be after. You line it up with that (.8) and put your zero there (2.0), then you add down, then bring down the decimal point.

I: So the 2 you can think of as 2.0? Does it make any difference if you put the zero in? Is it the same number?

S: Same number.

I: Could you put another zero in?

S: Then it would be different.

I: Why would that be different?

S: Well, it wouldn't really be different because after the decimal point, if there are zeros, they don't really have to be there.

I: Would it change the answer if you used this number (2.00)?

S: Yes.

Many students seem to have several different, contradictory rules for treating zero. One prescribes appropriate actions in computation situations, another operates in response to questions about equivalence. The seventh grader above continued by correctly solving .7 − .04, writing

$$\begin{array}{r} .70 \\ \underline{-.04} \\ .66 \end{array}$$

The student indicated that only one zero could be inserted with the .7; otherwise the answer would be too large. However, on the very next task, the student correctly identified all forms equivalent to .8 (e.g., .800, .800000, etc.) One fifth-grade student captured the perceptions of many students when asked whether .7 and .70 have the same value. The student said, "Um . . . well . . . it depends on what you're doing with it." In other words, the context determines what rules are accessed and how zero is perceived.

Students' treatment of zero illustrates a more general feature of their procedural knowledge. Many procedures, such as that for solving .7 − .04, can be viewed as compositions of subprocedures. The advantage of this view is that subprocedures, such as transforming .7 to .70, can be extracted from the larger procedure and recognized as applications of general concepts, in this case "equivalence." Considering subprocedures in this way has two advantages. First, one subprocedure is sufficient for applying the referenced concept in all contexts. Using a single subprocedure ensures consistent application of the concept. For example, .7 is equivalent to .70, .700, and so forth, regardless if one is adding, subtracting, ordering, or generating equivalent values. A second benefit is that a few core subprocedures can be used flexibly and combined in various ways to create many larger procedures. This reduces the number of separate procedural moves that must be learned and remembered. Thus, one subprocedure is sufficient to deal with zero and ensures consistent treatment in different contexts. But the picture that emerges from the data just presented is that many students do not view procedures this way. Students seem to learn procedures as a whole, indivisible. Subprocedures are not extracted and considered independently. Most students treat zero differently in different contexts because they manipulate zero only as a part of the larger procedural sequence.

To summarize, an important semantic component of the decimal numerical symbol has its origins in the place value concept of whole numbers. If students are to establish appropriate meanings for written decimal symbols they must link them with their conceptual understandings of whole numbers. Such links would promote generalization of appropriate concepts and encourage the recognition of powerful subprocedures. However, it appears that rather than bringing along their place value concepts, students overgeneralize syntactic conventions and apply syntactic rules as indivisible sequences. Tasks that involve ordering decimal fractions and dealing with zero reveal some of the conventions that are overgeneralized and some of the procedures that are inviolable. Often it appears that symbols are given meaning solely by the role they play in symbol manipulation procedures.

Connecting Symbols with Fraction Concepts.   Decimal fractions are one representation form for rational numbers; common fractions are another representation form for the same numbers. Two syntactic systems are connected to one semantic base. Relationships between fractions and decimals depend upon the fact that two different symbols represent the same concept. However, it appears that many students do not recognize the semantic linkage. They do not recognize, for example, that .3 is equivalent to $\frac{3}{10}$ because both represent three-tenths of a unit. Rather, most students relate common fractions and decimal fractions directly through syntactic rules.

A question that taps directly the relationships between fractions and decimals asks students to write an equivalent expression in one form given the other. The National Assessment data suggest that about half of 13-year-olds can translate between decimal and fraction forms in the easiest situations—when the denominators are powers of 10 (Carpenter et al., 1981). Our data show a similar level of expertise and, based on error responses, suggest that translation strategies change as students move from relative novices to relative experts. About one-fourth of our fifth graders simply converted the numerals of the given number to the alternate form (e.g., .09 = $\frac{0}{9}$). This represents an extremely simple kind of syntax rule: write a common fraction with the given numerals. Older students used strategies that produced answers that conform more closely to appropriate form. For example, when seventh and ninth graders were asked to write a fraction for .09, the most frequent error was $\frac{9}{10}$. It is difficult to tell whether these "more reasonable" errors reflect more conceptually informed responses or an equally rote application of syntax rules that are based on increased knowledge of syntax conventions (e.g., converting decimals to fractions always begins by placing a 10 or 100 or 1000, etc., in the denominator).

Responses on other tasks suggest that the second of the explanations is most plausible. Even many older students have not connected decimal symbols with fraction concepts and rely heavily on syntax rules. For example, students were asked to write a decimal fraction to represent the shaded part of a unit rectangular region. One region was divided into 10 equal parts with three shaded; a second was divided into 100 equal parts with four shaded; and a third was divided into five equal parts with one shaded. Not more than half the students, even in grade nine, responded correctly to any of these items. The most frequent errors on the three tasks in all grades were 3.10, 4.100, and 1.5, respectively. The frequency of these errors declines from about 50% in grade five to about 15% in grade nine. A plausible explanation for these responses is that students called up a common fraction response ($\frac{3}{10}$, $\frac{4}{100}$, $\frac{1}{5}$, respectively) and then manipulated the symbols into a decimal form. Notice that the responses are conceptually or semantically unreasonable but syntactically appropriate—one decimal point and at least some numerals to the right.

In general, students appear to work at a syntactic level that remains isolated from semantics. The two systems of common and decimal fractions are related through manipulations of the written symbols directly rather than through the intermediary of conceptual referents. This may be due in part to an impoverished conceptual base (Behr, Wachsmuth, Post, & Lesh, 1984), in which case linkages are severely constrained (Carpenter, this volume). But even in those domains where rudimentary part–whole concepts probably are in place (Pothier &

Sawada, 1983), linkages between symbols and concepts simply do not exist. As one seventh grader said after denying that .6 is equivalent to $\frac{6}{10}$, ".6 is 'six-tenths' and $\frac{6}{10}$ you say the same way, but it's different."

Connecting Operation Symbols with Arithmetic Actions. When first graders recognize that the joining action in the story "Susan had 5 marbles. Her father gave her 3 more marbles. How many marbles did Susan have altogether?" is a conceptual referent for "+" in $5 + 3 = \square$, then they have created meaning for the written symbol. Similarly, arithmetic actions involving "take away" or separating, making multiple groups of a particular size, and determining how many groups of a particular size can be formed from the total, are appropriate initial referents for the symbols $-$, $\times$, and $\div$, respectively. Other meanings, such as the difference or comparison meaning for "$-$," and the combinatorial or Cartesian product meaning for "$\times$," also are appropriate referents and, as they become connected, help to provide a more complete meaning for the symbols. It is important to note that the meanings do not include knowledge of methods that might be used to calculate the results of these actions; the meanings only convey the aim or intent of the calculations.

Two kinds of tasks provide some measure of whether students have established appropriate meanings for the operation symbols. One is estimation, in which students are asked to produce an approximate answer to a computation problem without using a conventional algorithm. For example, what would be a good guess for $3.012 \div .96$? A second type of problem is one in which students are asked to relate a computation expression to a story problem. The assumption here is that if students know the meaning of, say, "$\div$," they should be able to relate the expression $3.012 \div .96$ to a story that describes such a situation. The estimation tasks assess connections at Site 3 as well as Site 1 and consequently are presented later; what follows is a description of students' facility with computation story problems involving decimals.

By the time students reach upper elementary school, the symbols $+$ and $-$ are quite familiar, and primitive notions that often accompany these symbols, such as "$+$ makes bigger" and "$-$ makes smaller," can be brought to decimal numbers with no adverse effects (as long as the numbers are positive). In other words, the meanings of $+$ and $-$ can be generalized from whole numbers to positive decimal numbers without extension or modification. Since most students of this age can interpret one-step addition and subtraction whole-number stories (NAEP, 1983), they should be able to interpret simple addition and subtraction decimal-number stories as well. This expectation is confirmed by our students, who performed at the same level on story problems as on parallel symbolic computation problems.

Students' performance in multiplication and division situations presents a different picture. Unlike the case for addition and subtraction, primitive notions of multiplication and division cannot be transferred wholesale from whole numbers to decimals. Decimal numbers may be (and often are in students' experience) less than 1. Thus, multiplication does not always "make bigger," and division does not always involve "taking a smaller number into a bigger number." Students must extend the meanings of "×" and "÷" and suppress certain primitive notions that may develop in whole number contexts. Performance data suggest that many students do neither.

Students in our project, as in others (Bell et al., 1981; Fischbein et al., 1985), performed quite well on story problems in which the numerical values supported the primitive notions of multiplication makes bigger and division involves taking a smaller number into a bigger number. For example, Fischbein et al., (1985) report that most students (ages 10–15 years) identified multiplication as the operation needed to solve a story involving 15 groups of .75. However, in all studies performance drops dramatically on problems where the numerical values conflict with students' primitive meanings. The most striking example of this is reported by Bell et al. (1981). Many students (ages 12–15 years) correctly selected multiplication as the operation needed to solve a problem with n gallons of gasoline at m per gallon when n and m were whole numbers, but selected division for the *same* problem when n and m were decimal numbers with n *less* than 1.

As with numerical symbols, it appears that students overgeneralize certain aspects of their whole-number knowledge of operation symbols. Primitive meanings of multiplication and division are inappropriately transferred from whole number to decimal contexts. Conceptual referents that would give a more complete meaning to the symbols may be absent from many students' conceptual networks and at the least remain unconnected to the written symbols.

One final distinction should be noted. Whether or not students select the correct algorithmic procedure when they encounter an operation symbol is a question different from whether they have established a semantic meaning for the symbol. Selecting the appropriate syntactic rule is important, but the connection between the written symbols and the rule can be made entirely within the syntactic system. The meaning of the symbol, on the other hand, necessarily appeals to conceptual knowledge for connections and provides an entirely different kind of information. The meaning of the symbol tells you, in very general terms, what the algorithm is doing for you.

To summarize the situation at Site 1 and to anticipate what is to come, we will borrow an idea presented nicely by Byers and Erlwanger (1984). They point out that the content, or semantics, of mathematics is absolute, but the forms, or syntactic systems, that represent the content can vary. Keeping this distinction straight, they say, is the heart of mathematical competence. "Inability to distinguish between inferior form and incorrect content is one of the surest signs of not understanding mathematics" (p. 272). An overreliance on syntax can lead to a perceived reversal of these roles. Syntactic features become the primary guiding force in mathematical behavior. The number .06 is thought to be unequal to

$\frac{6}{10}$ because the syntax is different; the conceptual identity of .6 and $\frac{6}{10}$ is inconsequential. The initial value given in the story is less than 1, so the operation is thought to be something other than multiplication; the semantics of the story is inconsequential. It appears that few students have developed meaning for decimal symbols by connecting them with appropriate conceptual referents. Many students acquire decimal fractions as a new symbol system, isolated from semantics. The consequences of this separation will be seen at the remaining two sites.

Connections Between Conceptual and Procedural Knowledge at Site 2

"When once the notation is understood, addition and subtraction of decimals can offer no difficulties, and we pass them by to consider multiplication" (McLellan & Dewey, 1895, p. 263). We do not quarrel with McLellan and Dewey's claim, but since the information at Site 1 suggests that many students do not understand the notation, we might expect that difficulties in addition and subtraction do exist. In fact, we will focus our discussion at Site 2 on addition and subtraction and consider whether students have connected the procedures they use to compute with the rationale that motivates them.

One of the procedural rules that students first encounter when learning to add and subtract with decimals is "line up the decimal points." The rationale for the rule is that one can make sense of the answer when things are combined that have been measured with the same unit. The same rationale motivates lining up the numerals on the right before adding whole numbers, finding common denominators before adding fractions, adding like units when combining measurements, and combining like terms in algebra. Applied to decimals, it says that decimal points are aligned so tenths are combined with tenths, hundredths with hundredths, and so on. There is precedent for this idea in students' previous work (with whole numbers and fractions), it is conceptually rather simple (and powerful), and students spend time practicing it. The question is whether students use it appropriately and understand why it "works."

The first part of our written tests consisted of decimal computation items. The items were presented in horizontal form and were free response. The addition and subtraction items led to predictable errors if the line-up-the-decimal-points rule was not used. Table 8.1 lists the items that depend on using the line-up-the-decimal-points rule and shows the percentage of students at each grade that failed to follow the rule. The figures are a conservative estimate because they include only the students who chose the whole number rule—line up the numerals on the right—and not the students who used an alternate procedure. Clearly, not all students used the decimal rule appropriately, even after several years of instruction.

The next question is whether the students who correctly used the rule knew why it worked. During the third individual interview, students were given computation items like those on the written tests and were asked to explain their

TABLE 8.1
Percentage of Responses Resulting From Lining Up
Digits on the Right Rather Than Lining Up
Decimal Points

Item	Grade				
	4[a]	5[b]	6[c]	7[d]	9[e]
Addition					
5.3 + 2.42	25	42	30	14	3
5.1 + .46	46	36	50	19	7
6 + .32	71	72	86	47	15
4 + .3	90	84	84	53	14
Subtraction					
4.7 − .24	35	46	52	22	7
.86 − .3	71	69	86	43	18
7 − .4	85	88	88	59	20

Note. Data are from fall tests. Students performed similarly
in the spring, except for a lower incidence of this error on some
items in Grade 6.
[a]$N = 48$
[b]$N = 113$
[c]$N = 50$
[d]$N = 279$
[e]$N = 223$

procedures. If they described lining up decimal points on the addition and subtraction problems they were asked why they used the rule. Students were pressed
quite hard to describe all possible reasons for the rule. Later in the interview they
were asked to "teach" addition or subtraction to their friends who supposedly
had missed class, and they again were asked to justify lining up the decimal
points. The following percentages of students in each grade referred at *some* time
during the interview, even vaguely, to the values of the numbers or other conceptual bases for the rule: 0%, 12%, 33%, 60% in grades five, six, seven, and nine,
respectively. It appears that if the link between rule and rationale is established at
all, it is a late rather than an early development.

What seems to provide the bases for students' selection of procedures are
syntactic features of the problem. As noted earlier, the connections between the
written operation symbol and the related algorithmic procedure can be made
exclusively within the syntactic system. Indeed, many students in our project
displayed these syntactic links. Notice in Table 8.1 that the inappropriate line-
up-the-numerals-on-the-right rule nearly disappears (with age) on some items but
not on others. Notice also that the differences between problems that might
account for this change are syntactic rather than semantic. The problems are
conceptually nearly the same (adding or subtracting units, tenths, and hundredths) but are different syntactically (numbers have different number of digits

and some do not show a decimal point). The differential performance between items, then, suggests that even in the upper grades the line-up-the-decimal-points rule is tied to the form of the written symbols rather than conceptual considerations. As further support for this interpretation, we note that many students justified using the correct line-up-the-decimal-points rule by citing acceptable forms of symbol expressions. The following interchange is typical:

Interviewer (I):   Let's go back and talk about this one (.23 + .41). How did you know to add this like you did: .23
.41
―――
.64

Seventh-grade Student (S):   There are two places past the decimal. You have to line the decimals up.

I: Why do you have to line up the decimals?

S: Because otherwise it wouldn't come out right.

I: Why not?

S: You would have two decimals in two different places.

I: Where?

S: In the answer.

Apparently, the student believed that if the decimal points were not aligned, then two decimals would need to be placed in the answer. This would violate syntactic conventions and consequently would be incorrect. "Answers don't have two decimal points" is an example of well-formed answer rules described by Matz (1980). Students use these syntactic rules rather than conceptual knowledge to determine the acceptability of a response.

Another expression of students' reliance on syntax is the belief that rules can be mutually contradictory if they operate in different syntactic contexts. The belief is illustrated by the fact that a number of students assumed that identical problems presented in different formats called for different rules or methods and could yield different answers (additional instances of this belief are presented in chapters by Baroody and Ginsburg, by Carpenter, by Schoenfeld, and by Silver). During our second interview students were asked to compute the answers to four addition and subtraction problems with paper and pencil and then with base ten blocks. All the students had the information they needed to compute using the blocks due to the activities of the first interview. Using our previous experience, we selected problems to maximize the likelihood that students would get different answers on paper than with the blocks. When students got different answers, the results were compared and the students were asked whether it was acceptable to get different answers to the same problem. If they said it was not acceptable they were asked which answer they preferred, and why.

Many fifth and sixth graders believed it was permissible to get different answers to the same problem. Most often the justification for this belief was that they had used "different methods." In grade five, 6 of the 10 students who got different answers resolved this conflict in at least some cases by accepting both answers. In grade six, 6 of 11 students who found themselves in this situation accepted both answers as correct. In grade seven, none of the 7 students faced with this conflict accepted both answers. It appears that as students increase their facility with decimals the notion that different methods may produce different answers disappears. However, there is some evidence to suggest that the belief that different situations call for different methods and may produce different answers to the same problem is not eradicated as students get older but simply reappears in other contexts where the content is challenging. Such a belief is held by some students in some contexts at least through college (Kaput, 1982).

Believing that answers can change with different methods points again to an over-reliance on procedures and a lack of awareness of conceptual content. Using Byers and Erlwanger's (1984) terms, the appropriate roles are reversed— the form of the problem becomes the essential feature and the content is allowed to vary. Different methods for the same problem are not viewed as variants of a theme because the key to recognizing their similarities—the underlying conceptual content—is not connected with the methods and remains untapped. Thus, answers remain tied to procedural methods rather than to the conceptual content of the problem, and students come to believe that a single problem can have several different answers.

In summary, data from a variety of tasks suggest that students learn procedures for which they do not connect the conceptual rationale. At the least, conceptual rationale does not influence performance (see also Davis & Mc-Knight, 1980; Resnick, 1982). As we have seen, many students line up numerals on the right for decimal addition and subtraction; certainly these students are not influenced by the conceptual notion of adding like quantities. Even many students who perform correctly are not able to cite a rationale for the rules they have memorized. The absence of links between procedures and rationale is expressed further in the fact that many students who are beginning to learn about decimals believe that the answer to a computation problem depends on the procedure used rather than its conceptual content. The reliance on syntactic features that is evident for the few computation procedures considered here extends to all of decimal computation and is evident in older as well as younger students (Hiebert & Wearne, 1985). Site 2 shows a marked separation between conceptual and procedural knowledge.

Connections Between Conceptual and Procedural Knowledge at Site 3

Site 3 is the point in the problem-solving process when the written answer has just been obtained. Mathematical competence expresses itself through an ability to evaluate the reasonableness of the answer. Gelman and Meck (this volume) identify a similar competency in nonsymbolic contexts and propose it as an important mechanism of learning. We believe that such a competency in written contexts requires connections at Site 1, connections between both the numeric and operation symbols and appropriate conceptual referents. Connections at Site 2 (between procedural rules and concepts) are not required.

For example, consider the problem 3.152×24.98. Judging that an answer close to 75 is reasonable depends on possessing some appropriate meaning for the numerical symbols 3.152 and 24.98, and some intuitive notion of " $\times$ ", such as repeated addition or multiple groupings. It is not necessary to know why the conventional algorithm for decimal multiplication "works," or even how to perform it. In other words, it is not necessary to have established connections at Site 2. In a sense, connections at Site 3 represent an application of connections at Site 1.

Considering that many students lack connections at Site 1, it is not surprising that connections at Site 3 seem to be largely missing. A first indication that many students do not check the reasonableness of their answers comes from error analyses on written computation items. Tables 8.2 and 8.3 present the most frequent error response given on each of several select computation items. All of the error responses in the tables are in some sense unreasonable.[1] Accepting unreasonable answers as correct in decimal tasks is not limited to our sample but has been reported widely (Bell et al., 1981; Brown, 1981; Carpenter et al., 1981; Ekenstam, 1977).

One explanation for the frequency of unreasonable responses is that students simply do not think to check the reasonableness of their answers. If students remembered to "look back" and check their answers they might recognize the implausibility of the responses and correct the errors. Such an explanation places

TABLE 8.2
Percentage of Responses Accounted for by Most
Frequent Errors

Item	Most Frequent Error	Grade			
		5[a]	6[b]	7[c]	9[d]
5.3 + 2.42	2.95	31	22	4	2
4 + .3	.7	51	68	51	14
4.7 − .24	.23	13	22	8	1
7 − .4	.3	50	76	55	18

Note. Data are from fall tests. Students performed similarly in the spring, except for a higher incidence of frequent errors in Grade 5.
[a]$N = 113$ [c]$N = 279$
[b]$N = 50$ [d]$N = 223$

---

[1] "Unreasonable" refers to the fact that, mathematically, the response is quite far from the correct answer and possibly quite far from an answer that students themselves know to be correct (outside the classroom). The term does not imply that we cannot trace the immediate causes of the error, explain the error in terms of rule selection and use, and even describe the procedure flaws as "reasonable" given instructional practice.

TABLE 8.3
Percentage of Responses Accounted for by
Most Frequent Errors

Item	Most Frequent Error	Grade		
		6[a]	7[b]	9[c]
6 × .4	.24	40	35	15
42 ÷ .6	.7		52	23
3 ÷ .6	.2		51	31

Note. Data are from fall tests. Students performed similarly in the spring.
[a]N = 50   [c]N = 61
[b]N = 81

the burden on metacognitive processes (Garafalo & Lester, 1985). Metacognitive explanations seem plausible and may be appropriate in some cases but the evidence presented below suggests that they are not sufficient. Students' difficulties involve cognitive deficiencies as well.

Work in other areas as well as decimals (see Silver's chapter in this volume) suggests that many students provide unreasonable answers in a variety of contexts, even if given clues that should help them catch their mistakes. We asked students during one of the interviews to focus directly on the reasonableness of answers. They were shown an addition and a multiplication problem and asked to pick from several choices the number that would be the closest to the actual answer. Calculating the complete answer was prohibited. Table 8.4 shows the

TABLE 8.4
Estimating Answers to Decimal Computation Problems

Item	Possible Responses	Percent of Sudents at Each Grade Selecting a Given Response			
		5[a]	6[b]	7[c]	9[d]
3.51023 + .4625	.7	58	27	25	10
	3	17	27	17	0
	4*	8	9	33	60
	6	0	0	17	0
	7	0	9	8	10
	8	17	27	0	20
.92 × 2.156	18	0	0	0	10
	180	33	27	17	20
	2*	8	18	33	30
	.00018	25	36	50	30
	.21	33	18	0	10

[a]N = 12   [d]N = 10
[b]N = 11   *correct response
[c]N = 12

percentage of students at each grade who selected each of the choices. Even in ninth grade many students were unable to identify reasonable responses.

The causes for students' inability to judge the reasonableness of answers often can be traced to an absence of connections at Site 1 and to an overreliance on syntactic rules. As a first example consider the explanation of a ninth-grade student for writing 5.1 directly underneath .36 when adding and getting .87 for the answer: "If you're adding .36 and 5.1 it would make a lot more sense if it came out to .8 or so." It is clear that checking whether an answer makes sense is not enough. One also must know what the numerals mean.

TABLE 8.5
Strategies Used to Place Decimal Points in Calculator-Produced Answer

| Strategy | Percentage of Students in Each Grade Who Used a Strategy Consistently | | | |
	5[a]	6[b]	7[c]	9[d]
Syntactic Maneuvers				
Count digits from right, all multiplication and one or both division		27	59	60
Count digits from right, multiplication only		18	17	10
Count digits from left, all problems				10
Place after first nonzero digit	8			
Place so position matches position of one number given in the problem	8	9		
Uncodable[e]	83	45	8	10
Semantic Considerations				
Check for reasonableness of numerical value on the easier calculation problems, count digits from right on the others			8	10
Check for reasonableness of numerical value on all problems			8	

Note. Students were asked to place the decimal point in the answer for the following problems, without doing any calculation

    $2.42 \times 3.610 = 0\ 8\ 7\ 3\ 6\ 2\ 0\ 0$
    $3.20 \div .08 = 0\ 0\ 4\ 0\ 0\ 0\ 0\ 0$
    $.42 \times .23 = 0\ 0\ 0\ 0\ 9\ 6\ 6\ 0\ 0$
    $30 \div .6 = 0\ 0\ 5\ 0\ 0\ 0\ 0\ 0\ 0$
    $4.5 \times 51.62 = 0\ 2\ 3\ 2\ 2\ 9\ 0\ 0\ 0$

    [a]$N = 12$
    [b]$N = 11$
    [c]$N = 12$
    [d]$N = 10$
    [e]Included here are students with identifiable but inconsistent strategies. Most involved counting digits or an apparently random process; all yielded incorrect solutions.

In the absence of connections between symbols and meaningful referents, students resort to applying syntactic rules. Consider students' strategies in solving some multiplication and division estimation problems during one of the interviews. The students were asked to place the decimal point in an answer produced by a slightly malfunctioning calculator. They were told that the calculator sometimes put extra zeros in front or back of an otherwise correct response, and always forgot to insert the decimal point. Table 8.5 shows the problems students received and the strategies they used to place the decimal point. *Three* of the 45 students considered the values of the numbers and the meaning of the operation in placing the decimal point for at least one problem; only one student used "reasonableness" criteria on all problems. Most students used syntactic maneuvers, such as counting digits, and matching the decimal placement in the answer with that of the numbers in the problem.[2] In some sense it appears, as noted by Byers and Erlwanger (1984), that students' excessive focus on syntax precludes the notion of verifying solutions using semantic criteria. Students believe that syntactic rules must be applied to get the problems right; no other criteria are thought to be relevant.

In summary, the separation between procedural and conceptual knowledge culminates at Site 3. If connections are absent at Site 1, students have no chance of evaluating the reasonableness of answers at Site 3. The only criterion available is the appropriate configuration of symbols (e.g., one decimal point) or well-formed answer rules, using Matz's (1980) terms. Although unreasonable answers may be explained by students' forgetting to check the answer, the tendency to accept unreasonable responses seems also to spring from fundamental problems involving separations between conceptual and procedural knowledge.

CONCLUSIONS

To observe students work with decimal fractions is to observe students struggling with written symbols they do not understand. The decimal symbols are perceived by most students as a new symbol system with a new set of rules representing new concepts. Many students fail to connect the new form with old and familiar conceptual content of common fractions and whole numbers. The consequences of failing to connect procedural and conceptual knowledge are profound.

We have identified three sites in the problem solving process where procedural and conceptual knowledge could be linked. The sites provide one way of organizing an analysis of the relationship between conceptual and procedural knowledge in mathematics learning. The sites also help to localize students'

---

[2]It should be noted that the sample contained some students in each grade who were high achievers in school mathematics. Apparently, the dependence on syntax is not restricted to those who are doing poorly on conventional measures.

difficulties and help to trace back, at least one step, toward the origins of the difficulties.

The data suggest that many students lack connections at all three sites, but some gaps seem to be especially crucial. Connections at Site 1, between symbols and meaningful referents, are the most critical because they provide the foundation for mathematics learning. Without connections at Site 1, that is, without knowing what the symbols mean, students have little chance of developing connections at either of the remaining sites. Indeed, without connections at Site 1 students have little chance of succeeding in mathematics at all (Van Engen, 1949).

Connections at Site 3 also are essential for mathematical competence. These connections are highly dependent on prior connections at Site 1. Perhaps the most disturbing feature of our students' performance was their lack of concern when providing answers that were mathematically unreasonable. Often the unreasonable answers violated their own conceptual knowledge as demonstrated on other written or interview tasks. What seemed to be missing was a link between their conceptual knowledge and a notion that written answers should be reasonable.

Suggestions for improving instruction can be formulated in a straightforward way from the preceding discussion. The instructional priority is to help students create meaning for symbols. However, the suggestion connotes more than its simplicity conveys. Creating meanings for symbols first requires establishing a rich store of conceptual knowledge that can provide the appropriate conceptual referents (Carpenter, this volume). This means designing instruction to promote meaningful experiences that support quantitative concepts (to hook with numerical symbols) and arithmetic concepts (to hook with operation symbols). Consider an example from the system of common fractions. Instruction that successfully aids students in creating meaning for written symbols would place them in the position of thinking something like the following when encountering $1\frac{3}{8} \div 2\frac{8}{9}$: "This is about $1\frac{1}{2} \div 3$, which means how many 3s will fit into $1\frac{1}{2}$. Since 3 is more than $1\frac{1}{2}$, the answer will be less than 1." Some students might continue, "The problem is really *how much* of 3 will fit into $1\frac{1}{2}$, so the answer will be close to $\frac{1}{2}$." Notice that this reasoning can proceed without students knowing anything about the algorithm that generates the exact answer. Instructional implication number one is that more time must be devoted to creating meanings for written symbols in order to permit the kind of reasoning just illustrated.

The second implication complements the first and perhaps is controversial: The extra instructional time needed for Sites 1 and 3 should be taken from activity at Site 2. Actually, our suggestion involves only part of Site 2. As students move into upper elementary school, some of the algorithms they are taught (e.g., dividing common fractions and dividing decimal fractions) are quite complex. It is not clear that students' mathematics background and cognitive capabilities are sufficiently developed at this point for them to understand the complexities of these algorithmic procedures. We are quite certain, on the other hand, that most students are able to develop connections for the same problems at Sites 1 and 3. So, in spite of the traditional research and instructional focus on helping students understand the rationale for complex symbolic algorithms (see, e.g., Payne, 1976), it may be wise to shift our focus to other sites.

Where the algorithms are simpler and their rationale more transparent (e.g., whole-number arithmetic, addition and subtraction of decimals) time should be devoted to connecting the symbol procedure with its rationale. An example will illustrate one way of proceeding. Lining up decimal points in addition and subtraction is a special case of the more general procedure of combining like quantities. Instruction might exploit students' tendency to induce from examples (VanLehn, this volume) and make explicit the relationship between lining up decimal points, lining up whole numbers on the right, finding common denominators, and so forth. Such instruction may even promote the development of conceptual knowledge through reflection on procedures (compare chapters in this volume by Baroody & Ginsburg, Gelman & Meck, and Sinclair & Sinclair).

Suggesting that we need to facilitate the construction of links between conceptual and procedural knowledge, and prescribing *exactly* how to do this, are two different issues. Building connections between written symbols and conceptual referents is not an easy task. Making the links between a symbol system and a set of concepts or intuitions is, in some sense, the crowning achievement of intelligent human activity (Hofstadter, 1979). It should come as no surprise, then, that it is a difficult task for students, and that the process of doing it is not entirely understood.

We are left with some questions that must be answered before we can further our understanding of students' learning difficulties and, in turn, be more precise in our prescriptions for instruction. First, how is conceptual knowledge formed? Second, how do mathematical symbols become viewed as representations of conceptual content? Third, how do algorithms become viewed as prescriptions for carrying out with symbols what are meaningful operations on conceptual content? The answers are not yet available, but we believe the questions are the right ones and that these questions will guide productive research in the immediate future.

ACKNOWLEDGMENTS

The data reported in this chapter were collected with the support of National Science Foundation Grant No. SPE-8218387. Any opinions, findings, or conclusions expressed herein are those of the authors rather than the National Science Foundation.

REFERENCES

Behr, M. J., Wachsmuth, I., Post, T. R., & Lesh, R. (1984). Order and equivalence of rational numbers: A clinical teaching experiment. *Journal for Research in Mathematics Education, 15,* 323–341.

Bell, A., Swan, M., & Taylor, G. (1981). Choice of operation in verbal problems with decimal numbers. *Educational Studies in Mathematics, 12,* 399–420.

Brown, M. (1981). Place value and decimals. In K. M. Hart (Ed.), *Children's understanding of mathematics: 11–16* (pp. 48–65). London: John Murray.

Byers, V., & Erlwanger, S. (1984). Content and form in mathematics. *Educational Studies in Mathematics, 15,* 259–275.

Carpenter, T. P., Corbitt, M. K., Kepner, H. S., Lindquist, M. M., & Reys, R. E. (1981). Decimals: Results and implications from the second NAEP mathematics assessment. *Arithmetic Teacher, 28* (8), 34–37.

Carr, K. (1983). Student beliefs about place value and decimals: Any relevance for science education? *Research in Science Education, 13,* 105–109.

Davis, R. B. (1984). *Learning mathematics: The cognitive science approach to mathematics education.* Norwood, NJ: Ablex.

Davis, R. B., & McKnight, C. (1980). The influence of semantic content on algorithmic behavior. *Journal of Mathematical Behavior, 3* (1), 39–87.

Ekenstam, A. (1977). On children's quantitative understanding of numbers. *Educational Studies in Mathematics, 8,* 317–332.

Erlwanger, S. H. (1975). Case studies of children's conceptions of mathematics—Part I. *Journal of Children's Mathematical Behavior, 1* (3), 157–183.

Fischbein, E., Deri, M., Nello, M. S., & Marino, M. S. (1985). The role of implicit models in solving verbal problems in multiplication and division. *Journal for Research in Mathematics Education, 16,* 3–17.

Garofalo, J., & Lester, F. K., Jr. (1985). Metacognition, cognitive monitoring, and mathematical performance. *Journal for Research in Mathematics Education, 16,* 163–176.

Grossman, A. S. (1983). Decimal notation: An important research finding. *Arithmetic Teacher, 30* (9), 32–33.

Hart, K. M. (Ed.). (1981). *Children's understanding of mathematics: 11~16.* London: John Murray.

Hiebert, J. (1984). Children's mathematics learning: The struggle to link form and understanding. *Elementary School Journal, 84,* 497–513.

Hiebert, J., & Wearne, D. (1984). *Children's understanding of decimal numbers* (Contract No. SPE-8218387). Washington, DC: National Science Foundation.

Hiebert, J., & Wearne, D. (1985). A model of students' decimal computation procedures. *Cognition & Instruction, 2,* 175–205.

Hofstadter, D. R. (1979). *Gödel, Escher, Bach: An eternal golden braid.* New York: Vintage Books.

Kaput, J. (1982, March). *Intuitive attempts at algebraic representation of quantitative relationships.* Paper presented at the annual meeting of the American Educational Research Association, New York.

Matz, M. (1980). Towards a computational theory of algebraic competence. *Journal of Mathematical Behavior, 3* (1), 93–166.

McLellan, J. A., & Dewey, J. (1895). *The psychology of number and its applications to methods of teaching arithmetic.* New York: Appleton.

National Assessment of Educational Progress. (1983). *The third national mathematics assessment: Results, trends and issues.* Denver: Educational Commission of the States.

Payne, J. N. (1976). Review of research on fractions. In R. A. Lesh (Ed.), *Number and measurement* (pp. 145–187). Columbus, OH: ERIC/SMEAC.

Pothier, Y., & Sawada, D. (1983). Partitioning: The emergence of rational number ideas in young children. *Journal for Research in Mathematics Education, 14,* 307–317.

Resnick, L. B. (1982). Syntax and semantics in learning to subtract. In T. P. Carpenter, J. M. Moser, & T. A. Romberg (Eds.), *Addition and subtraction: A cognitive perspective* (pp. 136–155). Hillsdale, NJ: Lawrence Erlbaum Associates.

Resnick, L. B., & Nesher, P. (1983, November). *Learning complex concepts: The case of decimal fractions.* Paper presented at the annual meeting of the Psychonomics Society, San Diego.

Van Engen, H. (1949). An analysis of meaning in arithmetic. *Elementary School Journal, 49,* 321–329; 395–400.

9 On Having and Using Geometric Knowledge

Alan H. Schoenfeld
University of California, Berkeley

OVERVIEW

This chapter focuses on what might be called the "cognitive support structure" underlying competent performance on straightedge and compass construction problems in Euclidean geometry. The current section begins with a brief introduction to the issues addressed in this chapter. The subsequent discussion provides an attempt to place those issues in a larger context, in order to provide a unifying framework for examining the issues described in this chapter and in the chapters that precede it. At first glance, the subject that is the focus of this chapter, Euclidean geometry, may appear to differ substantially in kind from the subject matter of other chapters. It is more advanced, and the obstacles to mastering it may seem different from the obstacles to learning more elementary mathematics. From the appropriate vantage point, however, the issues of understanding versus performance are seen to be the same in Euclidean geometry as they are in every other subject area dealt with in this book. This opening section is designed to sketch the view from that vantage point.

The detailed discussion of geometry begins in the second section. We begin with an attempt to deal with a persistent false dichotomy, which stipulates that a logical, deductive approach to geometric knowledge is antithetical to an empirically based inductive approach to the subject. Segments of two problem-solving sessions (a typically deductive session recorded by a faculty member and a typically empirical session recorded by two students) illustrate behavior representative of the two conflicting approaches. The extended analysis of a complex problem solving session follows. In that problem session, the use of deduction as a means of discovery and the development of intuition by means of empirical explorations are quite compatible; indeed, each is strengthened by interaction with the other. Thus, it is argued (as Imre Lakatos (1977) argued regarding mathematics in the large, and Charles Saunders Peirce (1931) argued in regard to epistemological issues), the inductive/deductive dichotomy in geometry is a false dichotomy. It is further argued that having a solid conceptual grasp of geometry requires both the use of empirically induced knowledge and having skill at deduction. In short, the foundations on which geometric performance are based include both inductive and deductive competencies.

The third section offers a brief discussion of extant research characterizing students' abilities to grasp both the empirical and the logical underpinnings of geometry. There is a fairly extensive body of research describing students' intuitive apprehension of geometric concepts, based largely on the work of Pierre van Hiele (1957) and Dina van Hiele-Geldof (1957). The basic thrust of that work is described. The literature on students' acquisition of proof skills is more sparse, but some interesting recent work by John Anderson and colleagues provides some ideas regarding ways to teach students to write deductive proofs in geometry. That, too, is outlined briefly.

The work described in the third section characterizes some of the skills necessary but (alas) not sufficient for students' competent geometric performance. In the fourth section some examples from ongoing research indicate that students can be competent at deduction and competent at constructions, but that they will often compartmentalize their knowledge in inappropriate ways. The result is that much of their knowledge goes unused, and the students' problem-solving performance is far weaker than it might (and should) be. In brief: Unless the students learn to take advantage of both deductive and empirical approaches to geometry and learn to profit from the interaction of those two approaches, the students will not reap the benefits of their knowledge. Moreover, it will be argued that—contrary to what is obviously intended for the mathematics curriculum—students develop the inappropriate compartmentalization of deductive and constructive mathematics as a direct result of their mathematics instruction. Examples from a year-long series of classroom observations are used to document this claim. Finally, some suggestions are made regarding ways to teach geometry in such a way that the empirical and formal aspects of the domain can be seen as flip sides of the same coin.

Toward a Unifying Framework

The mathematical subject matter discussed in this chapter is significantly more advanced than the mathematics discussed in earlier chapters. Moreover, the issues on which the chapter focuses—the roles of empiricism and deduction as components of underlying geometric competence—may seem to be different from the issues discussed in the earlier chapters. For these reasons it may be worth drawing some parallels between this work and other investigations of conceptual and procedural knowledge. It will be useful to back away from the immediate issues and to try to frame the issue of competent performance in mathematics more broadly than in terms of conceptual/procedural dichotomy. Examples are drawn from place value subtraction, from elementary word problems, from fractions, and from geometry.

In broadest terms, the generic issue explored in this book can be phrased as follows: What does an individual need to "understand" in order to develop competency in a particular mathematical domain? What, if anything, will assure that a student (a) becomes fluent in performing the symbolic manipulations in that domain, and (b) comes to understand the deep meaning of the mathematical notions represented by the symbols and the procedures that are used to operate on them? At some slight risk of oversimplification, the sequel presents an abstraction of prevailing assumptions regarding the acquisition of such understanding in typical mathematical domains. The assumptions are first elaborated in the case of base 10 arithmetic. Then the parallel case in geometry is illustrated, and the generic case encompassing both domains is abstracted. Subsequent discussions are based on the abstracted generic case.

We begin with base 10 arithmetic. Figures 9.1 and 9.2 illustrate two typical hypotheses regarding ways to promote students' understanding of base 10 algorithms, and the underlying rationales for them. Dienes blocks are concrete manipulative materials designed to provide tangible models for arithmetic base 10. The physical objects designed to represent canonical base 10 numbers—ones, tens, hundreds, thousands—are designed so that their physical properties correspond to the symbolic properties they represent. Lining up 10 "ones," for example, results in a shape identical to the shape that represents 10; placing 10 "tens" side by side yields a shape identical to the shape that represents 100, and so on.

Figure 9.1 illustrates one intended use of Dienes blocks. The figure captures an explicit research hypothesis made by Lauren Resnick and colleagues (Resnick & Omanson, in press). The idea is that procedures for addition and subtraction can first be learned by way of concrete operations (trades) on Dienes blocks. The trades (e.g. a "ten" for 10 "ones") seem natural because of the physical properties of the blocks, and in consequence addition and subtraction should become meaningful operations in that particular symbolic domain. Suppose, then, that there is direct "mapping instruction" from Dienes blocks to base 10 numerals. Students are taught how number representations correspond to configurations of Dienes blocks and how borrowing and carrying in the base 10 symbol system are the precise analogues of trades with Dienes blocks. The map appears to be an isomorphism of symbol systems. Physical entities (the blocks) correspond uniquely to digits in place, and operations on those entities (trades) correspond uniquely to operations on symbols (borrowing, carrying). The working hypothesis is: If a student understands number representation and the operations of addition and subtraction in the Dienes blocks domain, and the student under-

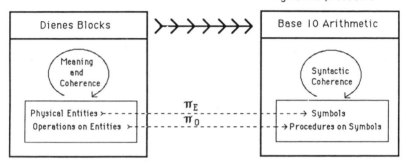

(1) A solid understanding
of how Dienes Blocks
are combined...

(2) and a good mapping from the
concrete manipulatives to
the symbolic procedure...

(3) should produce understanding
and mastery of the
symbolic procedure

| Dienes Blocks | ⟩⟩⟩⟩⟩⟩⟩ | Base 10 Arithmetic |

Meaning
and
Coherence

Syntactic
Coherence

Physical Entities ➤- - - - - - - - - - π_E - - - - - - - - - - ➤ Symbols
Operations on Entities ➤- - - - - - - π_O - - - - - - - ➤ Procedures on Symbols

FIG. 9.1.   Phase 1: Concrete representations serve as a vehicle for making sense of abstract symbolic operations.
*Note: A detailed explanation of the mappings π_E and π_O, and a discussion of the boldface feathered arrow between the reference domain (Dienes blocks) and the symbol system (Base 10 arithmetic), are given in the discussion of the general case illustrated in Figure 9.4.

stands the mapping of entities and procedures from the Dienes blocks domain to base 10 numerals, then procedural competency with Dienes blocks should carry over to procedural competency with base 10 numerals. In short, error-free performance on Dienes blocks and a solid mapping to base 10 numerals should produce error-free performance in addition and subtraction.

Figure 9.2 represents a subsequent hypothesis about understanding, which has been advanced by Greeno and Resnick. The idea is that, having identified the parallel structures in the two symbolic domains—the structure of base 10 arithmetic as reflected by the trade operations on Dienes blocks and as reflected by borrows and carries in the base 10 algorithms—students can abstract the deep structure of base 10 arithmetic as a generalization of the two specific symbol systems they have encountered. Of such abstraction, it is hypothesized, a deeper sense of the nature of numbers and operations on them will emerge.

The nature of the abstraction process is clearly illustrated in the case of geometry. In Fig. 9.3, both phases of the learning and abstraction process are indicated at once. The bottom part of the diagram illustrates the way an understanding of "real-world" geometric objects and their properties is hypothesized (by researchers such as the van Hieles and others, whose work is discussed later) to be essential for an understanding of formalizations of those objects, in Euclid-

228

ean and Cartesian geometry. In the example given, having a sense of a circle as a physical object is hypothesized to be necessary for understanding the locus definition of a circle, or the algebraic characterization of one. From experience with all the ways of characterizing circles (and triangles, and all other geometric objects), it is hypothesized, the student comes to understand the fundamental natures of those objects.

For the purpose of subsequent discussions, the commonalities in the preceding diagrams are presented in abstract form in Fig. 9.4. The generic situation represented in Fig. 9.4 deals with (a) the mapping from a reference domain to a symbol system, with the intention of using the reference domain to impart meaning to the symbols and procedures in the symbol system; and (b) the abstraction over similarities in both systems (reference domain and symbol system) to a deeper understanding of the underlying notions being represented.

First, there is a reference domain, **W.** There are entities in **W,** and a consistent set of operations defined on those entities; **W** is closed under those

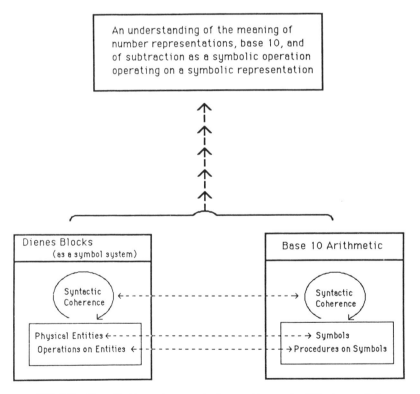

FIG. 9.2.   Phase 2: Abstracting over the isomorphic aspects of the two symbol systems leads to an understanding of the underlying mathematical notions and procedures.

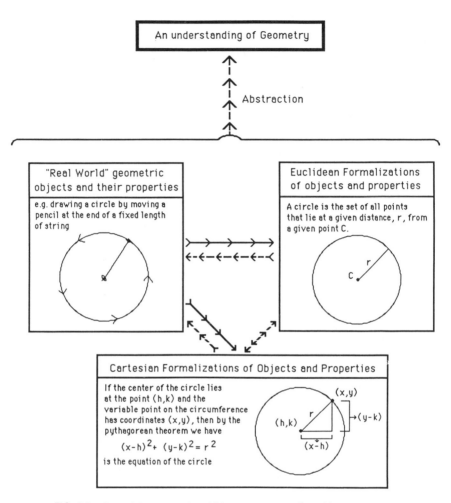

FIG. 9.3. Part of the process by which one comes to grips with geometry.

operations. (Consider, for example, trades on Dienes blocks.) It is essential to recognize that **W** has a dual nature. On the one hand, **W** serves as a *reference world:* individuals dealing with **W** perceive the objects in **W** as meaningful entities with a full range of attributes and associations, and of operations on those entities as being consistent with, and deeply embedded in, that broad meaning structure. Often, in fact (for example in the case of concrete manipulatives chosen to introduce a topic), it is the richness of **W** as a reference world that makes it (at least intuitively) an attractive choice for the first domain in which a student is exposed to particular kinds of ideas. On the other hand, **W** can also be thought of as a *symbol system* (although, one notes, it may seem strange at first to think of the physical objects in Dienes blocks world as symbols). The point is that **W** is a representation of a mathematical idea: The objects in **W** are tokens of particular mathematical entities, and operations on those objects are procedures, the results of which correspond to actions on the mathematical entities.

Second, there is a symbol system **w**, which is both a symbolic representation of some underlying mathematical idea and a mathematically consistent abstraction of selected important aspects of **W**. Symbols in **w** represent entities in **W** (note that the mapping may not be 1–1), and procedures in **w** represent the corresponding operations on entities in **W**.

Third, there is a clearly defined structure morphism π: **W**→**w** that maps entities and procedures in **W** to the symbols and symbol manipulation procedures of **w**. π has two components. The first, which carries entities in **W** to symbols in **w**, is denoted π_E. The second, which carries procedures in **W** (which, again, may be physical operations on physical objects) to procedures in **w**, is denoted π_O. The idea, as in the case of Dienes blocks, is that π is chosen such that the coherent meaning structure in **W** (entities and operations on entities) is mapped cleanly into the syntactic structure of the symbol system **w**. That is: Let upper-case letters {A,B, . . .} denote entities in **W**, and let the mapping π_E associate with those entities the symbols {$\pi_E(A)$, $\pi_E(B)$,. . .}. Let P be a procedure in **W**

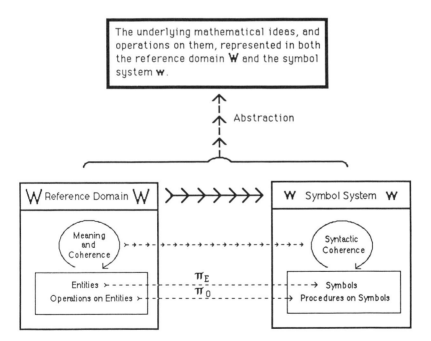

FIG. 9.4.   A generic representation of (first-order) hypotheses regarding (1) mappings from reference domains to symbol systems and (2) the abstraction of mathematical ideas (Notation explained in text.).

for operating on those entities, and let $p = \pi_O P$ be the procedure in **w** that is the image of P. Then $\pi_E[P(A,B, \ldots)] = p(\pi_E(A), \pi_E(B), \ldots) = \pi_O P(\pi_E(A), \pi_E(B), \ldots)$. These mappings are indicated by the thin dotted arrows in Figs. 9.1, 9.2, and 9.4

Finally, the boldface feathered arrows in the diagrams represent what might be called "comprehension mappings." The common assumption regarding the role of reference domains as springboards for mastery of symbol systems was made explicit in Fig. 9.1. That assumption can be summed up as follows:

Assumption 1

If an individual has a solid understanding of the meanings of objects and procedures in the reference domain **W**, and of the relationships among them; and

If the individual understands the nature of the symbolic abstraction that yields the symbol system **w** (the mapping from **W** to **w** denoted by feathered arrows),

then the individual should have a solid understanding of the symbols and procedures in the symbol system.

The assumption underlying the abstraction process symbolized in Fig. 9.2 is similar.

Assumption 2

If the individual understands the structures in the different symbolic domains that stand as representations of a particular mathematical idea; and

If the individual perceives the underlying structural morphisms among those representations,

then the individual should be able to abstract the underlying mathematical idea.

It should be noted that the framework elaborated and the assumptions embodied in it apply to all the topics discussed in this book. As examples, consider the techniques used to help students model the solutions of elementary word problems ("John had 8 apples. . . ."), and the various representational techniques used to teach students about rational numbers. Thus, the framework provides a general way to look at the relationship between developing an understanding of particular subject matter and being competent at performing certain symbolic manipulations—or, in short, between conceptual and procedural knowledge.

Unfortunately, the idealization captured in Fig. 9.4 represents a "best of all possible worlds" scenario. (Recall that it was an attempt to capture a mainstream perspective regarding the acquisition of mathematical ideas and procedures, not necessarily to address the full complexity of the issue.) The balance of this section presents a series of arguments that the issues involved are indeed more complex than Fig. 9.4 would lead one to expect. The point of these discussions is not to cast doubt on the generic utility of the perspective reflected in Fig. 9.4, but rather to indicate that the issues involved in mathematical knowledge acquisition are extremely subtle—and that researchers and developers of instructional materials ignore such subtleties at their own peril. Five complicating factors are discussed.

Complicating Factor 1: The "Reference World" versus "Reference Domain" Dilemma.   This dilemma, which one faces when using any concrete manipulatives, is clearly illustrated in the case of Dienes blocks. Although Dienes blocks do stand on their own as a symbol system (a consistent representation of the integers base 10), they were, of course, designed with additional properties to make the representation seem "natural." It is hardly an accident that a "ten" is the same size as 10 "ones" lined up against each other, that a "hundred" is the same size as 10 "tens" placed side by side, and so on. If the representation were all that mattered, we could use pennies, dimes, and silver dollars to teach base 10 arithmetic—but we don't, and for good reason. What contributes to the power of the Dienes blocks as a representation of base 10 arithmetic is that the nature of the representation capitalizes on extra-mathematical notions—the child's notion of fairness, for example. The act of trading a dime for ten pennies makes no sense except by convention, a matter of mutual agreement. On the other hand, the act of trading Dienes blocks consists of exchanging one quantity for another whose shape is identical. That does make sense. It appeals to an inherent sense of conservation of volume, conservation of mass, and so forth. Thus, what makes Dienes blocks a "good" representation is that, for the child, Dienes blocks form a coherent reference **world.** Such other than symbolic aspects of the entities in the Dienes blocks domain as physical properties, an appeal to an inherent sense of fairness, and the like are the basis of the coherence of the representation system. Indeed, the more natural the representation seems to be in the reference world, the easier it is to comprehend manipulations on the entities in it (e.g. addition and subtraction as trades). And if the reference world coheres naturally, then the symbol system that it maps to should cohere naturally as well. This fits well with phase 1 of the process, as illustrated in Fig. 9.1

The difficulty comes in phase 2. Hypothetically, the student comes to understand the underlying mathematical ideas (in the present case, number, number representations, and arithmetic operations base 10) by abstracting over the isomorphism between the symbol system of numerals base 10 and the symbol system of objects in the Dienes block domain. What made the reference domain cohere, however, was that it was much more than a symbol system. The more natural the representation, that is, the more the representation domain coheres because of its implicit properties as a reference world, the more difficult it may be to see past those properties to perceive its structure as an abstract symbol system. Thus the more natural the representation, the harder it may be to abstract the underlying mathematical ideas from the morphism between reference domain (reference world) and the target symbol system. This paradox is illustrated in Fig. 9.5

Complicating Factor 2: Like Beauty, Isomorphisms May Be Only Skin Deep. This argument, from John Seely Brown (personal communication, July 5, 1985), goes as follows. Again for purposes of illustration, we take **W** to be the domain of Dienes blocks and **w** to be base 10 arithmetic. Let *P* be the manipulative procedure for subtracting one set of blocks (in canonical form) from another, and let *p* be the standard base 10 subtraction algorithm that corresponds to *P*.

The triple $(\mathbf{W},\mathbf{w},\pi)$ appears to satisfy all of the constraints required for Fig. 9.1. **W** and **w** are well defined. The morphism π is also clearly defined—in the sense that its component mappings π_O and π_E are well defined. The mapping π_O defines the isomorphism between *P* and *p*, which is clear. The mapping π_E defines an isomorphism between entities in the reference world and digits in place. Digits in the place to the far right represent a number of ones; digits in the

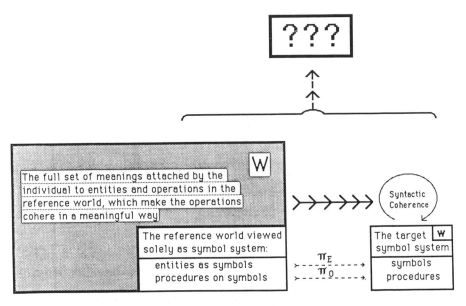

FIG. 9.5. If the mapping from **W** to **w** relies heavily on other-than-symbolic aspects of **W**, it may be quite difficult to perceive of **W** as a symbol system. Thus it may be quite difficult to perceive the similarities between **W** and **w** when they are considered as symbol structures—and in consequence, difficult to abstract the underlying mathematical structure that they both represent.

next place over represent a number of tens; and so on. So far, so good. This should permit the conclusion suggested in Fig. 9.1: If a student has a solid grasp of how Dienes blocks are combined (i.e., the student can perform subtraction procedures reliably and in error-free fashion in the Dienes blocks domain), and a solid grasp of the mapping from Dienes blocks entities and procedures to the symbol manipulation on numerals base 10 (i.e., the student can explain how each entity in one domain can be converted to its isomorph in the other, and how the procedures match), then the student's performance of the base 10 subtraction algorithm should be (relatively) reliable and error free.

Empirical evidence gathered by Lauren Resnick and colleagues (Resnick & Omanson, in press) suggests otherwise. Students in the studies reported were carefully trained to use Dienes blocks, and, as far as the investigators could tell, they mastered arithmetic procedures in that domain. Performance of the addition and subtraction algorithms on Dienes blocks was consistent, reliable, and error free. The students were taught the mapping between the Dienes blocks representation and the base 10 representation. They were taught the mapping between the manipulative procedures on Dienes blocks (trades) and the corresponding arithmetic procedures (borrows and carries) on base 10 numerals, and experimental evidence indicated that the students could provide clear and lucid explanations of the correspondence between them. Despite all this, there were persistent bugs in the students' performance of base 10 algorithms. Brown's (1985) explanation for this difficulty is as follows.

As a preliminary caveat, it should be noted that the base 10 structure of Dienes blocks is not quite as "natural" as it would appear. Though trades may seem reasonable, the use of canonical forms—where no more than 10 tokens of any category are allowed; and when one has more than 10, one must trade up for tokens in the next category—is arbitrary. (What's "wrong," for example, with having 16 dollar bills, 22 dimes, and 14 pennies? Absolutely nothing, unless you have made an artificial agreement to the contrary.) Thus the operations on Dienes blocks represent a partitioning of the Dienes blocks world into equivalence classes, with addition and subtraction being performed on designated representatives of the equivalence classes. Resnick and Omanson (in press) indicate, however, that students are willing to accept appropriately constructed "cover stories" that induce them to make trades in accord with canonical representations. The problem is deeper than the artificiality of base 10 representation. The core of the problem lies in the interaction of π_E and π_O, or, perhaps more precisely, in the different relationships between procedures and entities in the two domains. In the base 10 symbol system, the subtraction procedure is column independent: In problem 2 below, one performs precisely the same operations on the digits in the second and third columns (from the right) as on the digits in the first and second columns of problem 1. This is because the standard procedure for implementing the subtraction algorithm considers only whether the digit on the top line is larger or smaller than the digit below it, and not the column in which the digit is placed.

Problem 1:   763   Problem 2:   7639
              −327   −3275

If, however, one performs the same two problems in the Dienes blocks domain, there is a world of difference. In problem 1, the individual converts one of 6 "tens"—physical objects that are rectangular solids—to 10 "ones," which are little cubes. In problem two, one converts one of 6 "flats," or "hundreds"— physical objects that are substantial squares of relatively small height—to 10 "tens." These trades are hardly equivalent. At this level, the isomorphism breaks down. Despite the match at the level of π_E and π_O, there is no morphism $\pi{:}P{\to}p$, because the symbol system **w** consists of more than just symbols and procedures that operate on them. It is a coherent system to which people attach meaning, just as they attach meaning to entities, operations, and structures in the reference domain **W**. An isomorphism at the level of syntax (between **W** and **w** considered as symbol systems) may not extend to an isomorphism at the level of attributed meaning and coherence. See Fig. 9.6

Complicating Factor 3: Interference Phenomena From Multiple Reference Domains.   Figure 9.4 describes a situation in which a single "natural" choice for a reference domain serves as the basis for the mapping to a symbol system. Often, however, there is no one natural choice: Particular aspects of many different reference domains may seem appropriate for explicating particular aspects of a symbol system, but no single reference domain may map cleanly to the symbol system. Consider the case of rational numbers, for example, and the operations of (a) multiplying two fractions and (b) reducing a given fraction to lowest terms.

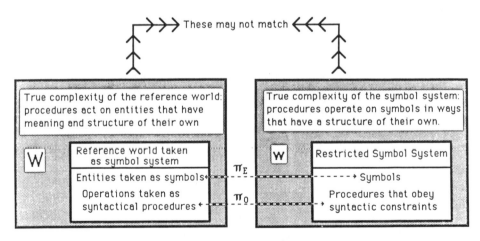

FIG. 9.6.   Even though π_E and π_O may be isomporphisms when **W** and **w** are considered purely as symbol systems, the attributions of meaning to the operations in both domains may not be isomorphic.

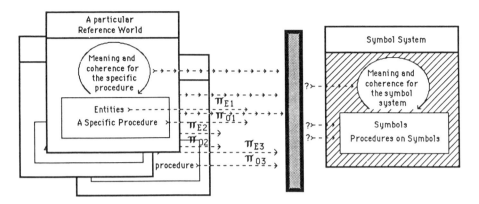

FIG. 9.7. The mappings to a symbol system that has multiple reference worlds with different meaning structures may interfere with each other. This may make it difficult to develop a coherent view of the symbol system.

Kieren (1976) indicates seven different ways that fractions can be conceptualized. Unfortunately, one or another of these conceptualizations may be differentially useful in providing the conceptual underpinnings for any particular procedural operation on the symbols. Thinking of fractions as unitary stretching or shrinking operators may, for example, be a useful way to understand the procedure for multiplying fractions. In these terms, multiplication consists of applying operators in sequence. That is, taking $(\frac{5}{2})(\frac{3}{4})$ can be imagined as shrinking a given object to $\frac{3}{4}$ of its size, and then stretching the resulting object to $\frac{5}{2}$ of its size. However, viewing fractions as stretching operators may make it extremely difficult to grasp the correctness of the procedure for reducing fractions to lowest terms. Conversely, thinking of the rational number $\frac{m}{n}$ as "a selection of m out of n equal subdivisions of a given entity" may help to understand the procedure for reducing fractions to lowest terms, but the student who thinks of fractions in this way may find it very hard to make sense of the procedure for multiplication. A similar example is discussed by Silver in his chapter in this volume. Silver attributes remedial students' "freshman error" in adding two fractions, using the incorrect algorithm $\frac{a}{b} + \frac{c}{d} \rightarrow (a + c)/(b + d)$ to "an overdependence on a single mental and physical model for the fraction concept, . . . the part/whole model expressed as sectors of a circle" (p. 189). To sum up this discussion in more formal terms, the symbols and procedures that operate on them in the symbol system **w** may themselves have multiple meanings for which there are multiple, and perhaps conflicting antecedent reference domains {**W**}. (See Fig. 9.7.)

Complicating Factor 4: The Nondeterministic Nature of **W**. Often the use of a particular procedure requires that one construct for oneself the appropriate reference world **W** (entities, procedures, and relationships among them) rather than simply working from a given reference world. In the case of elementary word problems, for example, one must create token sets to represent "John's eight books," or more problematically, token sets to represent as yet unspecified sets designated by the phrase "John has some books." As work by Greeno and Johnson (1984) indicates, there is decidedly nontrivial interaction between the kinds of knowledge representations that one has available for use (e.g. does one have access to the part–whole schema?) and the kinds of reference worlds one can construct. (See Fig. 9.8.)

Complicating Factor 5: There Are Connections . . . and There Are Connections. In formal terms, this issue deals with the question of necessary versus sufficient conditions on the morphism π. Seeing connections between the domains **W** and **w** may be one thing, but being able to exploit those connections may be something else entirely. This theme is raised quite clearly by Gelman and Meck earlier in this book. In discussions of counting, they distinguish among conceptual, procedural, and utilization competence. The idea is that people may have a sufficient understanding of a domain to recognize correct and incorrect performance and label them as such, but they may lack the competence to generate those procedures for themselves. Conceptual understandings "specify characteristics that correct performance must possess but they do not provide recipes for generating these correct performances. . . Conceptual competence or principled knowledge is coordinated with the planning and procedure-generation system that makes up procedural competence, and thus helps determine the actual procedures used." (p. 30).

One obstacle to carrying procedures from **W** to **w** is that there may be subtly hidden enabling conditions required to complete the mappings between reference domains and symbol systems. Translating declarative statements into implementation procedures may require additional steps that, at first glance, seem so trivial as to not need mention. For us, the statement "You can't go out without your shoes on" carries an implied procedural consequence, "If you want to go out, you must first put your shoes on." As Gelman and Meck indicate, translation from the declarative to the procedural form is not always so obvious—or at least, doing the

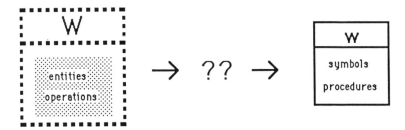

FIG. 9.8. Making the relevant mappings may be impossible if the individual is unable to create the appropriate representations in the reference world

translation calls for implementation knowledge (or "enabling conditions"). The following discussion offers an example from geometry. Consider the following line of reasoning:

> *Given:* In a geometric construction problem, you wish to locate the center of a circle, C, by construction. You know the following: (1) There is a given line segment PV, and P is known to be a point on the circle. The radius CP—if you had it—would be perpendicular to PV at P. (2) The line segment from C to a given point V (again, if you had C and could draw the segment) must bisect a given angle with vertex at V.
>
> *Conclusion.* Locate the point C (1) by constructing the perpendicular to line segment PV at P, (2) constructing the bisectors of the angle V, and (3) identifying the intersection of those two line segments.

Drawing this conclusion seems as obvious as drawing the conclusion, in the example given earlier, that to go outside you put your shoes on. However, drawing the conclusion does not really follow directly from what is given. In addition to background knowledge about locus constructions (e.g. that points are uniquely identified at the intersection of any two constructible loci that they satisfy), drawing the conclusion depends on the following knowledge:

> *Enabling condition.* If a point is known to lie on a line that has certain properties, then constructing the line with those properties yields a locus for the point.

A second obstacle, reflected in the title of this paper, is the following: The fact that a person knows something provides no guarantee that the knowledge will be called upon in situations for which it is appropriate. Examples are given later indicating that students may make virtually no connections between reference domains and symbol systems that we would expect them to think of as being nearly identical. In

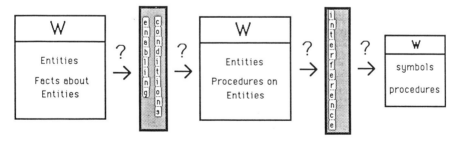

FIG. 9.9.   The mapping between domains may not be completed for lack of an enabling factor or because of interference (e.g. from inappropriate belief systems.)

240

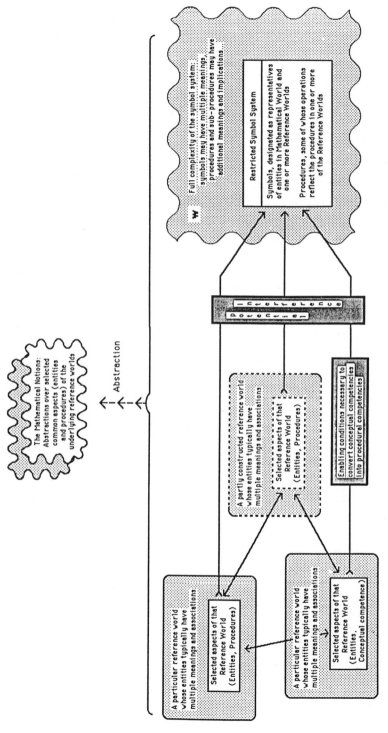

FIG. 9.10. The web of connections that need to be made in order to meaningfully comprehend symbolic operations.

consequence, the students will make hypotheses about entities in **W** that flatly contradict results they have obtained about the corresponding entities in **w**. This issue is explored at length in the balance of the paper. (See Fig. 9.9.) Adding all of these "complicating factors" to the conceptual scheme elaborated in Fig. 9.4 yields, alas, a diagram of frightening complexity. (See Fig. 9.10.) Like it or not, that complexity is precisely what we confront in trying to help students to make sense of subtle mathematical ideas—and, as the preceding discussion indicates, most mathematical ideas are more subtle than they first appear to be. Indeed, the extended discussion up to this point serves to flesh out the substance of the sentence that began this paper: "This chapter focuses on what might be called the 'cognitive support structure' underlying competent performance on straightedge and compass construction problems in Euclidean geometry." As indicated by the preceding discussions, the issue of "cognitive support structure" must be interpreted quite broadly. In dealing with constructions, for example, it will not suffice to ask "What mathematical knowledge will enable students to do well at constructions?," a question that presumes that learning will proceed as smoothly as suggested in Fig. 9.3. Understanding what would enable students to make sense of geometric constructions calls for exploring how the knowledge (and knowledge organization) of various reference domains (e.g. deductive geometry, intuitive geometry, Cartesian geometry) map into the meaning structures imposed by the person on the straightedge and compass construction domain, and how the meanings imposed on the construction domain map back into those of the reference worlds. It calls for exploring conditions that support or obstruct the development of those mappings; it calls for exploring conditions under which students will or will not make the linkages among the various kinds of knowledge in the deductive, intuitive, and constructive universes. Such explorations occupy us for the balance of this chapter.

THE RESOLUTION OF A FALSE DICHOTOMY

In *The Foundations of Science,* Henri Poincare (1913) referred to a classic mathematical dichotomy. There is "intuition" on the one hand, and "logic," or deduction, on the other; like the proverbial east and west, the two are supposed to be disjoint entities. Poincare expressed a preference for intuition over logic, but he also expressed concern about that preference. Hilbert, he noted, was a proponent of logic—and that provided substantial evidence for the other side. Poincare found himself "troubled."

Poincare had reason to be troubled, but not because of the weight of evidence favoring either side over the other. The two ostensibly disjoint approaches to mathematics—a deductive approach to mathematical discovery, in which new pieces of information are logically deduced, and an empirical intuitive approach, in which "insight" plays the major role, are in fact mutually reinforcing. The twain do meet, and each is the better for it. As noted in the introduction, this idea is not novel. Lakatos (1977) argued that mathematics as a discipline evolves as the result of the interplay of empirical observations and formal mathematics, and Peirce coined the term "abduction" to describe the synthesis resulting from the dialectic interplay of induction and deduction. However, the interplay occurs far more rarely than one would like.

To establish a context for discussions in the sequel, we begin with two clearcut examples of behavior, one deductive and one empirical. In both cases the subjects were asked to solve the problem given in Fig. 9.11.

A Mathematician's Deductive Approach

The entire transcript of the mathematician RD's approach to the problem follows. On reading the problem statement he said: "This one is so easy that I could guess the answer, but I ought to do it right. OK, let me sketch in the circle I want. . . [he does so; see his completed sketch in Fig. 9.12] and I'll put the center (C) here. All right, I'll draw in the radii. They're equal, and they're perpendicular to these two lines [marks diagram at P and Q], so if I draw in CV then the two triangles are congruent. I'm done. I can use the perpendiculars through P and Q, or the angle bisector if you like.

RD's opening comment appears to have been made for public consumption (he knows the tape will be analyzed afterwards) and may not reflect his customary problem-solving behavior. It does, however, make quite clear his view of the "proper" (purely deductive) method that should be used to solve construction problems.

It appears that the task in the given problem is one of discovery, to find a particular circle. Yet RD's discovery proceeds by proof. He begins with the known properties of the desired circle and sets about deriving the properties it must have. When he has derived sufficient constructible properties of the circle (two constructible loci determine the center, which, along with the given point P, determine the circle), he considers himself done. He does not bother to perform the

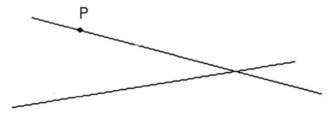

FIG. 9.11.   You are given two intersecting straight lines and a point P marked on one of them, as in the figure above. Show how to construct, using straightedge and compass, a circle that is tangent to both lines and that has the point P as its point of tangency to one of the lines.

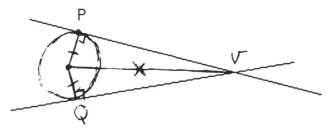

FIG. 9.12

actual physical construction: his proof provides assurance that it will work, and he feels no need to verify what he knows will be the case.

This behavior exemplifies the logical, or deductive, approach. It is a bit extreme, since RD behaves as though the constructive world is a purely formal domain and deliberately eschews any empirical actions. However, this protocol provides a clear illustration of the deductivist approach: "One knows what one proves, neither more nor less."

RD's approach stands in stark contrast to that taken by virtually all the students I have recorded (see Schoenfeld, 1985a, 1985b for extensive documentation). To sum things up briefly, most students from high school sophomore through college senior, all of whom have had a full year of high school geometry, are naive empiricists whose approach to straightedge and compass constructions is an empirical guess-and-test loop. That is, the student makes a conjecture and tries it out by performing the indicated constructions. If the construction looks sufficiently accurate, it is accepted as correct and the search is terminated; if it does not meet certain tolerance standards (the bounds of error considered reasonable for the tools at hand), the solution is rejected and the search continues. In various problem sessions students have rejected correct solutions because they did not look sufficiently accurate and have accepted incorrect solutions because they looked good; they have submitted mutually contradictory solutions as correct because both constructions met the same empirical standard. In a number of problem sessions, the students were asked to work both proof problems and related construction problems. In half of the recording sessions, the students first worked the proof problems, in which they derived the properties that would produce the desired circle in Fig. 9.11. They were then asked to do the construction problem. In working on the construction problem, a fair number of students ignored the results they had derived in the proof problems, making conjectures that flatly contradicted what they had just proved. In some cases this was the result of impetuous behavior, since there is a strong (and incorrect) perceptual bias toward a particular hypothetical solution to the construction problem. In other cases, however, the students simply did not see any connection between the deductive mathematics of theorem proving and the inductive mathematics of doing constructions—even though they were asked directly about it. Many students adopted a purely empirical standard for a construction's correctness: the procedure for a construction is correct if it produces an accurate figure. The following segment of a problem session illustrates that kind of behavior.

In their problem session, the students RO and LI first worked the construction problem and then the proofs. As it happens, their conjecture regarding the construction was incorrect, although it looked reasonably accurate, and they accepted it as being correct. (They were not told whether it was correct or not.) In a post mortem, the students worked the proof problems. They showed no signs of making connections between the two, so the investigator (AHS) asked about the relationship.

AHS: Can we look at the construction problem again? Does this one [pointing to the diagram from the proof problem] give you any ideas about that one [pointing to the diagram from the construction problem]?

RO: Oh! I would draw a perpendicular from this [pointing to P]. Would that be right? A line perpendicular to this. Would that be right?

AHS: How do you know whether it's right or not? I mean, I could tell you. . .

RO: [Pointing to the location she hypothesized to be the circle's center] *Put the center of the circle here and then draw the circle.* [emphasis added]

AHS: . . .but I won't always be around to answer your questions. And you could try it and see if it looks good, if you wanted. But could you know whether or not the construction ought to work, without trying it? Or do you have to try it out, or ask someone who knows whether it's right?

RO: I would try it myself.

Students with this perspective—and there is a substantial percentage of students whose empiricism is every bit as strong as RO's and many more whose nondeductive approach to construction problems is similar—lie at the opposite pole of the deductive/empirical dichotomy from the logicist mathematicians exemplified by RD. The logicist mathematicians are capable of performing the constructions, but they dismiss as superfluous the physical act of performing the constructions. In contrast, the empiricist students are (usually) capable of making the appropriate deductive arguments, but they either fail to see the connections or dismiss the proofs as being irrelevant. From both perspectives, there appears to be no middle ground.

There is, however, both an epistemological and pedagogical middle ground. At bare minimum, empirical knowledge and deductive knowledge are mutually reinforcing, with each enhancing the other in significant ways. At most (see the discussion of Kitcher that follows), empirical experience is the foundation upon which all knowledge, including the purely deductive, rests. Consideration of these issues also begins with the discussion of an illustrative problem solving session.

The problem is given in Fig. 9.13. A class of 20 talented students, working as a group and with my assistance (I had not solved the problem before we discussed it and did not know how to solve it) took nearly ¾ of an hour to find the solution. What follows is a brief description of certain key aspects of that problem session. A more detailed description may be found in Schoenfeld (1983, pp. 42–51).

There is a standard approach to such construction problems (see chapter 1 of Polya, 1980) in which one begins by copying one of the given parts of the triangle. This is followed by an attempt to determine, at the intersection of two constructible loci, the location of a point that uniquely determines the triangle. (As an example, note that the customary procedure for constructing a triangle, given its three sides **a, b,** and **c,** is of this type. One begins by copying one of the sides, say **a.** Then the location of the vertex **A** opposite side **a** is determined at the intersection of two arcs: one of radius $|\mathbf{b}|$ with center at one endpoint of **a,** the other of radius $|\mathbf{c}|$ with center at the other endpoint of **a.**) The class was familiar with this approach, with which it began.

First attempts in that direction were unsuccessful, as were numerous other efforts. After 20 minutes or so, the students returned to the initial idea, although they had little sense of what directions might be useful to pursue. Some discussion

Construct a triangle, given:

    1. One side of the triangle, **a**.
    2. The radius, **r**, of the triangle's inscribed circle
    3. The measure of the angle **α** that lies opposite **a**.

That is, your completed diagram would like like this:

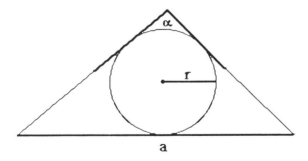

if you were given the darkened entities **a**, **r**, and **α**.

FIG. 9.13

led the class to decide that side **a** was the best of the three "givens" with which to start the construction. Given that the construction starts with side **a,** the solution might proceed in one of two directions.

Possibility 1. There is a known construction for obtaining the locus of points that make a fixed angle, α, opposite a given line segment **a.** This gives one locus for the vertex **A.** A second locus for **A** would finish the problem.

Possibility 2. There is also an obvious locus for the center, **C,** of the inscribed circle: a line parallel to **a** and at distance **r** from it. A second locus for **C** would provide the precise location of the circle. Then the construction could be completed as suggested in Fig. 9.14.

Thus the class had the following two options.

Option 1. Determine the locus of vertex **A,** given the side **a** and the (variable) inscribed circle of radius **r.**

Option 2. Determine the locus of the center **C** of the desired circle, given the side **a** and the (variable) vertex **A** that makes an angle α opposite **a.**

The class was unfamiliar with a construction of either type and had no idea which (if either) was likely to prove tractable. For that reason the students decided to try some rough sketches, in the hope the sketches would suggest fruitful directions to pursue. The sketches corresponding to Options 1 and 2 are given in Figs. 9.15 and 9.16 respectively.

While the sketch in Fig. 9.15 was not suggestive, the sketch in Fig. 9.16 was: It indicates that the locus of centers of inscribed circles might be the arc of a circle. This appeared to be worth pursuing, so the class turned to a new problem:

Problem (equivalent to option 2): Prove that the locus of **C,** given fixed side **a** and variable vertex **A** of fixed measure α, is a circle that has **a** as a chord.

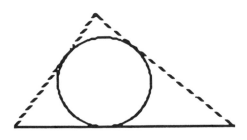

FIG. 9.14

Option 1: The locus of the variable vertex **A**, given the fixed
side **a** and the variable inscribed circle of radius **r** ...

does not appear suggestive.

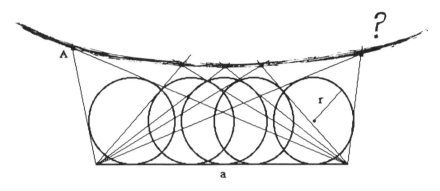

FIG. 9.15

Option 2: The locus of the centers, **C**, of the inscribed
circles with base **a** and third vertex the variable point **A**
that makes an angle **α** with **a** ...

might just be the arc of a circle.

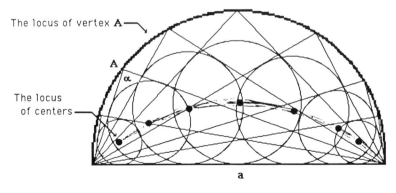

FIG. 9.16

247

This, in turn, led to a

Reformulated problem: Show that in Fig. 9.17, δ is a function of α alone.

Working with Fig. 9.17, the class eventually managed to prove that δ = 90 + α/2. Since α is constant, it follows that δ is constant, and thus that **C** makes a fixed angle opposite the given chord **a.** This fact yields a second constructible locus for **C.** Hence, the location of the inscribed circle is determined, and construction can be finished by constructing the tangents to the circle as suggested in possibility 2 above. The problem was solved.

Perhaps the most interesting aspect of this problem session is that it demonstrates the dynamic interplay between empiricism and deduction during the problem-solving process. Contributions both from empirical explorations and from deductive proofs were essential to the solution. On the one hand, the class (myself included) was absolutely stymied after preliminary attempts to solve the problem were unsuccessful. Options 1 and 2 had been generated as possibilities to consider, but the class had no idea whatsoever of how to proceed and no idea of what the relevant loci might be. Had the class not embarked on empirical explorations—and discovered that the locus of **C** in option 2 appeared to be the arc of a circle—the class would have run out of ideas and failed in its attempt to solve the problem. On the other hand, an empirical approach by itself was insufficient. The best that the class could tell from its sketches (e.g. Fig. 9.11) was that the locus of **C** in option 2 *appeared* to be the arc of a circle. No matter how many sketches it drew, there was no plausible way for the class to discover from those sketches that the locus of **C** travels at a constant angle of δ = 90 + α/2 opposite the given side **a.** This piece of deduced information is as essential for solving the problem as was the empirically derived observation that the locus

<u>Problem:</u> Determine the relationship between α and δ .

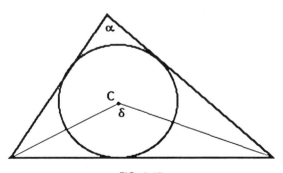

FIG. 9.17

appears circular. More to the point epistemologically, empiricism and deduction were necessary components of each other's workings during this problem session. Given what the class knew, the deductive argument ultimately proving that $\delta = 90 + \alpha/2$ would not have been embarked upon were it not for the information gathered from empirical explorations. (To characterize the issue somewhat differently, the empirical explorations determined the deductive problem space.) Thus, empiricism was an essential component of the machinery of deduction. Conversely, however, deduction made possible a discovery that was inaccessible to insight or empiricism. In the short run, that discovery simply added one more fact to the students' knowledge base. They were now familiar with one more property of geometric objects, and perhaps saw another connection or two among such objects. In the long run, the accumulation of such facts, first learned through deductive means, results in a body of knowledge and experience sufficiently rich to serve as fodder for insight and intuition. In that way, deduction is an essential component of the machinery of empiricism. In short, deduction and empirically based intuition are hardly dichotomous. They are, to borrow a phrase, "deeply intertwingled."

COGNITIVE UNDERPINNINGS: THE RELEVANT LITERATURE

For the most part, the literature dealing with students' learning of geometrical concepts reflects the empirical/deductive dichotomy discussed in the preceding section. The research was motivated by the perceived failure of the traditional curricular offerings, where students received their first formal classroom exposure to geometry in its deductive-axiomatic form—usually in a tenth-grade course that placed a very heavy emphasis on proofs. Wirszup (1976) described the prevailing state of affairs as follows.

As a result of unsuccessful experience and convincing evidence, the so-called axiomatic methods of initiation into geometry have been recognized by modern educators the world over as unpedagogical. A review of the teaching of geometry in the United States indicates at once that only a very small number of elementary schools offer any number of organized studies in visual geometry, and where they are done, they begin with measurements and other concepts which correspond to levels II and III of thought development in geometry. Since level I is passed over, the material that is taught even in these schools does not promote any deep understanding and is soon forgotten. Then, in the 10th grade, 15 and 16 year old youngsters are confronted with geometry for almost the first time in their lives. The whole unknown and complex world of plane and space is given to them in a passive axiomatic or pseudo-axiomatic treatment. The majority of our high school students are at the *first* level of development in geometry, while the course they take demands the *fourth* level of thought. It is no wonder that high school graduates have hardly any knowledge of geometry, and that this irreparable deficiency haunts them continually later on. (p. 96)

Wirzup's argument, in brief, is that formal symbolic manipulations in the deductive geometric universe **w** are meaningless for those students who lack a deep intuitive understanding of the properties of the elements in the empirical reference world **W** from which the abstract objects manipulated in **w** are abstracted. (That is, proof *qua* proof cannot be meaningful until the entities manipulated in the proofs are meaningful.) This argument is based on the empirical studies of two Dutch educators, Dina van Hiele-Geldof (1957) and Pierre van Hiele (1957). A recent translation of some of the original studies (Fuys, Geddes, & Tischler, 1984) makes that work more accessible to an English-speaking audience. Contemporary research in the United States based on the van Hieles' work is described in Hoffer (1983). For the sake of completeness, it should be noted that there has been a fair amount of work on geometry in the Soviet Union (see, e.g. Volumes 1, 4, 5, 10, and 13 of the Soviet Studies [Kilpatrick & Wirszup, 1969–1975]). Freudenthal's (1973) eclectic and often elegant arguments about the role of axiomatics in geometry also draw heavily on the van Hieles' work.

The van Hieles' Perspective on Geometry: Empirical Foundations for Proof

The van Hieles (1957; 1957) propose a psychological/pedagogical theory of thought levels in geometry. The most recent version of the theory proposes that an individual passes through five separate thought levels on the way to a complete mastery of the subject matter. Before the levels are described, however, some context is in order. First, the number of levels is still a matter of some controversy. However, determining the precise number of levels (Are there four, five, or six?) is not a central issue with regard to the theory. The theory does not provide a determinist, structuralist view of a fixed progression of cleanly divided "stages" through which individuals must pass. Rather, it offers an empirically based description of what appear to be relatively stable, qualitatively different states or levels of understanding. Second, there is no developmental timetable determining a progression through the various levels. As indicated by Wirszup's (1976) comment, high school students as well as third graders may be at the first level—and they may remain at the first level long after they have begun collecting social security benefits. Third, the van Hieles' is a psychological/pedagogical theory. There is a heavy emphasis on pedagogy, or the structuring of the students' experiences with the mathematical universe, as the means of promoting transitions between thought levels. Fourth, understanding the van Hieles' goals for the teaching of mathematics is important for understanding the nature of their theory. The purpose of teaching mathematics, as they see it, is to develop *insight* in their students. That is, students should have a sufficient grasp of their mathematical knowledge in any domain (e.g. geometry) to deliberately and consciously apply their knowledge not only in circumstances replicating those in which they have been trained, but also in novel circumstances that call for the application of that knowledge. That context having been established, there are two remaining aspects to the theory: a description of the thought levels, and of the phases of learning that provide the means of transition between levels.

The five thought levels in geometry

First level: Gestalt recognition of figures. Students recognize entities such as squares and triangles, but they recognize them as wholes; they do not identify the properties or determining characteristics of those figures.

Second level: Analysis of individual figures. Students are capable of defining objects by their properties (e.g. "a rhombus is a four sided figure in which all four sides are the same length") but do not see relationships between classes of objects (e.g. "a square is a rhombus with a right angle.")

Third level: Analysis of relations. Students can conclude (for example) that every square is a rhombus, because of the properties of squares (e.g. "all four sides of a square are equal, and a quadrilateral with four equal sides is a rhombus"). However, they have not attained. . .

Fourth level: Deductive competence, the goal state of 10th grade geometry. If asked to prove (for example) that the inscribed angle subtending a given arc of a circle has a measure half that of the central angle subtending the same arc, the student can do so by producing a series of statements that logically justify the conclusion as a consequence of the "givens."

Fifth level: Understanding of axiomatics (rarely achieved). Students appreciate the role of axioms and the role of logic in deductive systems, and recognize that Euclidean geometry is one of a number of possible ways to describe an abstract mathematical universe.

Phases of Learning

The process of moving from one level to the next is, in essence, one by which the objects of inquiry at the lower level—objects that are accessible to inquiry, but whose structures are not yet comfortably grasped—become familiar and can serve as tools of inquiry in further explorations. The van Hieles propose a five-phase pedagogical sequence to effect this transition. In brief, those phases are: *inquiry,* in which the dialogue between teacher and student introduces the objects of discourse and establishes the students' current understandings of those objects; *directed orientation,* in which the student undertakes a carefully designed sequence of exercises chosen to unfold the structures of the objects of inquiry; *explicitation*, in which the newly discovered properties are discussed and codified; *free orientation*, in which students refine knowledge and develop facility in the domain by engaging in problem solving; and *integration*, in which the teacher helps to consolidate the students' knowledge by means of coherent summary presentations.

There are numerous gaps in the framework proposed by the van Hieles. One can quarrel with the pedagogical sequence, which rings more of common sense than it does of justified theory; its foundations are in pedagogical "experience" and teaching experiments, and the justifications offered for it are loose by any rigorous standard. Similarly lacking is a detailed explanation of cognitive processes that underlie competent performance. To examine the fourth level, for example, how does one actually go about constructing a proof? (That is, how does one undertake the dialectic between givens and goals that ultimately results in a linked chain of consequences from one to the other? How does one figure out the right things to look at)? To my knowledge, these issues have not been systematically addressed in van Hiele-based research, which focuses more on the empirical support structure of the reference world **W** and the linkages to the symbolic proof world **w** than on the workings of **w** itself. These caveats notwithstanding, some useful pedagogical points follow from the work. As Wirszup's (1976) comment indicates, people at different levels speak different languages; the teacher using terms meant to be understood at the third or fourth level may be completely misunderstood by the student at the first or second level. Distilled a bit further, this translates into the classroom advice, "Make sure that what is heard is what is being said"—old hat but still useful, and too often ignored. The framework provides a set of empirical guidelines for teacher–student communication. It also provides a template for textbook evaluation. Preliminary studies reported by Rosamond Tischler at the 1984 PME meeting in Madison indicate that textbook exercises corresponding to particular subject matter frequently differ by one or two van Hiele levels from the level of presentation of that subject matter; thus they do not provide the appropriate opportunity for consolidating information ostensibly learned in the lessons. This too is useful. But beyond the pragmatics, the theory raises some interesting epistemological issues. These are discussed briefly in the next section.

Anderson's View of Proof Skills:
Navigating the Search Space of Formal Deduction

Does one need to progress from the first through the fourth van Hiele level—or, in broader terms, does one need a solid empirical grounding—in order to grasp what proof is all about? Or, can one learn to construct formal proofs on their own terms, without concern for the empirical underpinnings that "support" an understanding of geometry? Perhaps what is needed, and what has been lacking, is an understanding of how proof really works. This is the perspective behind John Anderson's development of computer-based geometry tutors. (A nice overview of the work may be found in Anderson, Boyle, Farrell, & Reiser, 1985. Details on cognitive principles underlying the design of the computer-based geometry tutor are given in Anderson, Boyle, Farrell, & Reiser, 1984, and the psychological theory on which the work is based is described at length in Anderson, 1982.) The "product" of the work is a computer-based tutorial system that offers instruction in constructing geometry proofs.

A fundamental insight that drives the structure of the geometry tutor is that the final form in which proofs are generally presented obscures the complex processes by which proofs are in fact developed. As mathematics educators (e.g. Polya, 1945) and researchers in Artificial Intelligence have long argued, solving proof problems frequently involves heuristic search processes such as working forwards, working backwards, establishing subgoals, and the like. Yet the linear progression from givens to goals that one sees in most standard geometry textbooks leaves students with the impression that there is one logical, inexorable chain of reasoning that starts with the givens and ends with the goals—that is, there is one right way to do a proof, period. The geometry tutor presents, on the computer screen, a dynamic representation of the current state of the search. As a student begins to work on a problem, the diagram appears in the upper left-hand corner, the goal state at the top of the screen, the givens at the bottom. Figure 9.18(a), for example, presents the initial set-up for a proof problem. One is given that M is the midpoint of the segments AB and CD, and is asked to prove that M is the midpoint of EF. Figure 9.18(b) presents an intermediate state of the proof. Note there is both working forwards (from the givens at the bottom of the screen) and working backwards (from the goal at the top). The idea, of course, is to tie the top and bottom successfully together—a task achieved in Fig. 9.18(c), which provides a representation of the problem solution.

The instructional purpose of the tutor is to develop in students procedural competence at making deductive arguments in geometry. The tutor itself is based on Anderson's ACT* theory of knowledge compilation. Some of the instructional principles guiding the tutor's development are as follows (Anderson, Boyle, Farrell, & Reiser, 1984). As noted, the formalism on the screen reflects the semantics of the domain. (That is, proof is a nonlinear search process; this should be represented as such.) Anderson feels it essential to provide instruction in problem-solving contexts. In tutorial interactions one concept (e.g. the angle-side-angle postulate) is introduced at a time, along with a number of practice problems. Working the problems provides the student with the appropriate information about both how and when the concept is used. The "target skill" of tutorial interactions is an idealized competence at writing proofs, and tutorial sessions are designed to move students by successive approximations toward the target skill. Thus students are provided with immediate feedback regarding errors

a

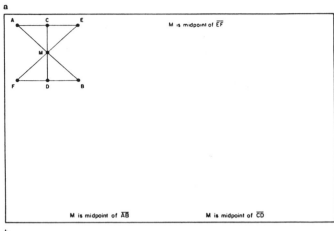

M is midpoint of $\overline{EF}$

M is midpoint of $\overline{AB}$ M is midpoint of $\overline{CD}$

b

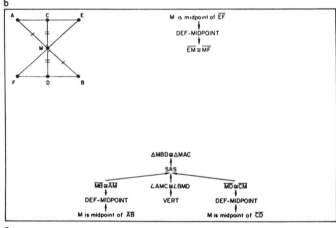

M is midpoint of $\overline{EF}$
↓
DEF-MIDPOINT
↓
$\overline{EM} \cong \overline{MF}$

$\triangle MBD \cong \triangle MAC$
↑
SAS

$\overline{MB} \cong \overline{AM}$ $\angle AMC \cong \angle BMD$ $\overline{MD} \cong \overline{CM}$
↑   ↑   ↑
DEF-MIDPOINT   VERT   DEF-MIDPOINT

M is midpoint of $\overline{AB}$ M is midpoint of $\overline{CD}$

c

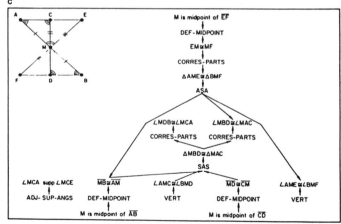

M is midpoint of $\overline{EF}$
↓
DEF-MIDPOINT
↓
$\overline{EM} \cong \overline{MF}$
↓
CORRES-PARTS
↑
$\triangle AME \cong \triangle BMF$
↑
ASA

$\angle MDB \cong \angle MCA$ $\angle MBD \cong \angle MAC$
↓   ↓
CORRES-PARTS   CORRES-PARTS

$\triangle MBD \cong \triangle MAC$
↑
SAS

$\angle MCA$ supp $\angle MCE$ $\overline{MB} \cong \overline{AM}$ $\angle AMC \cong \angle BMD$ $\overline{MD} \cong \overline{CM}$ $\angle AME \cong \angle BMF$
↑   ↑   ↑   ↑   ↑
ADJ-SUP-ANGS   DEF-MIDPOINT   VERT   DEF-MIDPOINT   VERT

M is midpoint of $\overline{AB}$ M is midpoint of $\overline{CD}$

(i.e. deviations from the "right" way to do things), so that they can be moved efficiently towards the target skill.

One can, as with van Hiele, argue over pedagogy. In particular, interactions with the tutor are extremely constraining. For any particular task, the tutor has determined the right way to do things. Deviations from that path, even if ultimately correct or potentially interesting, are regarded as "errors" and are not allowed. What happens when the student does something wrong or something that doesn't fit with the computer's model of the student? "Usually, this occurs when the student is confused. We have found that the best thing to do in such situations is to tell the student what to do next. If this is explained properly, the student is often able to get back on a right track" (Anderson, Boyle, & Reiser, 1985, p. 458). I find this approach troubling for a number of reasons, but these objections should not be allowed to overshadow the nature of the achievement. The tutor provides students with a dynamic representation of proof procedures (that is, it shows the dynamic nature of the search process in the deductive world w); in a theoretically based attempt to capture the idealized actions of a human tutor, it builds and updates cognitive models of students who are in the process of acquiring complex skills and uses those models as a means of moving the students towards mastery of those skills.

More interesting than arguments over pedagogy, however, are the underlying issues regarding the nature of geometric competence raised by the approach taken in the geometry tutor. As Anderson, Boyle, and Reiser (1985) state the issue, "We have found that only certain aspects of the theory are relevant to the tutoring of cognitive skills—in particular, the procedural assumptions" (p. 457). The key word in the statement is *skill:* The geometry tutor works in the world of proof *qua* proof, under the assumption that a skill—the ability to construct logical chains of reasoning—is what is being taught. The tutor's attention is restricted solely to developing fluency in chains of reasoning that take place in the symbolic proof world w; the meaning structures (I would say "semantics," but the term is problematic in this context and I have managed to avoid it until now) of the reference world W are not deemed relevant for the student-tutor interaction. If these proof skills are to be embedded in a larger context, then the issue of their acquisition as skills *qua* skills may not be problematic. But if they are not to be so embedded, it is worth quoting (if only for the rhetorical flourish) van Hiele's expression of concern about such approaches.

If one does not take the content of the symbols into consideration, but only their relations, one could say that from a mathematical point of view, everything is

---

FIG. 9.18. (a) The geometry tutor's initial representation of the problem; (b) a representation in the middle of the problem; and (c) a representation at the solution of the problem; SAS, side-angle-side. (From Anderson, Boyle, & Reiser, 1985, p. 459. Reproduced by permission.)

perfect. The student is capable of handling the relational system of deduction without mistakes. But from the pedagogical and didactic point of view, and from the social point of view, one has wronged the student! One has committed a pedagogical error because one has stolen from the student an occasion to realize his creative potential. From the didactic point of view, one has neglected to let the student discover how to explore new domains of thought by himself. Finally, one has wronged society because one has provided the student with a tool which he can handle only in situations which he has studied (quoted from "The child's thought and geometry," Fuys, Geddes, & Tischler, 1984, p. 248).

IN THE CLASSROOM

It is important to understand that the segment of dialogue with the student RO that was quoted earlier does not reflect singular or highly unusual behavior. RO was an average student who had finished a year of high school geometry. The vast majority of that course was devoted to proofs, and she was fairly competent at them. The course also included a unit on constructions, and she was relatively competent at those as well. The fact is, she simply saw little or no connection between the two topics. From her perspective the entities manipulated in geometric proofs were hypothetical objects, and the standard of correctness for a proof was its logical connectedness. On the other hand, the objects that she manipulated in constructions were (obviously) real, and the standard of correctness for a construction was its accuracy. Thus the result of a proof might suggest which procedures might be tried in a construction but did not serve to guarantee that the construction would be correct.

It should also be understood that RO's separation of geometry into non-overlapping deductive and empirical worlds was not the result of a local aberration, of a peculiar experience with one teacher or one school system. RO's behavior typified that of students in her local (upstate New York) high school district. It was not, however, at variance with the behavior of more than a hundred students from Hamilton College and the University of Rochester who were asked to work similar problems. Those students came from secondary school districts all over the country, and there is no reason to believe that their behavior is unusual; indeed, there is evidence to suggest that it is normative. In addition, it should not be assumed that being able to see the connection between the two geometries is simply a matter of intelligence, and thus that brighter students (rather than average students like RO) would make the relevant connections on their own. Indeed, some of the brightest students I have recorded showed the clearest signs of having constructed the empirical/deductive dichotomy for themselves. Such students solved the proof problems related to the construction problem without difficulty in 2 or 3 minutes; there is no question about their skill at producing deductive arguments. Yet many of them, given the construction problem immediately after they had worked the proof problems, made guesses that they would have been compelled to reject as incorrect if they had taken the results of the proofs to apply to the construction problems. These students, having made conjectures that violated the results of the proofs, then went on to test their conjectures by performing the constructions and accepting or rejecting the constructions on the basis of empirical accuracy. (One of the most devastating quotes on the videotapes comes from the brightest student in a problem-solving class at Hamilton. Having made a conjecture and being quite confident of its correctness, he mused: "But can we prove that now? Yeah—by drawing a circle and seeing if it works.")

There is some fairly clear evidence that the students' separation of deductive and empirical mathematics is learned behavior. Moreover, that behavior appears to have been learned in the students' geometry classrooms. In academic year 1984 a research project conducted in parallel with the interview sessions described earlier consisted of detailed observations of one high school geometry class (the "target class"), supplemented by periodic observations and questionnaire studies of a dozen other mathematics classes. (The classroom observations are described in chapter 10 of Schoenfeld, 1985a; the questionnaire data are given in Schoenfeld, 1985b.) The target class was not notably different from the other classes either in observed classroom behavior or in the patterns of questionnaire responses. Moreover, the pattern of responses on the questionnaire (N = 240) closely mirrored the pattern of responses on the third National Asessment of Educational Progress (N = 45,000). Thus, there is every reason to believe that the instruction observed in the target class typifies instruction taking place in high school geometry classes around the country.

The target class studied the classic year-long course of tenth-grade Euclidean geometry. Course content was carefully prescribed, since New York state had a mandated state-wide curriculum (which is now in transition) and a uniform end-of-year Regents examination. The school in which the class was given was a well-regarded secondary school in an affluent suburban school district. Instruction in this class was typical of instruction in other mathematics classes in school. The teacher was competent. He respected and liked his students; he had worked hard to create a relaxed atmosphere conducive to learning in the classroom. In short, what took place in his class was (within the bounds of freedom allocated individual instructors) precisely what was intended by those who had designed the curriculum.

What took place was skill acquisition, with performance criteria determined by the state-wide Regents curriculum. The major part of the course focused on developing skills at writing proofs, which played a prominent role in the curriculum. There were a number of "required" proofs, specifically designated arguments with which the students were expected to be familiar and at least one of which (worth 10 points out of 100) appeared on the exam; there were also proof problems that called for using proof skills on unfamiliar diagrams. Constructions played a relatively minor role in the course. There were roughly a dozen required constructions, one or two of which appeared on the examination. The constructions were worth only two points on the exam. They were graded only for their accuracy. The units on locus and constructions occupied 2 to 3 weeks of instruction, during which the students spent the vast majority of class time practicing the constructions.

The goal of the unit on constructions was to have the students rapidly and accurately perform the right sequence of straightedge and compass manipulations. It goes without saying that the students were supposed to understand why the constructions made sense. Thus, when each construction was introduced, the rationale for it was given in terms of the known theorems that justified it). Such rationales soon receded into the background, however, as performance became the focus of classroom and homework practice. The emphasis on speed and accuracy was clear, as indicated by these comments, which were made by the teacher shortly before an examination.

> You will have twenty-five questions. [A 54-minute long examination period thus allotted slightly more than two minutes per question.] *You'll have to know all your constructions cold so that you don't spend a lot of time thinking about them.* [emphasis added.]. This is where practice at home comes in. . . .
>
> I have to see the arcs. Now what I will not take will be a lot of trial and error on the constructions. . . As long as I can see all the marks so that I can follow your construction, then I will not take off if it's [off by] just a minimal distance. But if it's off by more than that, yes.

The students in this class learned what they were supposed to learn. The vast majority of class time during the unit on constructions was spent practicing the constructions, step by step. ("The next problem is bisecting an angle. All right, what is step number one?. . .") As a result of this practice the students became quite competent at carrying out the constructions. They also became reasonably competent at writing proofs. The students had, of course, committed the required theorems to memory; but they were also capable of working, with some skill, problems like the one posed in Fig. 9.18(a). The class did well on the Regents exam.

What the students also learned, however, was to make the strict separation between deductive and empirical geometries. The rationales for the constructions were presented when each construction was first introduced. In the particular classroom context, however, the rationales came to be interpreted by the students as "reasons suggesting why we do the constructions the way we do." The emphasis on accuracy when performing the constructions—ultimately the sole criterion for correctness on the examinations—became internalized as the students' sole, and purely empirical, standard for a construction's correctness. Proofs, on the other hand, had nothing to do with such "real" objects. They were sequences of operations on hypothetical entities that may have been abstracted from the real world, but whose real antecedents no longer mattered. What mattered instead was getting the proof right—making the right chain of logical connections, and then expressing them in the rigorous, two-column format. For these students, the proof universe was self-contained, and they came to think of the results of proofs as applying only to the (hypothetical) objects manipulated in those proofs. The coursework had not only failed to make connections between the empirical and deductive geometries, it had helped to erect barriers between them.

Why worry about this state of affairs? After all, the students demonstrated competence at the constructions; they demonstrated some competence at being able to write proofs. Isn't that what the course was designed to teach, and isn't that appropriate? I hope it is clear that the answer to this last question should be a resounding "no"—on mathematical, pedagogical, utilitarian, and epistemological grounds.

Let us deal first with the mathematical grounds. From the mathematician's point of view, the behavior just described reflects a clear failure of instruction, and it is essential to understand why that is the case. The business of mathematics is, in large part, one of abstraction and of perceiving structure. One of the reasons these processes are so important is that engaging in them gives the mathematician a tremendous amount of predictive power. A group, for example, consists of a collection of objects $G = \{g\}$ and a binary operation $*$ from $G \times G$ into G, such that there is an identity in G and every element in G has an inverse under $*$. The notion of group is an abstraction of common properties shared by otherwise very different-looking objects. For example, the integers mod 28 under addition, the set of all nonsingular 3×3 matrices under multiplication, and the set of all continuous strictly monotonic functions from [0,1] onto itself under composition are all groups. The abstraction allows one to see commonalities among these objects that might otherwise be obscured by their different forms. It provides great efficiency, because any theorem proved for an abstract group automatically applies to all of these. (For example, the cancellation law, "if $a*b = a*c$, then $b = c$" is true for all groups; hence one knows it is necessarily true for, say, the set of all continuous strictly monotonic functions from [0,1] onto itself under composition.) In fact, it provides more than efficiency; it provides predictive power. If the mathematician encounters a new collection of objects and demonstrates that that collection of objects is a group, then those objects automatically satisfy the cancellation law, and every other theorem that has ever been proved about groups. In that sense every mathematician, even the most "pure," is "applied." Much of the intrinsic power of mathematics comes from the perception of structure—from seeing connections and exploiting them. One of the primary reasons for learning mathematics is to develop such skills.

When students uniformly fail to see connections that should be apparent, something has gone seriously awry. To emphasize the point and to indicate its generality, it is worth repeating an example of a similar phenomenon at a more elementary level discussed by Wertheimer (1945). In this case, the domain is elementary arithmetic. Wertheimer asked schoolchildren to solve arithmetic problems like the following:

$$\frac{10638 + 10638 + 10638}{3} \quad \text{and} \quad \frac{303 + 303 + 303 + 303 + 303}{5}$$

The answers to those problems should be obvious. In the first case, adding a number to itself three times is the same as multiplying it by three, and dividing the result by three undoes the multiplication. Thus the original number (10638) remains unchanged, and no computations need to be done. The argument for the second case is similar.

Many students, who were familiar with all four of the basic arithmetic operations, solved each problem by laboriously computing the sum of the integers in the numerator, and then dividing that sum by the integer in the denominator. On the one hand, that procedure was technically correct. The fact that the students got the correct answers demonstrated that they were proficient at the symbolic manipulations; in a limited sense, they "understood" addition and division. On the other hand, there is something terribly wrong about the way they solved the problems. The students' blind performance of completely unnecessary algorithmic operations indicates that they had very little sense of the underlying structure and meaning of the arithmetic computations. That they eventually arrived at the right answers by using the algorithms is little consolation.

The case in geometry is similar. The proof skills studied in a geometry course are of intrinsic value. The construction skills, however, are not. Part of what makes them interesting is that the constructions take place in a domain to which the results obtained from pure mathematics can be applied (and vice versa); exploiting the parallels helps lay the groundwork for students' perceptions of mathematical structure and mappings of that structure to new domains. If students fail to see such obvious connections, they are missing what lies at the core of the mathematics. What hope is there, then, that they will learn the general reasoning and thinking skills that are supposed to be the consequence of learning mathematics?

The pedagogical and utilitarian grounds are dealt with more briefly (although we cycle back to them, implicitly, in the ensuing epistemological discussion). In terms of classroom performance, the students who fail to see the connections between the deductive and empirical geometric worlds wind up unable to solve a large class of problems that they could otherwise solve with ease. In utilitarian terms—regarding the students' abilities to apply, outside the classroom, the mathematics they learned in it—the situation is far worse. Students who fail to make the mapping from "ideal" geometric objects in the proof world to their paper-and-pencil counterparts in the construction world are hardly likely to map that knowledge onto physical objects in the real world. To recall the quotation from van Hiele, such students could use their knowledge only in situations they have studied.

The related epistemological issues are much more thorny, especially if one looks for the positive side: What collection of experiences is necessary for one to have the appropriately connected knowledge of geometry? What follows is sketchy, to say the least. It is based in part on ideas explored by Kitcher in *The nature of mathematical knowledge* (1983), and in part on a series of discussions in a seminar with Jim Greeno. Aspects of the approaches taken both by van Hiele and by Anderson mesh with the perspective taken here.

Kitcher explores the notion of an empiricist epistemology, in which the individual X knows the proposition p to be true if and only if (a) p is true, (b) X believes that p is true, and (c) X's belief that p is true was produced by an empirical, experiential warrant that justifies the belief. His argument is that one's knowledge of mathematical objects (or concepts) is derived from one's mathematical operations on those objects. Thus, for example, the following explanation of the origins of a child's understanding of number:

> Children come to learn the meanings of "set," "number," "addition" and to accept basic truths of arithmetic by engaging in *activities* of collecting and segregating. Rather than interpreting these activities as an avenue to knowledge of abstract objects, we can think of the rudimentary arithmetic truths as true in virtue of the operations themselves. By having experiences like [collecting a pile of two objects together with a pile of three objects to make a pile of five objects]. . . we learn that particular types of collective operations have particular properties: we learn for example that if one performs the collective operation called "making two," then performs on different objects the collective operation called "making three," the total is an operation of "making five." (Kitcher, 1983, pp. 107–108.)

According to Kitcher, the origins of knowledge of arithmetic (here that $2 + 3 = 5$) lie in such operations. Up to this point, he appears to be making more or less the classical constructivist argument. Now the realist clincher: Kitcher "consider[s] arithmetic to be true in virtue not of what *we can do* to the world but rather in terms of what *the world* will let us do *to it*" (p. 108). This perspective allows for the existence of a "real world" with which we interact and which we come to *know* through our operations on it.

In other words, we come to know mathematical objects (or learn about them) by operating on them. This perspective raises some interesting issues regarding the kinds of experiences students would have to undergo in order to understand the connections between the empirical and deductive geometries. (Note that this perspective rejects the obvious first order approach to the problem: Teach proof, then teach constructions, and then show how the two fit together.) On the one hand, this point of view lends support to some of the notions behind the van Hieles' (1957; 1957) work. It suggests that a solid empirical grounding is necessary for apprehending and then manipulating abstract geometric objects, that the objects themselves will not be meaningful to the students unless they have the appropriate experiential foundation. (Note that the question of when one should obtain that kind of grounding is very much open.) On the other hand, Anderson's (1982) thesis that learning takes place in a problem-solving context is also relevant here. In the context of the proof world, students are more likely to develop a sense of "meaningful proof structures" in the way Anderson describes than by studying formal, linear proofs. That understanding, however, remains within the formal proof world. For students to see how the various aspects of geometry fit together, and for them to have the potential to use their knowledge, it is likely necessary that there be a problem-solving context in which empiricism and deduction coexist and reinforce each other for example, an environment in which students work problems like the one discussed in the second section of this paper and are encouraged to see (and reflect upon) the relevant connections.

At issue here is a question of balance and synthesis, rather than whether empiricism is good or bad, for example, or whether there is too much or too little empiricism in any environment. The balance is delicate, and the right mix (and context) is not easy to predict or specify. As an example, the following story was passed on by Judah Schwartz. One of the technological microworlds currently being developed at the Educational Technology Center at Harvard is the "geometric supposer." The supposer "remembers" constructions, so that it can repeat them on new figures. For instance, a student can specify a sequence of operations to be tried on a particular triangle. If something interesting appears—say, all of the medians intersect at the same point—the student can have the supposer automatically repeat the sequence of steps on a new figure. Repeat constructions, which used to be tedious and time consuming, are now "cheap." I expressed some concern about this, because having this kind of tool available might encourage rampant empiricism. Because it would be easy for students to check conjectures, they might develop a *modus operandi* that consisted of making a guess and trying it on a large number of cases. If the guess worked for all of those cases, then it would be "right"—and the students would feel no need for proof at all. Schwartz pointed out that the knife cuts both ways. In one class where supposer was being used, for example, one student tried to convince another of the correctness of a construction by appealing to the large collection of instances (a dozen or more) in which the construction had worked. The response was "So what? We've seen lots of constructions that worked for lots of examples, and then turned out not to be right."

Geometry in the curriculum has taken a beating in recent years, and that is a shame. It is a fascinating mathematical microcosm, for a variety of reasons—not the least of which is that when it is taught properly, students have the opportunity to do real mathematics in precisely the same way that research mathematicians do. Such a goal for a high school course is not unrealistic. What it requires, however, is that we develop a thoughtful view of the kinds of things we expect students to learn—and the kinds of connections we expect them to make—in such a course. (Such connections range from the straightforward ones discussed in this chapter to deeper issues like understanding "logical thinking" or "the meaning of proof.") It requires that we elucidate the nature of the cognitive support structure that underlies such understanding and design instructional contexts conducive to the development of such cognitive structures. In particular, the various chapters of this book stand as examples of the kind of work that needs to be done. Detailed explorations of what it means to "understand" particular mathematical ideas, and what it takes to be able to implement mathematical procedures related to them, will help us to understand the nature and organization of those cognitive support structures. As the frightening complexity of Fig. 9.10 reminds us, this task will by no means be easy. There are, however, some signs that progress is being made.

ACKNOWLEDGMENTS

The author gratefully acknowledges the support of the Spencer Foundation for the research described in this paper. He also wishes to thank Jim Greeno, John Seely Brown, and Leon Henkin for their discussions of the first draft version of the paper. Those discussions resulted in the clarification of some significant issues, and the ways in which they were discussed.

REFERENCES

Anderson, J. R. (1982). Acquisition of cognitive skill. *Psychological Review, 89* (4), 369–406.
Anderson, J. R., Boyle, C. F., Farrell, R., & Reiser, B. J. (1984). *Cognitive principles in the design of computer tutors* (Tech. Rep. ONR-84-1). (Available from Advanced Computer Tutoring Project, Carnegie-Mellon University.)
Anderson, J. R., Boyle, C. F., & Reiser, B. J. (1985). Intelligent tutoring systems. *Science, 228,* 456–462.
Brown, J. S. (1985, July) Notes on arithmetical competency. Paper delivered at a conference celebrating the 20th anniversary of the University of Pittsburgh's Learning Research and Development Center.
Freudenthal, H. (1973). *Mathematics as an educational task.* Dordrecht, Holl.: Reidel.
Fuys, D., Geddes, D., & Tischler, R. (Eds.). (1984). *English translation to selected writing of Dina van Hiele-Geldof and Pierre M. van Hiele.* (Available from Dorothy Geddes, School of Education, Brooklyn College, The City University of New York.
Greeno, J. G., & Johnson, W. (1984). *Competence for solving and understanding problems.* Paper presented at the International Congress of Psychology, Acapulco. (Available from James Greeno, Education, University of California, Berkeley.)
Hoffer, A. (1983). van Hiele-based research. In R. Lesh & M. Landau (Eds.), *Acquisition of mathematical concepts and processes* (pp. 205–227). New York: Academic Press.
Kieren, T. E. (1976). Perspectives on rational numbers. In R. A. Lesh & D. A. Bradbard (Eds.), *Number and measurement* (pp. 101–144.) Columbus, OH: ERIC/SMEAC.
Kilpatrick, J., & Wirszup, I. (Eds. & Trans.). 1969–1975). *Soviet studies in the psychology of learning and teaching mathematics* (14 vols.). Chicago: University of Chicago Press.

Kitcher, P. (1983). *The nature of mathematical knowledge*. New York: Oxford University Press.

Lakatos, I. (1977). *Proofs and refutations* (revised edition). Cambridge, Eng.: Cambridge University Press.

Peirce, Charles Saunders. (1931). Collected papers of Charles Saunders Peirce (C. Hartshorne & P. Weiss, Eds.) Cambridge, MA: Harvard University Press.

Poincare, H. (1913). *The foundations of science* (G. H. Halstead, trans.). New York: Science Press.

Polya, G. (1945). *How to solve it*. Princeton, NJ: Princeton University Press.

Polya, G. (1980). *Mathematical discovery*. New York: Wiley.

Resnick, L. B., & Omanson, Susan F. (1986). Learning to understand arithmetic. In R. Glaser (Ed.), *Advances in instructional psychology (Vol. 3)*. Hillsdale, NJ: Lawrence Erlbaum Associates.

Schoenfeld, A. H. (1983). *Problem solving in the mathematics curriculum*. Washington, DC: Mathematical Association of America.

Schoenfeld A. H. (1985a). *Mathematical problem solving*. New York: Academic Press.

Schoenfeld, A. H. (1985b). *Students' beliefs about mathematics and their effects on mathematical performance: A questionnaire analysis*. Paper presented at annual American Educational Research Association Meeting, Chicago.

van Hiele, P. M. (1957). *De problematiek van het inzicht*. Unpublished doctoral dissertation (includes English summary). University of Utrecht.

van Hiele-Geldof, D. (1957). *De didaktiek van de meetkunde de eerste klass van het V.H.M.O.* Unpublished doctoral dissertation (includes English summary). University of Utrecht.

Wetheimer, M. (1959). *Productive thinking*. New York: Harper & Row.

Wirszup, I. (1976). Breakthroughs in the psychology of learning and teaching geometry. In J. L. Martin (Ed.), *Space and Geometry: Papers from a research workshop*. (pp. 75–97). Columbus, Ohio: ERIC.

10 Conceptual and Procedural Knowledge in Mathematics: A Summary Analysis

Robert B. Davis
University of Illinois, Urbana/Champaign

Anyone who doubts that mathematics education has become a serious discipline in its own right need only read the preceding chapters to have those doubts substantially resolved. Indeed, one probably needs to read no further than the first chapter, by Hiebert and Lefevre. Mathematics education nowadays clearly involves a serious and valuable study of problems that are important at both theoretical and practical levels.

At the same time—and this adds to the attractiveness of the subject—there are significant disagreements, there are important unsolved problems, there are difficulties in translating one conceptualization into another, and there is a quite reasonable prospect of further progress. In short, a very promising field for future research!

Personally, I am interested both in the theoretical matters—I wish to deepen my "understanding"—and also in the practical questions—I want to see major improvements in our educational programs and practices. But I ask the reader to view this final chapter especially in practical terms. Existing school and university programs have many serious shortcomings. We *can* do better, we *need* to do better, and we are beginning to know *how* to do better.

I do not for a moment doubt that the theory now being developed can help us to create better instructional programs in mathematics, from arithmetic through calculus, and perhaps even into more advanced courses beyond that.

WHAT'S WRONG WITH SCHOOL MATHEMATICS?

First, consider a few of the main criticisms of most existing mathematics programs. What is wrong?

265

Overemphasis on Written Symbols

School programs typically regard mathematics as primarily a matter of writing symbols on paper, according to certain prescribed rules. This is not what mathematics is. At the elementary levels, mathematics is a description of reality—a description that is sufficiently detailed to give us a considerable measure of control.

To be sure, someone "doing mathematics" may indeed make some marks on a piece of paper. This is not, however, what should usually be center stage in that person's thinking. Perhaps the point can be clarified if we imagine, say, that we are writing a script for a television drama. Here, too, we may write on paper. But our thoughts should be mainly on the action, the dialogue, the development of the characters, and the like. "Is this the kind of thing this character would say?" "Has this action been motivated enough beforehand so that it will seem reasonable, or even inevitable?" *Miami Vice* and *The Cosby Show* do not succeed because of intrinsic attributes of the way their writers make notations on paper, but rather because of social situations, interactions between characters, visual appeal, and so on.

Returning to mathematics, consider how schools typically deal with notation. For the first 6 years of schooling, written notations of arithmetic are the almost exclusive focus of interest. This is far from a realistic view of *mathematics* (though it may be a realistic view of parental expectations). Schools seem to deny three truths: (a) One needs to have a reality to describe *before* one can try to describe it; (b) using written notations is not the only way to do mathematics; and (c) it is usually important to *understand* the real meaning of what you are doing.

Let me say a few words more about each of these:

Real Experiences Before Symbols.   Children need a reality to write about, before they can do much writing. This is true whether they are writing (in English) about "What I did last summer" or (in some appropriate symbolism) about some actions in combining two collections of Dienes' MAB blocks.

Everyday Mathematics Is not Usually Dependent On Written Symbols.   Adults do not rely heavily on written algorithms, nor should they (see, e.g., Lave, 1982; Lave, Murtaugh, & de la Rocha, 1984; Cockcroft, 1982). Most readers can easily confirm this for themselves. Try to solve these problems:

(i) Anne and Linda hammered nails into different boards. Anne hammered a line of 15 nails into a board 3 feet long. Linda hammered a line of 45 nails into a board 9 feet long. On which board are the nails hammered closer together? Circle your answer.

   a) Anne's board
   b) Linda's board

   c) Their nails are spaced exactly the same.

   d) There is not enough information to tell.

Show how you figured out your answer.

(ii) Tom and Bob drove along a country road. Tom drove 8 miles in 32 minutes. Bob drove 2 miles in 10 minutes. Who was the faster driver? Circle your answer.

   a) Tom

   b) Bob

   c) They drove at exactly the same speed.

   d) There is not enough information to tell.

(iii) Tom invited some friends to be his guests for lunch at a Chinese restaurant. They occupied two tables, one large table and one small table, served by two different waitresses. When it was time to pay, the bill for the large table came to $36.50. The bill for the small table was $26.50. Tom handed both to the cashier, together with a check for $73.00 and asked her to give each waitress an appropriate tip. What did the cashier do?[1]

The reader is urged to solve each problem and notice the methods used. Here are solutions to the second and third problems.

Solution to the second problem (by a mathematician):

I must multiply 8 by 4 to get 32.

Does the same number work for Bob's trip? No—I must multiply 2 by 5 in order to get 10. So Bob's number is bigger. ["Bob's number" refers to the *multiplier*.]

Now, does that mean Bob is going *faster* or *slower*?

Let me use the strategy of going to extremes: if Bob's "10 minutes" were really big—say, 100 minutes—he would be going very slowly. Therefore, [putting this all together] Bob is going more slowly.

(Notice that this uses the *fact* that, if ax = y, if a, x, and y are all positive, and if x is kept constant, then a increases if and only if y increases. This *fact* is used, but *nothing was written on paper*.)

The third problem is based on an actual occurrence. Here is what happened:

Cashier: Can I give them [the waitresses] each $5?

Tom: I think you should divide it proportionally.

Cashier: All right. I'll give one $6, and the other $4.

---

[1]All three of these problems are from Tom Post's studies of proportional reasoning.

Tom: How did you decide?
Cashier: [responding with a question] What is the tip? Ten percent?
Tom: I think it probably should be 15%.
Cashier: Then I'll just give each 15%.
Tom: Suppose it doesn't add up to $10?
Cashier: Then I'll just give each waitress a little bit more.

How do these numbers work out?

Cashier's quick solution: $6 to one, $4 to the other.
Solution, by computing 15%:
   $5.00 plus 47½ cents to one waitress, $3.00 plus 97½ cents to the other; we'll
write this as $5.475 and $3.975 (total: $9.45).
   Preceding solution, if the "little bit more" is distributed equally: $5.75 and
$4.25.
   The "15% solution" if the "little bit more" is distributed roughly proportionally: $5.78 and $4.22.
   Solution if one writes out the problem and solves algebraically: $5.793650794
and $4.20634906.
   Preceding solution, rounded to the nearest penny: $5.79 and $4.21.
   It might be added that Tom decided on the $73.00 amount of the check,
intending a 15% tip, without writing anything down. (Notice also that one of the
cashier's immediate solutions, with no writing, differed from the "ideal" solution by only four cents to each waitress, and another of her solutions differed by
only one cent.)

   Underemphasis on Understanding the Problem.   The "third truth": if you
understand a problem, you can usually find the answer *with essentially no reliance on the methods usually taught in school.*
   To illustrate this, let me pretend to be the cashier in the following (imaginary)
episode:

   A customer selects an item costing 37 cents, and gives me a dollar bill. I must
give them change. I give them 3 pennies—that gets me to 40 cents. I give them a
dime—that gets me to 50 cents. I give them 2 quarters, and I am done.

   In simple arithmetic tasks, *understanding the problem nearly always guides
you to the method for solving it.* "Finding the answer" is hardly ever a difficult
matter. *It is only when I try to think of mathematics as writing symbols on paper
that I begin to experience difficulties.* (This theme is well discussed in preceding
chapters by Baroody and Ginsburg and by Carpenter, among others.)

Of course I *could* write something on paper to show how I made change. It might perhaps look like this:

$$
\begin{array}{ccc}
100 & & 100 \\
37 & \text{or even} & -\ 37 \\
\hline
3 & & 3 \\
10 & & 10 \\
50 & & 50 \\
\hline
63 & & 63 \\
\end{array}
$$

But which should come first? Which should I experience first? Which should play the central role in my thinking?

I would argue that *dealing with actual problems* should come first. Learning to use written symbols as cheap proxies for reality comes second—but we should not allow ourselves too long a period of total concentration on these proxies. Mathematics does not lie in its symbols, but in the ideas these symbols are supposed to represent.

Observational studies by Baroody and Ginsburg, and by Carpenter (reported in this volume) as well as by others (e.g., Whitney, 1985; Cochran, Barson and Davis, 1970) indicate that young children follow exactly this pattern. Reality, and ideas about reality, come first. It is only when school programs begin to disrupt this developmental pattern that difficulties usually appear. (See also Whitney, in press.)

We do not argue that school is unnecessary, nor do we argue that formal written methods should not be taught and learned. On the contrary, our argument is that, when school focuses almost exclusively on written symbols, mathematics is *not* learned. We advocate instead that schools pay attention (as they do not do at present) to the developmental needs and developmental processes of children. In particular, *provide experience before a child is asked to write about it.* And, when schools do deal with written records, *maintain the focus of attention on what the symbols mean, and not on the symbols themselves.*

Consider typical programs to teach the usual addition algorithm for whole numbers. Students who have already learned addition facts such as:

$$3 + 5 = 8 \qquad 2 + 7 = 9$$

and so on, are asked to deal with problems such as:

$$
\begin{array}{r}
2035 \\
+\ 1723 \\
\hline
\end{array}
\qquad (1)
$$

In typical school programs, this is presented as a paper-and-pencil task; symbols are everything—the meaning is nothing.

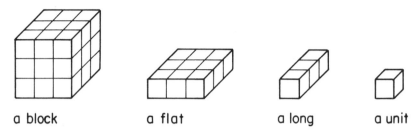

FIG. 10.1.   Dienes' MAB Blocks, Base Three

Problems such as (1) are seen as nothing more than four independent problems of the "addition facts" type:

$$2 + 1 = 3, \quad 0 + 7 = 7, \quad 3 + 2 = 5, \quad 5 + 3 = 8.$$

This provides no adequate foundation for addition where "carrying" is required.

By contrast, consider an alternative curriculum using Dienes' MAB blocks, as developed by the Madison Project (see Davis, 1984, pp. 9–14). First, children (who have *not* yet faced column addition problems—the experience must come *before* the notation) play "trading" games, using MAB blocks base 3. (See Fig. 10.1.) Base 3 is chosen here to simplify the counting tasks. The point is that three units can be traded, in either direction, for one long. Three longs trade for one flat. Three flats trade for one block. From a theoretical point of view, these experiences are creating an *assimilation paradigm* (Davis, 1984), in this case, a familiar idea of "trading" and how trading works.

Once trading with base 3 blocks is familiar, one can go on to trading with base 10 blocks.[2] (see Fig. 10.2). Here, of course, ten units trade for one long, ten longs for a flat, and so on.

After trading is familiar (and a suitable "assimilation paradigm" has been created in the child's mind), one begins a sequence of tasks using the wooden blocks. Two arrays of blocks are arranged, each array is somehow recorded (possibly using tally marks on paper where columns are separated by vertical lines [see Davis, 1984]), the two arrays are merged, and the result is recorded.[3]

The important points are these:

1. The experiences of creating the arrays with wooden blocks come *before* any attempt at writing on paper.

2. When writing on paper is done, its role is clear: it is a recording of what has actually been done.

---

[2]In actual practice it is important that the instructional sequence be adjusted to the intellectual maturity level of the children. For some children counting poses no problems, starting with base 3 blocks is unnecessary, and it is preferable to begin directly with base 10 blocks.

[3]A more complete explanation is given in Davis, 1984.

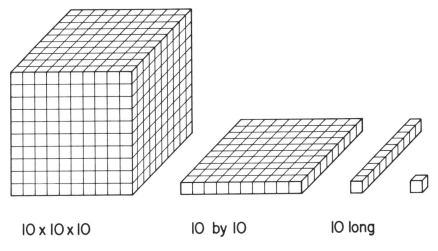

10 x 10 x 10   10 by 10   10 long

FIG. 10.2.   Dienes' MAB Blocks, Base Ten

3. The notation used will at first be a simple one, which will gradually evolve into the standard Hindu-Arabic decimal notation for positive integers.

4. Even when dealing with written notations, the teacher will speak about the wooden blocks. Thus, in talking about

$$237$$
$$+241$$

the teacher will say something like: "We have seven units here, and one unit here. When we push them all together, how many units will we have?" Similarly: "We have three longs here, and four longs here. When we push them together, how many longs will we have?" "And where will we write that?" The teacher does not say "ones", or "tens", or "hundreds." The actual experience of the children has been with wooden blocks called "units," "longs," "flats," and "blocks", and these are the words the teacher uses. Thus, "237" is a symbol that does stand for something; its meaning is: "2 flats, 3 longs, and 7 units". The children are not being asked to deal with meaningless symbols.

Notice that this sequence is very closely parallel to: (a) Having the experience of going to the circus. . . (b) . . . and, *after* that, writing about the experience of going to the circus.[4] Words such as chimpanzee, zebra, okapi, panda, and peacock might then be used with meaning.

---

[4]MAB blocks need to be used carefully, if we want to get good results. See Davis and McKnight, 1980.

The Too-Slow Pace

An obsession with notation is not the only error that schools are accused of making. Another is the too-slow pace.

In most U.S. schools students advance through the mathematics curriculum at a very slow rate, which is not dictated by student capabilities. On the contrary, there is by now a very large body of evidence that many students can progress *very much* faster, with *deeper* understanding.[5] It is feasible for academically inclined students to complete two years of calculus, with excellent understanding, before their 17th or 18th birthday. (This is routinely achieved at University High School in Urbana, Illinois.)

Why, then, is progress typically so slow? There are several answers (expectations is one), but the heavy reliance on rote, meaningless, unmotivated formalism is possibly the main answer. How long would it take anyone to memorize the Manhattan telephone directory?

Although there are practical reasons for the very slow pace, the relevance of many of the preceding chapters points in another direction. If theories of learning or of knowledge are inappropriate, they will tend to influence practice, and probably not for the better. We look further at the close relation between theory and practice in later sections of this chapter; now, however, we consider one other "practical" weakness in typical school curricula: their very narrow range of coverage.

Excessive Commitment
to Rote Arithmetical Calculation

As Robert Karplus (personal communication) has said:

> The United States will not soon have an elementary school science program because it believes it doesn't need one. The United States will not soon have an elementary school mathematics program because it believes it has one already.

Similar remarks have also come from Peter Hilton (personal communication). Mathematics is a subject that many children find fascinating, and this applies to many different aspects of mathematics (see, e.g., Davis, 1967; Hoyles, 1985; Lawler, 1985; Williams & Shuard, 1970; Schools Council, 1966). Why is nearly all of this subject absent from most school programs?

Clearly the answer is related to the other problems. If "mathematics" is seen as conformity to memorized rituals, if it is taught without meaning (and therefore

---

[5]Some of the best evidence comes from direct observation of student work, e.g., Suzuki, 1979; Kumar, 1979, 1980; Pandharipande, 1985; Secrest, 1985; Davis, Jockusch, and Mc Knight, 1978; and Davis, 1984.

hardly learned at all), if meaninglessness compels a slow pace and a vast investment in repetition, and if routine calculation is the main goal, very little mathematics will be included in the curriculum. Indeed, very little mathematics *can* be included in the curriculum.

A Wrong View of Mathematics

As one examines typical school mathematics programs, it becomes clear that theory and practice have influenced one another so as to make them inseparable. No small responsibility for other weaknesses can be traced to a wrong notion of what mathematical knowledge is like.

What does it mean to "do mathematics"?

Consider the cashier in the Chinese restaurant. At what point did she "do mathematics"? Some would say she began to do mathematics only when (and *if*) she started to write:

$$x + y = 10$$

$$\frac{x}{y} = \frac{36.5}{26.5}$$

I submit that this is a wrong view of mathematics. In my view (and that of most critics of school programs), she began "doing mathematics" *the moment she began thinking about the problem,* the moment she began to make a mental representation of the problem. To discard all these early steps as "not mathematics" is to separate "mathematics" from the real world, to confine mathematics within an arid ghetto, and to render "mathematics" very nearly unlearnable. James Faulkner was not "a writer" only when he took pen in hand; he was also a writer when he sat in the village square and watched what people did and how they talked.

Or consider this problem: On the left, we see three butterflies; on the right we see five flowers. Each butterfly flies over, alights on a flower, and remains there. Will every flower have a butterfly on it? If not, how many flowers will *not* have a butterfly?

If the butterflies are moveable—flannel cutouts, perhaps—every child who can count can solve the problem, by moving (if necessary) the butterflies over to "act out" the story. Was this mathematics? I (and the critics) would say yes.

A more experienced child can imagine or visualize this action even when the pictures of butterflies and flowers are printed on a page and cannot be moved together. Is this visualization, and the resulting solution of the problem, properly called "mathematics"? I (and the critics) would say yes.

Or consider this, a particularly telling example from John Anderson (Davis, 1985a): Do tenth-grade geometry teachers teach mathematics? In most cases it appears that they do *not*! Consider this typical sequence of events: (a) The teacher assigns the task of proving a certain theorem, the proof to be handed in the next day; (2) on the next day, some students (usually only a few) come to class with correct proofs and pass them in. Clearly, the teacher did not teach *these* students how to make the proof; they worked it out at home, either by themselves, or with parental help; (3) But most students come to class the next day without a proof and report that they were unable to make one. What does the teacher do for these students? Typically, the teacher *shows* them a proof. But this does not answer the question. The real question was: *How does someone who, initially, does not know how to make a proof, go about the task of analyzing the problem so that they ultimately ARE able to make a proof?* Typically the teacher does not attempt to deal with this question. (For a more extended discussion, see Davis, 1985a.)

"Doing mathematics" is a process of *thinking*. Because typical school programs do not see it this way, they focus on a small part of the subject which, in isolation, is not viable. "Doing mathematics" means creating, in one's own mind, a mental representation of the problem, and a mental representation of some relevant knowledge that can be used in creating a solution. Schools ignore these representations and do not help students to build effective representations. (Nor do they identify, and "de-bug," unsuitable representations. See, e.g., Erlwanger, 1973.) It has been argued that this unsatisfactory practice is largely a consequence of an unsuitable S-R Theory that focuses on what a student *does*, rather than on what a student *thinks*. Mathematics, however, is far more a matter of *thoughts* than a matter of *actions*. A teacher who is not concerned with how the students *think* will not succeed in teaching much mathematics.

A Wrong View of Learning

Increasingly over the past few decades it has been argued that schools are preoccupied with "putting knowledge into the child's mind" rather than perceiving their main task as one of helping children to develop useful and appropriate ideas by analyzing their own experience. Perhaps no one has argued this case more strongly than Whitney (1985). (See also Papert, 1980; Kamii, 1985; Lawler, 1985; or, for an earlier discussion, Schools Council, 1966.) Of course, as we argued earlier, the alternate view means that schools must make sure that children do have the appropriate experiences, and schools must work with children on the difficult task of interpreting these experiences. When this interpretive assistance is not provided, children often learn grotesquely inappropriate ideas (see, e.g., Erlwanger, 1973). The fact is that children develop *ideas,* whether we help them in this process or pretend that it does not occur.

There is a special case of this general criticism. Schools typically insist that students learn certain "conventional procedures" (Gelman and Meck's excellent phrase!)—procedures for counting objects, procedures for subtracting with place-value numerals, procedures for solving algebraic equations, procedures for evaluating indefinite integrals. As Gelman and Meck (this volume) say, the student is often led to judge "rightness" or "wrongness" by whether the conventional procedure has been followed and not by whether the essential criteria have been satisfied. (See especially the chapter in this volume by Baroody and Ginsburg, and also Ginsburg, 1982.)

This insistence on the prescribed ritual is particularly evident in many presentations of equation-solving (and also solving inequalities) in introductory algebra. A *criterion*-based approach would first of all put the task in context by considering some equations and inequalities, by demonstrating that some numerical replacements of the variable(s) yield false statements, and perhaps by going on to show that some numerical replacements produce true statements. The task, then, is to determine all numbers (or ordered pairs of numbers) that lead to true statements.

The second stage is to study this process and notice what patterns can be used to advantage. The most common *general* process is to construct a sequence of rewritings of the equation or inequality that either leave the truth set unchanged or change it in a way that is not too complicated—as, for instance, when one squares both sides of an equation. By the end of the second stage of study, one has identified a collection of rewriting rules that *may* be used, and one has begun to develop some skill in analyzing each novel equation so as to be able to determine a sequence of rewritings that will move toward a solution.

For a conceptually-oriented presentation, efficiency would probably not be a requirement—at least not until later, when efficiency might become a legitimate need. At that time it can easily be developed. Once a process is thoroughly understood, it can be made more efficient with little difficulty.

Of course, what schools typically do is quite different from this. Some procedure is determined in advance—"out of sight of the students," as it were (determined perhaps beforehand by the author of the textbook)—such as solving the equation

$$\frac{x - 3}{2 - x} = \frac{4 - x}{x - 1} \tag{2}$$

by "cross-multiplying." Students are then told to use this procedure on equations of this type. In most classes few students can answer why a certain procedure is considered acceptable, whereas some other procedure is unacceptable. Orthodoxy, not utility, has been the sole criterion for the operation. You do things "the way they are supposed to be done," without asking questions.

By contrast, a heuristically and conceptually oriented presentation might, instead, ask: What makes equation (2) difficult? Answer: The fractions. Can you get rid of one or both of the fractions? Answer: Well, whenever a fraction is multiplied by its denominator, the result is no longer a fraction (well, more or less, anyhow)." So if we multiplied

$$\frac{x - 3}{2 - x} \qquad (3)$$

by $2-x$, it wouldn't be a fraction anymore. Could we multiply (3) by $2-x$ without changing the truth set of the equation? Yes, provided we multiplied *both sides of the equation* by $2-x$. (Again, we may need to check for $x = 2$ as a possible extraneous root.) This kind of analysis leads reasonably quickly to a solution of the equation.

Notice how different the heuristic/conceptual approach is from the "prescribed-ritual" approach. It can hardly be said that both teach the same thing.

Typical school insistence on following a conventional procedure raises a number of questions. Is it the nature of children to want a conventional procedure? (In many cases, it is not. Our observational records show many children who make up their own solution strategies and would prefer to use them; indeed, some do, surreptitiously—suspecting the teacher would not approve.) Is it something in the nature of schools or the way schools (and many parents) relate to children? (More and more observers are coming to suspect that it is; there is a frequent expectation that children should learn to do many things the way the grown ups do—novelty is not necessarily welcome.) There are also some obvious implications for evaluation. Suppose, for example, that evaluation of both students and school programs included observing tasks such as the cashier-making-change task, included questions such as "Why is _____ not accepted as a legitimate rewrite rule in solving equations?" and included some novel types of equations that could not be solved by the common procedures, but could be solved by thinking about them. What would be the effect of these changes in evaluation procedures? Some examples of novel types of equations might be:

(i)   Solve $(x - 2)^2 + (y - 3)^2 = 0$ for all pairs (x, y) that will produce a true statement.

(ii) Solve $|x - 3| + |x + 2| = 0$.

(iii) Find all pairs (u, v) that make $2u + 2v = uv$ into a true statement, if u and v are required to be integers (Davis, 1985b).

I have argued that typical existing school mathematics programs are extremely unsatisfactory; that their main weaknesses are related to incorrect theories of what is going on (and what needs to go on); that much better curricula are possible; and that achieving these better curricula depends on the development and acceptance of better theoretical understandings.

Let us turn now to the question of what a better theory might look like.

THE SHAPE OF AN EMERGING THEORY

In order for a human being to think about a mathematical problem or situation, at least two kinds of representations must be present in "work-space" memory[6] in that person's mind. The problem, task, or situation must be represented, and some relevant knowledge must be represented. The nature of these representations is crucial to one's success or lack of success in creating a solution (see, e.g., Davis, 1985b).

Consider once more the cashier in the Chinese restaurant. When Tom asked her to give each waitress the appropriate tip, the cashier must have represented this in her mind as some kind of sharing or distribution task. How could she distribute the money beyond the total of the bills for each table? Nearly all humans beyond the age of 3 or 4—certainly nearly all adults—have had many experiences in "sharing" or "dividing up," and from these experiences they have synthesized a "sharing" schema of some sort.

The cashier then had to retrieve from memory some relevant knowledge and represent this knowledge within "work-space" memory. How to share? Give equal shares!

At this point an important process had to occur: specific "input" data from the problem representation had to be mapped into the knowledge representation. How many shares were required? Two, because there were two tables and two waitresses. Hence the cashier asked if she could give each waitress half. Presumably, had there been three waitresses involved, the cashier would have suggested thirds.

If we take this general view of the process of thinking about problems—focusing on mental representations—what questions must a theory attempt to deal with? At least these seven:

1. What sort of pieces are available as building blocks, to be used in constructing mental representations?

2. Where do these pieces come from?

3. Before we can move any "piece" from long-term memory into the small confines of "working-space" memory, we must locate it in long-term memory. How is this memory search carried out?

4. How are the "pieces" assembled together to make larger representations?

---

[6]Not everything in your memory is readily accessible to you. You cannot, for example, write down every male first name that you know. You will leave out many; you will think of some more tomorrow and still others some time next week. "Work-space" memory is that part of memory accessible to you right at this moment. It has limited capacity. Only a very small portion of the contents of your overall memory can be retrieved and transfered to work-space memory at any one time. For an extended discussion, see Davis, 1984.

5. How is input data mapped from the problem representation into the knowledge representation?

6. After the problem is solved, we store something in long-term memory. This is a main part of the "knowledge" we have gained from the experience of solving the problem. What can we say about this "record" that is now entered into long-term memory?

7. The processes listed above require some form of direction or control. What can we say about the *control processes* that direct the first six "tactical" processes?

One cannot, in the space of a single chapter, answer all seven questions; nor, for that matter, are complete answers yet available either from the preceding chapters of this volume or from anywhere else. But we can see some useful pieces of some of the answers. In what follows I consider briefly questions 1, 2, 5, and 6, referring the reader who wishes to pursue questions 3, 4, and 7 to the volume *Learning Mathematics* (Davis, 1984).

Cognitive Building Blocks and Their Origins

The first two questions are best considered simultaneously, and perhaps best by starting with an example—in this case, observations of a group of 6-, 7-, and 8-year-olds beginning to learn about area by using geoboards.[7]

Ben had made the shape shown in Fig. 10.3, by using a rubber band stretched over nails. He is having difficulty determining its area. He has cut two paper unit squares along the diagonal, getting triangles that he has labeled "$\frac{1}{2}$." But when he finally manages to fit these triangles into his square, he sees that his "diamond-shaped" figure is now divided into four equal parts, so he wants to relabel the triangular pieces "$\frac{1}{4}$," and he claims that the area of his "diamond" is *one*. There is just enough truth in each piece of his thinking to be troublesome. The triangles are each one-fourth of *his diamond,* but they are still each one-half *of a unit,*—and that is what counts. One might have used words in an attempt to explain all of this to Ben but would likely have failed. Ben might have continued to give priority to his diamond and refused to see why we insist on urging him to use our unit square—and not his diamond—as the crucial standard.

Fortunately Larissa, another student, observed Ben's problem and made the arrangement shown in Fig. 10.4. When Ben compared Larissa's figure to his own, he could see how his diamond really was made up of two unit squares. With the help of Larissa's figure, Ben could visualize rotations and translations that would transform two squares (see Fig. 10.5) into his diamond, or transform

---

[7]A "geoboard" is usually made by partially driving nails into a wooden board, leaving the heads protruding about $\frac{1}{2}$ inch, so that shapes can be made by stretching rubber bands over the nails. The nails are arranged in rows and columns (see Davis, 1980).

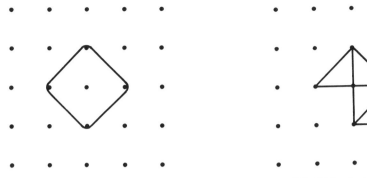

FIG. 10.3. Ben's Figure   FIG. 10.4. Larissa's Figure

his diamond into the two squares of Fig. 10.5. Ben had not arrived at a complete understanding, but he was beginning to make intellectual progress.

For our present purpose the question is this: What "cognitive building blocks" did Ben need to make use of? Triangles and squares, of course. Where could these ideas come from? They were mental representations of paper squares and triangles and of shapes made by stretching rubber bands over nails. These were things he had seen, touched, manipulated, built himself. It is not surprising that he had also created mental representations of them.

But he also needed more, he needed mental representations of the *acts* of rotating the triangles, of translating them, of putting them together to make other shapes, and even of creating them by cutting a unit square along a diagonal.

Because we adults do indeed possess mental representations for such things, we often assume that all children do. Many do not, *unless we provide them with the experiences that will lead to the creation of such mental representations.* This is why the nails and rubber bands and pieces of paper can be important. Notice, in particular, how mundane and "ordinary" the key experiences are: moving small objects, rotating them, rearranging them into patterns. Many powerful and abstract ideas have origins of this sort.

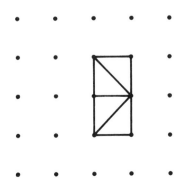

FIG. 10.5.   Rotating Two Triangles Appropriately Can Produce Ben's Figure.

279

These are not the only "cognitive building blocks" from which mathematical mental representations are synthesized. Among other building blocks that are recognizable, one finds:

1. learned, experienced, or practiced *sequences* (including so-called VMS sequences [Davis, 1984]), such as the "orthodox" sequence of steps for solving, say, a quadratic equation like

$$x^2 - 5x + 6 = 0$$

by writing:

$$(\quad)(\quad) = 0$$
$$(x\quad)(x\quad) = 0$$
$$(x - 3)(x - 2) = 0 \quad ,$$

so either $x - 2 = 0$ or else $x - 3 = 0$, whence either $x = 2$ or else $x = 3$;

2. general schema from life experiences (such as "adding more" sugar to coffee, or laying down more change on the counter, or pulling out a longer stretch of dental floss from the container, etc.);

3. "assimilation paradigms" (which are essentially metaphors);

4. previously synthesized representations.

The Role of "General Schema from Life Experiences"

When, say, column addition is taught in relation to concrete materials—whether MAB blocks, "beans on tongue depressors" (Davis, 1972), or whatever—the well-established schema for "trading ten longs for one flat", and the like serve to guide what should be written. Suppose, for example, that in addition to experience with MAB blocks, we have taught the children "Volkswagen numerals" (by analogy with "two Volkswagens parked at one parking meter" [Davis, 1971]), so that

$$1\ 7\ _{12}\ 3$$

means "three units, twelve longs, seven flats, and one block." We have a rule— the "thou shall not have ten" rule—which says that we must not hold ten of any single shape. We are presently in violation of this rule: we *do* have ten longs (plus even more, but having ten is already a violation). Hence we must trade. But the important attribute of MAB blocks is that fair trades "look right" and "feel right" (whereas trades between one dime and ten pennies do not). There is very little that need be remembered about the proper trade; we must trade ten longs for one more flat.

Hence

$$1\ 7\ _{12}\ 3$$

becomes

1 8 2 3.

Our great familiarity with handling physical objects guides our thinking and our writing. Or, to put the matter more theoretically, we can build mental representations by drawing on well-developed schemas relating to the handling of blocks. Notice that most of these schemas were not taught in school. They were created by a multitude of everyday experiences in handling physical objects and in observing the results.[8]

When, in typical school programs, the focus is almost entirely on writing notations on paper, the schema that represent concrete actions with blocks are not available to guide either our thinking or our writing. The result is the familiar writing errors studied by VanLehn, Brown, and their colleagues (e.g., VanLehn, 1982, this volume).

From this theoretical perspective, there is nothing surprising in the power of young children's mathematical thinking, as observed and reported in this volume by Baroody and Ginsburg, Carpenter, Sinclair and Sinclair, and others. The mystery is why schools fail to build on this well-functioning capability of children.

The question Where do schemas come from? can then be answered: They come from experience! (Sometimes one should add: . . .and from reflecting on that experience.) This process is turning out to be unexpectedly complex. Indeed, recent research has established rather firmly that episodic knowledge and more general "semantic" knowledge are quite different in their representations in the human mind. The biochemical processes for these two kinds of "memory storage" are different and there are known disease processes that disrupt one without damaging the other (Blakeslee, 1985; Graf, Squire, & Mandler, 1984; Greenough, 1984; Schimamura & Squire, 1984; Zola-Morgan & Squire, 1984; Squire & Cohen, 1984).

To quote Blakeslee (1985): "Amnesia victims can figure out how to solve difficult puzzles. . . . They do so just as well as normal people. When amnesiacs

---

[8]Notice how a "put more down or pick more up" schema reveals itself in an episode reported by Gelman and Meek: Child: "Because that way there was eight, and there's no way you can try and change numbers." Experimenter: "How could you change the number? What would you have to do?" Child: "You would have to put more things on the table or take things away."

It is these ordinary real-world schemas that are the true foundation of mathematical thinking (see Davis, 1984.)

master such learning, they cannot consciously remember doing it nor can they articulate how they do it" (p. 17).

But the fact is, they *can* do it. A familiar dramatic plot of a few years ago dealt with an amnesiac who could not remember his name, where he lived, whether he was married, or how he had earned a living. When confronted with surgical instruments, however, he held them correctly and could even perform surgical operations. This fictional dramatic theme turns out to correspond quite accurately with reality. Amnesiac subjects can be taught to solve the Tower of Hanoi puzzle. They learn this as quickly as normal subjects. A week later the amnesiacs deny ever having been in the laboratory, deny ever having met the experimenter, and deny ever having seen the Tower puzzle before. They insist they know nothing about it. If, however, they are persuaded to "sit there and just play with it for a moment," they solve it—again, just as quickly and correctly as normal subjects. But of course the amnesiacs insist they are just playing with the discs with no goal in mind, "just playing with the pieces." They say they don't know the rules, nor what one is supposed to do. But while their words deny all knowledge, their fingers solve the puzzle.

Squire (Blakeslee, 1985) calls one kind of knowledge *declarative,* and the other *procedural knowledge.* In his terms, these amnesiacs have not retained declarative knowledge, but have retained procedural knowledge. The dividing line is not precisely known; it may perhaps be better described by Brewer's terms *personal memory* (or episodic memory)—the knowledge that a certain event occurred and how it was experienced—as opposed to *generic memory* (or semantic memory), and *skill memory* (Brewer, 1982; Davis, 1984).

What is relevant to mathematics education is the evidence that even at the biochemical level at least two quite different processes are involved, and trauma to one need not affect the other. The alternatives that we discuss—conceptual knowledge, procedural knowledge, skill memory, verbal knowledge, episodic knowledge, and semantic knowledge—though we may not know the precise lines of demarcation between them, nor which are distinct from the others, are in fact real alternatives, both at the behavioral level that we can observe in the mathematics classroom, and even at the biochemical level.

Some distinctions are unambiguous: for example, much procedural knowledge is sequential in nature, whereas (in Hiebert and Lefevre's phrase, this volume) "conceptual knowledge is saturated with relationships of many kinds" and typically has a kind of "random-access" quality. Probably my knowledge of the layout of the house I live in is, in these terms, mainly conceptual. I can start anywhere in reconstructing a mental representation of the rooms, doors, stairways, windows, and other features, and I can answer any reasonable question. Of course, I have lived in the house for more than 10 years.

By contrast, my knowledge of how to walk between two buildings on an unfamiliar university campus is, at first, sequential. I do not at first see how everything relates to everything else. I could not draw an accurate map, and some of my routes may be far from optimal. I can retrace routes I have taken, but I have not worked out correct geometric relationships between the few buildings I have dealt with. (It is interesting to keep a personal "trip" diary when one is at a conference on an unfamiliar campus, including periodic attempts to sketch from memory a map of the campus. The gradual building up of more relationships usually becomes clear.)

For the purposes of mathematics education, I know of nowhere that the lines of demarcation between procedural and conceptual knowledge have been better described than in the chapters by Hiebert and LeFevre and by Carpenter.

Assimilation Paradigms.   The matter of *assimilation paradigms* deserves special consideration. From a theoretical point of view assimilation paradigms seem very similar to the *frames* of Minsky (1975), the *scripts* of Schank (1977), and the *metaphors* of Lakoff (in press). Each is something in memory that can be retrieved, that allows us to feel that we *recognize* (a lovely word!) our present input data as merely an instance of something we already know. Hence, we merely retrieve from memory the appropriate schema and enter input data into the variable slots in this schema.

When the cashier in the Chinese restaurant was faced with the task of allocating "a little bit more" money between the waitresses, she presumably retrieved a "sharing" schema that was an example of a simple assimilation paradigm. Assimilation paradigms have *slots* or *variables;* in the case of the sharing schema, the major variables were probably the answers to *how many recipients are there?* and *what is to be shared?* There being two recipients, each should get half.

Assimilation paradigms can be much more complex, and can be deliberately created as a result of the experiences we provide for students. Three good examples might be the "Guess My Rule" game, introduced by W. W. Sawyer (Davis, 1967), "Candy-Store Arithmetic", introduced by Gerald Thompson (Davis, 1967), and the "Pebbles-in-the-Bag" activity used by the Madison Project to introduce negative integers (Davis, 1967, 1984).

In "Guess My Rule," a committee of three students work together to "make up a rule," such as, "Whatever number we tell them, they will double it, add seven, and tell us the answer." In this way we accumulate a table, such as

$\square$	$\triangle$
0	-1
1	2
2	5
3	8
4	11

It is now our job to guess their rule, and to write the answer in $\square$, $\triangle$ notation, using $\square$ for the number we tell them, and $\triangle$ for the number they tell us in return. (For the table shown, this might be $(\square \times 3) - 1 = \triangle$). By the age of 8 or 9, children handle this easily, and it gives them experience on which they can draw in subsequent mathematical tasks. Properly developed as a classroom activity, it creates assimilation paradigms for the concepts of *variable, function,* and *formula,* and for the process of translating between tables, formulas, and graphs.

In the "Pebbles-in-the-Bag" activity, a bag contains some pebbles (no one knows how many). Additional pebbles are available in a pile on a nearby table. We mark a reference point in time by having Kwami clap his hands. We put, say, five pebbles into the bag, and record this as: 5. We now take three pebbles out of the bag and record this so that the record now reads: $5 - 3$.

Question: Are there more pebbles in the bag than when Kwami clapped his hands, or are there less? Answer: More. Question: How many more? Answer: Two more. We record this by writing: $5 - 3 = {}^+2$, where the "positive" sign tells us that there are two *more*.

Similarly, if Mary claps her hands, we put in five, and then take out six, then our record will read: $5 - 6 = {}^-1$, where the "negative" sign tells us that there is now one *less* pebble in the bag than when Mary clapped her hands.

If, in subsequent lessons, a child has difficulty with, say, $8 - 10 = \underline{\hspace{1cm}}$, the teacher would advise the child to think of this as a problem of the "Pebbles-in-the-Bag" type. In most cases, the child can then solve it without further help.

As a final example of an assimilation paradigm, the Madison Project curriculum (as used in Weston, Connecticut; see Davis, 1967) presented fourth, fifth, and sixth graders with many different views of mathematics. One among these was the "*logical*" view: the vast (infinite) array of possible mathematical statements can be generated from a few initial statements ("axioms") by using certain explicit rewrite rules ("rules of inference"). Children presumably come to school unequipped with appropriate assimilation paradigms for such tasks — they have not had the relevant prerequisite background experience. Hence the school program must provide experience from which children can synthesize appropriate assimilation paradigms.

At least two assimilation paradigms are needed: one to show that "new" statements can sometimes be inferred from certain "old" statements, and one to show the creative use of certain precise rewrite rules.

For the first, the children were shown one or two examples and asked to make up more. One, made up by a fifth grader, made use of the gender-ambiguity of the English word *cousin* and the fact that at that time Little League baseball was for boys only:

You are told: My cousin plays in the Little League.

Only boys play in the Little League.

You can infer: My cousin is a boy.

For the other assimilation paradigm (the creative use of explicit rewrite rules), the children worked on problems of a familiar type, where one starts with one word, say SOUP, and generates new lines under the rules:

1. To go from one line to the next, you may change only one letter.
2. Every line must be a legitimate word in the English language.

Some word is specified as the *goal*—in this case, our goal word might be ''nuts,'' and we reach this goal by inventing intermediate steps where every new line obeys the two rules above.[9]

Once these assimilation paradigms (and a few others) have been firmly established, the students are able to deal with derivations, such as the following (see Davis, 1967):

$$A + (B \times C) = A + (B \times C)$$
$$A + (B \times C) = (B \times C) + A$$
$$A + (B \times C) = (C \times B) + A$$

When schools fail to establish these assimilation paradigms, they report that tasks of this type are ''too difficult for the students,'' ''the children are not *ready* for such tasks.'' Of course not! Getting them ''ready'' means leading them to synthesize the necessary assimilation paradigms.

In simple terms, there are two ways to create a mental representation: (a) build it up from smaller pieces; (b) retrieve an assimilation paradigm ''whole,'' and map the present data into the variable slots in the retrieved schema. Clearly the second process, when possible, is in some ways easier, more productive, and more stable. Readers can easily demonstrate this for themselves. Consider the geometric figure described by saying: ABE is an equilateral triangle; EBCD is a square; point A does not lie inside square EBCD. In those terms one's mental representation is probably demanding in cognitive effort, and is fragile. Note how much easier it becomes when one is able to say ''Oh! It's a *house!*'' The instructional use, and theoretical analysis, of assimilation paradigms is discussed further in Davis (1984).

---

[9]One solution might be:

SOUP
SOAP
SOAR
SEAR
SEAS
SETS
NETS
NUTS.

Mappings Into Mental Representations

In the literature, too little attention has been paid to *mappings*. Suppose I have retrieved or constructed a general representation of the problem situation. I must still map into it specific input data. We saw one example of this when the cashier in the Chinese restaurant retrieved a "sharing" schema. Presumably, at least for adults, any schema for "sharing" must have a *variable* or *slot* for "How many shares?" In the Chinese restaurant case, the answer was: *two*. Presumably the cashier could have coped with the need for four shares, or ten, or more. The specific input data "two" had to be extracted from the general input data and mapped into the *problem representation*.

But there is another representation that often plays a role, namely, the *representation of relevant knowledge*. When it has been retrieved or constructed, data must be mapped from the *problem representation* into the *representation of relevant knowledge*. This is by no means always an easy task. To show how difficult it can be, consider this example. Kazuko Suzuki, when in grade 9, was asked to prove that, for $\varepsilon > 0$, there exists an integer N such that $\frac{1}{n} < \varepsilon$ provided $n > N$, by using the Archimedean postulate[10] (which says: if a and b are any positive numbers, then there exists an integer N such that $aN > b$). The Archimedean postulate can be put into words by saying: no matter how long a journey you want to make (b), and no matter how short your step is (a), you can go far enough if you take enough steps (namely, N of them).

Kazuko was, in effect, being asked to prove that

$$\lim_{n \to \infty} \frac{1}{n} = 0.$$

She had never seen this problem before, nor ever before seen the Archimedean postulate, so this was a new task for her, requiring originality and creativity. The key steps are, first, to transform

$$\frac{1}{n} < \epsilon$$

into its equivalent form

$$n > \frac{1}{\epsilon} \tag{A}$$

and, second, to show that inequality (A) is obtainable from the Archimedean postulate a N > b by making a correct replacement of the variables. Kazuko solved this novel task easily and immediately—a performance far beyond what one would ordinarily expect from someone her age—by making this mapping

---

[10]This classroom episode was videotaped, and the videotape is available from The Study Group for Mathematical Behavior, Inc., PO Box 2095 - Station A, Champaign, Illinois 61820; for a more complete description of the episode see Davis, Jockusch and McKnight, 1978, pp. 90–91.

from the problem representation into the representation of relevant knowledge (in this case, the Archimedian postulate).

Symbols in this example	Mapping Action	Variables in the general Archimedean postulate
$\dfrac{1}{\epsilon}$	$\rightarrow$	b
n	$\rightarrow$	N
1	$\rightarrow$	a

The main point of this instance, for our present purposes, is that mapping data into the variable slots in a *representation of relevant knowledge* cannot be taken for granted. Few people could have carried out the mapping that was needed in this case, and very few could have done it with the speed and seeming ease that Kazuko displayed.

What Is Stored In Memory Afterwards?

Clearly, students solve problems in order to learn something. After they have had the experience of solving a problem, what do they store in memory? Many things, undoubtedly, including some episodic knowledge, and, one hopes, some knowledge in other forms. One kind of knowledge, discussed by Stephen Young, has been called "key-feature representations" (Young, 1982; Davis, 1984). One clearly does not memorize every feature of, say, a tetrahedron, nor every feature of Pascal's Triangle. What is stored in memory is in fact a fairly minimal list, with the hope that other properties can be reconstructed or deduced when needed. (This is one of the major ways that mathematics differs from, say, the study of history or the study of literature, where logical reconstruction of missing knowledge is not equally straightforward.)

In one study, a proof by Marion Walter was shown to a mathematics teacher. When he was satisfied that he now "knew" her proof, he was asked to describe what he remembered about it. The problem, from Davis and Hersh (1981), can be stated as follows:

The length and width of a rectangle are both positive integers. The area equals the perimeter. Prove that the area must be either 16 or 18.

Here is Walter's proof:

Let u and v be the dimensions.
Then $2u + 2v = uv$
Solve for u:

$$u = \frac{2v}{v - 2}$$

Divide:

$$v - 2\overline{)\,\begin{array}{c}2 \\ 2v\end{array}}$$
$$\begin{array}{c}2 - 4 \\ \hline 4\end{array}$$

So

$$u = 2 + \frac{4}{v - 2}$$

Hence $v - 2$ must be either 1, or 2, or 4.
So v must be either 3, or 4, or 6.
Solutions:

$v = 3$,	$u = 6$,	area = perimeter = 18
$v = 4$,	$u = 4$,	area = perimeter = 16
$v = 6$,	$u = 3$,	area = perimeter = 18
		Q.E.D.

Now, after studying this proof until he was satisfied that he "knew" it, what did the math teacher report that he remembered:

1. A visual memory of $2u + 2v = uv$. (Of course, he could have been reconstructing this from his knowledge of perimeter and area, and even reported that he might be doing exactly that.)

2. The idea "solve for u" (but *not* the details of carrying this out).

3. The idea of *dividing polynomials*. (This had not occurred to him before he saw the Walter solution; in his own earlier solution of the problem he had proceeded quite differently.) He reported some sort of "hazy" visual memory, something like the following:

$$u = \frac{\text{some polynomial in v}}{\text{some polynomial in v}}$$
$$v - 2 \overline{)\,2v}$$

hazy, unsure what these polynomials actually were, but did remember that the binomial was the denominator, the monomial was the numerator (which made matters somewhat more complicated).

4. A hazy recollection of the result of this division process; some equation like:

$$u = 4 \pm \frac{2}{v - 2}$$

5. Hence the requirement that the algebraic fraction take on integer values, so that its denominator must be a divisor of its numerator.

6. A realization that the "proof" sketched above had been carried out with his attention focused mainly on strategy and algebraic forms. (Such a calculation is sometimes called "formal," in that it neglects meanings.) There could be difficulties with the range of some of the variables, possible division by zero, and so on. Hence, with this formal sketch in mind, he now needed to go through this carefully a second time, paying careful attention to ranges of variables, to possible zero factors before dividing, and the like.

He also remembered that when he had made this "second pass through the problem," it had been possible to construct a logically correct proof.

Two weeks later the teacher still remembered the Walter proof and still in essentially this same "key feature" form—even though before seeing the Walter solution he had not thought of this proof by himself. The really key idea that he now remembered was: "*divide!*" (see also Davis, 1985b; Pandharipande, 1985). This seems to be the main thing he stored in memory as a result of studying the Walter solution. Note that the memory seems to have been at least partly in the form of "hazy visual representations." Was it also partly *verbal*? The word "divide" played a prominent role—was this *word* part of the memory record?

The Role of Words

Omitted from our list of criticisms of schools is one that should be added: schools are typically very *verbal* institutions. In the beginning, in the middle, and at the end is the *word* (see, e.g., Mayer, 1961). Is mathematical knowledge largely *verbal* knowledge?

We need to be clear about the question. Three kinds of mental processes might exist:

1. Information in the mind is stored in the form of words and statements, retrieved in this form, and offered to the outside world in this form.

2. Information in the mind is stored in some *nonverbal* form, but can be converted to words and statements that can be spoken or written.

3. Information in the mind is stored in some nonverbal form, and cannot be converted into verbal statements.

Note that these are not mutually exclusive.

Clearly the first process does occur, as (for instance) when we memorize:

> Whose woods these are I think I know.
> His house is in the village, though;
> He will not see me stopping here
> To watch his woods fill up with snow.

These lines by Robert Frost are not *just* words—surely few words do more to conjure up pictures in the reader's mind (at least if the reader is from rural New England)—but *words* are the key ingredient. We know this because, having memorized these lines, we are able to repeat them *verbatim,* something that one cannot usually do with words one has heard or read.

It seems equally clear that the third process does sometimes occur. We have the evidence of the amnesiacs' fingers solving the Tower of Hanoi puzzle efficiently at the same time that their words are disclaiming any knowledge of the puzzle, its goal, its rules, or the strategy for solving it. There is also the evidence from anyone who can correctly identify Mozart, Brahms, or Bach as the composers of various unfamiliar pieces of music, without being able to say *how* they know that this particular composition must be by Bach, or that it most likely is by Brahms.

For mathematics, though, it is important to notice how much knowledge is nonverbal.[11] This fact is sometimes obscured by the operation of the second process—the putting into words of one's thought processes and ideas, even when the ideas themselves were neither stored nor used in verbal form.

Evidence for the nonverbal nature of much thought comes from many directions: people's usual inability to repeat statements *verbatim,* amnesia studies of the type discussed, the many things we can do without being able to say how we do them, studies of disruptions in mental functioning after certain lesions in the brain (Davis, 1984), and name-substitution errors commonly made by normal people,[12] to mention only a few.

---

[11]See, for example, this excerpt from Lean and Clements, 1981:

In a letter to Jacques Hadamard, Albert Einstein stated that he always thought about anything in terms of mental pictures and that he used words in a secondary capacity only (see Einstein's letter in Hadamard, 1954). In the field of mathematics, some mathematicians have claimed that all mathematical tasks require spatial thinking (see Fennema, 1979). Indeed, as early as 1935 H. R. Hamley, an Australian mathematician and psychologist, wrote that mathematical ability is a compound of general intelligence, visual imagery, and ability to perceive number and space configurations and to retain such configurations as mental pictures (McGee, 1979). Given statements such as these, it is not surprising that there is a substantial literature in which relationships between spatial ability, mental imagery, and mathematical performance have been investigated (Bishop, 1973, 1979; Fennema, 1974, 1979; Guay and McDaniel, 1977; Lin, 1979; Sherman, 1979; Smith, 1964.)

[12]Because of their relevance to mathematical thought processes, we have collected many such errors. Teachers at University High School, for example, often interchange "Green Street" and "Springfield Ave.", both in statements and in actual walking and driving. These are the two parallel, heavy-traffic, East-West streets north of the campus, both lined with campus-town stores and offices. Clearly the actual words that name the streets are *not* similar, but the *descriptors* of the streets are. What is stored in memory must often be some collection of nonverbal descriptors—indeed, probably an assimilation paradigm.

Is this relevant to mathematics education? I would argue that it is. Witness the ancient Chinese motto, recently popular in mathematics education circles:

> I hear, and I forget;
> I see, and I remember;
> I do, and I understand.

In the remainder of this chapter I consider two cases where the relation between words and nonverbal ideas seems to be critical; then, switching emphasis from humans to computers, I ask whether computer languages themselves show the same kind of distinction between "procedural" and "conceptual" knowledge.

Polya's Heuristics

What is a heuristic? From one point of view, it seems to be a verbally stated slogan that helps us construct a strategy for attacking a problem.

Examples include: "Do something you *can* do!" "Try to break the problem up into several smaller problems, and try to solve these smaller problems independently." "Chain backwards: if the goal is the last step in your work, what would the next-to-the-last step look like?" "What's making this problem *different* from those you know?" "What makes this problem difficult?" "Can you change this difficulty, or somehow avoid it?" "Can you make up a simpler, similar problem, solve it, and learn from that?"

Although stated in verbal terms, heuristics have a large nonverbal component as well—unless one has had some practice in using the heuristic, and has thereby built up this nonverbal component, the verbally stated heuristic is usually not much help.

The episode I want to consider is based on one of George Polya's heuristics: "Imagine that you already *have* the solution, and think of the properties it would have." This was, in fact, the heuristic that one mathematics teacher said he thought of when he was shown one of the mathematical problems in Schoen-

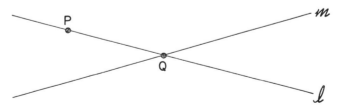

FIG. 10.6.   The Task Is To Construct A Circle Tangent To Line *l* At Point P, And Also Tangent To Line *m*.

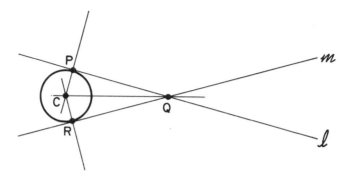

FIG. 10.7.   Pretend You Have The Answer, Then Study Its Properties.

feld's chapter (this volume): Given lines *l* and m (which intersect at point Q), and point P on line *l*. Using Euclidean ruler and compass methods, construct a circle tangent to line *l* at point P, and also tangent to line m. (See Fig. 10.6).

The moment he thought of the Polya heuristic, and reported that he had done so, the teacher had no difficulty in drawing the diagram shown in Fig. 10.7, after which the solution of the problem was immediate.

Angles CPQ and CRQ are right angles; triangle CPQ is congruent to triangle CRQ; point R is easily located since $d(R, Q) = d(P, Q)$; construct a perpendicular to line *l* at point P, and a perpendicular to line m at point R. These intersect in point C, which is the center of the circle, and CP is a radius.

Did *words* help? Did a verbally stated rule (the Polya heuristic) help in this case? Probably so, but the words alone did not solve the problem. A substantial amount of nonverbal knowledge was also necessary. As further evidence of its nonverbal nature, the teacher could not name the theorem he used to claim congruence for the two triangles. He could think of SAS, ASA, and SSS, but it was clearly none of those; nor could he immediately state the theorem in words. Yet he felt certain that such a theorem did exist; he could (somewhat fumblingly) state it; and he was correct.

A Difficult Integral Problem

Elizabeth Jockusch, when a 15-year-old junior at University High School, was in a calculus class that was asked to find the antiderivative

$$\int \sec x \, dx$$

without looking in any book. She began working on the problem at 10:00 a.m., worked on it during free moments at school, and worked on it more intensively that evening. "Working on it" involved thinking about formulas such as:

$$\sec x = \frac{1}{\cos x}$$

$$\int \cos x \, dx = \sin x + C$$

$$\int u^n \, du = \frac{1}{n + 1} u^{n + 1} + C$$

$$\frac{d}{dx} \tan x = \sec^2 x$$

$$\frac{d}{dx} \sec x = \sec x \tan x$$

$$\frac{d}{dx} u^n = n \, u^{n - 1} \frac{du}{dx}$$

$$\tan^2 x + 1 = \sec^2 x$$

$$\int \sec^2 x \, dx = \tan x + C$$

$$\int \sec x \tan x \, dx = \sec x + C$$

$$\int \frac{du}{u} = \ln u + C$$

$$\frac{d}{dx} (u + v) = \frac{du}{dx} + \frac{dv}{dx}$$

and $\int (u + v) dx = \int u \, dx + \int v \, dx$

and trying to fit a few of these together so as to be able solve the problem. This task is not like, say, long division, where a well-known algorithm provides us with a routine method of solution. For this problem no routine method exists. One must juggle many complicated pieces in one's mind until somehow some of them can be made to fit together.

When Elizabeth went to bed that night she had not yet solved the problem. . . but at 5:00 a.m. she awoke, realizing that she knew the solution.

This is not an easy problem. Elizabeth was the only member of her class to solve it (indeed, no one else known to us has solved it entirely alone—one ordinarily looks up the solution in a book).

What is involved in thinking about such a problem? It would seem to be similar to some of the problems studied by Baars and Kramer (1982), such as this:

What word is suggested by:
line   birthday   surprise?

Baars and Kramer give as the "answer" the word *party* (Davis, 1984, pp. 83–86).

The phenomenon involved in reaching the answer is usually described by a "spreading activation" model of human thought: the word "line" should raise the activation level of many other ideas (some of which are words, some of which are nonverbal) associated with it, perhaps including the word "drive," a visual image of Leon Durham lining out to the second baseman, the visual image of a linear graph, and so on. Perhaps none of these activation levels reaches the threshold level that brings the corresponding idea to conscious awareness. But we have more—there is also the word "birthday," which may raise the activation levels for, say, the word "cake," for a mental image of pastel-colored frosting, candles, children wearing party hats, ice cream, and so on—and, of course, also raise the activation level for the word "party." This increment is added to that caused by the input "line." If the threshold level for "party" is still not reached, we have one more input—the word "surprise"—and by now, with this third increment the threshold level is reached, and it suddenly occurs to us that the answer may well be "party."

Readers may find it instructive to see if they, independently, can solve the original integral problem.

For anyone who does not succeed in doing so, consider these facts, which become clear if we think about the preceding formulas:

1. Multiplying sec x by the tan x produces sec x tan x, which is the derivative of the sec x.

2. Multiplying tan x by the sec x produces sec x tan x, which is the derivative of the sec x.

3. Multiplying sec x by sec x produces $\sec^2 x$, which is the derivative of the tan x.

Now, observations (1) and (2) together tell us that multiplying by sec x can have an effect somewhat similar to differentiation. There is one small difficulty: multiplying the tangent in this way produces the derivative of the secant, and multiplying the secant produces the derivative of the tangent—so there is a kind of reversal or "cross-over". But suppose we had

$$u = \tan x + \sec x.$$

Now, multiplying u by sec x has the same effect as differentiating u:

$$u \sec x = \tan x \sec x + \sec^2 x$$

$$\frac{du}{dx} = \sec^2 x + \sec x \tan x$$

which are equal. Can we use this?

Yes, if we notice two familiar properties of fractions:

$$a = \frac{a}{1}$$

$$\frac{a}{b} = \frac{ac}{bc}$$

Combining these, we have:

$$\sec x = \frac{\sec x}{1} = \frac{\sec x \, (\sec x + \tan x)}{\sec x + \tan x}$$

So,

$$\int \sec x \, dx = \int \frac{du}{u}$$

and

$$\int \sec x \, dx = \int \frac{d(\sec x + \tan x)}{\sec x + \tan x}$$

$$= \ln \mid \sec x + \tan x \mid + C$$

This is what had fitted together in Elizabeth's mind by the time she awoke at 5:00 a.m.

Are such episodes better conceptualized by a "spreading-activation-and-threshold" type of model, or by the more discrete cognitive models (in terms of tree searches, subgoals, etc.)?

CONCEPTUAL VS. PROCEDURAL KNOWLEDGE IN COMPUTERS

Beyond any doubt, our experience with computers is giving us new metaphors for thinking about information processing as it must occur within the human mind. It is probably also true that the metaphors drawn from computers in the past have been very limited in their variety. The computer has been the quintessential *sequential* machine, tied inexorably to *explicit procedures;* human beings do not seem like this at all (see, for example, Hinton & Anderson, 1981).

All of this may be about to change. Besides the still exotic possibilities of "connection machines" (Lerner, 1985; Gabriel, 1986), there is the already existing alternative of "conceptually oriented" computer programing languages such as PROLOG, which begin to give us an entirely new collection of metaphors for information processing (Bobrow & Stefik, 1986).

Traditional computer languages such as BASIC bear an obvious resemblance to procedural knowledge: first you do this, then you do this, and so on. The result might look somewhat like this:

```
10 PRINT "WHAT IS YOUR AGE?";
20 INPUT A
30 IF A<18 THEN 60
40 PRINT "YOU ARE ELIGIBLE TO VOTE."
50 STOP
60 PRINT "YOU WILL BE ABLE TO VOTE IN"; 18-A; "YEARS."
70 END
```

BASIC is an example of what Cuadrado and Cuadrado (1985) call a "traditional imperative (or procedural)" language (p. 151). By contrast, "declarative languages" (or "logic-programming languages") are described as "fundamentally different." Cuadrado and Cuadrado analyze the distinction as follows:

> When we program in imperative languages (e.g., FORTRAN, Pascal, Ada), we are machine-oriented: we "prescribe" the manner in which we want the computer to go about solving the problem, i.e., we explicitly specify the detailed flow of control necessary to carry out a given computation. [By contrast]. . . in using logic programming to solve problems, we describe or "declare" the logical structure of the problems. (p. 151)

This distinction is described by Bharath (1985) in these words:

> In conventional programming languages the focus is on designing a step-by-step procedure that consists of commands that match the step-by-step . . . hardware operations. This is why these languages are sometimes referred to as procedural or imperative languages. But the concept of programming in logic emphasizes declarations or assertions of the relationships between, and the rules applicable to, the various objects or entities involved in the problem. The task of deriving the necessary results is left to the computer. (p. 49.)

One declarative language is Prolog. A Prolog program to solve a maze-traversing problem might look essentially like this.

```
/*Prolog representation of the maze*/

adjacent (cave-entrance, trolls).
adjacent (cave-entrance, fountain).
adjacent (fountain, mermaid).
adjacent (fountain, bandits).
```

adjacent (bandits, exit).
adjacent (mermaid, exit).

avoid (trolls, bandits).

traverse (Here, There):—

avoid (Dangers).

path (Here, There, Dangers, [Here]).
path (From, To, Dangers, Trail):—
adjacent (From, Intermediate)
adjacent (Intermediate, From)
not member (Intermediate, Dangers).
not member (Intermediate, Trail).
path (Intermediate, To, Dangers,
[Intermediate: Trail]).

The preceding lines of code are (essentially) the computer program. To make the program run, you call for:

traverse (cave-entrance, exit).

Clearly, this Prolog program has more the random access and rich interrelationships character discussed in the preceding chapters in relation to conceptual knowledge in humans. Equally clearly, BASIC has much more the characteristic flavor of procedural knowledge. Thus computer programming appears to be shifting its emphasis from procedural languages toward more concept-like languages. What this will mean—if anything—for our conceptualizations of human thought remains to be seen.[13]

It should also be remarked that Prolog, which is more conceptual and less procedural, depends on what might be called a more educated computer— more processing can be left to the computer because it already contains, within Prolog itself, more "knowledge." Does this suggest that teaching very young children should be more procedural, whereas teaching older students should be more conceptual?

In thinking about the possible implications of computer programing languages such as PROLOG, one needs to keep in mind certain reservations, particularly with regard to the role of *words* in human thought. As we argued earlier,[14] there

---

[13]Interestingly enough, another trend involves the design of computer hardware in a direction somewhat similar to spreading activation models in psychology. An example would be the non-VonNeumann "connection machine" now being developed at MIT (see Lerner, 1985). Thinking Machines, a recently created corporation in Cambridge, Massachusetts, plans to market its Connection Machine, a computer that has 64,000 processors working simultaneously. See also Hinton and Anderson, 1981.

[14]And so have others. See, for example, Bobrow and Collins, 1975.

is abundant evidence that humans are not limited to thinking in words or verbally coded mental representations. Computer programming languages seem usually to be limited to coding that is not very different from words. Thus, while PROLOG-type languages are interesting, they may not yet provide us with really adequate metaphors for true human conceptual thought.

CONCLUSION

How does this all add up? The various chapters in this volume achieve at least two results, their explicit result of considering the relationship between procedural and conceptual knowledge, and an implicit result of sketching out a more "cognitive-science-oriented" conceptualization of human mathematical thought and how such thought develops.

It is clear that this kind of theory is not an academic luxury, irrelevant to the needs of children, schools, and teachers. On the contrary, theory influences practice to a very considerable extent, and many of the shortcomings of typical school mathematics programs are closely related to reliance on weak conceptualizations of what mathematical knowledge really is and what is involved in acquiring such knowledge. The theory suggested in the chapters of this book shows real promise of being a substantial improvement. It also holds out hope for leading to improvements in what actually happens to children.

There is much here that deserves to be thought about.

REFERENCES

Baars, B. J., & Kramer, D. N. (1982, August). *Conscious and unconscious components of intentional control.* Paper presented at the Fourth Annual Conference of the Cognitive Science Society, Ann Arbor, MI.

Bharath, R. (1985). [Review of *Beginning micro-Prolog*]. *Byte, 10*(8), 49–52.

Bishop, A. J. (1972). Use of structural apparatus and spatial ability: A possible relationship. *Research in Education, 9,* 43–49.

Bishop, A. J. (1979). Visualizing and mathematics in a pre-technological culture. *Educational Studies in Mathematics, 10,* 135–146.

Blakeslee, S. (1985, February 19). Clues hint at brain's two memory maps. *New York Times,* p. 17.

Bobrow, D. G., & Collins, A. (Eds.). (1975). *Representation and understanding.* New York: Academic Press.

Bobrow, D. G. & Stefik, M. J. "Perspectives on Artificial Intelligence Programming," *Science,* vol. 231 (28 February 1986), pp. 951–57.

Brewer, W. F. (1982). Personal memory, generic memory, and skill: A re-analysis of the episodic-semantic distinction. *Proceedings of the Fourth Annual Conference of the Cognitive Science Society* (pp. 112–13).

Cochran, B., Barson, A., & Davis, R. B. (1970). Child created mathematics. *Arithmetic Teacher, 17* (3), 211–15.

Cockcroft, W. H. (1982). *Mathematics counts: Report of the committee of inquiry into the teaching of mathematics in schools*, under the Chairmanship of Dr. W. H. Cockcroft. London: HMSO.

Cuadrado, C. Y., Cuadrado, J. L. (1985). Prolog goes to work. *Byte, 10* (8), 151–58.

Davis, P. J., & Hersh, R. (1981). *The mathematical experience*. Boston, MA: Houghton Mifflin.

Davis, R. B. (1967). *Explorations in mathematics: A text for teachers*. Palo Alto, CA: Addison-Wesley.

Davis, R. B. (1971). *Helping children learn mathematics*. Syracuse, NY: Syracuse University, The Madison Project.

Davis, R. B. (1980). *Discovery in mathematics: A text for teachers* New Rochelle, NY: Cuisenaire.

Davis, R. B. (1984). *Learning mathematics: The cognitive science approach to mathematics education*. Norwood, NJ: Ablex.

Davis, R. B. (1985a). A study of the process of making proofs. *Journal of Mathematical Behavior, 4*, (1), 37–43.

Davis, R. B. (1985b). The role of representations in problem solving: Case studies. *Journal of Mathematical Behavior, 4* (1), 85–97.

Davis, R. B., Jockusch, E. & McKnight, C. C. (1978). Cognitive processes in algebra. *Journal of Children's Mathematical Behavior, 2* (1), 10–320.

Davis, R. B., & McKnight, C. C. (1980). The influence of semantic content on algorithmic behavior. *Journal of Mathematical Behavior, 3* (1), 39–87.

Dwyer, T. A., & Critchfield, M. (1978). *Basic and the personal computer*. Reading, MA: Addison-Wesley.

Erlwanger, S. H. (1973). Benny's conception of rules and answers in IPI mathematics. *Journal of Children's Mathematical Behavior, 1*(2), 7–26.

Fennema, E. (1974). Mathematics learning and the sexes: A review. *Journal for Research in Mathematics Education. 5*, 126–39.

Fennema, E. (1979). Women and girls in mathematics: equity in mathematics education. *Educational Studies in Mathematics, 10*, 389–401.

Frost, R. (1970). *The poetry of Robert Frost*, (ed. Edward Connery Lathem). New York: Holt, Rinehart & Winston.

Gabriel, R. P. "Massively Parallel Computers: The Connection Machine and NON-VON," *Science*, vol. 231 (28 February 1986), pp. 975–8.

Ginsburg, H. P. (1982). *Children's arithmetic*. Austin, TX: Pro-Ed.

Graf, P., Squire, L. R., & Mandler, G. (1984). The information that amnesic patients do not forget. *Journal of Experimental Psychology, 10*(1), 164–178.

Greenough, W. T. (1984). Structural correlates of information storage in the mammalian brain: A review and hypothesis. *Trends in Neuro Sciences, 7*(1) 229–33.

Guay, R. B., & McDaniel, E. D. (1977). The relationship between mathematics achievement and spatial abilities among elementary school children. *Journal for Research in Mathematics Education, 7*, 211–15.

Hadamard, J. S. (1954). *An essay on the psychology of invention in the mathematical field.*: New York: Dover Press.

Hinton, G. E., & Anderson, J. A. (1981). *Parallel models of associative memory* Hillsdale, NJ: Lawrence Erlbaum Associates.

Hoyles, C. (1985). Developing a context for LOGO in school mathematics. *Journal of Mathematical Behavior, 4*(3), 237–56.

Kumar, D. (1979). Limits, conic sections, and other problems. *Journal of Children's Mathematical Behavior, 2*(2), 183–200.

Kumar, D. (1980). The points nearest the origin. *Journal of Mathematical Behavior, 3*(1), 204–207.

Lakoff, G. (in press) *Women, fire and dangerous things* Chicago, IL: University of Chicago Press.

Lave, J. (1982). *Arithmetic procedures in everyday situations*. Paper presented at the Fourth Annual Conference of the Cognitive Science Society, Ann Arbor, MI.

Lave, J., Murtaugh, M., & de la Rocha, O. (1984). Recounting the whole enchilada: The dialectical constitution of arithmetic practice. In B. Rogoff and J. Lave (Eds.), *Everyday cognition: Its development in social context.* Cambridge, MA: Harvard University Press.

Lawler, R. W. (1985). *Computer experience and cognitive development* Chichester, West Sussex, Eng: Ellis Horwood.

Lean, G., & Clements, M. A. (1981). Spatial ability, visual imagery, and mathematical performance. *Educational Studies in Mathematics, 12*(3) 267–99.

Lerner, E. J. (1985). Parallel processing gets down to business. *High Technology, 5*(7), 20–28.

Lin, C. Y. (1979). Imagery in mathematical thinking and learning. *International Journal of Education in Science and Technology, 10,* 107–11.

Mayer, M. (1961). *The schools* New York: Harper.

McGee, M. G. (1979). Human spatial abilities: Psychometric studies and environmental, genetic, hormonal, and neurological influences. *Psychological Bulletin, 86,* 889–918.

Minsky, M. (1975). A framework for representing knowledge. In P. Winston, (Ed.), *The psychology of computer vision.* New York: McGraw-Hill.

Pandharipande, R. (1985). The Isis problem. *Journal of Mathematical Behavior, 4*(1), 101–03.

Schank, R. C. (1977). Representation and understanding of text. In E. W. Elcock & D. Michie (Eds.), *Machine intelligence 8: Machine representations of knowledge.* New York: John Wiley.

Secrest, D. (1985). Regular polyhedra. *Journal of Mathematical Behavior, 4*(1), 105–18.

Sherman, J. (1979). Women and mathematics: Summary of research from 1977–1979. Final Report, NIE Grant, University of Wisconsin.

Shimamura, A. P., & Squire, L. R. (1984). Paired-associate learning and priming effects in amnesia: A neuropsychological study. *Journal of Experimental Psychology, 113*(4); 556–70.

Smith, I. M. (1964).*Spatial ability.* London: University of London Press.

Squire, L. R. & Cohen, N. J. (1984). Human memory and amnesia. In J. L. McGaugh, G. Lynch, & N. M. Weinberger, (Eds.). *The neurobiology of learning and memory* (pp. 3–64). (Guilford Press, New York, NY).

Suzuki, K. (1979). Problems and solutions. *Journal of Children's Mathematical Behavior, 2*(2), 135–65.

VanLehn, K. (1982). Bugs are not enough: Empirical studies of bugs, impasses and repairs in procedural skills. *Journal of Mathematical Behavior, 3*(2), 3–71.

Whitney, H. (1985). Taking responsibility in school mathematics education. *Journal of Mathematical Behavior, 4*(3), 219–35.

Whitney, H. (1985). Coming alive in school math and beyond. *Journal of Mathematical Behavior, 5*(2).

Williams, E. M., & Shuard, H. (1970). *Primary mathematics today* London: Longmans.

Young, S. (1982). The mental representation of geometrical knowledge. *Journal of Mathematical Behavior, 3*(2), 123–44.

Zola-Morgan, S. & Squire, L. R. (1984). Preserved learning in monkeys with medial temporal lesions: Sparing of motor and cognitive skills. *Journal of Neuroscience, 4*(4), 1072–85.

Author Index

Subject Index